PENGUIN BOOKS

THE GREEN FLAG: VOL. TWO
The Bold Fenian Men

KT-149-867

An author, journalist and broadcaster, Robert Kee has
worked for many years for both ITV and BBC television on
current affairs series, such as *Panorama* and *This Week*, and
on other programmes, including a number of documentaries.
He has been a special correspondent for the *Sunday Times* and
the *Observer*, and was literary editor of the *Spectator*.

The Green Flag has been continuously in print since 1972. The
other two volumes in his monumental history of Irish nationalism are *The Most Distressful Country* and *Ourselves Alone*,
also published by Penguin. Robert Kee made a thirteen-part
series for BBC television based on *The Green Flag*. Entitled
Ireland: A History, it received great critical acclaim and was
widely shown both here and in the United States. He has also
written *Munich: The Eleventh Hour* (Hamish Hamilton 1988),
published to commemorate the fiftieth anniversary of the
Munich Agreement and *Trial and Error* (Penguin 1989).

The Green Flag
Volume Two:

The Bold Fenian Men

Robert Kee

PENGUIN BOOKS

PENGUIN BOOKS

Published by the Penguin Group
Penguin Books Ltd, 27 Wrights Lane, London W8 5TZ, England
Viking Penguin, a division of Penguin Books USA Inc.
375 Hudson Street, New York, New York 10014, USA
Penguin Books Australia Ltd, Ringwood, Victoria, Australia
Penguin Books Canada Ltd, 2801 John Street, Markham, Ontario, Canada L3R 1B4
Penguin Books (NZ) Ltd, 182–190 Wairau Road, Auckland 10, New Zealand

Penguin Books Ltd, Registered Offices: Harmondsworth, Middlesex, England

First published in a single volume (with *The Most Distressful Country* and *Ourselves Alone*)
under the title *The Green Flag* by Weidenfeld & Nicolson 1972
Published in Penguin Books 1989
3 5 7 9 10 8 6 4

Printed in England by Clays Ltd, St Ives plc

To the memory of my father,
Robert Kee (1880–1958),
and of my mother,
Dorothy Frances Kee
(1890–1964)

Contents

... The study of Irish history does not excite political animosity but leads to the very opposite result. Thoroughly to appreciate the history of this or any country it is necessary to sympathise with all parties ...

A. G. Richey, from *A Short History of the Irish People*, 1869

Nearly a million of our countrymen have fixed their homes in England and Scotland. Every family in the Kingdom is linked by domestic connexion with England – every British colony teems with the children of our soil ... Deep indeed must be the wounds inflicted upon our national pride, and upon our national interests, before we can consent to deplore the associations which belong to identity of language, similarity of constitutions, connexion of kindred, and community of glory ...

William Smith O'Brien, letter to the *Nation*, 30 December 1843

The National Flag is an uncrowned gold harp on a plain green background.

The *Irish Volunteer*, 18 March 1916

Preface to Volume Two

When I finished writing *The Green Flag* in the spring of 1971 the latest of the ancient troubles of Ireland had already been going on for nearly two years. It was not part of my scheme then to include any account of them, and it is not now. They are still confused, unresolved and impossible to treat with the historical detachment which I hope is part of the character of this book. What I have tried to do in *The Green Flag* is to unfold as dispassionately as possible a narrative of earlier events (principally from 1789 to 1925) of which some knowledge is indispensable for any understanding of what has happened or may happen in Ireland. Knowledge and understanding do not in themselves provide solutions but there can be no solutions without them. I cannot help hoping that this new edition will, however indirectly, contribute something to an ending of that shame which the events of recent years have brought upon the United Kingdom and Ireland.

The present volume, *The Bold Fenian Men*, covers the period from the foundation of the revolutionary Fenian movement to the end of the Dublin Rising of 1916, two events seemingly tied to one another by logical development. But it is one of the many paradoxes of Irish history that the times between in fact saw Irish nationalism develop in the quite different direction of a popular constitutional movement.

I must once again ask Irish readers to forgive me for often presupposing ignorance of material with which they are familiar. I hope too they may sometimes feel rewarded by finding it viewed in a slightly different light from that to which they are accustomed.

The first inspiration for *The Green Flag* came from a magical valley in Co. Wicklow to whose resident spirit – even if also resident elsewhere – I send across many years gratitude and affection. Among others who gave me help I should like to thank particularly Mrs Ralph Partridge, Sir Nicholas Henderson, Dr P. M. Turquet, my wife Cynthia, my son Alexander, Miss Marguerite Foss and Mrs Topsy Levan; also the staffs over many years of the British Museum Reading Room, the British Museum Newspaper Library at Colindale, the London Library, and of the National Library of Ireland.

ROBERT KEE
January 1976

PART ONE

PART ONE

1

Beginnings of the
Fenian Movement

In the autumn of 1858 respectable Irishmen reading their newspapers were made unpleasantly aware of a new phenomenon on the Irish scene.

Secret societies had been a feature of Irish agrarian life for over a century and a half, fluctuating in virulence and intensity with the district and the season, a fact of life Ireland had grown to live with. So far, the nearest thing to a national character which such societies had assumed since the days of the Defenders had been through the loose federation of lodges of the so-called 'Ribbon' society first founded in 1826 and relatively flourishing at local levels ever since. The name derived from the wearing of a white ribbon round the hat for purposes of mutual recognition at night. Occasionally, as in the days of the Defenders, vague political aspirations had been discernible in Ribbon Society transactions: references to 'freeing Ireland', 'liberating our country' or just 'uniting all Roman Catholics'.[1] Once, ambitiously, in the late 1830s, the phrase had been bandied about: 'The hour of England's difficulty is at hand, the Russian bear is drawing near to her in India.'[2] But the Ribbon Society was principally an agrarian secret society, concerned as such societies had always been with dealing out rough justice on the land, a nineteenth-century form of Whiteboyism. The naïve political parlance of such Ribbon lodges could hardly be taken as an organized threat to the constitution.

Apart from the abortive and amateurish efforts of Gray, Lalor, Luby and O'Leary in 1849 there had been no attempt to organize a secret society primarily for political purposes since the days of the United Irishmen. Now, in this autumn of 1858, reports began to appear of a new type of secret society active in the south-west of Ireland.

The *Cork Constitution* of 4 November, while describing the new phenomenon as a Ribbon society and talking of nightly oath-taking, remarked on one rather untypical characteristic. The society apparently appealed mainly to labourers and farm servants, while the tenant farmers themselves held aloof, being 'not altogether at ease with the activists'.[3] An anonymous letter to the paper from someone in Macroom a few days later gave a clearer

4

indication of what was up. Numbers, it said, had taken the oath, but others were not doing so 'because those who so acted before gained nothing by it but were shot down like dogs, hanged, transported and their families turned out of farms and became beggars'.[4] This was an unmistakable reference to '98.

On 29 November the *Cork Examiner*, speculating about the rumours, pronounced: 'If a secret club has been formed, it is in the furtherance of a national movement for the independence of Ireland.' It did its best to make light of the affair.

If it has sprung into life at all it is simply from the dreams of a few enthusiastic young men, who, not yet sufficiently experienced to read the lessons of the past, hope to make of this country a free nation ... they will before long not only see how utterly impracticable are their hopes, and how dead is all sympathy for such movements in this country, but they will find their organization falling asunder now, as it did before, in a more stirring time, like a rope of sand ...[5]

The lord lieutenant issued a proclamation on 3 December offering £100 reward for information about oath-taking, and the first arrests followed immediately. In fact, Dublin Castle had already been given much information by the parish priest of Kenmare, possibly first alerted in the confessional.[6]

The 'enthusiastic young men' turned out to be mainly clerks and National schoolteachers, with a shopkeeper or two. The name of one was to ring sporadically down Irish history for the next fifty years: Jeremiah Donovan (later O'Donovan) Rossa. The Cork newspapers commented that these young men were of a more respectable class than those usually associated with agrarian secret societies.[7] It appeared that the secret society had been functioning under the cover of an open and legal, if nationally-minded, club for self-improvement, the Phoenix National and Literary Society of Skibbereen. This had been founded at the beginning of 1857, with reading-room premises on the walls of which 'Ireland for the Irish' was inscribed in ivy-leaf lettering.[8] The flavour of the talk that had gone on there can be gauged from a letter found in the house of O'Donovan Rossa after his arrest, which ran:

'I am ever ready to do my utmost to promote the cause and acquire the reality of nationality ... but ... I don't believe the Saxon will ever relax his grip except by the persuasion of cold lead and steel ...'[9]

The oath administered to members of the secret society formed under cover of this literary club may have varied slightly from mouth to mouth, and was sometimes inaccurately recollected by informers, but appears to have run, then, along the following lines:

'I ... swear in the presence of God, to renounce all allegiance to the Queen of England, and to take arms and fight at a moment's warning, and to make

Ireland an Independent Democratic Republic, and to yield implicit obedience to the commanders and superiors of this secret society ...'*

The redoubtable O'Donovan Rossa (a member of the House of Lords once thought he was two people, 'Donovan' and 'Rosser')[10] had been doing his share of the swearing-in. When a soldier whom he attempted to suborn declared that 'he was a Queen's man', Rossa replied, so the soldier said, that there was no harm .n that, and 'that there was many a Queen's man joining, that no one would know it till the hop of the ball was up, and everyone could turn to whatever side he liked then'.[11]

Another court witness at this time reported that he had been fed with similar optimistic tidings. Someone, he said, had notified him in the summer of 1858 that 'the Constables of Dublin Castle were in it, but that it would not be prudent to depend on them, though ... it was strongly hoped that ... the whole affair would be done without spilling a glass of blood, there would be such good management'.[12]

Perhaps it was partly such language that helped mislead the authorities into thinking they had no very serious threat to contend with. Moreover, in their critical zeal and alarm they had unearthed a number of other oath-taking societies, all at first supposed to be 'Phoenixes', but which in the end turned out only to be old-style Ribbon Lodges operating with some political flavour, but with no apparent connection with the men in the south-west.[13] Some of these had been using a crude set of challenges and passwords, such as 'We expect a new war between England and France', to be countered by: 'Yes, the Irish Brigade is on the advance.' At night the correct words were: 'The night is dark.' Answer: 'As black as heresy.' And again: 'That the triumph of freedom may proclaim a war.' To which the correct reply was: 'And hoist the French Eagle and American star.' The right hand was then to be brought to the nose and the left hand to the ear.[14] A man arrested in Westmeath with these passwords on him was, according to the police, so drunk he didn't know what he was doing. He turned out to be a naturalized Irish-born citizen of the United States named Fallon, with £38 and the constitution of a so-called Shamrock Benevolent Society of New York in

* Another prescribed version of this famous oath of what later became the Irish Republican Brotherhood seems at this date to have been: 'I ... do solemnly swear, in the presence of Almighty God, that I will do my utmost, at every risk, while life lasts, to make Ireland an independent Democratic Republic; that I will yield implicit obedience, in all things not contrary to the law of God to the commands of my superior officers; and that I shall preserve inviolable secrecy regarding all the transactions of this society that may be confided in me. So help me God! Amen.' See John O'Leary, *Recollections of Fenians and Fenianism* (London 1896), p. 120; Ryan, *The Fenian Chief*, p. 91. The form quoted in the text above was given in court in two separate cases, see *Irishman*, 8 January 1859, 12 March 1859. A famous phrase about the Irish Republic being 'now virtually established' first entered the oath when it was revised in 1859.

his pocket. He had been in the country some ten or eleven months and now received a sentence of seven years' penal servitude.[15]

Of all the others arrested at this time only one other received a term of imprisonment and even he was respited within the year, for O'Donovan Rossa and the rest agreed to plead guilty and bind themselves over to be of good behaviour on condition that he was released. While they had been in prison Smith O'Brien had been one of those who subscribed to a Fair Trial Fund opened on their behalf, though he had at the same time strongly dissociated himself from all attempts to identify the national cause with secret organizations.[16]

Newspaper readers breathed a sigh of relief. But, for all the rather anti-climactic spirit of reassurance that now set in, the *Kilkenny Moderator* had been quite right when it had declared earlier: 'There cannot now be much, if any doubt, that secret and illegal societies, having a directing power or body in some particular place, and activated by a community of purpose, ramify throughout the country.'[17]

The 'directing power' had not been touched; the one really dangerous man had got away. He was in America at the time of the Phoenix trials and the authorities, who knew that he was out of the country, may have made the mistake of bracketing his abilities with those of the slipshod Fallon of Westmeath. If so it was a serious error, for they had out against them a determined and formidable, if himself by no means infallible, opponent.

This man had cropped up in evidence more than once in the course of the Phoenix trials, figuring sometimes under the mysterious name of Shook or Shooks and at others under his real name of Stephens.[18] 'Shook' was merely an anglicization of the Irish 'An Seabhac', or 'the Wandering Hawk', a pseudonym under which for two years now Stephens had been travelling, mainly on foot, sometimes alone, and sometimes with one or two companions, over large tracts of Ireland. Stephens was that same young Kilkenny railway engineer, James Stephens, who had joined Smith O'Brien in the week before Ballingarry, and after weeks of adventurous wanderings during which he was reported dead, had eventually escaped to France.

In Paris Stephens had been with other Irish refugees, principally Michael Doheny and John O'Mahony. He had become particularly friendly with O'Mahony and together with him had made the acquaintance of some of the French and other social revolutionaries then active in the capital. It seems that Stephens and O'Mahony fought together on the barricades in the popular resistance to Louis-Napoleon's *coup d'état* of 1851.[19] Certainly they had contact with, and Stephens made a study of, the international secret societies through which revolutionary democratic activity was then carried on. He was anxious, in the words of an approved panegyrist writing fifteen years later, to acquire 'those secrets by means of which an indisciplined mob can be most readily and effectually matched against a mercenary army'.[20] Certainly, when he again turned his attention to Ireland his political thought contained obvious traces of revolutionary socialist thinking, a small instance of which was the reference to an 'Independent Democratic Republic' in the early oaths quoted at the Phoenix trials. It had, however, been some time before Stephens in Paris again turned his active attention to Ireland. As with most exiles the business of day-to-day living absorbed most of his energies. He taught English, and learned French so well that he was able to join the staff of the *Moniteur* and translated Dickens's *Martin Chuzzlewit* for it in serial form.[21]

Stephens's friend, John O'Mahony, left France for America in 1853. Stephens himself left Paris late in 1855, and after a stay in London came to Ireland again early in 1856. He seems to have returned partly out of a natural wish to see his family and friends again, and partly with some deliberate desire to assess the state of Irish national feeling and see if some of the political lessons he had learnt in France might not be applicable there. His own thoughts for Ireland were based firmly on the need for total separation and republican independence. But he was not just a doctrinaire abstract nationalist, and soon after his arrival he declared in private conversation his general creed, which was to remain constant all his life, namely that '... unless the Irish land were given to the Irish people, Irish national independence was not worth the trouble and sacrifice of obtaining it'.[22] Since, however, his entire active life was to be spent on attempts at organization, political details of the independent Irish Republic for which he strove remained largely undeveloped.

The Ireland of 1856 to which Stephens returned was one in which virtually the only nationalist thinking was that represented in constitutional form by the 'independent opposition' in Parliament. An occasional radical voice cried in the wilderness. One such was Philip Gray's new paper the *Tribune*, which, analysing the demand for Tenant Right, maintained that the real demand was for something much more fundamental than that. It allowed that a landlord had a right to do what he would with his own but asked whether the land really was the landlord's own. 'The truth is,' it declared in italics, 'that all the land of Ireland belongs to the people of Ireland, in the aggregate, to be distributed and made use of just so as best may serve the happiness, prosperity, peace and security of the People of Ireland.'[23]

The *Tribune* went out of business after fifteen weekly issues. Before it did so it published another leader headed 'No True Idea of Nationality in Ireland'. In this it deplored Irishmen's 'existing incapability of comprehending the large idea of an Irish Nation. It is true they talk of their country very plausibly, and in the most high flown terms; but behind all this there is no clear and comprehensive idea of the universal Irish nation, taking in ...

the entire population. All notions of country in the popular mind are vague and confused . . .'[24]

The *Wexford Guardian* commented bitterly on the fact that when O'Connell was alive and had talked about 'England's difficulty being Ireland's opportunity' everyone had thrown their hats into the air and 'dinned the ear of heaven with our acclamations'. Now England's difficulty in the Crimean war had come and gone and they looked like mountebanks or fools or worse. 'Is it to be said that we are men of Gascony, who boasted what we dared not perform?'[25] It was certainly a question extreme Irish nationalists would often need to ask themselves, none more so than Stephens, the man about to try and remedy the situation.

'The ardour of Young Ireland', wrote Stephens later, 'had evaporated as if it had never existed.'[26] He made contact with the surviving members of the youthful secret societies of 1849, with Gray and, later, with Luby, but all reported that such societies had now collapsed for want of any unifying force and that the thoughts they represented were totally isolated. Abandoning a temporary inclination to leave Ireland altogether, Stephens decided to set out mainly on foot to feel Ireland's pulse for himself.

He must have made a curious figure with his slightly foreign appearance and cut of clothes acquired in Paris. In the course of what he later called his 'three thousand mile walk' over much of southern and western Ireland he was frequently mistaken for an actor.[27] He found much to make him pessimistic. A revenue officer in Athlone told him that all was now so quiet in the country, with the '48 men crushed or out of the way, that 'in a few years more Ireland will be as content and as happy as Scotland'.[28] He was shocked to find a sense of national unity so little developed in Connaught that they considered there that there was 'little or none of the Irish in the Leinsterman, he's like any other foreigner and we don't like them'.[29] More than once he asked himself bitterly, 'Did Christ ever die for such a people?'[30] The closest he got to any ground for hope on this tour in 1856 seems to have been in Longford where he came across the age-old 'prophecies' of St Columbille. These had long figured as a mystical untutored inspiration in Irish country life. 'After a time', so ran the legend, or 'when the right time comes', then, and not till then, would Ireland wake from her trance and liberate herself. It was never precisely known what such liberation would involve, but the prophecies in this form probably dated back to the days of the great Tudor confiscations of land, and it was the return of the lost lands that was enshrined in the legend.

But if Stephens found little external encouragement, his own sense of purpose and determination had somehow acquired strength from his long walk. His health, too, which had been poor when he first arrived in Dublin was now greatly improved. And though he lacked almost all the qualities required of a great revolutionary leader, being jealous and boastful, capable of small-mindedness and untruthful at least to the point of serious self-deception, his extraordinary egotism was always allied to an extraordinary capacity for organization and work.

By the end of this tour of 1856, though he was still 'feeling his way' politically, his mind was moving in favour of some secret oath-bound revolutionary organization with ramifications throughout the country which would be dedicated to separation from England and the establishment of an Irish republic.[31] There was, after all, a tradition for such a republican organization in Ireland older than those secret societies which had so caught his attention in Paris. 'Such a movement,' he wrote, on looking back many years later, 'had not been inaugurated in Ireland since '98; but did not the United Irish society give me hope that their attempt would be improved upon by our avoiding the errors they fell into, and by a close adhesion to more Continental clubs where traitors were "few and far between".'[32] And though much of his tour had been discouraging, he had at least become clear about certain realities, not all of which were unfavourable.

First, it was a waste of time to bother any longer about winning the upper classes for nationality. In a conversation he had had with Smith O'Brien, himself only just returned from exile, in his home near Limerick, O'Brien had told him bluntly: 'You see, Mr Stephens, the respectable people of the towns especially are quite indifferent to, if not hostile to, nationality.'[33] Stephens accepted the fact and thus disencumbered himself of the most fatally preoccupying illusions of Young Ireland. The tenant farmers also, Stephens acknowledged, were temporarily mainly interested in their better harvests and 'apathetic' towards nationality. But among the labourers, small tradesmen and the sons of peasants he had discovered a great deal of general 'disaffection', and saw that 'even now it would not be hard to stir them up into insurrection'.[34] To this end he devoted, with little consideration for his own material well-being, the next ten years of his life.

Apart from the needs of his ego, it was the socially radical nature of the task that was Stephens's inspiration as much as any emotional Irish patriotism. He was to write in his diary not long afterwards that it was the principle of liberty and right that he was fighting for: if, he said, England were a republic battling for human freedom against an Ireland in league with despots he would unhesitatingly take up arms against his native land.[35] And this unabashed linking of Irish republicanism with those at the lower end of the social scale – an affirmation in European terms of the native principles of Lalor – was thereafter to remain one of its permanent features, with important consequences long after Stephens's own death. Another factor in the Irish republican tradition, which Stephens consciously formulated, and which was also to be of great importance after his death, was that of the need for continuity in the tradition at all costs, even the cost of dismal failure. There was inevitably some *post hoc* rationalization in which Stephens was to write of his own efforts. But this rationalization was picked up and consciously adopted as a principle by a later generation of nationalists.

'I came to the resolve', Stephens wrote, reminiscing years later, 'that the attempt was not only worth trying, but should be tried in the very near future if we wanted at all to keep our flag flying; for I was sure as of my own existence that if another decade was allowed to pass without an endeavour of some kind or another to shake off an unjust yoke, the Irish people would sink into a lethargy from which it would be impossible for any patriot ... to arouse them ...'[36]

In fact, in 1856, to James Stephens contemplating a republican organization there were quite other favourable factors besides those he had been able to detect in Ireland. Across the Atlantic existed a vast potential of hitherto little organized Irish money and Irish manpower which might be brought to Ireland's aid. Some attempts had already been made to organize this Irish power realistically for Irish purposes, but so far to little effect. The poverty of the vast majority of American-Irish immigrants and their primary wish to settle down successfully in their new lives meant for a long time that far more eloquence and emotion was readily available for Ireland than hard cash and practical intent. Irish nationalism was often more important in what it did for the emigrants' status in America than in what it did for Ireland. Some Irish republican clubs had been first formed in New York in 1848, but had proved their military effectiveness not in Ireland but in their transformation into a regiment of the New York State militia.[37] Shortly after Mitchel's escape from Tasmania and arrival in New York there had been founded under his inspiration, in April 1854, an 'Irishmen's Civil and Military Republican Union' with the object of liberating Ireland from English oppression.[38] But it came to nothing, and at the end of the year Mitchel left New York for Tennessee.

Mitchel's 'Republican Union' had a number of successors forming themselves on similar lines, and a Massachusetts Emigrant Aid Society actually held a convention to discuss the speediest and most effective means of promoting action 'leading to ensure the success of the cause of liberty in our native land'.[39] Another such organization was the Emmet Monument Association, whose purpose was plainly expressed in its name, recalling Emmet's wish to have no epitaph until his country took its place among the nations of the earth. Stephens's friend, John O'Mahony, who had gone to America in 1853, had helped run the Emmet Monument Association together with Michael Doheny, the former Young Irelander and Stephens's old companion on the run. They had even sent an emissary of their own to Ireland in 1855, a man called Joseph Denieffe, who was given *carte blanche* to organize and to inform the faithful that 'they' – Doheny and co. – were ready to land thirty thousand men in Ireland in the autumn.[40] Given the wild improbability of such a boast it was as well for Denieffe he got little further than founding a small organization in the neighbourhood of Kilkenny, and, after meeting Gray, Luby and others in Dublin, found it more relevant for a while to concentrate on the practical business of earning a living.[41]

When Stephens on his return to Dublin at the end of 1856 heard again of his old friend O'Mahony, it was to the effect that O'Mahony was so disgusted with Irish political agitation in America that he was going to give it up altogether. 'I am sick of Young Ireland and its theatrical leaders', he had written, '... I am sick of Irish Catholics in America. I am sick of Yankee-doodle twaddle, Yankee-doodle selfishness and all Yankee-doodle-dum! ... It is refreshing to my heart to turn from Irish tinsel patriots, the people's leaders on gala days, and from American retrogression, to the stern front and untiring constancy of the continental apostles of liberty and the ceaseless preparation of their disciples.'[42]

A man possessed of less demonic and egotistical pertinacity than Stephens might have taken this letter as discouragement. But Stephens seems by now to have made up his mind that something could be done. 'I have no hesitation', he once said, 'in saying that I think very highly of myself. I have grasped more of the truth than almost any other man.'[43] In any case, he had himself long thought Irish America worthless for want of a proper organization.

It was [he wrote later] a wind-bag, or a phantom, the laughing stock of sensible men and the El Dorado of fools. For what was the sum total at that time of Irish-American patriotism. ... Speeches of bayonets, gala days and jolly nights, banners and sashes ... bunkum and fulsome filibustering. ... The oratory of the Young Irelanders was the immediate cause of this scandalous state of things. They introduced into the Irish-American arena the pompous phrases of the old Nation suppers and the gilded harangues of Conciliation Hall. ... Irish patriots sang songs and responded in glowing language to glowing toasts on Irish National Independence over beakers of fizzling champagne.[44]

To all this Stephens felt convinced that he could put a stop. He wrote back to John O'Mahony at once to dissuade him from giving up Irish agitation in America and presumably gave him some inkling of the organization at home that was in his own mind.

The Emmet Monument Association, which had been inactive since 1855 and the dispatch of Denieffe to Ireland, began to revive. Meanwhile, Stephens extended his contacts in Dublin and elsewhere, meeting Thomas Luby for the first time and attending with him and speaking at the funeral of Philip Gray who died early in 1857. Stephens also found himself a satisfactory means of earning a living by teaching French. Two of his pupils were the sons of John Blake Dillon, with whom nine years before he had faced Captain Longmore of the Dragoons on the barricade at Killenaule. Stephens apparently proved a satisfactory tutor to the sons, but wholly failed to

12

convince the father that there was anything but futility in his proposal for a secret revolutionary organization.[45]

In the autumn of 1857 another Irish American from the Emmet Monument Association arrived in Ireland. His name, Owen Considine, is known to history only because of the historic message he brought. That message itself might have been grounds for no more than a historical footnote, and the Emmet Monument Association of no more significance than the Shamrock Benevolent Institution which had dispatched Fallon of Westmeath, but for the personality of the man to whom the message was addressed.

The message brought by Considine to Stephens came from O'Mahony and Doheny, and positively asked Stephens to set up a revolutionary organization with which they and other American exiles could cooperate. The available extent of the practical cooperation from America was not precisely stated, and Stephens, typically, seems either to have optimistically assumed it was adequate, or at least taken for granted his own ability to make it so. He sent a message to Doheny and O'Mahony to be carried by Denieffe, whom Stephens disinterred for the purpose from the tranquillity of a job in the North. Calmly Stephens stated that if, as suggested, he could be guaranteed money, and a spearhead force of some five hundred men from the States, preferably armed with Lee Enfield rifles, he would undertake, within three months of Denieffe's return to him with an official Yes, to have at least 10,000 men organized – 1,500 with firearms, the rest with pikes – ready to move at twenty-four hours' notice.[46]

It was the beginning of a near-decade of such optimistic statements. Stephens's message concluded with a warning which was equally characteristic of a whole future pattern of events.

'I believe it essential to success,' wrote Stephens, on this 6 January 1858, 'that the centre of this or any similar organization [i.e., himself] should be perfectly unshackled; in other words, a provisional dictator. On this point I can conscientiously concede nothing. That I should not be worried or hampered by the wavering or imbecile, it will be well to make this out in proper form with the signature of every influential Irishman of our union ...'[47] The man who was soon to be known as the Chief Organizer (sometimes Chief Executive) of the Irish Republic was beginning as he intended to go on.

Nearly three months later Stephens's messenger, Denieffe, returned from the States with the results of a fund-raising operation on the part of the American organization. This had brought in precisely £80 – the very minimum Stephens had stipulated as a necessary monthly income.[48] A man less obsessed by his own will than Stephens might have been daunted by such a puny result. Denieffe also had to make clear to Stephens that there was in New York as yet no proper organization, only a body of sympathizers. Nevertheless, the very evening of Denieffe's return, appropriately St

Patrick's Day, 17 March 1858, Stephens formally founded in his lodgings behind Lombard Street, Dublin, a secret society dedicated to the establishment in Ireland of an Independent Democratic Republic. This was the society later to be known as the Irish Republican Brotherhood, though it did not generally assume that name for some years.*[49]

Stephens, Denieffe, Thomas Luby and others who were present all swore themselves into the society. The very next day Denieffe was sent back to America for more money and Stephens and Luby set off on an organizing tour of the south and south-west of Ireland.

The organization of this new secret society was presumably partly modelled on what Stephens had learnt during his contacts with the international revolutionary societies in Paris. It was, however, also similar to the organization of the old United Irishmen. At the head of the society was the Chief Organizer, or Chief Executive, James Stephens himself, sometimes known as the Head Centre. Below him were four Vice-Organizers or 'Vs' – one for each province of Ireland – and below them came numerous Circles each of which had an A as 'Centre' or 'Colonel', with nine Bs or captains under him.[50] Under each B in turn came nine Cs or sergeants, and under each C, nine Ds or privates. The theory was that no member should be known to any other members except those in their own circles. This was not strictly adhered to, but Stephens's primary aim of establishing a system of security superior to that of the United Irishmen was for some time achieved. This was all the more remarkable since, as in the days of the United Irishmen and the Defenders, much of the oath-taking was conducted in and around public houses.

Although Stephens had many personal failings his ability as an organizer in the primitive and difficult conditions of rural Ireland was outstanding. All who in the course of time arrived from America to inspect the 'Home Organization', or 'men in the gap' as they came to be called, were impressed by the extent of the organization they found in Stephens's day and even those who, writing later, were fully alive to his defects as a leader continued to praise his qualities as an organizer. Luby and John O'Leary, the young student rebel of 1849, whom Stephens soon drew into his organization, were to come to refer to him as 'The Great Sir Hocus Pocus' and 'vain, arrogant, with a most inordinate belief in his own powers';[51] yet they retained to the end admiration for his organizing ability. And the French General Cluseret, who for a brief moment found himself caught up in Stephens's organization, described him as 'vain, despotic and overbearing beyond any

* In Devoy's *Recollections*, which was followed by Desmond Ryan in both his *Phoenix Flame* (1936) and his *The Fenian Chief* (1967), the exact place of the founding of the IRB is given as Peter Langan's timber yard in Lombard Street. But Devoy, who himself professed to be following Denieffe, more than once does so inaccurately and the versions of Denieffe, who was there, and of O'Leary who was merely repeating what he had been told by Luby who was also there, seem more reliable.

14

man I ever saw' but at the same time 'an organizer to the fingers' ends'.[58]

As yet, in the spring of 1858, the organization was in a totally embryonic state. The secret society had at this stage no official name, probably as an intentional feature of Stephens's security system. Members referred to it as 'Our Body', 'Our Movement' or 'Our Organization'.[53] And later in 1858 this certainly turned out to its advantage, for those corners of it that were revealed in the 'Phoenix' arrests were identified only with the name of the Phoenix societies thus put down.

It was in May of 1858 that Stephens and Luby had first made contact with the young men of the Phoenix Society of Skibbereen and had sworn in O'Donovan Rossa and his associates with promises of help coming from beyond the seas. However, Denieffe returned from America during the summer, this time with only £40, and Stephens thereupon undertook to go to America to put things on a better basis there himself. He sailed for the States in October 1858. Working there virtually from scratch he managed to collect some £600 in six months. This sum would have been larger, but for the discovery of the Phoenix societies and publication of details of the trials in the Irish American press during the winter. These reports induced a certain sudden wariness in the attitude of those whom Stephens had at first often impressed favourably. Thus he failed to get his hands on what was left of the sum of money collected on behalf of Gavan Duffy's tentative organization in 1848.* He also failed to secure the total confidence of the two Irishmen who were then still the most colourful patriots in the States, Meagher and Mitchel. But he left behind him in the States on his return to Ireland in March 1859 the embryo of an effective organization. This was to be headed by John O'Mahony and was soon to be known as the Fenian Brotherhood.

The name Fenian was given to the new organization by O'Mahony who, as a Gaelic scholar, found inspiration in the legend of the ancient Gaelic warrior Fiona MacCumhail and his élite legion, the Fianna.[54] Stephens, on sailing for Ireland, left O'Mahony in no doubt at all that he (Stephens) was in overall charge and that O'Mahony was subordinate to him. This O'Mahony reluctantly accepted. But the name under which those who worked in both halves of the movement – in America and in Ireland – were to go down to history was the one O'Mahony had given the American branch of the organization: the Fenians.

* See *The Most Distressful Country*, Volume 1 of *The Green Flag*, p. 271.

2

James Stephens at Work

For over a year after leaving America in the spring of 1859 Stephens did not return to Ireland at all but lived in Paris, out of reach of the British authorities. He sent O'Leary to America for a time to work with John O'Mahony, while Luby acted as his agent in Ireland, quickly re-organizing the South after the release of the Phoenix prisoners and creating for the first time an effective organization in Dublin.

Stephens himself in Paris soon began to show signs of enjoying the conspiracy for its own sake, rather than for the sake of its practical objective. The important thing for him was that he held the threads of the conspiracy in his own hands. The letter of introduction which he gave John O'Leary to take to America proclaimed that he expected for O'Leary 'the highest possible courtesy, respect and even deference, as my representative; and through me, the representative of the Irish cause'.[1] He protested continually to O'Mahony of the inadequate funds he was receiving from the States and strongly resented O'Mahony's dispatch of envoys to Ireland on his own initiative to see what progress the organization was making.

Stephens at this stage had no undue sense of urgency about planning a rising. He spent agreeable hours visiting picture galleries and pointing out the details of the bas relief on the Arc de Triomphe to other conspirators.[2] But though his main reason for not returning to Ireland was, sensibly, to avoid the authorities so soon after the Phoenix trials, he managed also to convince himself that he was not wasting time. He hoped to obtain help from the French Government, remembering undoubtedly the analogous situation of Wolfe Tone, who unlike Stephens had not had the advantage of knowing what was going on in Ireland.

But in an admittedly far less favourable international situation Stephens had no success with the French Government at all. He wrote to O'Mahony in America in lame self-justification: '... the very parties I relied on for putting me in touch with those I had to expect anything of consequence from, were not here, and the letters I addressed to each of them remained unanswered ...'[3] Even when Napoleon III embarked on his Italian campaign and Stephens's hopes of 'complicating' Franco–British relations were again raised, nothing came of them. He told O'Mahony: 'I succeeded in getting introduced to parties who, from the very first, showed a willingness to forward my views, of which disposition I found it impossible to avail myself, owing to my inability to meet the expenses incidental to important negotiations.'[4]

The curious strain of bombast and incompetence which was to mix with much that was idealistic and courageous in the Fenian movement was already at work. But at least there was in Stephens's thinking at this stage some appreciation of what was realistic and what was not. He wrote to O'Mahony from Paris in September 1859: 'I give you once more to understand that we cannot strike this year', adding that if anyone was suggesting that they ought to strike whatever happened they could never have got the idea from him.[5]

This was partly in response to some dissatisfaction with Stephens's leadership which had already been expressed in Ireland but which was quickly crushed by Luby and other supporters of Stephens. Among these was that eye-witness who had had such singular glimpses of Smith O'Brien smoking a cigar in his dreamy state in July 1848. This was Charles Kickham of Mullinahone. Kickham, though he had since become almost blind and totally deaf as a result of a shooting accident, had rallied to Stephens's organization early, and was one day himself to become its head centre. Now, as peacemaker, he tried to reduce the tension developing with O'Mahony as a result of Stephens's continual and often arrogant complaints of lack of financial support from America. Stephens had grounds for such complaints. Very little money was in fact sent from the States to the organization in Ireland for several years.[6] But O'Mahony's task was not easy, for a financial crisis in the United States in 1857 had depleted Irish emigrant savings and for a long time words remained easier to raise than money for the Irish cause. As Doheny himself was to remark frankly on one occasion: 'God knows, if eloquence could free or save a people we ought to be the freest and safest people on the face of the globe.'[7] In addition to this, however, many Irish in America in 1859 had to be convinced that there was anything realistic to subscribe for.

Stephens showed small patience with O'Mahony's difficulties. But O'Mahony, gentle and more likeable than Stephens, was a weaker personality. Moreover, O'Mahony's political future was for better or worse linked with Stephens. He had little alternative but to submit to the taunts and insults Stephens heaped on him. At the end of 1860 he came personally to Ireland for the first time since 1848 and to meet him there Stephens himself returned from Paris to Dublin. Personal relations were left little better as a result of the meeting, but some clarification of what was expected from America was agreed on. The arrival of five hundred men from America, with arms and officers, plus at least fifty thousand rifles, was accepted as the prerequisite of any rising of the Irish people. Stephens would continue to organize in Ireland itself. But the onus of making it possible for the Irish people to use their organization was placed squarely on the American half of the conspiracy.

An air of inactivity and apathy seemed to settle over the movement in Ireland for a while. John O'Leary allowed himself to get out of touch with it altogether and went off to make his life in London.[8] He lacked the willingness to dedicate himself professionally to the thankless and grinding tasks of humdrum revolutionary work. This was Stephens's own most notable quality. His presence in Ireland was a guarantee that the organization would not fade away. But the initiative for an event that was really to give the organization significance in Ireland came originally from outside Ireland altogether.

On 15 January 1861 there had died in a San Francisco hospital Terence Bellew McManus, the Young Irelander who at the prospect of a rising in 1848 had abandoned his very successful shipping agency in Liverpool, and rushed over to Ireland to join Smith O'Brien in his ineffectual progress round Tipperary. The gesture had ruined McManus's commercial career, for although he had escaped from Tasmania, where he had been transported, he had been unable to make a success of business life in America and had died in poverty. Little had been heard of McManus in a decade and he had not figured with any prominence in Irish American politics, despite a letter to Gavan Duffy soon after 1848, in which he had written: 'Whenever a death-blow is to be struck at this vile despotism that crushes our land, I trust in heaven I will be there to strike.' Now at last, in death, he was to be almost as good as his word.

The Fenian Brotherhood in America was an open and legal organization, keeping only its inner policies and contacts with Ireland as secret as possible. Some San Francisco Fenians proposed that McManus's body should be sent back to Ireland as a national gesture. The Brotherhood as a whole took to the project and the coffined body was brought with due Irish patriotic emphasis through a number of American cities to New York. There it was given a lying-in-state in St Patrick's Cathedral by the Catholic Archbishop Hughes, who reminded Catholics in his address that the Church in some cases found it lawful to resist and overthrow a tyrannical government.[9]

In Ireland, constitutional nationalists like A. M. Sullivan, the editor of *The Nation*, were hoping to acquire prestige from the mood of national solemnity evoked by McManus's return. But Stephens seized the opportunity to take control of the arrangements for the funeral himself and to work up national enthusiasm through his own organization. In doing this he challenged two groups of political opponents in Ireland: constitutional nationalists like Sullivan, and the Catholic hierarchy.

In a Lenten Pastoral as early as 1859 at the time of the Phoenix trials Archbishop Cullen had already made clear his interpretation of the Church's attitude to secret societies. He had not only condemned them along with 'improper dances, such as the polka' as repugnant to the Church. He had specifically stated that the Catholic Church solemnly excommunicated all her children who engaged in secret societies, and that no member of any secret society could receive absolution.[10] Although Cullen was to spend some years wresting from the Vatican a specific sentence of excommunication against Fenianism as such, his own clear attitude, expressed so early, presented Stephens with a formidable difficulty in his attempts to organize the Irish people. Though Stephens was to succeed in amassing much general popular sympathy for Fenianism, the Church's condemnation was always one additional telling reason why in the end people should be careful about committing themselves to it.

Cullen forbade the use of Dublin Cathedral for McManus's lying-in-state, and the coffin had to rest the day before the funeral at the Mechanics' Institute. But Stephens managed to score something of a triumph by reminding people that the Church did not always speak with one coherent voice. He secured for the funeral arrangements the cooperation of a radical priest named Patrick Lavelle, who was always to show sympathy with Fenianism and who, though more or less permanently embattled with Cullen, enjoyed a certain favour with the next most important member of the Catholic hierarchy, John MacHale, Archbishop of Tuam.

Stephens's practical organization of the funeral was an outstanding success. On the cold and cheerless morning of 10 November 1861, with the pavements deep in slush from the heavy sleet and rain of the night before and a drizzling rain which settled in by noon, an estimated crowd of between twenty and thirty thousand Dubliners turned out to watch the Young Irelander McManus brought to his final rest in Glasnevin cemetery, while the bands played the Dead March of Saul.[11] A measure of the whole manoeuvre's success had already been registered the day before when the very respectable constitutional paper, the *Freeman's Journal*, had commented of the crowds who attended the lying-in-state in the Mechanics' Institute the day before: 'the demonstration ... owed its origins and its magnitude to the cause with which he was identified.'

The whole event was an advertisement for 'the cause' of a dimension which Stephens could never have achieved by other legal, or even illegal means. His horsemen, wearing black scarves and armlets and carrying batons, kept the crowds in disciplined order. An official delegation from America, including Doheny and O'Mahony, were present. The four pall-bearers were all members of Stephens's organization and three thousand of an open 'front' organization, the National Brotherhood of St Patrick, followed close behind the coffin. There was not the slightest disorder or confusion in the procession. The formal funeral oration, rather starchily composed by Stephens, was delivered at Glasnevin by torchlight by a member of the American delegation. But before this, as night descended, Patrick Lavelle, the radical priest who was not afraid to risk Archbishop Cullen's anger, gave an impromptu address by the graveside. He seemed embarrassed by and deplored the occasional cheers by which he was interrupted. But he must have known he was inviting them.

'I am proud,' he said, 'to see that the people of Ireland and of Dublin are not dead – that they have hope – that though the prophet be dead the spirit he evoked will outlive him, and even in the present generation raise his country from degradation to the glory of a nation.'[12]

From the time of the McManus funeral Stephens's organization in Ireland began to flourish. Though referred to mysteriously rather in the same sort of way as people spoke of the fairies, it came eventually to be known popularly, from association with the open Brotherhood in the States, as 'the Fenians'.* Early in 1862 Stephens, accompanied by Luby, continued the series of organizational tours of Ireland which were to be a regular feature of his activity whenever he was in the country.[13] He kept up an active network in Dublin. In the summer of 1863, in an attempt to raise funds of which he was still desperately short, he started his own weekly newspaper, the *Irish People*, inducing John O'Leary to come back from London to help edit it, and installing O'Donovan Rossa as business manager.

The *Irish People* was not financially the success that had been hoped for and it never succeeded in Ireland in getting much circulation away from the constitutional nationalist paper, *The Nation*.†[14] But it was a propaganda platform for Stephens of major importance and wholly under his control, unlike the only other extreme nationalist paper, the *Irishman*. Though keeping within the bounds of legality the *Irish People* preached a much stronger message than *The Nation*, flirting continually with the language of violence and openly proclaiming that parliamentary agitation was a useless way of trying to achieve the Irish independence which was unequivocally its goal.[15] Like the old *Nation* under Davis it spoke of the need for 'National Self-Reliance'[16] and published patriotic songs and verses, which O'Leary, the editor, tried to keep to a certain literary standard, complaining bitterly on at least one occasion of the poor literary quality of many of the poems submitted – the endless repetitions of green, dear and poor Erin and the inevitable rhyming of sheen with green and crag with flag.[17] It kept constantly in front of the Irish people reminders of the existence of the open Fenian Brotherhood in the United States, and though the outbreak of the civil war there temporarily overshadowed the Irish American scene, there were

* This was true at least by the spring of 1864. See, e.g., *Irish People*, 26 March 1864, and thereafter Irish and British newspapers generally.

† Note, however, that in England and Scotland, where it would have been bought more, and passed from hand to hand or read aloud from less, it 'almost annihilated' *The Nation*.

continual hints of the eventual significance of that war for Ireland. A song
published at Christmas 1863 entitled 'An Irish Maiden to her American
soldier' concluded:

> Come home, come home, to your waiting bride – come home to your
> plighted vows, love,
> But never come back like a cringing slave, with the brand on your stain-
> less brow, love.
> Come home with the heart you bore away – to your kindred and home and
> sire-land.
> But stay away if you bear not back your manhood's resolve for Ireland.[18]

And when some New York ladies presented a green silk flag specially made
by Tiffany's to the 1st Regiment of the Phoenix brigade, commanded by
John O'Mahony, the fact was reported in faithful detail.[19]

The outbreak of the American civil war had obviously been a set-back
for Stephens, confining American Irish energies for several years primarily
to the other side of the Atlantic. On the other hand, it did provide the
American Irish, who were fighting for both North and South, with unequalled
experience of modern war. If they could afterwards be persuaded to turn
their attention to Ireland the delay might even prove to have been worth
while. But they needed organization and Stephens was increasingly dissatisfied with O'Mahony as an effective leader, actually sending Luby to
the States early in 1863 with powers to suspend or even depose him, if
necessary.[20] He himself kept up a continual pressure on O'Mahony with
accounts of his own success in Ireland, while deploring the small amount
of financial support from the States. 'One Hundred and Thirteen Pounds
from the whole American organization in a whole year!' he wrote in 1862,
and continued '. . . our numbers are in all places I have heard from increasing,
in some places the increase is next to incredible. Thus, a centre who, three
months ago, did not count a hundred men, sent me last week a return for
eight hundred.'[21]

As late as 1864 the Fenian Brotherhood in the States numbered only some
ten thousand men, but in that year Stephens himself went to America, and
carried out a most energetic and successful tour of the Union Armies recruiting for the Fenian Brotherhood. He wrote to O'Mahony in New York that
there were a hundred thousand men ready to fight for Ireland, adding: 'Don't
say any more that I exaggerate.'[22] And as the civil war moved towards
its conclusion Stephens increasingly sounded a note of optimistic urgency.
'Let no man, for an instant, forget,' he wrote to O'Mahony in December
1864, 'that we are bound to action next year ... I ask you in the name of
God to believe that no others, after us, can bring the cause to the test of
battle and that our battle must be entered on sometime in the coming
year.'[23]

In January 1865 the Fenians in the States themselves began to show signs of effective consolidation and firmness. At the Fenian Convention at Cincinnati in that month O'Mahony proclaimed that 'this Brotherhood is virtually at war with the oligarchy of Great Britain ... the Fenian Congress acts the part of a national assembly of an Irish Republic. Our organized friends in Ireland constitute its army ...'.[24] Supplies of money to Ireland increased considerably and a number of envoys were sent over to report back on whether in fact the organization there was in as good shape as Stephens maintained. Though the implied suspicion inevitably irritated Stephens, these envoys in fact all confirmed his own account, reporting back enthusiastically on the widespread nature of the organization.

One envoy, Captain T. J. Kelly (soon to be colonel), who had fought in the 10th Ohio Regiment of the US army, arrived in Ireland in March 1865.[25] He reported in June that everyone in Ireland was now ready, that property was being sold and rent withheld and that half the militia was Fenian-minded.[26] 'Only this inspection with its possibility of postponement implied is a dampener,' he added.[27]

The business of seducing the militia and other British soldiers from their loyalty to the queen and transferring it to the Irish Republic, which in terms of the 'The Brotherhood's' oath was 'now virtually established', had been in the hands of a young man named John Devoy, a member of Stephens's organization since the early days, who in 1861 had spent a year in the French Foreign Legion to acquire military experience which he hoped might one day be useful to Ireland.[28] Assisted effectively by a colourful character known as Pagan O'Leary and other agents, Devoy had managed to get a number of British soldiers to take the Fenian oath, though their eagerness to do so may often have owed more to the attractions of the public houses where the ritual was performed than to idealism. In addition to these successes Devoy had brought over from England some seventeen deserters from the British Army to act in Dublin as drill-masters for the Irish Republic in return for board and lodging and one shilling and sixpence a day – twopence more a day than they had been getting before.[29]

Meanwhile, Stephens himself, often known colloquially as 'the Captain', but operating under many different aliases (Power, Watson, Kelly, Wright, Daly, etc.),[30] had been perfecting his organization. Fenian meetings, held in fields under the cover of football matches, had proliferated.[31] Drilling proceeded regularly in groups of fifty to sixty in halls in the towns, while in the countryside and especially at night mysterious bodies of Fenians were parading and manoeuvring. A contemporary song ran:

> See who comes over the red-blossomed heather,
> Their green banners kissing the pure mountain air,
> Heads erect! Eyes to front! Stepping proudly together ...
> Out and make way for the bold Fenian men.

> ... Pay them back woe for woe,
> Give them back blow for blow,
> Out and make way for the bold Fenian men.

> Side by side for the cause have our forefathers battled
> On our hills never echoed the tread of a slave,
> In many a field where the leaden hail rattled,
> Through the red gap of glory they marched to the grave.

> And those who inherit their name and their spirit
> Will march with the banners of liberty then
> All who love foreign law, native or Sassenach,
> Must out and make way for the bold Fenian men.

During 1864 some arrests had been made for illegal drilling associated with the Fenians. The Brotherhood was known to have ramifications over most of Ireland, but considering its extent remarkably little hard evidence about it had come publicly to light.[32] Altogether, by the beginning of 1865, Stephens reckoned that he had some eighty-five thousand men effectively organized in Ireland and the only difficulty he foresaw was in keeping them together while delay occurred in supplying them with arms. He had established schools of engineering and musketry, manufacturing percussion caps, cartridges and shells and even, so he said, founding cannon. 'Nothing shall be wanting,' he wrote to America, 'if our American brothers do their duty.'[33]

When, therefore, after the South's surrender, the Union and Confederate armies began to disband in June 1865, the prospects for a rising in Ireland seemed good. Former American officers, recognizable from their felt hats and square-toed boots, were soon making their way across the Atlantic to Ireland.[34] In August, after further confirmation by Fenian envoys in Ireland of the readiness of the organization there, O'Mahony issued the 'final call' for money in the States, raising some $30,000 in two weeks.*[35] The idea of fitting out Irish privateers, 'to hoist the green flag and ... sweep English commerce from the seas' was openly advertised in the American press.[36] Ten Irish pilots arrived in New York to help bring Fenians into Ireland. But ominously O'Mahony found it 'maddening' that people in Ireland should think his plans so far advanced.[37]

A worrying incident of another kind had occurred in Ireland the month before. The last set of Fenian envoys, P. W. Dunne and Patrick J. Meehan, had on the very day of their arrival in Dublin lost some vital documents, including a letter from O'Mahony introducing them as plenipotentiaries to the Chief Executive of the Irish Republic.[38] This letter, together with another which compromised O'Donovan Rossa and a draft for £500, had been pinned to Meehan's underwear but had dropped out.[39] The whole day was spent looking for the documents, but in vain, and the possibility that they

* The total for 1865 was to top a quarter of a million dollars altogether.

might have fallen into the hands of the police was disconcerting. In fact this was exactly what had happened, for they were picked up by a small boy at Kingstown railway station about 4.30 that afternoon. But the authorities did not move.[40]

By September 1865 Ireland was tense. The gentry in Clare and Limerick were sending their plate in boxes to the Bank.[41] Boatmen on the Shannon saw large boatloads of men crossing silently by night from Clare to the Limerick side of the river, their arms glinting in the moonlight.[42] There was continued talk of the Fenians everywhere in the Irish and English press. Instances of Fenian drilling and marching became more and more blatant, the *Cork Herald* supposing correctly that 'some of those who have returned from America are disseminating the spirit of disaffection among the people'.[43] The police were said to be on the alert, but the *Dublin Evening Mail* warned against complacency. It reminded its readers that the authorities were not now dealing with hot-headed enthusiasts as in 1848, but with determined and clever men; 'and nothing has shown this more than the clever organization of the Fenians, which never leaves a password, paper or any other tangible means by which they can be discovered, and at the same time they appear to be under perfect control from some unseen authority'.[44] To Unionists there was certainly something sinister and mysterious about the quality of their opponents, but the *Mail* in fact was going too far. The loss of the documents from envoy Meehan's underwear had not been their only mistake.

On 8 September 1865 Stephens in Dublin wrote a letter on the subject of organization to the Fenians in Clonmel. It concluded: 'There is no time to be lost. This year – and let there be no mistake about it – must be the year of action. I speak with a knowledge and authority to which no other man could pretend and I repeat, the flag of Ireland – of the Irish Republic – must this year be raised. . . . Yours fraternally, J. Power.'[45]

The letter was to be taken to Clonmel by hand. But instead of proceeding there at once the messenger went and had a number of drinks. He then went to the *Irish People* office to sleep things off, and half-sleepy and half-drunk was making water into a chamber pot when the letter was taken from his pocket by a former folder of parcels and writer of labels at the office named Nagle. Nagle was a Fenian and former National schoolmaster. He had been giving detailed information to the authorities in return for money for the past eighteen months.[46]

3

Stephens In and
Out of Trouble

Even the careful John O'Mahony in the States had succumbed to the
wave of euphoria among the Fenians. 'Ere long,' he declared, 'there shall be
an Irish Army on the Irish hillsides ready to do battle for Irish independence
and drive back from the green and sacred Isle of Erin those ruthless tyrants
who have desolated our homes and driven us wandering exiles over the
whole earth.'[1]

Four days later A. M. Sullivan, the editor of *The Nation*, was woken in
the morning in the northern suburbs of Dublin by his brother telling him
excitedly to get up and hurry into town.

'Quick – quick. There is desperate work. The *Irish People* is suppressed;
the office is seized; Luby, O'Leary and Rossa are arrested; telegraphic com-
munication with the South is stopped ...'[2]

All this was true. The government had struck during the night.

It had been a thorough operation, with only one disappointment. Stephens
himself had not been caught. A. M. Sullivan thought this meant that there
would be barricades up in the city by nightfall. But there were to be no
barricades up in Dublin either that night or for many thousands of nights
to come.

Though Stephens had begun his organization determined to improve on
the security of the United Irishmen, and had succeeded in that, his security
was by no means watertight. What was surprising in the circumstances
was that it was as effective as it was.

The very openness with which the technically legal activity was carried
on must in itself have been confusing to the authorities. Stephens himself,
O'Donovan Rossa, O'Leary, Luby and others long associated with separatism and republicanism were regularly to be found in or around the *Irish
People* office. And the paper always made the most of the fact that the
Fenian Brotherhood in the United States was not a secret organization; it
quoted with approval a contemporary weekly which with mock-naïvety
declared that it had searched through the American papers for information
about that society and discovered 'there is no more secrecy about it than there

is about ordering a joint of meat from your butcher'.³ In Ireland, too, a body calling itself the National Brotherhood of St Patrick was an open legal organization, which by its very unabashed avowal of the cause of separation and its sympathy with the Fenian Brotherhood in the United States must have added to the government's difficulty in deciding exactly how much more there was in all this than met the eye.

But though the authorities were often in the dark about details of Stephens's organization, the broad lines of what was going on in secret and the identities of all the important people involved had long been known to them through their system of informers. Nagle, who had been giving information since March 1864, was not the only source. A detective named Thomas Talbot passed himself off so successfully as a water-bailiff called John Kelly at Carrick-on-Suir that local Fenians, thinking he was the head centre for the South of Ireland, used to come to him for promotion. He attended many a Fenian meeting at which drinking and the singing of Fenian songs took place, though he was overcome by scruples when 'Out and Make Way for the Fenian Men' came up, simply letting on he was singing it, but only moving his mouth up and down.⁴

Just as important as the penetration of the organization in Ireland was the fact that very close to John O'Mahony in America was a man named James MacDermot ('Red' Jim, after his beard), who had been working for the British secret service for years, and in 1865 was selling every secret of the Fenian Brotherhood to the British Consul in New York. Many Fenians, including Stephens, strongly mistrusted MacDermot, but O'Mahony's trust in him could not be shaken and it was many years before he was finally exposed.

But though the government information net was fairly widely spread, the organization itself was so large that there were always many secrets unpenetrated. Stephens himself was able to remain free in Dublin for two months after the *Irish People* arrests, living as Mr Herbert with Kickham and two other leading Fenians in a house in Sandymount which they left only at night.⁵ From his hiding-place he got a message out to America to the effect that the organization in Ireland was, despite the arrests, in all its essentials still intact. The arrests, he said, had only made its members more impatient than ever and men and supplies must be sent without delay.⁶ And one of the American officers whom O'Mahony had sent over as yet another envoy, William Halpin, reported back that the determination to strike was as strong as ever.⁷ Nevertheless, the rot was beginning to set in for those American rank and file who had now been hanging about Dublin for some months without anything to do. They were becoming hard-up and discouraged, and were applying to the American Consul in Dublin to send them home with a free passage.⁸

Then on the morning of 11 November the rented house in Sandymount in which Stephens had been living was surrounded while he was still in bed, and he, Kickham and the others were arrested. They had eventually been betrayed by yet another informer.[9] The reaction to the news by the average non-Fenian Dubliner was probably accurately summarized by A. M. Sullivan when he wrote, later: 'The dreaded Chief Organizer of the Irish Republic was now in custody. Now everyone might sleep with an easy mind. No "rising" need be apprehended. No lurid flame of civil war would redden the midnight sky.'[10] But Stephens still had some counter strokes in store.

The secret 'military council' of the Fenians – consisting of Kelly, Halpin, Devoy and others – now met and elected a temporary head for the movement, the American officer, General Millen, who at once sent a message to the States saying that they still intended to strike before the end of the year. Then Stephens made his most dramatic single contribution to the cause of Fenianism to date. With the help of two warders named Byrne and Breslin, who were sworn Fenians, he escaped from gaol. Breslin led him out of his cell in the middle of the stormy night of 24 November 1865, and with Byrne's help brought him to where an organized party, headed by Captain Thomas Kelly and John Devoy, threw a rope-ladder over the outer wall and got him away.[11]

Sometimes it seems that all the bungling during these years was on the Fenian side. But the escape was a masterly achievement. Nor was the government innocent of blunders. The governor of the prison remarked frankly at the subsequent inquiry that he had no confidence generally in any of his officers. And on more than twenty occasions since June 1861 the warder Byrne had been reprimanded, cautioned or fined for neglect of duty, once being temporarily suspended for allowing a prisoner to escape.[12] Stephens's escape gave a great boost to Fenian morale, and confirmed the worst fears of many loyalists that the tentacles of the conspiracy had spread everywhere.

In spite of the offer of a reward of £1,000 for Stephens's capture, or of £300 for information leading to his arrest, he remained in hiding in the centre of Dublin, just opposite the Unionist Kildare Street club, for nearly three months.[13] The fact is a tribute both to Fenian security when not already penetrated by an informer and to the unvenal idealism of the best Fenians, many of whom must have known of Stephens's whereabouts.

Before he finally left the country he was responsible for a decision only possible to a man whose reputation was at its height with his fellow conspirators. From the moment of his escape there had been strong pressure on Stephens both from the American and Irish Fenians in Dublin to keep the much repeated vow to strike before the year was out. But now on Stephens's part a distinct cooling-off suddenly became noticeable.

The later history of the Fenian movement is so full of personal quarrels and recriminations and charges of cowardice or other defects of character levelled against individuals – many of them centring on Stephens – that it is often difficult to sort out genuine charges from mere factional propaganda. Stephens's own motivation in the years 1865 and 1866 is particularly difficult to assess. For all the strain of self-aggrandizement in his activity to date there was much about it that was realistic. The organization was after all in being on a considerable scale, and was almost entirely the result of his own hard work. And at least until his arrest there had been a genuine note of urgency and determination about his final plans for a rising. Only in the field of coordination with the vast potential in America had there been something of a failure. There had been piece-meal help certainly with men and money, but given the number of men fresh from the civil war and the sums of money available it should have been possible to organize something much more like the well-supplied spearhead that Stephens had originally stipulated. For all the talk there was still no such well-organized expedition forthcoming.

The note of urgent determination in Stephens's statements about striking in 1865 may always have been partly a device for forcing O'Mahony and the American Fenians into more effective action. Partly, too, it was simply characteristic of Stephens's moral bombast. More than one factor may have been at work in his mind as he now decided to abandon hope of a rising for that year. But to give preponderance at this stage to the fright his arrest may have given him seems unfair. His personal experience may have made him rather more cautious. But then there was plenty to be cautious about. For, in addition to other shortcomings, in America a serious disaster had just overtaken the Fenian cause. At the very moment when the concentration of all efforts for Ireland was more necessary than ever, the movement in America had split into two rival sections. One, the more powerful, led by a Colonel Roberts in opposition to O'Mahony, and therefore outside Stephens's control, now favoured the direction of all Fenian efforts against the more easily accessible territory of Canada in the first phase of the battle for Irish independence.

With only weeks of the year to go, Stephens with some political skill succeeded in bringing leading Fenians in Dublin, both Irish and Irish American, reluctantly to accept his view that the rising must be postponed. The most effective argument he had to overcome was a purely military one, presented with particular strength by John Devoy, who had had charge of the seduction of British soldiers. A considerable part of the British garrison then in the country, particularly that part in Dublin, had been, nominally at least, seduced from their allegiance to the queen by the Fenian oath. Stephens himself conceded that about one-third of the total garrison in Ireland were Fenians – some twelve thousand trained men to be added to the two hundred thousand Irishmen sworn altogether, fifty thousand of whom he maintained were 'thoroughly armed'.

The argument for immediate action, pressed by Devoy, but strongly supported by most of the Dublin 'centres' and the American-dominated military council of which Kelly, promoted now to colonel, was chief of staff, persisted until February 1866. Such action would have had a desperate quality about it, as its advocates recognized, but that desperation need not have made it unsuccessful. Looking back with hindsight, as many Fenians and particularly Devoy were later to do, it was easy to say that any action taken then would have been more successful than what finally happened. But Stephens's feelings at the time were probably dominated by a typical conviction that his own ability could straighten out the difficulties in America and bring about that properly coordinated rising which had always been planned and which, if achieved, would have had at least a better than desperate chance of success. A less charitable interpretation of Stephens's attitude, even leaving out of account considerations of personal safety, would be that his ego had become so wedded to the business of conducting and managing the conspiracy that he preferred to spin it out indefinitely on one rational excuse or another rather than bring it to a climax. Probably shades of these different motivations were at work in him simultaneously at different levels. Of course, the longer he remained in Dublin without taking action the weightier became the arguments for postponement. The elements of suddenness and surprise necessary to all desperate actions were fading all the time, and the government itself became better and better placed to meet the situation. Arrests of American officers had been taking place since before the end of the year. In February 1866 Habeas Corpus was once again suspended, and most of those whom the government had so far failed to lay their hands on were arrested too.

On 21 February 1866 Devoy himself was arrested with a number of his Fenian soldiers in a public house in Dublin. Those who had so far only accepted most reluctantly Stephens's argument for postponing action now had to agree that there was no longer any other immediate alternative left. Stephens himself was smuggled with Colonel Kelly on to a collier and took to the Irish Sea. Blown by adverse winds up to Scotland, they landed there and came down by train to London, where they spent a night at the Palace Hotel near Victoria. They then passed on to France, en route for America, where Stephens was determined to heal the disastrous split in the Fenian Brotherhood.

This split had originated squalidly, as did many quarrels in the Fenian movement, over the handling of money, but its real cause had been the normal political factor of personal ambition. O'Mahony's rival, Colonel John Roberts, now dominated what was called the 'Senate' or Roberts's wing of the Fenian Brotherhood, and his half of the movement was numerically the stronger. There had been superimposed on the personal rivalry and the quarrel over handling of the funds a serious division of opinion about strategy. Roberts and his followers now held the view that an attempt on Canada would be of more immediate advantage to the Irish cause than coordination with the movement in Ireland because it was more likely to achieve immediate success. Stephens, for all his old taunts against O'Mahony, naturally sided with him and did all in his power to restore his authority. But when he reached America the split had gone too far. In any case, now that the civil war was over, the whole movement had now grown too big an American phenomenon for the limited magic of Stephens's strong personality to be able to control it. All he could really do was to try to use his formidable energy to rally support for the O'Mahony wing and its policy of a rising in Ireland in 1866, while the Roberts wing went its own flamboyant way.

'We promise,' declared the Roberts-wing Fenian general in charge of the Canada plan, in February, 'that before the summer sun kisses the hill-tops of Ireland, a ray of hope will gladden every true Irish heart. The green flag will be flying independently to freedom's breeze, and we will have a base of operations from which we can not only emancipate Ireland, but also annihilate England.'[14] The theory was that if only a foothold could be won on which the Irish flag could be raised, then independent Ireland would be recognized as reality.

Meanwhile, the O'Mahony wing, much to Stephens's disapproval, itself made an attempt in April to capture the island of Campo Bello off the coast of New Brunswick. This proved totally abortive, and the ship which had been purchased for the expedition for $40,000 never even set sail. The British Government had been kept informed of the project throughout by Red Jim MacDermot, who also reported that the idea of an expedition to Ireland was not totally exploded, and that six of the Irish pilots who had arrived the previous summer were still in the States.[15]

American Fenian energies now switched to the Vermont border with Canada where the 'Right Wing of the Army of Ireland' was soon poised. Some three thousand armed Fenians had assembled in Buffalo. On the night of 31 May 1866, eight hundred of them, commanded by a Colonel O'Neill, crossed the Niagara river and occupied the village of Fort Erie on the Canadian shore. On the morning of 2 June they won an engagement with some Canadian student volunteers at Lime Ridge, also known as Ridgeway, but with his rear threatened O'Neill retired on Fort Erie again hoping for reinforcements to reach him across the lake from Buffalo. But this was now being patrolled by the United States Government, which though it maintained a carefully ambivalent attitude towards the Fenians (finding their nuisance value against the British diplomatically too handy to throw away), felt obliged to enforce the neutrality laws now that an actual invasion had taken place. Cut off on the foothold he had won for the green flag O'Neill had no alternative but to withdraw again. In the skirmish at Ridgeway the Canadians had lost twelve dead and forty wounded, while the Fenian losses had been eight dead and twenty wounded. About sixty Fenians had been captured and there had been some desertions.[16] 'The Irish Republican Army', as Fenian headquarters described it, had been in action for the first time.[17] This fact alone gives the incident greater historical interest than it might otherwise merit.

Its sponsors seemed in no way dismayed by the failure. 'Arise, Irishmen,' proclaimed Roberts, 'a glorious career has opened for you. The Green Flag has waved once more in triumph over England's hated emblem...'[18] But as the US Government gently sent the Fenians home from the frontier with their passages paid – though seizing their arms which they later returned to them – the net effect of this rather empty demonstration in Canada was to lend force to Stephens's exhortations to the Brotherhood to strike in Ireland.

He had already been in the States, since his escape, for some months. In July and August 1866 he was promising that an army would be fighting on Irish soil before the year was out.[19] On 28 October he declared at a rally that they would next hear of him leading his troops against the Saxon aggressor.[20] A final appeal for arms and money was issued. But the response so far had not been good. Once again, as in the previous year, a situation had arisen in which Stephens was defiantly committed to rising in Ireland before the year was out with only a few more weeks of the year to run and the American end of the movement in disarray.

The moment of truth had again arrived. But how with any dignity or prestige left could Stephens face it for the second year running? The answer was that he could not.

In some ways, though accusations of personal cowardice were soon to multiply thick and fast, not least from Kelly,[21] the course he now took was a most courageous one, though the element of humbug present in so much of his activity should not be discounted.

It was in fact reasonable of him to urge as he now did, in the light of inadequate armament and American support, a further postponement of the rising. But it had not been reasonable of him to talk of the coming fight with such bombast and flourish if he had been unsure – as he had been throughout the seven months of his 1866 campaign in America – whether that support would materialize. In September in New York he had even hinted that whether or not the arrangements for a rising were adequate he would go to Ireland in any case for the men could be held back no longer. 'If I thought it would be any gain to delay, I would do so and risk all my popularity,' he had said. 'But I cannot for they are determined on fighting this year, and I am fully determined on being with them, come weal or woe. No matter what others say, take my word I will be in Ireland, and the people will strike a blow for liberty.'[22]

Having said that, he could not now, with any dignity or reasonable hope of being listened to, counsel his own Fenian officers in the States to postpone the rising. However, that was what he now tried to do and he paid the inevitable political penalty. At a series of meetings in his lodgings in New York beginning on 15 December 1866 they heard him detail as a reason for postponement the inadequate resources available for Ireland. There were, it appeared, only four thousand rifles out of the minimum of thirty thousand considered necessary.[23] His behaviour at these meetings, faced with charges of cowardice, seems sometimes to have approached hysteria. Once he even melodramatically offered to go to Ireland at once 'to get hanged' to prove his personal courage, a suggestion which no one took seriously.[24] Soon afterwards he was to confuse the issue, when justifying himself to the centres of the organization in Dublin, by writing that his health had been a reason for inaction, describing himself as having been 'apparently not long for this world'.[25] But in the same letter he urged his men, should Colonel Kelly call on them to rise, to do so '... and prove the stuff that is in you ...'.[26] He would, he said, be among them himself soon afterwards. He did not return to Ireland for almost another thirty years.

For all practical purposes the Fenian movement was taken out of Stephens's hands as a result of these meetings in New York. He was deposed from his recently assumed position of Head Centre of the Fenian Brotherhood in the States. To salve his pride the officers let him remain for a time the nominal civil head of the organization in Ireland, but Kelly became head of the all-important military sector, and was soon to be known as Acting Chief Executive of the Irish Republic.[27] The real control of the Fenians in Ireland passed into Kelly's hands, and Stephens, though he was to spend much of the rest of his life jockeying to regain position and was not to be without occasional supporters particularly in Ireland, passes out of Irish history as an effective force. Kelly's own appearance in the limelight was to be brief but sensational, and in one respect at least to have an indirect effect of enormous importance for the future, so that his name today is probably better known in Ireland than that of Stephens himself who virtually founded the Fenian movement.

Having deposed Stephens the next step taken by the officers assembled in his lodgings in New York was themselves to volunteer to cross the Atlantic and start a rising in Ireland. Thus the impetus for the dramatic events that were about to occur came from a group of tough, footloose Irish emigrant soldiers of fortune whose occupation had gone with the end of the civil war and was made good by the cause and livelihood provided by the Fenian Brotherhood. But that revolution happened to suit them was only one element in their motivation. After all, to be sustained by the hopes and funds of the Fenian Brotherhood there was no need to cross the Atlantic and risk their necks, as some of the Canadian or Roberts wing of the movement could demonstrate. Those who under Kelly now proceeded to engineer the Fenian rising of 1867 in Ireland were all – with one or two exceptions – idealists of one sort or another. Most had bitter first-hand memories of poverty and degradation in Ireland to avenge. All had been in battle. Many, like Kelly and Captain John McCafferty, a former Confederate soldier who had been particularly contemptuous of Stephens's prevarication in the New York meetings, had already risked their freedom in Ireland the year before and McCafferty had been actually arrested there as a suspect, though as an American-born US citizen he was released after American diplomatic intervention.*

Even John Mitchel, in Paris at the end of 1866 as an agent for Fenian funds, was opposed to a rising by this date on the grounds that it had no chance of success. But, without responsibility for any decision himself, he described the situation of any Fenian leader at the time as being like that of a man holding wolves by the ears.[38] The character of those who had escaped from Stephens's grasp justified the simile.

Among those who sailed with Kelly and McCafferty from New York to Europe in the second week of January 1867 was, for instance, Captain Richard O'Sullivan Burke of the 15th New York Engineers. He had been born in Macroom, County Cork, and had been a corporal in the South Cork militia before emigrating to the States in 1857. He, too, had spent part of the last year on British soil, negotiating, under different aliases, large commercial purchases of arms and ammunition with a Mr Kynoch of Birmingham.[39]

Some officers now assumed with sometimes dubious entitlement the rank of general. General William Halpin, a close associate of Kelly's, who had been one of O'Mahony's envoy-inspectors in 1865, and was soon again to be operating in Ireland under the alias of Bird, seems to have been at least a colonel in the Union Army in the civil war. But a more questionable figure altogether was 'General' Gordon Massey, a native of County Limerick and a former corporal in the British Army, who had served in the Crimea and then emigrated to America. Illegitimate, he had been known then and throughout his service with the Confederates in the civil war under his mother's name of Condon – Patrick Condon. After joining the Fenians in Texas in 1865 he came to New York late in 1866, and, perhaps because there was another Patrick Condon active among the upper echelons of the Brother-

* The British law's attitude to Irish-American nationality was, however, severe. Those Irish who had become naturalized Americans and had thereby specifically renounced all earlier allegiance were nevertheless held by British law to be subject to the allegiance under which they were born, and as liable to charges of high treason as any Briton. American-born US citizens were in any case subject to the normal British criminal law.

hood, he began to be known as Gordon Massey, after his father.[30] But a more profound question mark still remains over his name to this day. Before many months were out he was to turn queen's evidence, but whether his defection dated only from his own arrest or earlier is unsure. What is certain is that when he sailed from New York on 11 January 1867 he was high in the Fenian military councils.

Though Kelly was the 'acting Chief Executive of the Irish Republic' after Stephens's deposition, he had at his service a purely military command headed by a man who was not an Irishman at all. This was an adventurous Frenchman named Cluseret, who at least had every right to call himself a general and became the Fenian 'Commander-in-Chief'.[31] Cluseret's military career had begun in 1848 in the Garde Mobile of the Second Republic when he was awarded the Legion of Honour for storming eleven barricades during the suppression of the June insurrection.[32] Thereafter in thought at least he had gravitated more and more to the revolutionary left. His fighting career had continued in Algeria, the Crimea, in Sicily under Garibaldi and finally in the Union Army during the civil war under McLellan, where he achieved the rank of brigadier general.[33] He had met and made friends with Stephens in the States during 1866 and felt drawn to Fenianism partly because he was a natural soldier of fortune, but also undoubtedly because its identification with the cause of the poor of Ireland, and its republicanism appealed to his own radical sentiments.[34] As a practical soldier, however, he had driven a bargain with Stephens. He would agree to take over all military command of the rising only when he could be guaranteed that ten thousand men had already taken the field in Ireland.[35]

Cluseret had attended the meetings in New York in December 1866 at which Stephens had been deposed, and had agreed to go along with Kelly on similar terms. He selected as his military adjutants two other foreign veterans of the American civil war, Fariola and Vifquain, shadowy figures whose names flicker momentarily across the brief scene of the Fenian Rising.

One more name among the band of 'wolves' now on their way to Europe deserves mention. It is that of Michael O'Brien, a native of Cork, who had taken a formal part in the arrangements for McManus's funeral in 1862, but had then emigrated and emerged from service with the Union Army in the American civil war with the rank of captain. His name, with that of two Fenian companions, was soon to assume a heroic position in the history of nineteenth-century Ireland beside those of Mitchel and Emmet.

4

1867: Bold Fenian Men

Kelly set up his operational headquarters in London where, since Habeas Corpus was not suspended as in Ireland, freedom of movement and general security was that much easier.[1] He and Halpin took rooms under the names of Coleman and Fletcher off the Tottenham Court Road, while Burke and Massey, known as Wallace and Cleburne, took other rooms at 7 Tavistock Street.[2] The heads of the conspiracy were all lodged within a square mile of each other. General Cluseret and his adjutant Fariola took up residence at 137 Great Portland Street,[3] but they had no need to adopt aliases. They had obtained through Fenian political influences in America a commission to inspect British military organizations on behalf of the State of New York, and were furnished with documents to do so signed by the innocent American legation in London.[4] A directory, or provisional government of the Irish Republic, consisting half of civilians and half of military men was established.[5]

The military plan was for guerrilla warfare. In many respects it did not differ in general intention from the scheme of action finally adopted more than fifty years later by the Irish Republican Army of that day. The fighting of pitched battles was not contemplated. Bodies of fighting men were to assemble flexibly in different parts of Ireland, with a concentration round Dublin and the south-west. These were to destroy rail and telegraph communications, attack police barracks and have a general harassing effect on government movements until the army of the republic could be recognized as belligerents and substantial aid received from America.[6] This was the theory.

The speed with which the plotters moved into action after their arrival in London at the very end of January was a tribute both to their determination and the extent of the organization already existing in England and Ireland. The first intention was for the rising to start in Ireland on 11 February, preceded by a most daring action into which Kelly afterwards felt that McCafferty had too rashly precipitated them.*[7] This had as its objective no

---

* It was said by Kelly that the raid on Chester was attempted without agreement from London from him, but this was contradicted at the Trial of Flood (*Report of Dublin Special Commission*, p. 882).

less than the capture, with the aid of the man-power of the well-organized Fenians in the north of England, of the large British arms and ammunition store at Chester Castle, which was less a castle than a military barracks with a gaol attached.[8] Simultaneously, trains between Chester and Holyhead were to be seized and the arms rushed to Holyhead where the mail boat would also have been captured. With all rail and telegraph communications cut to prevent government intervention, the vast stock of supplies would then be rushed to Ireland for the rising which would have started the same day.*[9]

All this was to take place on Monday, 11 February, and early that morning strangers, mainly working men, began arriving at Chester station in large numbers by trains from Warrington, Crewe, Manchester and other towns of Lancashire and Cheshire. By the early afternoon there were well over a thousand in the town.[10] The day before, at Kelly's lodgings in London, an important meeting had taken place at which three of the four provincial 'centres' for the organization in Ireland were present and a number of military men. A statement of political aims had been drawn up. After the meeting 'General' Massey, who was to take charge of the first assembly phase of the rising until Cluseret felt conditions ready for him to take overall command himself, left for Ireland.[11]

It is not clear when the decision to postpone the rising was taken, but it seems at least likely that it was linked closely with what happened at Chester on the afternoon of 11 February. Certainly one Fenian close to the top of the organization believed this to be so.† In which case, the speed and efficiency with which news of the postponement was carried to every part of Ireland but one was commendable. For it was not until one o'clock on Monday afternoon, 11 February, when the trains crowded with strange working men from other towns were continuing to arrive at Chester, that McCafferty himself learnt that the authorities had been alerted to his plan.[12] The guard on the Castle had been strengthened; the Volunteers had been called out; a detachment of the Guards was on its way from London. It was too late to stop at least half the Fenians assembling. Most were already there. But with considerable skill McCafferty and his agents succeeded in calling the operation off and the police afterwards found large quantities of ammunition and revolvers dumped in the neighbourhood of the railway station and in the ponds and canals of the town.[13] Next day and for several days afterwards the police in Ireland met steamers arriving at Dublin and Dundalk and arrested dozens of young Irish working men who had been seen crowded together on the boats and, though without money in their pockets, had given up jobs in England to return to their native country.[14] McCafferty, calling himself William Jackson, was arrested on suspicion as

* 'If the Chester affair had succeeded, there was to have been a rising in Ireland.' (Corydon.)
† The informer, John Joseph Corydon. See, e.g., *The Times*, 30 April 1868.

he attempted to row away with a companion from a collier which had anchored in the Liffey after crossing the Irish Sea.[15] He continued to maintain he was William Jackson until those searching him found sewn into the lining of his coat a ring inscribed 'Erin I love thee and thy patriots – Presented to Captain John McCafferty IRB by the Detroit Circle of the Fenian Brotherhood, a token of esteem.'[16]

What McCafferty did not then know was how the authorities had learnt of his plan to raid Chester Castle. The information had been given them by one of his own men, John Joseph Corydon, a well-trusted Fenian who had acted as the principle carrier of dispatches between Ireland and America in 1865. A man of disreputable private life, he had been giving information to the authorities since September 1866 because, he said, he 'did not think the Fenian organization worth spilling one drop of blood for'.[17]

Only in Kerry did notice of the postponement of the rising fail to get through. Some men assembled in arms at Cahirciveen. But though a certain panic was caused among the gentry who flocked for refuge to the Railway Hotel, Killarney, the affair was more one of rumour than of real menace, for the Fenian Head Centre for Kerry, J. J. O'Connor, soon discovered his mistake and his men, estimated by the newspapers at anything between nine hundred and one hundred (including '20 Americans'), melted away.[18] James Stephens himself, chief Fenian bogeyman, of whose fall from grace the public were not yet aware, was widely reported to be in the district in person.[19]

Meanwhile, plans to bring the postponed rising to a new climax were being worked on. Massey, who had been in Ireland since 11 February, had conferred with the Irish centres, in Dublin, in the West and in the Cork district – where the most widespread effort was to be made – and returned to London on 24 February to report to Kelly and Cluseret.[20] On the strength of what he had learned of the available resources in Ireland he considered the prospect hopeless.

There was not, he thought, the least chance of the Fenians holding the field for a day.[21] Though there were fourteen thousand men organized in Dublin and twenty thousand in Cork, the proportion of arms to men, and of modern rifles to shot-guns and pikes, was absurdly low. Nevertheless, as Massey himself afterwards declared: 'I knew it would be destruction but I did not like to go back having gone so far.'[22] In any case, his seemed to be the only voice saying it was hopeless. A meeting of all the top military men, including Cluseret and Fariola, was held in London under Kelly and the decision was taken to rise on 5 March.

When Massey returned to Dublin to tell the centres there of the new date, he again told them frankly that he thought there was not a chance of success. 'To do them justice,' he said later, 'they were all for "shoving it on".'[23]

The Commander-in-Chief, Cluseret, had himself been unimpressed by his experiences with the Irish since arriving in London. Instead of receiving the news he wanted of adequate stocks of arms, he had to listen to endless discussions of an almost theological nature as to who should succeed James Stephens as Head Centre. He had been overwhelmed with complaints, recriminations and accusations. 'Everybody,' he recalled five years later, 'came to me with their personal grievances but with nothing else.'[24] He found many of the American-Irish Fenians too fond of drink, including Massey, on whom his verdict was that 'as captain or corporal he would do very well, but as a general he was deplorable'.[25] He himself thought there was not a chance in two thousand of success, but engaged as he was only to take the field once the rising had established itself in the field the prospect may not have appeared too personally disastrous. Cluseret, like Massey, paid tribute to the Irish 'centres' who took the decision with Kelly to strike on 5 March. He describes them as 'noble' and 'with fine natures'. They insisted to him that they would keep their word, even though Stephens may not have kept his. 'The people will know,' they told Cluseret, 'that, if there are some who deceive them, there are others who know how to die for them.'[26]

This iron, selfless dedication to a cause which, though often viewed with sympathy by the Irish people, was made consistently ludicrous by events, became an important feature of the Fenian movement. Tenacity to the extreme republican cause in spite of every failure, continued seriousness in the face of every absurdity, became a quality that won at least some respect, even if it gained little positive support.

When Massey went back to Ireland to inform the organization there of the new date for the rising, the informer Corydon went with him.[27] The commands for the various districts had been allotted in London. Halpin was to have the Dublin area, subordinate to Massey, whose own base would be the large railway centre just outside Tipperary, Limerick junction. There his only specific orders were to coordinate the various gatherings in the south-western districts. Halpin's orders from Massey were, in case of a reverse in the Dublin area, to withdraw to the Wicklow Mountains, like Holt and Dwyer seventy years before, and from there harass government communications. Vifquain, one of Cluseret's French aides, was to take command in the west of Ireland, but his arrival was held up at the last minute for lack of funds. Cluseret's other aide, however, Fariola, arrived in Cork on 1 March to put finishing touches with Massey to the arrangements with local commanders: Dunne and Moran for the county of Cork, William Mackey Lomasney and Michael O'Brien for the city of Cork, Deasy for Millstreet, McClure for Midleton. At last, on the evening before the rising, 4 March 1867, Massey set out by train from Cork to take up his command at Limerick junction.

In London the provisional government of the Irish Republic sent a copy of their proclamation to *The Times*. It began:

'We have suffered centuries of outrage, enforced poverty and bitter misery. Our rights and liberties have been trampled on by an alien aristocracy, who, treating us as foes, usurped our lands and drew away from our unfortunate country all material riches ...'[28]

The essential Fenian myth was thus established that the 'foes', the owners of the soil, were alien. In fact, most had been Irishmen for centuries, often of the same religion and racial extraction as the suffering multitudes. But making allowance for this political colouring, the description of what had actually happened in Ireland was acceptable enough.

'The real owners of the soil,' continued the proclamation, 'were removed to make room for cattle, and driven across the ocean to seek the means of living and the political right denied to them at home.... But we never lost the memory and hope of a national existence ...'

Again, the folk-memory of better times on the land was equated with modern nationalistic aspirations. A retrospective national gloss was given to the turmoil of '98, the Emmet débâcle, and the feeble gyrations of Smith O'Brien. But the desperate spirit of the proclamation rang tragically true:

'We appealed in vain to the reason and sense of justice of the dominant powers.... Our appeals to arms were always unsuccessful. Today, having no honourable alternative left we again appeal to force as our last resource. We accept the conditions of appeal, manfully deeming it better to die in the struggle for freedom than to continue an existence of utter serfdom.... All men are born with equal rights.'

The influences of international socialism with which Stephens and Cluseret had been in contact joined forces with the radical teachings of the United Irishmen, and of Fintan Lalor twenty years before:

'... We aim at founding a republic based on universal suffrage, which shall secure to all the intrinsic value of their labour. The soil of Ireland at present in the possession of an oligarchy belongs to us, the Irish people, and to us it must be restored. We declare also in favour of absolute liberty of conscience, and the complete separation of Church and state ...'

The final section had an unmistakably Marxist ring, for it was Marx's teaching, totally at variance with the facts of British life, that Irish freedom would be brought about by English workmen supporting their cause. Kelly had founded an English Republican Brotherhood, within two miles, as he liked to boast, of Buckingham Palace itself.[29]

'Republicans,' the proclamation concluded, 'Republicans of the entire world, our cause is your cause.... Let your hearts be with us. As for you, workmen of England, it is not only your hearts we wish but your arms. Remember the starvation and degradation brought to your firesides by the oppression of labour. Remember the past, look well to the future, and avenge yourselves by giving liberty to your children in the coming struggle for human freedom. Herewith we proclaim the Irish Republic.'

In Ireland the Army of the Irish Republic was about to go into action. Its senior commander on Irish soil, General Massey, stepped off the train from Cork at Limerick junction shortly after ten o'clock on the evening of 4 March to take up his secret command. Someone tapped him on the shoulder as he was walking along the platform.[30] He was under arrest, betrayed by the informer Corydon, together with all the Fenian plans.

Word got to Fariola, Cluseret's chief of staff, within hours. He fled from his hotel in Cork in the middle of the night, leaving behind him an unpaid bill for thirty-five shillings, and a revolver.[31] He was only arrested several months later, walking along Oxford Street, London.[32] But on the evening of the 5th, unaware as yet of the disaster that had overtaken its high command, the Irish Republican Army in Dublin, Drogheda, Cork, Tipperary, Clare and Limerick was on the march.

Considering the detailed information the government had received from Corydon, a curious feature of the affair was the relative state of unpreparedness of the police which was now revealed. It was a dark night and the moon was not yet up when a constable called McIlwaine in Stepaside barracks near Dublin, lying on his bed with his shoes off, heard what he afterwards described as 'the weighty tramp of a number of people ... going near the barracks'.[33] He had had some information that 'there might be a stir' but clearly so far he had not taken this very seriously. Now he hurriedly called his four men to arms and on investigation found himself required by a man wearing a green feather in his cap to surrender the barracks to the Irish Republic. This the Irish constable refused to do at first. There was an exchange of shots. Then, threatened that the barracks would be set on fire, he complied. Outside, he and his men were placed with some other police whom the rebels had captured en route. To one of these the local rebel 'captain' had remarked in an early moment of exaltation: 'I suppose you did not think we would rise as sudden as we did? You did not imagine we had so many arms concealed without your knowledge?'[34] This same leader, Peter Lennon, now reconnoitred the town of Bray, but, deciding it was too strong,[35] marched his men with his captives to the police barracks at Glencullen which he also called upon to surrender to the Irish Republic. It did so after the captured police had been placed as hostages in the line of fire between the rebels and the barracks. It was then about 6 a.m. Lennon told Constable McIlwaine that he hoped to have between fourteen and fifteen thousand men on the hill at Tallaght by midday.[36]

All through the night Halpin had been sending up signal rockets in the Green Hills round Tallaght to show the rebels where to rally.[37] Apart from Lennon's victorious column other bodies of men had marched out of Dublin in that direction but with less success. All seem to have arrayed themselves at first in fair military order, forming fours and marching off from their first assembly points with sloped arms, some of which at least were Lee Enfield rifles with fixed bayonets.[38] But discipline does not seem to have been good or morale particularly high. More than one group of men transporting ammunition fled at their first haphazard encounter with the police, and one rebel leader was heard calling out that he would shoot on the spot the first man who flinched from his duty.[39]

Marching into the small town of Tallaght itself, which Halpin had specifically wanted them to avoid, one body of several hundred rebels found themselves confronted by fourteen men of the Constabulary under the command of a Sub-Inspector Burke. He had already succeeded in forcing another such party to retreat by calling out to them: 'Disperse, or so help me God, I'll fire!'[40] It had withdrawn in disorder to the shelter of a stone wall some two hundred yards away. Now he called upon the second party to halt and surrender. Answered by a volley of stones, he threatened to fire. Thereupon a rebel leader himself called out: 'Now, boys, fire, fire.' There was a volley, estimated later by Sub-Inspector Burke at about fifty shots, but none of the police were hit. They then fired back. The rebels immediately fled, leaving one man wounded behind them.

The effect of this defeat seems to have been devastating, for it virtually ended the attempt to assemble in the neighbourhood of Tallaght. In any case, soon after first light, news of the arrest of Massey over twenty-four hours before and the collapse of the entire high command must have penetrated to Halpin and the victorious Lennon making clear to them the forlorn nature of their enterprise. They vanished underground and were not arrested for several months.

But many stragglers among the rank and file were picked up in the course of the night and next morning. Near Stepaside, where the barracks had been taken, a green flag was found on a broken staff. The flag bore the slogan 'God and Our Country', beneath which were the Irish Harp without the Crown and the words 'Remember Emmet'.[41]

There had been clashes elsewhere in Ireland on the night and morning of 5–6 March, but nowhere were the Fenians much more successful than round Dublin – in some places considerably less so. A body of about a thousand men assembling in the middle of the night in the Potato Market in Drogheda were totally routed after a brief exchange of shots with a force of less than forty police.[42] In County Limerick a party of fifteen police at Kilmallock barracks held off a strong Fenian attack under a captain wearing a dark green uniform and a slouch hat with a feather in it. The barracks were eventually relieved after a three-hour fight in which at least two Fenians were killed. One of the constables firing from a window had kept an open notebook beside him, in which, in the intervals between firing his gun, he noted down the names of those assailants he recognized.[43]

Elsewhere in County Limerick a party of some 250 Fenians had been unable to take the barracks at Ardagh, though they did succeed in breaking into the ground floor. In Sligo a party assembled by Drumcliffe churchyard, where Yeats was one day to lie, but were easily dispersed.[44] In County Cork there was a Fenian success when some two thousand men headed by J. F. X. O'Brien, William Mackey Lomasney and Michael O'Brien captured the police barracks at Ballyknockane.* The same party also successfully carried out sabotage of the Great Southern and Western Railway, according to the guerrilla plan, tearing up rails, destroying points and cutting telegraph wires, and actually derailing the Dublin express but without injury to the passengers.[45]

In County Cork, too, a party of Fenians captured a coastguard station at Knockadoon and made off with the arms they found there. But the impossibility of any significant follow-up without orders from above meant that even where there had been a success there was little to do afterwards but disperse. (Cluseret packed his bags for France as soon as he heard of Massey's arrest.) In addition to which, military flying columns were soon busy over the whole of the south-west and west of Ireland, dispersing such bodies of Fenians as were still intact. A sudden bout of severe weather with heavy falls of snow made the plight of the scattering rebels more desperate still.

On the morning of 6 March itself one of the first of these military columns approached an old Danish earthwork named Ballyhurst just outside the town of Tipperary. It was circular and surrounded by a hawthorn hedge.[46] A force of Fenians had assembled there during the night and early morning under an Irish-American 'general' with a shrunken leg, T. F. Bourke. They had earlier destroyed some telegraph poles and torn up railway lines. They were better at sabotage than fighting in the open. They fired a volley at the approaching soldiers, but as soon as the fire was returned they fled in disorder. With a cry of 'To the mountains! To the mountains!', their commander, Thomas Bourke, galloped off in a different direction from the main body of his men, but a soldier spotted him and brought him down from his horse with a shot at about three hundred yards.[47] A quarter of an hour later he was arrested creeping along a bank with the aid of a stick. In his pocket, together with a Catholic prayer book, a prescription for an eye infection, three photographs of girls and a Bradshaw's Railway Guide map, was found a Fenian oath which differed from the usual formula. It ran:

'In the presence of Almighty God, I solemnly swear that I will not bear arms against, or by word or act give information, aid or comfort to the enemies of the Irish Republic until regularly relieved of this obligation. So help me God.'

It was one clearly designed to be administered to less than enthusiastic Irishmen in the tide of the Fenian advance.

---

* Lomasney eventually blew himself up in 1884 trying to destroy London Bridge. O'Brien was to end on the gallows in Manchester; see below, pp. 46-7.

But the tide of the Fenian advance was already past its peak. If anyone had taken that oath during the night the moment when they could feel relieved of the obligation was at hand.

Thomas Bourke, though he had not proved much of a field commander, made amends from the dock. Shortly before being sentenced to be hanged, beheaded and cut into four quarters he declared:

'I accept my doom and I hope that God will forgive me my past sins. I hope that inasmuch as He has for seven hundred years preserved Ireland, notwithstanding all the tyranny to which she has been subjected, as a separate and distinct nationality, He will also assist her to retrieve her fallen fortunes, and raise her in her beauty and mystery, the sister of Columbia, the peer of my nation in the end.'[48]

A quarter of a century later, even the miserable action at Ballyhurst had become part of heroic myth. At a time when physical force as a means of righting Ireland's wrongs or awarding her national pride appeared to have been abandoned for ever in favour of parliamentary and constitutional agitation, a poet, looking back to the Fenians, could write:

> Thus, handicapped on every side, what wonder that we failed,
> And none but knaves and cowards say our spirit ever quailed,
> And Ballyhurst did more that day to raise all England's fears,
> Than all the 'blatherskite' I've heard these five and twenty years ...
>
> It makes me sick to talk to you and those who agitate* —
> Oh, give us but ten thousand men with rifles up to date
> Then Saxon laws and Saxon rule may do their very worst
> To men behind the rifles like the men of Ballyhurst.[49]

Desultory mopping-up operations by the military flying columns continued for several weeks. The last dramatic action was fought on the last day of March, when the three leaders of the successful raid on Knockadoon coastguard station, Peter O'Neill Crowley, McLure and Kelly were surprised in Kilclooney Wood in County Tipperary. After a running action among the trees Crowley was killed and the other two arrested — one with a small green flag and a manual of military tactics in his pocket.[50] These were the sort of men who, if the Fenian military high command had not been obliterated by the betrayal of Massey, might have been able, in spite of local defeats, to have given the rising the persistently harassing, continuous character that had always been part of the main plan. The defeats in the actual engagements with the Constabulary were disappointing and humiliating, but need not have been totally decisive if there had been any central command available to coordinate further guerrilla warfare as intended. It is significant that, for all the immediate disaster, Kelly himself at the time did not consider all further opportunity for action lost. On 15 March, ten days after the catas-

* i.e., for concessions from England.

trophe of the rising's opening, he wrote from London to America: 'Aid before two weeks and Irish independence is a fixed fact.... Fit out your privateers.... A landing in Sligo at the present time would be of infinite service.'[51]

Such a privateer was in fact fitted out – the *Jacknell Packet*, a two-hundred-ton brig – but did not sail from New York until the following month. On board were thirty-eight officers holding commissions in the army of the Irish Republic, signed by Colonel Kelly.[52] In the hold, packed in piano cases, sewing-machine cases and wine casks labelled for Cuba, were about five thousand modern breech-loading and repeating rifles, and a million and a half rounds of ammunition.[53] There were also on board three unmounted cannon taking a 3 lb shot which were fired from time to time during the voyage.[54] The ship was under the command of General Nagle, though it also had on board General Millen, who had been in Ireland under Stephens in 1865.[55] Whenever they met another ship on the high seas they hoisted the English colours, but just before noon on Easter Sunday, 21 April, they hoisted a green flag with a sun bursting over the horizon and re-christened the ship the *Erin's Hope*.[56] A month later the *Erin's Hope* slipped warily into Sligo Bay.

To meet it there, disguised as an English tourist, was Richard O'Sullivan Burke, the Fenian armaments' organizer who had come to England with Kelly in January and was now his second-in-command. Burke rowed out in a small boat to the *Erin's Hope*, whose officers had already pressed a reluctant pilot called Gallagher into service, threatening him with a revolver and at the same time telling him that they had come with a cargo of fruit from Spain.[57] Burke's news was that there was not the slightest hope of getting any support from the people of Sligo by this date, so the *Erin's Hope* sailed southwards down the coast of Ireland, looking for somewhere more suitable to land.

It was a desperately inconclusive and unsatisfactory voyage. A senior member of the crew afterwards reported that he could have landed the arms anywhere if only there had been anyone to receive them.[58] The fact that they had sailed unmolested as far south as Dungarvan in County Waterford before taking any further decision seems to bear him out. By then it was the beginning of June. Provisions were running out and it was decided simply to land a few of the officers and sail the ship back to New York. A Waterford fisherman named Whelan, who came alongside, agreed to land two officers for £2, but twenty-eight men altogether jumped aboard his boat, and fearing intervention by the coastguards, he landed them all in three feet of water off a spit of land called Cunnegar. Four were arrested soon afterwards, soaked through to the waist, and all the rest were in gaol within twenty-four hours.[59]

Fenian fortunes could hardly have been at a lower ebb. Yet they retained a general sympathy among the people for all their failure, and for all the people's failure to support them more positively. In Waterford the police escorting some of those from the *Erin's Hope* to gaol were attacked by a mob of eight thousand, one of whom was killed in the subsequent fracas, while thirty-eight of the police were wounded.[60] Corydon, the informer, who came to give evidence, was stoned in the streets of the town. Elsewhere in Cork, Limerick and other towns of Munster there were demonstrations of sympathy with the rebels. Yet the sympathy was emotional and confused rather than expressive of identity with specific political aims. The crowds who stoned the police in Waterford calling out 'Hurrah for the Fenians' also called out in a fine upsurge of deeply preserved resentment of old injustices 'Hurrah for Carrickshock', the site of a famous victory over the police during the tithe war nearly forty years before.[61]

But the most effective Fenian action, one that was to have an immediate consequence for policy in Ireland, was still to come.

5

The Manchester Martyrs

In spite of all the débâcles of the spring and summer, the Fenian organization still existed on a formidable scale. Its headquarters remained in England and there towards the end of the year it made itself felt with greater impact than any it had been able to achieve in Ireland.

A Fenian convention had already unanimously elected Kelly chief executive of the Irish Republic. An intensive search for him by the authorities had yielded no results. With Corydon and Massey exposed and removed from Fenian councils the organization now maintained a much more effective level of security. Then, on 11 September, the police arrested two men for acting suspiciously in a doorway in Manchester.

They gave the names of Wright and Williams and were charged with loitering, but, possibly because they had already been recognized by the informer Corydon,[1] their real names were soon known to the police. The arrest was of major importance. The loiterers were none other than Kelly himself and that Captain Deasy who had had a command in County Cork on the night of the March rising. A week later, on 18 September, the most important Fenian action of the year was fought in the streets of Manchester.

As an unescorted prison van conveying Kelly and Deasy in handcuffs from the police court to Belle Vue Gaol passed under a railway arch it was stopped and surrounded by about thirty Fenians who had been lying in wait for it, some of them armed with revolvers. These forced the unarmed police on the outside of the van to get down, and kept them and anyone else who might intervene at bay, while others tried to batter open the locked van and rescue Kelly and Deasy from the cells inside.

Inside the van with the two Fenians and some common criminals was a Police Sergeant Brett. Called upon through the ventilator of the locked back door by the Fenians to surrender, he refused to do so. Attempts to batter in the roof with stones were only partially successful and, eventually aware that help for the beleaguered sergeant would soon be on its way from the nearby gaol, a Fenian named Peter Rice fired his revolver through the ventilator, whether with intent to kill or merely to frighten the sergeant or simply to break open the door will never be known. In any case the bullet mortally wounded Sergeant Brett. It has been said that the shot was fired through the lock of the door in order to break it and that the sergeant had his eye to it and was killed accidentally. But a gunsmith who examined the van afterwards found that there was no mark of a bullet on the door, though one appeared to have smashed the ventilator. In any case, the desired effect was achieved. One of the women criminals in the van was so frightened by the shooting of Brett that she took the keys out of the dying sergeant's pocket and passed them through the ventilator. In a minute Kelly and Deasy, still in their handcuffs, had been released from their cells and were down from the van. 'I'll die for you, Kelly,' one of the rescuers is said to have shouted in the confusion. Still in their handcuffs the two men made their way over a wall and across the railway line. They were never recaptured.

Large numbers of Irishmen in Manchester were soon rounded up. The identification procedure employed by the police was so questionable, and much of the eye-witnesses' evidence so doubtful, that the surprising thing was not that one of the five men eventually put on trial for their lives should have been entirely innocent, but that the other four were in fact all involved in one way or another in the rescue attempt. The five were Maguire (an Irish Marine on leave who had never been near the scene of the rescue in his life), Edward Condon (tried as 'Shore'), who later claimed to have master-minded the whole escape, William Allen, Philip Larkin and Michael O'Brien (tried under the alias of 'Gould'). In court it was repeatedly maintained and generally accepted that Allen had fired the fatal shot. In fact this was not so and the man, Rice, who did, eventually escaped along with Kelly and Deasy to America. But in English law it was immaterial who had fired the shot, for anyone taking part in an illegal act as a result of which someone is killed is guilty of constructive murder. In law, Allen, Larkin, O'Brien and Condon were undoubtedly guilty of murder. They were found so, together with the unfortunate Maguire who pathetically asserted to the end that he had not been present and knew nothing of Fenianism.

Allen, Larkin, O'Brien and Condon, denying that they had fired the shot, all regretted the death of Brett and made idealistic speeches from the dock, clearly raising the level of their action above that of common murder.

'I want no mercy – I'll have no mercy,' said Allen. 'I'll die as many thousands have died, for the sake of their beloved land and in defence of it. I will die proudly and triumphantly in defence of republican principles and the liberty of an oppressed and enslaved people.'[2]

Larkin referred to Kelly and Deasy as 'those two most noble heroes'.

O'Brien, after giving his true name and saying that he was proud to be a fellow parishioner of the man killed in Kilclooney wood in March, went on: 'Look to Ireland; see the hundreds of thousands of its people in misery and want. See the virtuous, beautiful and industrious women who only a few years ago – aye and yet – are obliged to look at their children dying for want of food. Look at what is called the majesty of the law on one side, and the long, deep misery of a noble people on the other. Which are the young men of Ireland to respect: the law that murders or banishes their people, or the means to restrict relentless tyranny and ending their miseries forever under a home government. I need not answer that question here. I trust the Irish people will answer it to their satisfaction soon.'

Condon made the most famous remark of all. 'I have nothing to regret, to retract or take back,' he declared. 'I can only say: God Save Ireland!' And, as *The Times* man in court reported, the other prisoners all called out 'in chorus and with great power: "God Save Ireland!"'

The last spoken words of any of them as they left the dock after being sentenced to death were Larkin's: 'God be with you, Irishmen and Irish-women.'[3]

Anyone who knew anything of Ireland knew that, though the Irish people had not 'risen' to support the military projects of the Fenians any more than they had risen in 1798, 1803 or 1848, the sort of mood which Allen, Larkin, O'Brien and Condon had expressed in the dock had sufficient roots in Irish everyday reality to make an emotional appeal to the Irish people. One might have expected that the British Government's chief concern now would be to prevent any further identification of Fenianism with Irish disaffection. Instead, it saw as its highest priority only the need to carry out the letter of the law and avenge the killing of a brave member of the Manchester police force. With some embarrassment it had to recognize that in Maguire's case at least a miscarriage of justice had taken place and the bewildered marine was granted a free pardon. The decision inevitably cast doubt on the quality of the evidence in the other cases. Condon, who was an American citizen, was reprieved a few days before the date of execution after pressure from the American legation in London. Its intervention on behalf of O'Brien, however, was unsuccessful, as he had already been released from British justice as an American citizen once before, in 1866.[4]

Allen, Larkin and O'Brien were executed in public on the foggy morning of 24 November 1867, Larkin and O'Brien suffering much agony as a result of bungling on the part of the hangman.[5] The atmosphere was so tense that when, a few seconds after the triple drop two loud explosions were heard on the left of the gallows, everyone assumed it was a Fenian attack, and the riflemen of the 72nd Highlanders, who had been placed with fixed bayonets round the scaffold, got ready to use their arms. But it was only the detonation of two fog signals placed on the railway which passed close to the gaol.[6]

The reverberations of the execution in Ireland were heard for over half a century to come. Quite apart from any legal doubts about the fairness of the trial it was impossible for most people in Ireland, however critical of the Fenians, not to feel that Allen, Larkin and O'Brien had been executed because they were Irish rebels. They were the first Irishmen since Emmet to be executed for political action. In a country where even constitutional opinion had now accepted Emmet and the United Irishmen as legendary heroes, it was impossible that Allen, Larkin and O'Brien should not too become enshrined as martyrs for the nebulous cause that was Ireland's. Their names became words with which to heighten the emotion behind any particular aspect of Ireland's cause. A few days after the execution A. M. Sullivan, the constitutional nationalist who was editor of *The Nation* and had been one of the Fenians' most bitter Irish opponents, published some verses in his paper written by his brother, T. D. Sullivan, which soon attained a wide popularity:

> 'God save Ireland!' cried the heroes,
> 'God save Ireland!' say we all ...

Set to the American civil war tune of 'Tramp, tramp, tramp, the boys are marching' the song became virtually the national anthem of Ireland for the next fifty years.

When some years later, in June 1876, a British Home Secretary, Hicks-Beach, speaking in a debate on Home Rule made a reference in the House of Commons to 'the Manchester murderers' he was interrupted by a cry from the Irish benches of 'No! No!'

The interruption seems in fact to have been directed at the particular argument the Home Secretary was then elaborating rather than at the phrase. For Hicks-Beach was accusing an Irish member of saying that one of the first acts of an Irish parliament in Ireland would be to order the release of the Fenian prisoners in England. It was being denied that this was what the member had said.

Skilfully, however, Hicks-Beach turned the interruption with the remark: 'I regret that there is any Honourable member in this House who will apologize for murder.'

But the sally rebounded on him. For the member for County Meath, a Protestant land-owner who had been elected the year before and had recently been attracting some notice in the House, rose in his seat and declared: 'The Right Honourable member looked at me so directly when he said that he regretted that any member should apologize for murder, that I wish to say as publicly and as directly as I can that I do not believe, and I never shall believe, that any murder was committed at Manchester.'' This member's name was Charles Stewart Parnell, and he was soon to blend the emotional legacy of Fenianism with the procedures of a constitutional campaign in a manner that would change Anglo-Irish relations for ever.

The government's obtuseness in carrying out the Manchester executions seems in retrospect all the greater since they had confronted similar situations earlier in 1867 more wisely. Indeed, ever since the arrests of Rossa, Luby, O'Leary and others in September 1865 the government had dealt with the conspiracy to rise in arms against the queen relatively mercifully. All those convicted at the Irish People trials had received substantial terms of penal servitude, but only Rossa was sentenced to life imprisonment because of his previous release on condition of good behaviour after the Phoenix trials. Penal servitude in English prisons of the mid-nineteenth century was a hard and often crushing experience, but it was noticeably more humane than the treatment that had been meted out to many of the conspirators of '98.

After the rising of March 1867 Bourke, the Fenian commander at Bally-hurst, J. F. X. O'Brien, the victor of Ballyknockane barracks, and McCaf-ferty, the organizer of the Chester raid, had all been sentenced to death, and for a time it looked as if the government were determined to carry out the sentences. Bourke was the test case. Balanced pleas for the commutation of his sentence came from all shades of political opinion in Ireland. One memorial from Trinity College, the stronghold of Unionism, carried 320 signatures, including those of 18 Fellows, 8 Professors, 13 QCs and 67 members of the outer bar.[8] Bourke's execution, wrote the Irish correspondent of *The Times*, 'would be a terrible expiation, at this stage of the world, for a political crime committed by men of otherwise blameless life, who abstained in an impressive manner, from perpetrating outrages that were in their power'.[9] When, finally, the government changed its mind on the specific grounds that the deterrent effect intended would not be achieved by the execution, *The Times* man in Dublin reported with relief that the 'anxious angry feeling, which was deepening and spreading every hour, has given place to grateful expressions of loyalty to the queen'.[10]

All other death sentences imposed after the March rising were eventually commuted and the rank and file among the Fenians who had been picked up, cold and hungry, in the fields and on the highways in the days after the fiasco, had been treated with remarkable leniency. Most were tried only under the Whiteboy Acts and given sentences of from twelve to fifteen months' imprisonment, while others were discharged altogether on giving sureties to be of good behaviour.[11] It was an intelligent policy, the benefits of which were virtually obliterated by the Manchester executions.

One other Fenian incident in 1867, also in England, also had an effect on the future more profound than any of the haphazard skirmishes round Irish police barracks in March. This was an attempt to rescue Richard O'Sullivan Burke, the Fenian armaments' organizer, who had been arrested in London in December 1867, and placed on remand in Clerkenwell prison to await trial.

On the afternoon of Thursday, 12 December, Burke was being exercised with other prisoners in the prison yard when he was seen by a warder to go over to the wall and take off his boot as if looking for a stone in it and then knock his boot against the wall.[12] At about the same time a man in the street outside noticed two men stop by the wall with a truck out of which they tipped what looked like a barrel of paraffin. They seemed drunk and he went into his stables remarking to someone there: 'Here's two fools with a truck.'[13] When he came out again a few minutes later they and the barrel had gone and he thought no more about it. Inside the prison yard a warder saw a white indiarubber ball come over the wall, but as things were frequently coming over that wall from the street, particularly shuttlecocks and dead cats, he too thought no more about it.[14] In fact the barrel had contained gunpowder and an attempt had been made to blow up the wall, but failed owing to difficulty in getting the fuse to burn.[15] The white ball presumably was a prearranged signal for postponement.

So many warnings of a possible rescue attempt at Clerkenwell had already been received by the authorities that a state of alert had become a way of life in the prison, and Burke, though allowed to receive visitors, was moved constantly from one cell to another. It had even been rumoured that an attempt would be made to blow the prison up, but for some reason it was assumed only that the Fenians were trying to undermine the building, possibly by tunnelling through the sewers. Nevertheless, on the night of this Thursday the 12th, a special state of alert was ordered and half the prison officers remained on duty throughout the night, armed with revolvers. Those in the towers overlooking the prison yard were given carbines. Definite information had been received that an attempt was about to be made to free Burke and another Fenian, Casey, but not how it would be done. Next day the prisoners were exercised in the morning instead of the afternoon, and Burke, it was noticed, was particularly agitated by this change of routine.[16]

That afternoon some boys were playing much as usual in the street outside the wall, and a woman was talking to the milkman. Seeing two men come and place a barrel against the wall and try to light something sticking out of the top the woman said to a policeman who happened to be coming down the street: 'I wonder what sort of a game that is.' As the policeman moved towards them one man threw the other a second box of matches, from which he took one, struck it and applied it to the object at the top, which began to spark. The man turned and ran, and the policeman, who was then about five or six yards away, also prudently turned and ran in the opposite direction.[17] The ensuing explosion wrecked the prison wall, totally destroyed a number of houses in the street, and damaged others over a wide area. Altogether twelve Londoners were killed and some thirty others badly wounded, losing their limbs, their eyesight or being permanently disfigured.[18] The prison yard was, of course, empty. It was showered with bricks and rubble, but explosives experts testified afterwards that a man crouching just where Burke had crouched the day before to adjust his boot would have escaped injury.[19]

The combination of the Manchester rescue and the Clerkenwell explosion brought home to the English public a sense of Irish danger as nothing had ever quite done before. The very remoteness of Irish problems had always made failure to deal with them seem a somehow natural and acceptable state of affairs. Now, in the crudest way, the Irish situation had landed on the Englishman's own doorstep. It was something which had to be dealt with, if not on its own merits, at least for the sake of comfort. As if to compensate for previous neglect of Ireland, the Fenian menace now assumed hideous proportions in the English mind. In Worcestershire, Cumberland, Bedfordshire, Surrey, Derbyshire, Suffolk, Kent – all over the country – special constables were sworn in to defend life and limb and the British constitution. More than five thousand special constables were enrolled in the City of London alone, and even in the Channel Island of Jersey pensioners held themselves ready to spring to arms on hearing three guns fired from the fort.[20]

The English statesman, William Ewart Gladstone, in anticipation of the premiership which finally came his way in 1868, had long been turning over the problems of Ireland in the labyrinthine recesses of his remarkable mind. He now found public opinion prepared as never before to contemplate measures that might be necessary to give Ireland peace and justice. As he himself put it, Fenianism conditioned the British population 'to embrace in a manner foreign to their habits in other times, the vast importance of the Irish controversy'.

PART TWO

1

Beginnings of Home Rule

Popular national feeling in Ireland had so far been mainly a negative expression of resentment at intolerable living conditions reinforced by a law made beyond the Irish Sea. It had taken only the vaguest traditional patriotic form, because there was no realistic patriotic tradition for it to conform to. Available traditions dwelt either in the dim regions of Celtic legend or in the eighteenth century where, formulated by the Protestant ascendancy, Irish nationalism had even seemed remote from the majority of the Irish people altogether. Only O'Connell, with Repeal of the Union, had temporarily succeeded in giving a single political and patriotic shape to national demands, and he had been beaten by the famine. In any case, he had been at a serious disadvantage in an age before the widening of the vote when popular support was not automatically an effective political instrument. After him the Irish tenant farmer had again lowered his sights to the problems of escaping starvation and eviction and paying the rent.

The Fenians, it seemed, had failed to create a widely accepted national tradition almost as dismally as the United Irishmen, from whom they took part of their inspiration. They had accumulated popular sympathy but little positive popular support for republican separatism. Even this sympathy stemmed much less from political idealism than from the inherited tradition of resentment at a special time when harvests were bad and the number of evictions on the increase. Evictions had risen steeply from 1860 to 1864 when the number – nearly two thousand – was three times the average of the next ten years. In 1865 they dropped to 842, and thereafter continued to decline until the end of the decade.[1] 'The accompanying drop in emigration in the improved seasons 1865–7 probably also helped the Fenians.* More young Irishmen than usual, who had just been through a bitter experience and who in other seasons would have emigrated, were at large in the country.

Though the Fenians had strengthened the emotional heritage, even leaving popular martyrs, they had otherwise changed nothing. In fact, for the next decade even martyrs were less in demand than usual, for harvests were universally good until 1877 and evictions dropped to the lowest numbers recorded since records had been kept.[2]

* From 114,169 in 1864 to 72,000 in 1867. (*The Times*, 28 January 1868.)

And yet, looking ahead at Ireland some forty years after the Fenians – an Ireland entering the second decade of the twentieth century – a fantastic transformation is seen to have taken place. The two major features of the Irish scene have been irrevocably changed. First, the poverty-stricken insecurity of the great majority of the population on the land, with its attendant menace of starvation, eviction and enforced emigration, has disappeared for ever. The landlords have virtually vanished and the great majority of Irish holdings are actually owned by Irish peasant proprietors, sons and grandsons of men who had often been treated with less respect than cattle. Second, for the first time since O'Connell and in the setting of modern parliamentary democracy a coherent and well-organized nationalist movement exists on a popular basis. Its aim is much more modest than that of the Fenians, but unlike that of the Fenians it enjoys active popular support. The aim is Home Rule, or the establishment of an Irish Parliament to deal with internal Irish affairs within the British connection and under the Crown.

How has such a double transformation come about?

Partly it can be explained by the general progressive evolution in British democracy which took place during the period. Until 1867, the year in which Allen, Larkin and O'Brien were hanged at Manchester, the electorate had been virtually the same as at the time of the Reform Act of 1832. A new Reform Act in 1867, concerned primarily with the urban vote, was only of limited significance to Ireland compared with England, but the Irish borough vote went up about twenty-seven per cent altogether as a result of it.[3] In 1872 the secret ballot was introduced. This, in Ireland, had a double-edged effect, for intimidation at open elections had come from the popular as well as from the landlord's side; but, on balance, secrecy in the polling booth probably strengthened the ability of the tenant farmer to express his wish for a better life. The long-expected further extension of the vote to the agricultural labourer, which came in 1884, was to treble the Irish vote. That more consideration and attention should in such circumstances be given to the needs and wishes of the humbler classes of the community was inevitable. Yet the extent of the revolution brought about on behalf of the Irish peasant was far more sweeping than anything comparable achieved on behalf of the British industrial working man in the same period.

For this there were two principal causes. First, even before the implications of the evolving democratic process had fully made themselves felt in the British political arena, there came to office in Britain a man who combined in a way unique in the history of British democracy an eye for the main political chance with the highest moral principle and deep intellectual perception and understanding. This man was William Ewart Gladstone, who formed his first ministry in 1868. Until his final retirement in 1893 at the age of eighty-six he was to concern himself with the affairs of Ireland to a greater extent than any other English statesman since the making of the Union.

The second cause also lay in the impact of personality on events. For thanks primarily to the work of two Irish politicians, Isaac Butt and Charles Stewart Parnell, the latter a political genius, Gladstone's own natural inclination 'to do justice to Ireland' was allowed no rest. Where their pressure for this justice was resisted either by Gladstone himself or by his Conservative political opponents, that resistance was bitterly contested. The momentum of the vast social revolution thus set in motion was inexorable and was only fully implemented by the Conservatives themselves some years after Gladstone's death.

To help engineer this revolution a new practical nation-wide organization had to be created in Ireland, and it was this which was the work first of Butt, and then of Parnell. It found all the old powerful emotional traditions automatically at its disposal.

But the Fenians too made their contribution to the end result. For they left on the Irish political scene, after their own cause had failed, a small élite of diehard radicals, backed by financial resources in the United States. This élite, while dedicated in theory to militant republican separatism, provided an organizing spearhead of general radical national activity which Parnell in particular was to turn to most effective use. Perhaps more important still, their impact in advertising Irish disaffection so publicly had convinced large sections of opinion not only in England but in Ireland too that, after Fenianism, something much more than a mere return to the *status quo* was required.

As an indication of the way new winds were soon blowing in Ireland after the Fenian débâcle, a body of Roman Catholic clergy met in the George Hotel, Limerick, as early as January 1868 and announced that they already had 198 signatures from the clergy for their Repeal Declaration.

'We simply ask,' they declared, 'the Repeal of the Union and the Restoration of an Irish Parliament; and we ask it by no other means than those consecrated by the long years of O'Connell's teaching – constitutional and legal means. ... We feel certain that the restoration of Ireland's nationality will do more to conciliate the empire than the greatest power or the greatest severity which the government could employ.' And they passed a resolution 'that a national legislature means neither revolution, nor weakening of the power of the empire, but on the contrary its better consolidation and progress'.'

This was an expression of opinion in advance of the clergy as a whole. But later in the same month another powerful statement, though less ambitious in its political demands, came from an even more august source. Some of it might almost have been part of a Fenian manifesto.

'Our poor country,' it ran, 'has been reduced to a state of the greatest misery and destitution. Our towns and cities are filled with poor men, women and children half starved, without shoes or stockings or proper clothing to preserve them from the snows and frosts of winter. More squalid poverty of this kind is to be seen in Dublin alone than in all the great cities of France, Austria or Spain. The country has lost more than 3,000,000 of inhabitants who have been obliged to brave the dangers of the wide Atlantic in order to save themselves and their families from starvation. About 400,000 cottages of the poor have been levelled to the ground, lest they should ever again afford shelter to their former inmates . . .'[5]

But this was followed by a strong condemnation of Fenianism. For the statement was a Pastoral Letter from the ultra-conservative Archbishop Cullen of Dublin, to be read in all the churches and chapels of his diocese. He concluded by exhorting his flock to obtain redress of the many grievances from which they suffered by electing Members of Parliament who would defend their rights. The following immediate objectives were listed: the disestablishment of the Protestant Church, freedom of education and a law for the regulation of relations between landlord and tenant so that the fruits of their capital and labour might be secured to the agricultural classes.

From the extreme wing of the constitutional movement, the Dublin newspaper the *Irishman*, came more spectacular advice addressed to the Members of Parliament themselves. It cited the Dual Monarchy in which Hungary had just obtained equal partnership with Austria, and suggested that MPs should 'act like the Hungarians to win for their native land what Hungary rejoices in; let them, complying with all forms legal and constitutional, withdraw from London to their Irish homes'. There they should establish themselves as an Irish Parliament.[6]

In England, Gladstone had been coming to his own conclusions. He took office in 1868 with the declared intention of doing justice to Ireland. 'My mission,' he proclaimed, before proceeding to Windsor to kiss hands, 'is to pacify Ireland.'[7] To the extent that the Manchester rescue and the Clerkenwell explosion had prepared English opinion for the need to do some such thing his task was, as he conceded later, easier. But it was still not easy.

Gladstone seems at first to have imagined that he could solve the problem of Ireland for ever by two measures: first, by disestablishing the Irish Protestant Church and, second, legislating to compensate a tenant financially on eviction. That he should have thought like this is not the absurdity it now appears. Even in Ireland itself there were those, naturally mainly among the Catholic hierarchy, who thought that the grievance of the Established Church lay at the root of all others. And to begin to think at all of allowing the State to intervene in the relationship between landlord and tenant on behalf of the tenant was at that time itself a revolution.

To ridicule Gladstone, as it is tempting to do, for declaring that with Disestablishment of the Church 'the final hour' in Ireland was 'about to sound',[8] underestimates what seemed then the boldness of the step he was undertaking. In disestablishing the Protestant Church he was tampering with the Act of Union, and his Conservative opponents did not let him forget the fact. Before considering his proposal to go into a committee of the House of Commons on the subject, they insisted on the reading of the fifth article of that Act to the House:

'... The doctrine, worship, discipline and government of the said United Church,' members heard, 'shall be and shall remain in full force for ever.'[9] Conservatives declared that Disestablishment would mean 'the most violent shock to the Constitution since the Reformation'.[10]

Many fundamental and far-reaching political emotions were stirred by the introduction of the measure. To decide that the Church, which represented only one-sixth of the country's population, should no longer be that country's established Church might ha /e seemed an overdue technical adjustment. But even the English radical Roebuck scented danger. There was no knowing where this would lead to, he said; nothing was going to content the Irish until they had total separation from Britain and Independence. '... Cut off Ireland from England and you cut off her right arm. As long as I have a voice in this great Assembly that voice shall be raised in maintenance of Imperial rule.... No sentimental talk about oppression to Ireland, and indeed nothing on earth shall move me from that position.'[11]

A Conservative member also sensed in Disestablishment the beginning of the end, declaring that they were making the concession 'to that very class of the Irish population who wilfully shut their eyes to the advantages of the incorporation of the two countries ... who rather choose to regard themselves as members of a conquered race than of a triumphant united Empire'.[12] To this a Liberal presented the classic reasoned reply on which all Gladstonian and indeed future Liberal policy was to be based, namely that 'it was a mistake to suppose that when symptoms of nationality arose they must either succeed in suppressing them or else must give them full sway and allow them to lead to absolute separation and independence'.[13]

Stanley, replying to Gladstone for the Conservatives in the Disestablishment debate, in a restrained and sensible speech merely warned Gladstone against 'that common and tempting fallacy of believing that certain political consequences will follow from what you are doing, merely because from your point of view you think it just and right that they should'.[14] And even some of Gladstone's Liberal supporters failed to share their leader's optimistic hopes that Disestablishment would eliminate Irish disaffection. 'I fear,' said one, 'that the youngest member of this house will never live to see Ireland what she might have been if our ancestors in their dealings with her people had not read backwards every precept of Christianity and every postulate of policy.' But the measure, he thought, would at least 'purify the air'.[15]

It did more than that. It showed that the Union was not itself sacrosanct, and thus opened up the possibility of a fundamental re-adjustment of attitudes. It was in fact no part of Gladstone's intention to disrupt the Union, only to make it work. But that in itself was the beginning of a revolution.

The Act disestablishing the Protestant Church over the whole of Ireland became law in 1869. *The Nation* hailed it as 'the greatest victory ever won in the British Parliament',[16] and the statement is not the exaggeration it may seem. Of the sixty-seven years of the Union only just over half had seen a normal functioning of the British Constitution in Ireland at all. The other thirty had been marked by so-called coercion acts of every style, all restricting the normal liberties of the subject – Peace Preservation Acts, Arms and Insurrection Acts and Acts proclaiming Martial Law and the suspension of Habeas Corpus. Habeas Corpus itself had been suspended for rather more than one-sixth of the whole period. During that time the population had been depleted by a quarter. A million people had died of starvation and its after-effects. Another million had felt compelled to emigrate. Disestablishment of the Irish Protestant Church, though marginal to the Irish people's welfare, was the first measure the Union Parliament had passed solely because the majority of the Irish people wanted it. It was indeed, in a sense, the beginning of the end.

But the vital issue was the issue of the land. Gladstone's first Land Bill, introduced in 1870, was as inadequate as Church Disestablishment to do proper justice to Ireland. But it too was of the greatest significance as the beginning of another aspect of revolution. Introducing this Land Bill in the House of Commons, Gladstone said in a masterpiece of understatement: 'I sorrowfully admit that neglect is chargeable (upon Parliaments since 1832) in respect to the question of Irish land tenure', and he cited, from a quarter of a century before, the Devon Commission's recommendations for security of tenure which had never been acted on.[17] His own bill was not to go so far as those recommendations. But even so, one apprehensive member of the House, while prepared to vote for it in the hope that it would tie the Irish people to the Empire, saw in it 'the principles of communism' in the way in which it dealt with property.[18]

In the context of the time he was not far wrong. For the new Act made clear that, in defiance of laissez-faire tradition, a man no longer altogether had a right to do what he would with his own. Henceforth a landlord who wanted to evict a tenant for any other reason than non-payment of rent would have to pay over a sum of money to the tenant for the improvements his occupation had made to the property.

Almost every Irish member who spoke in the debate pointed out that this really missed the heart of the problem altogether. What the Irish tenant wanted was not compensation for eviction, but freedom from eviction. Gladstone, by imposing a sort of fine on the landlord, sought to discourage the landlord from eviction. But the competition for land in Ireland was still such that a landlord legally liable to pay compensation could always re-coup himself financially by making a new tenant pay either a premium or an increased rent, and could anyway insure himself against any future need to pay compensation by raising the rent immediately for the incumbent tenant. Finally, if he really wanted to evict without penalty all he had to do was to raise the rent to a level the tenant could not afford to pay and, provided that it was not what the law courts would define as 'exorbitant', he could evict the tenant for non-payment without the need to pay any compensation at all.*

Really to ensure security of tenure for the Irish tenant farmer, what was necessary was to establish by law rents which the tenant could afford to pay and to make any eviction illegal so long as he paid them. Twelve years later this was to become the principle embodied in Gladstone's second Land Act. But the inadequacies of the first Land Act did not immediately make themselves felt with any severity, for the early seventies saw continued agricultural prosperity. It was when that prosperity suddenly collapsed towards the end of the seventies that the Act's failure was to have immediate political repercussions.

Quite a wide section of opinion in Ireland reacted to Gladstone's policy of intended justice to Ireland in a cooperative manner at first. It was to be the contribution of Isaac Butt to Irish nationalism that, in spite of this cooperative atmosphere, he first organized Irish public opinion to reject the principle of piecemeal justice from a British Parliament. His theme, taking its cue from O'Connell, was that only an Irish Parliament itself could give Ireland the full justice she required.

In September 1870, a so-called Home Government Association held its first public meeting in Dublin. This was a curious alliance at first, embracing a number of Protestant supporters motivated by actual resentment of Gladstone's new measures, particularly a feeling of betrayal over the Disestablishment of the Protestant Church. Somewhat naturally, therefore, the Home Government Association in this first phase had little success in promoting any wide national movement. To be effective such a movement had to have the Catholic Church behind it and the Catholic Church was obviously not happy about the support of Conservative Protestants converted by spite, as the former Young Irelander, John Martin, put it.[19] The Archbishop of Cashel declared that the Protestant Home Rulers looked on the movement as identical with a movement against (sic) 'Rome Rule'.[20] Even in the following year, when Conservative Home Rulers, increasingly appreciating the inappropriateness of their liberal nationalist bedfellows, began to

---

* The original word in Gladstone's bill had been 'excessive', but this was amended by the House of Lords to 'exorbitant', thus giving the landlord greater latitude.

withdraw, the Church still disapproved of the movement. The imperial government, wrote Dr Moriarty, the Bishop of Kerry, was for the first time heading in the right direction and he feared that a barrage of agitation for Home Rule would enable Gladstone to feel released from a sense of obligation to do something for specifically Catholic education in Ireland.[21]

Although Home Rulers won a number of spectacular by-election victories in 1871 and 1872, Irish Catholic liberals willing to cooperate with Gladstone could still, as late as November 1872, trounce them at the polls. Moreover, there were other elements making for discord on the national scene. Between the remnants of the Fenians and those Irishmen agitating for a reform of the land system as the most important goal, there was even downright hostility.

In 1869 a wide section of Irish opinion had been mobilized in an amnesty campaign for the Fenian prisoners serving grim terms of penal servitude in English prisons. The drive in the amnesty movement came from those Fenians who had remained at liberty. It was an early example of their new spearhead activity on the political scene and was organized by a Fenian, John ('Amnesty') Nolan. This movement made the most of the undoubted severities to which Fenians were subjected by prison rules. It particularly publicized details of the sufferings of O'Donovan Rossa who, for throwing the contents of his chamber pot at the prison governor, had on one occasion spent thirty-five days with his hands manacled behind his back throughout the day except at meals, when they were manacled in front.[22] He had spent some of the time reading a copy of D'Aubigny's *History of the Reformation* by turning pages over with his teeth.[23] The government commission of inquiry, a consequence of the amnesty agitation, found the punishment to have been out of order, though as the governor of Chatham prison pointed out, Rossa was lucky by the standards of the day to have escaped a flogging for such an offence.

A further propaganda success of Nolan's, who organized vast mass meetings on behalf of the amnesty campaign – one of them at Cabra was said to have been attended by 200,000 people – was to put Rossa himself up as a candidate for the by-election in Tipperary at the beginning of 1870, while still in prison, and get him elected, although he was of course subsequently unseated as a convicted felon. But the amnesty movement, which in any case was disapproved of by the Catholic hierachy for its Fenian association, was very far from representing any politically coordinated national movement. The less heroic day-to-day issue of Tenant Right preoccupied many Irishmen. The amnesty men, being good orthodox Fenians, thought that no issue should be allowed to blur the single over-riding goal of an independent Irish Republic. Clashes actually took place between Amnesty meetings inspired by the Irish Republican Brotherhood – as the Fenians were now more and more commonly called – and Tenant Right meetings.[24] O'Donovan

Rossa had triumphed in Tipperary not over a Unionist but over a tenant righter.

The significance of Isaac Butt was that he was a figure common not only to the cause of Tenant Right but also to the Amnesty Movement of which he was the cover 'President', and at the same time to the Home Government Association with which he had been connected from the beginning. He was eventually to pull all three strands together into one Home Rule movement, and thus establish that movement in a position where it naturally acquired the support of the Church.

Butt was a distinguished QC who had defended both Smith O'Brien and Meagher in 1848, and the Fenians from 1865 onwards. He was himself a Protestant, and a Conservative by instinct, but even when early in his career he had opposed O'Connell on Repeal he had always shown a national pride in being born an Irishman. It was the famine which had begun his disenchantment with the Union. What alternative was there for any Irishman, he had asked in 1847, as the full horror of the calamity made itself felt, but to think that the Union Parliament had abdicated the functions of government for Ireland and to demand for his country a separate existence?[25]

Addressing himself now to the clashes between the IRB amnesty meetings and the tenant righters, he foreshadowed what in IRB parlance was later to be known as 'the new departure', namely a participation of the IRB, for all their iconoclastic separatism, in constitutional politics.

'I believe,' he said of tenant right and nationalism, 'that the two objects, so far from being antagonistic, help each other.... No proceeding,' he added, was 'more mischievous than any attempt to sever the cause of the Irish tenantry from the cause of the Irish nation.'[26]

Butt has been much disparaged by latter-day nationalists, and was indeed left behind by events even in his own lifetime. But the credit for first coordinating the movement from which latter-day nationalism was to draw its strength must be his.

'Bide your time,' Butt told the Amnesty Association in December 1869, echoing Davis. '... Next session will prove the utter impotency of the English Parliament to legislate for Ireland's people.' And by consciously working to discredit Gladstone's 'justice to Ireland' as inadequate, he eventually succeeded in substituting for it the more ambitious aspiration of Home Rule.

Like O'Connell's Repeal, Home Rule in the early stages combined the attractions of national sentiment with the attractions of a social panacea. But no movement in Ireland could effectively become a national movement without in the end securing at least the benevolence of the Catholic Church. And for a time Cardinal Cullen's satisfaction with the British Government for carrying the Protestant Church's Disestablishment made it difficult for the hierarchy to bestow this, however much individual priests might see that the

Home Rule movement was developing a popular dynamic of its own. The gradual withdrawal of Protestant support from the movement made things easier. Increased Catholic support made Protestant withdrawal faster. Instead of the movement being regarded as a movement against Home Rule, the belief that 'Home Rule means Rome Rule' now took root as the traditional basis of opposition to the movement. This in turn inevitably made it increasingly sympathetic to many Catholics.

In a famous election in Kerry in 1872, a Home Ruler, Blennerhassett, was elected with the support of many priests against a pro-Gladstone Liberal Catholic backed by the hierarchy. Butt himself, after one defeat, had been elected in September 1871 as a Home Ruler for Limerick, and as part of his attempt to polarize all demands round Home Rule he made a point of raising during the election not only the issues of tenant right but also those of a Catholic university and denominational education. It was actually Gladstone's failure to satisfy the Catholic Church with his provisions for education that finally turned conventional Catholic thought towards the need for something more than mere piecemeal 'justice'. Gradually the Church came to identify itself with Butt's Home Rule altogether. And the Bishop of Clogher was soon heard declaring that he had had enough of 'a Parliament that confessedly loathes our religion and loathes ourselves because of that religion'.[27]

On the other wing of national sentiment Butt secured at least the neutrality of the IRB for a trial period of three years. Thus under-cover Fenians took part in the first Home Rule Conference which met in Dublin in November 1873, together with twenty-five members of Parliament and fifty Catholic priests. The Fenians were 'determined that within certain limits, Mr Butt's projects should have fair play'.[28]

What Butt's 'projects' amounted to was simply separate parliaments for the domestic affairs of England, Scotland and Ireland. Details seemed at this stage hardly relevant. The likelihood of achieving any such goal seemed so remote that discussion among Home Rulers centred at this stage more on the tactics to be adopted and the extent of party discipline to be exerted than on the precise form Home Rule was to take. Butt's tactical proposal at the conference was that the only pledge which sitting Home Rule members should take should be to vote for an annual Home Rule motion in Parliament and otherwise vote as their consciences dictated. In discussion of such things there was inevitably recall of the Sadleir–Keogh fiasco of twenty years before. One of the Fenians at the Conference, Joseph Biggar, a Belfast pork butcher then a member of the Supreme Council of the IRB and soon to be Member of Parliament for Cavan, outlined the shape of things to come in what seemed to many a disturbing amendment. This was to the effect that Irish members should act compactly together by majority decision on all parliamentary issues.[29] But such a proposal was still regarded as unthinkable by the majority of Home Rulers at the conference, and Butt's original resolution was carried unanimously.

As a result of this conference in 1873, the Irish Home Rule League was founded, and at the General Election of 1874 a few weeks later fifty-nine nominal Home Rulers were elected for Ireland. This was really the peak of Butt's achievement. Though the driving forces in Irish politics were still primarily other than national, they were now incorporated in a Home Rule movement, and Home Rule as a national aspiration was at least on the political map. Only two out of thirty-eight non-Home Rule Liberal candidates at the election had thought it politic actively to oppose Home Rule.[30]

However, under Butt's leadership the performance of the Home Rule party in Parliament was ineffective. This was partly because Butt himself, caught in the personal trap of trying to lighten a long accumulated burden of heavy debt by increasing his burden of work at the bar, could not give the party more than part-time political leadership. But the party's ineffectualness was mainly due to the fact that its fifty-nine Home Rulers elected in 1874 were a far more disparate body than their nominal triumph then made them appear. The election had taken place only three weeks after the end of the Home Rule League's conference and long before it had been possible to get any professional coordination into the party, even of those who had any real disposition to accept it. Of the famous fifty-nine soon only between twenty and thirty acted in any way like a regular party when they got to the House of Commons.[31]

On 30 June the first Home Rule motion was put to the House of Commons. At the meeting of the party which had agreed the wording only thirty-two members had been present.[32] The motion was that the House should go into committee to consider parliamentary relations between England and Ireland. If this was accepted, Butt was to propose:

'That it is expedient and just to restore to the Irish nation the right and power of managing all exclusively Irish affairs in an Irish Parliament.

'That provision should be made at the same time for maintaining the integrity of the empire and the connection between the countries by reserving to the imperial parliament full and exclusive control over imperial affairs.'[33]

This set the framework of the Home Rule demand for the next forty years, during which it became the Irish nationalist creed for the vast majority of the Irish people. Compared with the ambitious phrases about national independence in which the United Irishmen and the Fenians or even the Young Irelanders had indulged, the demand may seem an almost absurdly modest national one for Ireland. Yet nothing re-emphasizes more clearly the irrelevance such earlier phrases had held for the majority of the Irish people than the fact that even for this modest demand enthusiasm was quite difficult to arouse. Any prospects of fulfilment seemed at this stage remote.

On this first occasion in 1874, fifty-one Irish members out of a total of

103 voted for the motion. Together with the tellers and those who were paired this comprised almost the whole of the so-called Home Rule party – not at all a bad turn-out considering that party's essentially flimsy structure. But only ten English members voted for the motion, whereas Butt had earlier claimed that twenty-nine were sympathetic to Home Rule.

Clearly, if the movement were to take hold more effectively, even to seem in Ireland something seriously worth going for, then a more active and vigorous procedure than merely presenting a similar motion once a year was required. The tenant farmers did not in any case have too much enthusiasm for a cause that might well push into the background of parliamentary affairs their more pressing immediate interests on the land. At the other extreme a small doctrinaire majority felt that Home Rule did not go far enough. The Fenians in particular soon became disillusioned by their experiment in cooperation with Butt, but other non-IRB nationalists also voiced their disapproval. John Mitchel, now allowed to return to Ireland, declared that he was 'savage against the helpless, driftless concern called "home rule" . . .'.[34]

Mitchel, as a nationalist seeking something more advanced than mere Home Rule, accepted nomination for a by-election in Tipperary. This embarrassed Butt who was unwilling to antagonize the Church by endorsing him but also unwilling to antagonize the Fenians by opposing him. Mitchel was elected, but immediately disqualified as an undischarged felon, an affront to national pride which made it easier for Butt to support him in a second campaign. In this Mitchel was also helped by young John Dillon – spirited son of John Blake Dillon, co-founder of *The Nation* in 1842 – who was himself later to occupy a major position in Irish national politics. Mitchel was again elected, but the seat was at once awarded to his Tory opponent, and Mitchel himself died a week later. The contemporary comment: 'Poor Mitchel's last legacy to Ireland is a Tory misrepresentation of Tipperary'[35] was literally true and in one sense justified as a caustic judgement on his whole erratic political career. But his true legacy was something more than that: the idea that there were times when Irish republicanism must defy reason to assert itself, and this idea, it might be said, passed into the Fenian subconscious.

The small handful of Fenians actually in Butt's parliamentary party soon showed their restlessness in the parliamentary dead end in which they found themselves. As early as 1874, Joe Biggar, the IRB pork butcher from Belfast, was already practising the technique of obstruction in the House of Commons by reading long extracts from previous Acts of Parliament to delay the passage of a bill to continue the government's special powers in Ireland. Butt's own distaste for such tactics was immediately apparent, but on the night of 22 April 1875, when Biggar spoke for four hours against a new coercion bill, reading extracts from newspapers and government blue books until finally sitting down because he was 'unwilling to detain the House any longer', a new member entered the House. He was soon to become Biggar's most powerful ally, eclipse Butt altogether and earn himself the popular title of the Uncrowned King of Ireland. This was the new member for County Meath, a tall, elegant, bearded man, a former high sheriff of County Wicklow which he had captained at cricket and in which he owned over four thousand acres: a Protestant, Cambridge educated, who spoke with the precise accents of an Englishman. His name was Charles Stewart Parnell. Four days later, in his maiden speech, he objected to a reference made by a former Chancellor of the Exchequer to Ireland as a 'geographical fragment'. Ireland, said Parnell, was 'not a geographical fragment but a nation'.

2

Parnell and the Land Crisis

It is unnecessarily melodramatic to suggest that any man in history may have been indispensable to events. By the time Parnell appeared on the scene a new economic inexorability was at work in Irish politics which would have brought about great political changes whatever the personalities involved. Yet to match that inexorability history could hardly have timed a better manipulator of events than Charles Stewart Parnell. It is relatively easy to see how other men who played important roles in the next decade could have been duplicated, even men of the stature of Michael Davitt and John Devoy. Parnell alone dominated events, forging from them a political movement from which there eventually grew at last a modern popular Irish nationalism.

1877 was a key year in the gradual revolution on which Ireland, thanks to Gladstone and the impact of the Fenians, was now embarked. Politically it saw a wider use of obstructionist methods in Parliament by that very small group of Irish MPs who were trying to draw forcible attention to the demand for Home Rule – methods of which Butt, the party's nominal leader, increasingly disapproved. Joseph Biggar and F. H. O'Donnell, about to be the irascible member for Dungarvan, were early advocates of obstruction, but the new member for Meath, Charles Stewart Parnell, with an iron stamina, a cool indifference to the clubman's atmosphere of the House of Commons, and his concern only for the way in which what was said there would strike people in Ireland, soon made himself a master of the technique.

Descended on his father's side from a Protestant Irish patriot of the eighteenth century, a strain which in any case conferred a certain remoteness from the Ireland of his own day, Parnell had an American mother whose dislike of the British had not prevented her from having her daughters presented at Queen Victoria's court, or sending him to Cambridge. Her own father, Charles Stewart, nicknamed 'Old Ironsides', had been an American admiral and a scourge of the British in the war of 1812. And it was Parnell's emotional detachment from both England and in a way Ireland, too, that was to be his chief strength as an Irish politician. His least favourite colour was green: and during one critical period of three years in the next decade he never even visited Ireland at all. He had incorporated early into a natural aloofness a sympathy for the Irish peasantry in their distress and having once engaged in politics on their behalf treated the subsequent problems which arose rather like problems in engineering or science, of which he was an enthusiastic amateur.[1] He made inscrutability and unpredictability into political techniques which baffled colleagues and opponents alike. 'We feared him,' an English viceroy was to say, 'because we never knew what he was up to.'

Never before had there been a man who thus deployed the essentially English qualities of inborn superiority and arrogance in the cause of the Irish peasant. For this his colleagues forgave him much and his countrymen, after his tragic death, everything. 'An Englishman of the strongest type moulded for an Irish purpose', the Fenian Michael Davitt called him when he first met him in 1877.[2] And so he was to prove.

Not the least of Parnell's political merits was that he felt under no obligation towards any form of Irish national dogma. His definition of the Irish national goal was constantly criticized by Englishmen as equivocal, but that was its virtue: it was wholly pragmatic. 'I'm not sure he knows exactly where he is going,' observed another Fenian early in Parnell's career while saying that he had qualities which should endear him to Fenians.[3] Irish nationalism did not know where it was going either and had suffered from too many people trying to force it to go where it could not. Parnell never worried about where he was going. 'None of us,' he once said, 'whether we are in America or Ireland, or wherever we may be, will be satisfied until we have destroyed the last link which keeps Ireland bound to England.' But he was also quite happy to deny that he ever said it.*[4] He subsequently often categorically rejected a separatist republican goal but never made it clear whether he did so as a matter of principle or policy. In so far as he had a basic national position it was the infinitely flexible one now inscribed on his monument in O'Connell Street, Dublin: '... no man has the right to fix the boundary to the march of a nation. No man has the right to say to this country "Thus far shalt thou go and no further", and we have never attempted to fix the *ne plus ultra* to the progress of Ireland's nationhood and we never shall.'[5]

'They will do what we can make them do,' he said once of the British Government, and this was the only national principle on which he operated.[6]

In the summer of 1877, taking advantage of the generous rules of debate and the latitude then given by gentlemanly custom to individual members

* During the debate on the first Home Rule Bill in 1886 Parnell, challenged with these words by the then Liberal–Unionist, George Trevelyan, denied that he had ever uttered them. He had, he said, only been in Cincinnatti once in his life and held verbatim accounts of the two speeches he made that day and neither contained the words in question (Hansard, iii, 306, 99). Trevelyan then correctly gave the *Irish World* reference, with its report of Parnell using the words in Cincinnatti on 23 February 1880. This does not rule out the possibility that the *Irish World* may have misreported him, but it seems on the face of it improbable.

to assert their rights against the government machine, Parnell and his small group of half a dozen or so supporters began holding up government business to a point where ministers desperately sought the help of Butt himself in restraining them.

'I regret,' said Butt, dragged in from the smoking-room on the night of 12 April 1877 when Parnell was holding up the passage of the Mutiny Bill with innumerable amendments and unnecessary divisions, 'I regret that the time of the House has been wasted in this miserable and wretched discussion.... I am not responsible for the member for Meath and cannot control him. I have, however, a duty to discharge to the great nation of Ireland and I think I should discharge it best when I say I disapprove entirely of the conduct of the honourable member for Meath.'[7]

Though the House itself rang with cheers,[8] Butt could hardly have struck a more unsuitable note for Ireland. He was in fact sounding his own political death-knell. For while throughout that summer Parnell and his friends, equally contemptuous of Butt and the House of Commons, persisted in their obstruction, forcing the House on 31 July 1877 into its longest ever continuous session of twenty-six hours over the South Africa Bill, an agricultural slump was looming in Ireland and an imperative need was arising that the always discordant voice of the Irish peasant should be properly heard. The tenant farmers faced their gravest crisis since the great famine of the forties. To take political charge in such a crisis Parnell was ideally suited.

The season of 1877 had been disastrously wet in Ireland but a deeper economic cause underlay the Irish tenant farmer's troubles. The opening up of the corn-growing areas of the American West, together with the development of efficient transport by rail and fast steamship across the Atlantic, was flooding Europe with cheap grain with which the United Kingdom could not compete. Prices began to fall and with them went the Irish farmer's ability to pay his rent. Evictions loomed. The wet summer, and a consequent reduction in the potato crop to less than half the value of the previous year, complicated the prospect with the additional threat of famine.[9] The number of evictions more than doubled in 1878 to the highest figure for over a decade.[10] By 1880 they had more than doubled again and literally half the population of Ireland was living on private charity, with the proportion in the south-west of the country as high as nine-tenths.[11] 'Charity alone,' the Lord Mayor of Dublin's Mansion House Committee was later to report, 'stood between the vast masses of the population and a terrible death ... a Famine ... was stayed by the hand of private charity ...'[12] As in the forties much of the private charity came from England. But that after eighty years of the Union the vast majority of the population should still be ultimately dependent for survival only on private charity, from whatever source, was a terrible condemnation of government, if not of the Union itself, and certainly of that mood of civilized self-satisfaction at Westminster which Parnell and his supporters had been so busily disturbing.

As early as August 1877 a natural Irish political alliance had begun to suggest itself. There were only two positive national forces in Irish politics: those extreme nationalist elements in Ireland represented by the IRB, isolated as they were from the great body of Irish opinion by their obsession with the dogma of armed national revolt, and the new force in the constitutional sphere first created by Butt but active only in the small group round Parnell.

The Irish Republican Brotherhood had been reorganized in 1873 under the leadership of the deaf and almost blind novelist Charles Kickham, who as a young man had observed Smith O'Brien's trance-like perambulations in Tipperary. But remoteness from political reality was now the IRB's own chief characteristic. Most of those IRB men, who had been at first prepared to cooperate with Butt, were disillusioned with the experiment. One critic had expressed his disappointment in Butt graphically but unkindly by saying he 'would not give the snuff of a farthing candlelight for all the nationality that existed in that man'.[13] The IRB leadership itself therefore had deduced that only total abstinence in future from any such parliamentary compromise could guarantee the purity of the republican separatist doctrine. But it was not unreasonable to question the point of preserving such a doctrine, however pure, in totally ineffective isolation.

Joseph Biggar and another Fenian member of Parliament, John O'Connor Power, together with other members of the Supreme Council of the IRB, recognized the absurdity of such an attitude and decided to continue to work through Parliament as the only avenue available. They were consequently expelled or forced to resign from the IRB for their heresy. But more and more former Fenians were, like them, becoming impatient with classical Fenian orthodoxy and looking round for ways in which they could at least be active. And though Fenians of any sort were relatively few, their political significance in Irish politics was always out of proportion to their numbers. The total membership of the IRB in Ireland in 1877 was only about nineteen thousand,[14] but because of their close affiliation with the wealthy Irish revolutionary organizations in the United States they were a political force which any more practical political operator in Ireland had to take seriously into account.

In the summer of 1877 an Irish-American journalist named James J. O'Kelly, a close friend of the exiled Fenian John Devoy who was now the most effective figure in Irish-American politics, came on a visit to Europe and, in the course of it, held two long conversations with Parnell. In the first of these Parnell told O'Kelly that he was thinking in terms of some political collaboration between the radical extremists and constitutional nationalists. O'Kelly, writing to John Devoy in August, commented approvingly: 'With the right kind of support behind him and a band of *real* nationalists in the House of Commons he would so remould Irish public opinion as to clear away many of the stumbling blocks in the way of progressive action.'[15]

The next month Parnell himself, speaking to one of those members of the Supreme Council of the IRB who had just been expelled from the organization, used a phrase which was soon to become famous. 'I think there must be quite a new departure in our party,' he said. 'We are only at the beginning of an active forward policy but it must be pushed to extremes. A few men in the House of Commons can do nothing unless they are well-supported in the country . . .'[16]

The 'New Departure' was the term soon to be given by extremist republicans in the United States, headed by Devoy, to a new public policy of their own. This consisted of temporarily shelving the single uncompromising goal of an Irish Republic to be won by force of arms, and substituting a more gradualist approach of short-term objectives to be won at Westminster under the leadership of Parnell. The theory was that this would help activate popular nationalist feeling, and parliamentarians were in turn to accept as a final goal a totally independent Ireland.

To make this compromise and work with parliamentarians demanded considerable heart-searching on the part of former Fenians. The IRB itself, under the leadership of Kickham, could not bring itself to do so and this in turn led to its further ineffectualness and a further splintering off of its members into would-be more active groups. Devoy, however, who had received favourable personal reports on Parnell and his attitude not only from his journalist friend J. J. O'Kelly, but also from his chief revolutionary collaborator in the States, Dr William Carroll, who saw Parnell during a long visit to Europe in 1878, finally swung the full force of his Irish-American organization, the Clan-na-Gael, over to the principle of such an alliance. He himself referred to it as a New Departure when he published details of a proposed offer of collaboration with Parnell in his paper the *New York Herald* on 26 October 1878. The chief terms were named as the substitution of 'a general declaration in favour of self-government' for the federal demand of Home Rule, and 'vigorous agitation of the land question on the basis of a peasant proprietary, while accepting concessions tending to abolish arbitrary eviction'.

Soon afterwards Devoy himself visited Europe, and in two meetings with Parnell came to an unwritten understanding about the sort of way in which the new alliance should work. It seems fairly clear that Devoy, who had also been corresponding with the old Fenian John O'Leary on the matter, thought of the alliance as soon leading to some sort of practical nationalist climax, if possible to coincide with the centenary of the 1782 meeting of the Protestant Volunteers at Dungannon.* It also seems fairly clear that Parnell, mak-

* See *The Most Distressful Country*, p. 35.

ing use throughout his life of any effective instrument to further immediate political advantages, encouraged Devoy to think in such ambitious terms, though his own eye was in fact set on down-to-earth political objectives. Later in his career it was to be in Parnell's interest to play down any suggestion that he had originally entered into collaboration with revolutionaries for revolutionary aims. But contemporary evidence suggests that at the time of the new departure, and even as late as 1881, to keep the extreme revolutionaries working for him, he certainly allowed them to think that he worked for the same goal of total separation as themselves.

According to Devoy, part of the undertaking agreed at his own meeting with Parnell was that the direction of their combined energies into the land crisis should not prevent preparations for an armed uprising from going forward. Dr Carroll in a later description of his first 1878 interview with Parnell wrote: 'I asked him if he was in favour of the absolute independence of Ireland. He replied that he was and that as soon as the people so declared he would go with them. ... I met him several times afterwards in London, always on the most friendly terms and with the same understanding.'[17] And a contemporary letter of Carroll's to Clan-na-Gael, dated March 1878, seems to confirm this, saying that Parnell and his friends expressed themselves 'at the firm's service for anything they can do in their line'.[18] As late as February 1881, William Lomasney, a former Fenian who had helped capture Ballyknockane barracks in the '67 rising and within a few years was to blow himself up with dynamite in an attempt to destroy London Bridge, met Parnell in Paris. He wrote to Devoy that Parnell meant to go as far as both of them 'in pushing the business' of national independence, and that Parnell had told O'Leary 'as soon as he secured the means he would start in business with us and smash up the opposition firm'.[19] Finally, in June of this same year, 1881, Parnell was seen at the House of Commons by an Englishman living in America named Thomas Beach. Beach called himself Henri Le Caron, which was the name under which for years he had been posing as a French-American Fenian and supplying information to the British Government about American-Irish revolutionary circles, with which he had the highest contacts. He had been instrumental in frustrating the Fenian raid into Canada in 1868. Now, in 1881, writing to Devoy, he passed on to him a reassuring message from Parnell (having first passed it on to the British Government), to the effect that an armed rising was still his (Parnell's) ultimate goal.[20] Parnell, in fact, was having difficulty with the IRB in Ireland at the time and needed Devoy's and the Clan-na-Gael's support in preventing their hostility.

Such was the nature of Parnell's political pragmatism that it is of little value to try to assess how far he may or may not have meant what he said in such conversations. He himself avoided the need to inquire into his own sincerity. He was already making a political art out of not knowing precisely where he was going provided he went in a direction which he thought would help Ireland. He was content in his active plans to have his hands full with immediate political objectives. By instinct rather than by well-calculated intent he made use of the revolutionary extremists at this period as he was later to make use of both the great English parties, Liberal and Conservative, and, in the end, turn back again to make use of 'the hillside men' with whom he had begun.

Whatever the degree of sincerity with which Parnell had managed to secure the support both of Devoy and his American financial resources, and that of many dissident IRB men in Ireland, two salient facts emerge in retrospect. First, he did secure their support, and, second he put it to a purpose which, whatever his continued assurances, reversed the priority of the terms on which the New Departure had been formally based. In those terms agitation on the land had been seen as a means to the end of fairly immediate nationalist revolution. What Parnell did was to turn the policy inside out. He used the energies of idealist nationalists to work the land problem into an urgent and overriding political consideration in national life. This he did, not out of any particular principle, but because to a politician like himself looking for an area in which to be effective, the land situation clearly presented itself as the more promising. Effectiveness alone was Parnell's political criterion; when he could not be effective he did nothing.

Much of his political skill lay in his ability to master forces which others had set in motion. It was largely thanks to the efforts of another man altogether that he found the critical situation on the land politically so promising: that very Fenian who, meeting Parnell in December 1877, had seen in him 'an Englishman of the strongest type moulded for an Irish purpose'. His name was Michael Davitt, and he had then just been released on ticket of leave from Dartmoor after seven years in prison.

Davitt had been born at the height of the famine and his mother and father had been evicted from their smallholding in County Mayo in 1852 when he was five. They had emigrated to Lancashire where, as a boy of eleven, he had lost an arm in a factory accident. Almost inevitably in such circumstances, being a young man of spirit and feeling, he had become a Fenian. He had gone to Chester on the morning of 11 February 1867 to take part in McCafferty's abortive raid on the castle. Later he had helped to run rifles and revolvers to Ireland, and in 1870 had been sentenced to fifteen years' penal servitude for his alleged part in an assassination plot. In prison, handicapped in his ability to work in the stone quarries by his one arm, he had been harnessed to a cart like an animal. He had thought much about the future of Ireland. Recognizing realistically, on his emergence from prison, that 'the vast mass of our population had grown politically indifferent or apathetic'[21] and that the Irish revolutionary movement as represented by the IRB needed a new outlook, Davitt felt immediately drawn towards

Parnell, whom he actually asked to join the IRB of which he himself remained for a time a member. Parnell refused. But he expressed much sympathy with Davitt's general ideas for future action, which largely coincided with his own, and included a proposal that a new type of parliamentary party drawn from men of strong nationalist convictions should make a reasoned demand in Parliament for Repeal of the Union and, if this was refused, withdraw in a body and form a national assembly in Ireland. Parnell immediately endorsed the proposal in a public speech.[22]

On a visit to America soon afterwards Davitt discussed at length with Devoy the prospects of future collaboration with Parnell. But Davitt was not himself party to the formal inauguration of Devoy's new departure, being apprehensive that too public an identification of Parnell with extremists might prejudice Parnell's opportunities for effectiveness. Davitt's own political preoccupation was with the relationship between nationalism and the problem of the land; and he was to become increasingly obsessed with land reform as an end in itself. Now, in a speech in Boston in December 1878, he had publicly asked himself the pertinent question: 'Why is the Irish farmer not an active nationalist?' and replied on behalf of that farmer: 'If the nationalists want me to believe in and labour a little for independence, they must first show themselves willing and strong enough to stand between me and the power which a single Englishman, a landlord, wields over me.'[23] With the reservation that the landlord was in fact far more likely to be an Irishman and that the nationalist element in the tenant farmer's mind was therefore even more remote than Davitt postulated, this was a reasonable diagnosis.

Back in Ireland in 1879 Davitt found that in his own home county of Mayo the situation on the land was nearing desperation. Under the pressure of the agricultural crisis the peasantry confronted the classical pattern of disaster. Unable to pay their rents because of the slump in prices they were threatened with eviction. There was nowhere for them to go except out of the country. Simultaneously, the failure of the potato crop meant that there was nothing to eat. The spectre of the Great Famine, for thirty years never far from the back of any Irish peasant's mind, was suddenly out in the open again.

The protection from eviction supposed to have been conferred on the tenant by Gladstone's Land Act of 1870 was revealed as useless. The would-be deterrent effect on the landlord of having to pay compensation for eviction did not apply because, under the Act, compensation only applied to cases of non-payment of rent where the rent demanded was 'exorbitant', and the tenant could not now pay even a normal rent.

On one estate in County Mayo administered by an Irish Catholic priest, Canon Burke, the tenants made a stand and called a protest meeting at Irishtown near Claremorris on 20 April 1879. The meeting, which Davitt himself helped to organize, demanded a general reduction of rents and denounced the landlord system. It had an immediate local effect, for the priest, Canon Burke, reduced his rents by twenty-five per cent within a few days. It also set the pattern for a whole new land agitation in the rest of Ireland where similar conditions of hardship were soon experienced.

Davitt proceeded to extend the Irishtown principles on a national scale. When he organized a similar meeting to take place at Westport, County Mayo, on 8 June 1879, he secured Parnell's promise to speak at it. Parnell, carefully weighing up the situation, had recognized the vast social forces that now stood ready to be harnessed to a political movement.

Intimidation and agrarian violence of the traditional Irish secret society type had already begun to manifest themselves. This was intensified by the participation of former Fenians who on the principle of the new departure now became active in the land movement. Because of this the venerable Archbishop of Tuam, John MacHale, O'Connell's former supporter, felt obliged publicly to criticize Parnell's decision to speak at the Westport meeting. Parnell displayed that bland indifference with which he was to confront all opposition whether from Church, State, Liberal, Conservative or his own party for the next eleven years.

'Will I attend?' he said to Davitt who went to see him at his Dublin hotel the day before the meeting and the day after the publication of the Archbishop's pronouncement. 'Certainly! Why not? I have promised to be there and you can count on me keeping that promise.'[24]

At the meeting itself he set the tone of the whole subsequent Land League agitation.

'A fair rent,' he declared, 'is a rent the tenant can reasonably afford to pay according to the times, but in bad times a tenant cannot be expected to pay as much as he did in good times.... Now, what must we do in order to induce the landlords to see the position? You must show them that you intend to hold a firm grip of your homesteads and lands. You must not allow yourselves to be dispossessed as your fathers were dispossessed in 1847. ... I hope ... that on those properties where the rents are out of all proportion to the times a reduction may be made and that immediately. If not, you must help yourselves, and the public opinion of the world will stand by you and support you in your struggle to defend your homesteads.'[25]

He was as good as his word. In August Davitt summoned an assembly of 150 tenant farmers of Mayo who founded the Land League of Mayo with no less an ultimate objective than the transference of the ownership of the soil from the landlords to the cultivators, with compensation payable to the landlord. It was the first open convention in Ireland for eighty-five years, for the Convention Act of 1793 had just been repealed. And that autumn, while men with blackened faces were increasingly shooting at or otherwise intimidating landlords and their agents – more particularly terrorizing those Irishmen who were prepared to occupy land from which another had been evicted – and while threatening letters were being received, signed this time not by Captain Right or Captain Rock but by Rory of the Hills ('who always warns before he kills'), the National Land League of Ireland was founded on 21 October 1879 with, as its president, Charles Stewart Parnell.

The Land League's object was, by promoting the organization of the tenant farmers, to bring about a reduction in rents, protect those threatened with eviction, and finally obtain 'such reform in the laws relating to the land as will enable every tenant to become the owner of his holding by paying a fair rent for a limited number of years'.[26]

This latter objective enshrined the principle known as 'land purchase' by which, in the course of the next fifty years, a complete transfer of the land-ownership of Ireland was to be brought about.

The principle of land purchase had been first introduced by Gladstone in his Church Disestablishment Act of 1869 and Land Act of 1870. Land purchase clauses in these acts made it possible for tenants to buy their holdings by putting up a proportion of the purchase price and paying off the remainder in annual instalments over a period of years, the whole of that remainder being meanwhile advanced to the landlord by the State. Little advantage had, however, so far been taken of these provisions because the proportion of the price which the tenant had to put up – as much as a third – was far beyond the means of the average Irish tenant, and the period over which repayment was to be made too short. But an extension of the principle on more and more generous terms over the fifty years that followed the foundation of the Land League meant that by the time of the Anglo-Irish Treaty in 1921 out of 470,000 holdings, 400,000 were owned by their occupiers, who were paying off the purchase price by an annual sum considerably less than their rent would have been and for a limited period only.*

However, this goal of full Irish peasant proprietorship seemed almost utopian at the time it was first formulated by the Land League in 1879. Starvation and large-scale evictions were then the immediate order of the day, and concessions to prevent these were the immediate objectives. Final victory on the land was only achieved after a so-called Land War which the Land League then inaugurated, and which was to be fought out in spasms for more than twenty years. Though it was to be fought out in many phases and by organizations with different names it was fought in the first formative and crucial phase by Parnell and Davitt, with twin offensives on the land in Ireland and in Parliament at Westminster.

A new generation of polite society had now to be reminded of what eviction meant in Ireland. An Irish Member of Parliament recalled a sight

* Vindication of those who had always maintained that it was the system itself and not the fecklessness of the Irish tenant that made land tenure in Ireland unworkable was found in the fact that out of a total of some £120,000,000 advanced to the Irish peasant in the course of the entire operation, only £12,000 was not repaid.

witnessed long ago by the Roman Catholic Bishop of Meath, who had seen seven hundred people evicted in one day with winnowing sheets placed over the forms of sick and unconscious people lying in bed while the roof was pulled down over their heads.[27] Nothing now prevented a repetition of such things for, as no less a patrician figure than Lord Hartington told the House, the exceptional circumstances of the time had placed in the hands of a bad landlord a power which enabled him absolutely to defeat the purpose of the Land Act of 1870. If he wanted to clear his estate, now was the time to do it without pecuniary loss.[28] The report of a Quaker committee from the West of Ireland insisted that it was absolute poverty alone that prevented payment of rent, for many of the people there had even pawned their shawls and were without any other food than that supplied by charity.[29] A case was cited of a small farmer in Kerry who in 1854 had been threatened with eviction if he did not take an additional ten acres of marsh land, and had agreed to do so. He had drained and fenced this land and for twenty-three years had regularly paid the rent but now, hit by the slump, had been unable to pay for two years and had been evicted. He and his wife and five children had taken shelter with a neighbour, but the landlord's agent then threatened the neighbour with eviction for sheltering them. Whereupon the man and his family in desperation had returned to the house from which they had been evicted and two days later had had the roof pulled down over their heads.[30]

A letter quoted in *The Times* in 1880 from that pillar of Empire, General Gordon himself, described the prevailing condition of the Irish peasantry in terms uncannily reminiscent of other witnesses over two centuries. He found them 'patient beyond belief. ... Loyal, but at the same time broken-spirited and desperate, living on the verge of starvation in places where we would not keep our cattle. ... The Bulgarians, Anatolians, Chinese and Indians are better off than many of them are ...'[31]

Loyal, in a constitutional sense, most of them were, but this time they were not taking things lying down.

The popular power of the Land League, organized in Ireland largely by ex-Fenians, spread rapidly throughout the country. Mass demonstrations to secure reductions of rents were successfully mobilized. Many evictions were physically prevented. Where they could not be prevented, victims of eviction were sheltered and supported while private charity kept the majority of the people fed. The Land League operated by a combination of above-ground official action and underground violence. On the one hand there were the meetings, the speeches, even official Land League Courts replacing the normal administration of justice in some parts of the country – all largely financed by Devoy from America under the working of the New Departure. On the other hand there were the shots fired into windows, the threatening letters and the visits in the dead of night to those paying rents which the League regarded as excessive or taking holdings from which another had been evicted. Sometimes shots were fired into their thighs or pieces of ear removed from them or other physical torture applied. In this traditional agrarian activism many rank-and-file ex-Fenians of the New Departure school could now take part in the rather blurred conviction that they were in some way promoting that national uprising to which their original creed had been dedicated. On the official level, both the Secretary of the Land League, Thomas Brennan, and the Treasurer, Patrick Egan, were ex-Fenians.

The leadership of the Land League officially deplored violence, as of course did Parnell from his position in Parliament. But it was often a case of the Land League's right hand not being particular to inquire what its left hand was doing. And Parnell's ally in Parliament, the outspoken member for Belfast, Joseph Biggar, crudely summarized something of this ambivalent attitude when he opposed the shooting of landlords on the grounds that it was wrong because the assailant frequently missed and hit someone else. At the same time, the officially correct character of the movement, with its determination to right the poor man's wrongs, made it possible for the Land League to enlist that support of the parish priests without which no movement in Ireland could flourish. The priests worked almost to a man to help their people fight a possible repetition of the 1840s. Even some of the Catholic hierarchy and in particular the popular Archbishop Croke of Cashel proclaimed the Land League's principles of justice to the tenant to be moral and right. And the official organ of the Vatican itself declared that 'in consequence of the unsupportable state of the Irish peasantry the people must shake off their oppression. The crimes committed in Ireland are not attributable to the Land League...'[32]

By 1880 there were parts of Ireland where the queen's writ no longer ran. Reductions of rent from between ten and fifty per cent had been forced from many landlords, and where landlords refused to yield to pressure or to their own moral promptings in face of the Irish peasant's distress, it was made often physically impossible for them to carry out an eviction at all. The Irish correspondent of *The Times* described the Land League as 'a very distinct and potent government which is rapidly superseding the Imperial government.... It rules with an iron hand and with a promptitude which enforces instant obedience. Its code is clear, its executive resolute, its machinery complete and its action uniform. There is a Government *de facto* and a Government *de jure* – the former wielding a power which is felt and feared, the latter exhibiting the paraphernalia and pomp, but little of the reality of power.'[33]

This was the situation which Parnell now exploited to maximum political advantage in the British Parliament, elevating the Irish question to that Parliament's chief preoccupation for the first time since the Union, so that as one member complained soon it was 'occupying all minds to the exclusion of everything else'.[34]

Parnell and Home Rule

Butt had died in 1879, and his place as leader of the Home Rule party had been temporarily taken by another moderate, William Shaw. But a general election took place in April 1880 in which significantly it was not the still rather abstract question of Home Rule but that of the land that was the issue. This was the first election fought with the principles of the New Departure in operation, and former Fenians with advanced ideas sympathetic to Parnell not only took part in the electoral campaign but were elected in some constituencies. Joining Biggar and O'Connor Power in Parliament were now other former Fenians, such as John Barry, Thomas Sexton and T. P. O'Connor, together with other radicals of a new type, of whom the most striking was John Dillon, the son of the Young Ireland founder of *The Nation*, and already a pillar of the Land League. Though it was not until the election of 1885 that the Irish Party finally became a closely-knit and efficient radical machine with strict party discipline and officially paid members, yet some suggestion at least of this new radical phenomenon was felt after the election of 1880 and was almost immediately signalized by the election of Parnell himself to be the party's leader in May 1880. A few of its members had even probably received some clandestine financial support from Land League funds.¹ By the end of the year the party under Parnell had already taken the decision to sit in opposition to Gladstone's new Liberal government – itself a striking departure from the traditional Irish parliamentary practice of looking for what crumbs might come Ireland's way at the Liberals' table.

Yet at this stage Parnell's real source of strength was still the extent to which the Land League in Ireland was making Ireland ungovernable. And here he walked a political tightrope.

The parliamentary party was a relatively moderate force, and even the decision to sit in opposition to Gladstone had led to a rupture within it. Yet on his other wing, the Land League with its neo-Fenian elements and extravagant aims was a remarkably independent organization. And the most delicate consideration of all in the balance of forces he commanded was this: the government he was fighting was led by a man who in the past decade had shown a genuine concern to solve the problems of Ireland equitably. While pressing Gladstone, therefore, to do much more for Ireland than Gladstone saw his way clear to do, Parnell had to remember that up to a point Gladstone was a potential ally. Only while Gladstone did nothing but introduce special repressive legislation against the Land League, and before the good intent in his mind had had a chance to show itself, was an outright challenge to him safe tactics.

In such a situation, Parnell, while identifying himself with Land League policy, had to be careful to deplore violence in itself, merely explaining crimes where necessary, as the Vatican did, as the inevitably evil products of an evil system. In fact, the most extreme offensive measure which either he or the Land League ever officially sanctioned was the one he proposed in a famous speech at Ennis, in September 1880: that 'species of moral Coventry', as he called it, into which a proclaimed enemy of the Land League was to be placed by a rigid denial of all social or commercial contact on the part of his neighbours. The policy itself was not new and had been advocated as Land League technique by John Dillon in 1879. But its endorsement by the new leader in graphic phrases about isolating such a man from his kind 'as if he were a leper of old' and showing him 'your detestation of the crime he has committed' in bidding for a farm from which his neighbour had been evicted, gave Irishmen a firm new spirit of self-respect with which to gird themselves. The next month the technique was employed against a man whose name is still identified with it all over the world, a much disliked but courageous evicting land agent on Lough Mask, County Mayo, named Captain Boycott. Fifty volunteer Orangemen from Ulster crossed Ireland to help harvest Captain Boycott's crops when no one else would touch them, and seven thousand men, one-sixth of the entire British military force in Ireland, was required to protect them. It was, said a local carman, 'the queerest menagerie that ever came into Connaught'.[2] Boycott's crops were saved, but there was no slackening of the campaign against him, and when he tried to retire to a hotel in Dublin even the proprietor there refused to let him stay, and he had to withdraw temporarily from Ireland altogether.

But for all the Irish popularity Parnell won by speeches endorsing boycotting, the balance of forces he had to manipulate was soon to become almost intolerably delicate. The Land League agitation emboldened by success was growing increasingly wilder and demanding nothing less than the total compulsory buying-out, on terms favourable to the tenantry, of all landlords.

Gladstone's method of dealing with the crisis, which reached its climax in the winter of 1880–81, was to introduce a severe Coercion Bill to restore law and order before any land reform. Parnell and his supporters fought the Coercion Bill in the House of Commons with all the persistence and ingenuity in obstruction which past experience gave them, and his supporters were now many more than in the previous Parliament.

82

On the night of 31 January 1881 they far outdid the previous record of 1877, by forcing the House into a continuous session of forty-one hours in an attempt to hold up the Coercion Bill. Whereupon the Speaker on his own initiative arbitrarily suspended the time-honoured rules of the House and forced the closure of the debate. This called the bluff of obstruction, and a formal reorganization of the House's rules later in the year confirmed the eclipse of obstruction as an effective technique. But meanwhile, after a last gesture of defiance on the day following the Speaker's historic ruling, Parnell and thirty-five other Irish members were suspended from the House of Commons and temporarily ejected from the Chamber.

A situation had come about as envisaged in Parnell's conversation with Davitt a few years before, when the possiblity of a withdrawal from the British Parliament altogether and the establishment of some self-styled national assembly in Ireland was discussed.* The decision Parnell now took against this was epoch-making, though it would have been out of character if he had thought of it as such. It was based on a firm grasp of political realities: chief of which was the fact that at most one-third of the party would have followed him to Ireland.³ While keeping the radical wing among his New Departure supporters in the Land League as happy as possible, by being, as one historian has put it, 'adept at the cape-work of the pseudo-revolutionary gesture',⁴ Parnell directed his mind towards the future which included the all-important question of Gladstone's new Land Bill.

Two Royal Commissions on the tenure of land in Ireland had just reported. These were the Bessborough Commission, appointed by Gladstone himself to inquire into the working of the 1870 Land Act, and the Richmond Commission, appointed in the previous administration of Disraeli, to inquire into agricultural conditions in Great Britain and Ireland. In the light of these, quite apart from the pressure of the present crisis, the argument for some new measure to regulate relations between landlord and tenant was unanswerable. Gladstone's first attempt to devise one, a relatively tame affair, the principle of which was expressed in its title, the Compensation for Disturbance Bill, was thrown out by the House of Lords in August 1880.

Any land reform short of the total abolition of landlordism was going to dissatisfy the extremists among the Land League organizers. But their persisting intransigence made it easier for Gladstone to present and eventually get accepted by Parliament a Land Bill that was of much more revolutionary dimensions than the Compensation for Disturbance Bill and yet which could by then seem, if not moderate, at least acceptable by contrast with the Land League's increasingly violent demands. The new bill became the Land Act in August 1881.

Basically it granted the three F's, long demanded by tenant righters from the days of Sharman Crawford and O'Connell: fixity of tenure, provided the

* See above, p. 85.

rent was paid; free sale by the tenant of the tenant's interest and improvements in a holding on his vacating it; but above all, fair rents. The Act laid down that the definition of a fair rent no longer rested ultimately with the landlord but with a government Land Court to be especially appointed for the purpose. Given the prevailing notions of the rights of property, it was in the context of its time perhaps the most revolutionary social legislation any British Government has ever introduced.

Parnell, confronted with what he knew to be a relatively excellent measure, had to reconcile this with the knowledge that it would not satisfy his extreme friends in Ireland who wanted a total transfer of the land to the people. Above all, it would not satisfy his New Departure supporters in America with their all-important financial resources, who wanted an independent Irish republic. They, after all, had embarked on the New Departure intending land reform to be only a secondary consideration, the means by which the temperature was to be raised to white hot national heat. The temperature had in fact been raised to white heat but to fashion not a nationalist revolt but land reform. Nationalism, though thus partly aroused, was still a long way secondary in the peasantry's mind to concern for their own economic situation. How was Parnell to welcome and rest on the major success he and his supporters had won from Gladstone without giving many of those supporters the feeling that they had been sold or at least cynically exploited?

At first, in public and in the House of Commons, he refused to support the bill, on the grounds of its inadequacy, thereby going so far to please his extreme supporters that his more conservative supporters began to doubt his political wisdom. But he knew that while the Land League and even the more iconoclastic land reformers among his parliamentary group, like John Dillon, were assailing the bill for not abolishing the landlords outright, the benefits of the Act would be extended to Ireland whether he opposed it or not.

In fact, he played a classical political game of keeping the movement together by not altogether satisfying either wing. Croke, the nationalist Archbishop of Cashel, condemned Parnell's decision not to support the bill, and almost a third of the Home Rule members in the House of Commons even voted for Gladstone. Parnell, replying to the Archbishop's public criticism of himself, maintained that there had been a need to mark the imperfections of the bill by 'making a demonstration ... which` ... will not affect the division'.[5] Those on the left, who rightly suspected from such remarks that Parnell was at heart inclining towards moderation and some eventual compromise with Gladstonian policy, were partly placated by his launching at this time a new newspaper, *United Ireland*, under the editorship of the ex-Fenian, William O'Brien. In *United Ireland*, O'Brien unleashed the wild and colourful verbal violence in which his journalistic talent revelled, backing the stern public policy of Parnell with papery battle cries and trumpet calls which were almost a parody of traditional Irish revolutionary language. The working of the Coercion Act, with sporadic arrests of prominent land leaguers like Dillon for rash speech-making, made this sort of reaction obligatory. But reality in the form of the passing of the Land Act and the practical prospect which this opened to tenant farmers of lowered rents secured through government Land Courts was an equally obligatory consideration. Parnell, a politician interested in concrete results, had to take up a concrete position. He finally devised the masterly formula of 'testing the Act', or letting the Land League put forward a number of selected cases to see what sort of reduction in rents the government was really prepared to give, thus skilfully placing the onus of cooperation on the government rather than on the Land League.

To the extremists, however, particularly in America, who thought the only policy for the tenant was to hold the harvest and refuse to pay rent until the government abandoned coercion altogether and transferred the land to the tenant, 'testing the Act' was a dangerously soft attitude. Parnell typically did his best to reassure them by the toughness of his speeches in Ireland. He talked of the hollowness of the Act and used increasingly militant language to denounce the British Government, reminding them that behind all this lay Ireland's national aspirations. Things were made easier for him by attacks on him from England, particularly a famous speech of Gladstone's at Leeds in October 1881 in which the Prime Minister reminded Parnell that 'the resources of civilization in Ireland were not yet exhausted'.

Finally, Gladstone rescued Parnell from his awkward spot altogether by putting the resources of civilization into action. As the contemporary balladmaker had it:

... Before this wrong all other wrongs of Ireland do grow pale,
For they've clapped the pride of Erin's isle into cold Kilmainham jail.

Parnell was arrested.

It was the best thing that could have happened to him. William O'Brien, John Dillon and others prominent in the Land League agitation were soon in Kilmainham gaol with him. From there they issued at last a desperate and often envisaged call for 'a general strike against rent' in the form of a 'No Rent Manifesto'. On 20 October the government suppressed the Land League.

To subscribe to this No Rent Manifesto was in many ways Parnell's master-stroke. It was to make things impossibly difficult for his opponents on both sides: his own and the government's. It did so at the very moment he was himself withdrawn from the scene, thereby suggesting his own indispensability and the need for both sides to take him on something like his own terms. Parnell had already said that Captain Moonlight would replace him if he were imprisoned, meaning that the time-honoured methods of the secret societies, always at the back of the Land League agitation, would take over completely. And Captain Moonlight, unlike Parnell, was inaccessible to the government and could be dealt with only by unpopular methods of repression, leading to further bitterness and chaos. At the same time Captain Moonlight would not in fact get the average tenant farmer anywhere, for the resources of civilization were indeed quite adequate to deal with him, particularly since they also included the advantages of the new Land Act. Parnell 'on the shelf'* automatically became a catalyst who could make things easier for everyone.

In a private letter on the day he was imprisoned Parnell admitted that the Land League movement was already breaking up fast. The principal cause of this was the success of the new Land Act. Though he later blamed the clumsy repressive measures of the government for giving the agitation a longer lease of life than it would otherwise have had, the tenants were soon obtaining substantial reductions of rent from the Land Courts and often getting a fairer deal than many of them had dreamt of as possible. The extremists in Ireland and America were thus increasingly isolated from the majority of Irish opinion and Parnell could more cavalierly afford to disregard them. One practical problem remained. It concerned holdings on which considerable arrears of rent had accumulated. The Act had failed to make adequate allowance for such cases, and the need for further legislation on this score became an important item in the clandestine and unofficial negotiations between Parnell in Kilmainham and Gladstone, which were first tentatively entered into as early as November 1881† and seriously taken up in the New Year.

These negotiations were carried on through two sets of intermediaries. On Gladstone's side was Joseph Chamberlain, the young radical Birmingham politician who was one of the Liberal leader's brilliant young supporters. On Parnell's side there were two intermediaries. One was Captain Willie O'Shea, formerly of the 18th Hussars and now Liberal Home Rule MP for County Clare. O'Shea was a dashing and feckless character who hoped to achieve through politics that worldly wealth and influence which had so far eluded him in bloodstock breeding and company promotion. The other intermediary

* It was the tyrant Gladstone and he said unto himself,
  'I nivir will be aisy till Parnell is on the shelf
  So make the warrant out in haste and take it by the mail,
  And we'll clap the pride of Erin's isle into cold Kilmainham Jail'.

The ballad is given in Jules Abels' *The Parnell Tragedy* (London and New York, 1966), p. 126.
  Conditions for Parnell in Kilmainham were by no means as bleak as the ballad-maker envisaged. Like O'Connell some forty years before, he received privileged treatment.

† W. H. Duignan, a friend of Chamberlain's, went to Ireland in November 1881 with an introduction from Chamberlain to the Chief Secretary, Forster. He saw the 'suspects' in Kilmainham, but, he added later, rather disingenuously 'by no means on Mr Chamberlain's account'. (Letter from Duignan in *Freeman's Journal*, 8 July 1893.)

on this side was O'Shea's wife, Katharine, who had been carrying on a passionate love affair with Parnell since the winter of 1880. She was, in April 1882, about to bear him his first child.

The extent to which Captain O'Shea was or was not a complaisant husband at this stage is a complex one of considerable human interest but of no immediate significance to Irish history. Parnell's own personal involvement is more relevant.

The extent to which any personal considerations affect the decisions of professional politicians must always be difficult to assess. But the strength of Parnell's attachment to Mrs O'Shea and the fact that she was about to bear him a child must have made it at least easier for him to continue in the political direction in which he was already moving, and have confirmed an inclination away from revolutionary politics towards some sort of understanding with Gladstone.

The understanding eventually arrived at became known as the Kilmainham Treaty, though there was no document or even formal agreement of any sort. The terms were that in return for legislation to protect tenants with heavy arrears from eviction and a repeal of the Coercion Act together with the release of Parnell and his fellow detainees Parnell should call off the agitation on the land and cooperate in working the Land Act. The further implications of the understanding were that Parnell should in future use his strength in Ireland and in the House of Commons to collaborate with the Liberals in continuing Gladstone's whole policy of 'justice to Ireland'. And since the Irish party was after all a Home Rule party, even though the land and not Home Rule had so far been its chief preoccupation under Parnell's leadership, 'justice to Ireland' would inevitably one day include some recognition as yet unspecified by Gladstone of Ireland's aspiration to self-government.

The situation within the Liberal party on the one hand, and between Parnell and his extremist supporters on the other, was still much too delicate for any such prospective final development to be aired. But a grim fortuitous event occurred within a few days of Parnell's release to complicate and considerably set back the implementation of the new alliance at all levels.

The Chief Secretary for Ireland, W. E. 'Buckshot' Forster, had felt betrayed by Gladstone's decision to release Parnell and had resigned.* When Gladstone told the House of Commons that his place was to be taken by

---

* Forster had been a member of a Quaker Famine Relief Committee in 1847 (see above, p. 23). He earned the epithet 'Buckshot' because it was in his period of office as Chief Secretary that an earlier administrative decision was implemented by which the police on certain occasions were to be armed with buckshot rather than the more lethal ball cartridge. There has been so much injustice in Irish history that the anomaly by which this marginally humanitarian administrative gesture, which was not his, should have earned the well-meaning Forster an ineradicable reputation for brutality must seem of trifling importance. See *I.H.S.*, Vol. xvi, no. 62 (September 1968), p. 238.

Lord Frederick Cavendish, younger brother of Lord Hartington and his own nephew by marriage, the announcement was greeted with jeers and laughter. Though an agreeable and intelligent man, Cavendish had hardly made the sort of mark on politics that seemed to qualify him for such a post. 'We will tear him in pieces within a fortnight,' jocularly commented one of the Irish party's brightest newcomers, Tim Healy.[6] Before the week was out Cavendish was found at about half past seven on the evening of his arrival in Dublin lying outside the vice-regal lodge in Phoenix Park, hacked to death by twelve-inch long surgical knives. Killed with him was the Under-Secretary, a diligent Catholic Irishman named Thomas Burke. Their assassins, who had earlier hoped to kill Forster, were members of a recently formed secret society named the Irish National Invincibles. This was composed mostly of former IRB men operating independently of the IRB in the general atmo-sphere of the New Departure, though they seem to have modelled themselves on the IRB assassination committees for dealing with traitors, and the IRB itself issued a statement after the deed that the men who had carried out 'this execution ... deserve well of their country'.[7] The Invincibles' leader was the Irish-American ex-Fenian, McCafferty, who had made the attempt on Chester Castle. As head of the Invincibles he had the connivance of senior officials of the Land League itself, principally an organizer named P. J. Sheridan, the Treasurer Patrick Egan, and the Secretary, Frank Byrne. The man given the job of supervising the Dublin end of the operations, a com-mercial traveller named Tynan, had been recruited by Byrne in the Cham-bers in Westminster which the Land League shared with the Irish party.[8] The surgical knives for the deed had been purchased in Bond Street and brought over to Dublin by Mrs Byrne, then seven months pregnant, in her skirts.[9]

The Invincibles and their leaders in the Land League represented that very strain of idealist extremism from which Parnell was trying to extricate him-self before embarking on the new phase of collaboration with Gladstone. In this respect the assassination could not have come at a worse time and Parnell's immediate reaction was one of political despair. He thought for a moment of resigning his leadership of the Irish party, but was dissuaded by Gladstone himself. Parnell's denunciation of the murder – sincere enough because it made his own political task so very much more difficult – had on the whole a convincing effect on English opinion at the time, and was echoed from almost all quarters in Ireland except the IRB. But the murders post-poned the day when Gladstone and the majority of the Liberals on the one hand and Parnell and his party on the other could finally present a united front on Home Rule. Gladstone's first preoccupation inevitably was to ap-pease English opinion. This meant further coercion which Parnell equally inevitably had to oppose. Even without the consequent delay there were in any case considerable internal difficulties to be resolved on the Liberal side before the full alliance implicit in the Kilmainham Treaty could be implemented. Gladstone, at the time of Kilmainham, was in his mind moving in the general direction of Home Rule, but he was much too skilled a politician to be explicit even to himself on such a point when finding himself, as he did, so far ahead of his own party. His final public commitment to Home Rule did not in any case come about until Parnell had once again applied considerable political pressure.

In order to force Gladstone to realize his good intentions over the land, Parnell had made use of crude violence in Ireland. The form of pressure which he continually applied to help Gladstone manifest his conversion to Home Rule was subtler and played out on the parliamentary scene in England.

No attempt was made to resurrect the suppressed Land League. Instead, in October 1882, Parnell founded the Irish National League, the object of which, now that the agricultural crisis had temporarily subsided, was no longer agrarian but specifically national. It expressed a popular national demand for Home Rule, which had been considerably stimulated by the general anti-government feeling aroused during the recent land agitation. The importance of the new National League in practical terms was that it gave the Irish party for the first time its own national structure at constituency level, and with this structure the party went into the General Election of 1885.

This election of 1885 was the first fought with the new enlarged electorate introduced by the Franchise Act of the year before, which had granted household suffrage to the country as well as the towns. It was also the first election fought in Ireland mainly on the issue of Home Rule. From it Parnell emerged triumphant, with Home Rulers victorious in 85 out of 103 Irish seats, including an actual majority of 17 to 16 in Ulster itself. He also now had at his disposal in the Irish Parliamentary Party a far more tightly disciplined and effectively fashioned instrument than ever before. It was the first British democratic political machine of modern times.

In Parliament in the months before the election Parnell had manoeuvred with tactical ingenuity. He had put the ultimate logical pressure on Gladstone by actually voting with the Conservatives to turn him out of office, thus demonstrating to the Liberals that they could hardly afford in the end not to implement the full implications of the Kilmainham Treaty. For seven months of minority government the Conservatives under Lord Salisbury, dependent on the Irish, themselves flirted obscurely with Parnell through their Viceroy Carnarvon, a personal but unrepresentative convert to the idea of self-government for Ireland. Deftly Parnell had suddenly made Home Rule the principal issue in English politics.

At the General Election Parnell had called on his supporters in England to vote for the Conservatives. It is reckoned that this cost the Liberals some twenty seats. But the final result was ideally calculated to make Gladstone commit himself. The Conservatives won 249 seats, the Liberals 335 and the balance was held by 86 Irish Home Rulers.*

Gladstone, adroitly blending true statesmanship with political interest, had hoped that the Conservatives might raise Home Rule above party politics altogether, and would have supported them in conceding it. Quite apart from allowing Parliament to devote its time to other issues in the national interest, this would have spared himself the awkward task of trying to make Home Rule the special cause of his own party. Both the right wing of the Liberals, represented by the Whig Lord Hartington, and the left wing, represented by the radical Joseph Chamberlain, were deeply uneasy about Home Rule though prepared to concede a limited form of local government. But given the Conservatives' natural leanings towards imperial grandeur the chances of any agreed solution between the two parties was remote. The Conservatives were in any case at this time looking round for an issue on which to mould an effective political identity, and were soon to realize that they had found a good one in 'patriotic' opposition to Home Rule.

Gladstone, seeing the balance held in the Commons by the Irish and feeling in his own conscience the need for Home Rule, inevitably played for Irish support and introduced a bill to grant it. The Conservatives gratefully made the most of the role with which he had presented them. Quite apart from the solution to their identity problem it gave the Conservatives the immediate prospect of a return to power in alliance with the dissident Liberals, those followers of Hartington and Chamberlain who opposed Home Rule and were soon to be known as Liberal Unionists. When the vote came on the Home Rule Bill's second reading in June 1886, Hartington, Chamberlain and 91 other Liberals voted against it and the measure was rejected by 341–311. A new General Election followed and a Conservative–Liberal–Unionist alliance then held power for the next six years.

Paradoxically, this defeat of the first Home Rule Bill in the House of Commons was of less moment than the great victory which its introduction marked for Irish nationalism. It was the climax of a great achievement engineered by Parnell. He had not only effectively coordinated Irish nationalists feelings into a wide popular movement for the first time since O'Connell but, unlike O'Connell, had succeeded in securing for it at the centre of political power the nominal adherence of one of the great English parties.

The mood in Ireland, immediately after the defeat, did not reflect despair but rather a proud recognition of what had been achieved. The reaction of the *Cork Examiner* was typical:

'The progress of the cause of Irish Nationalism,' it wrote, 'has suffered a check, but it has at the same time reached a point at which five years ago

* The seat additional to the 85 in Ireland was won in Liverpool by T. P. O'Connor.

it would have been deemed simply impossible to reach within that period of time. The Irish question now is to the forefront of politics and the defeat of last night cannot relegate it to a minor place.'[10]

Ten days later the paper was talking about nationalists being actually 'on the eve of the triumph of their principles'.[11] Parnell, speaking at Manchester in the election campaign that followed Gladstone's inevitable dissolution of Parliament, spoke of the Irish having 'nothing before them now but the prospect of hope'.[12] Even when the new election results began to come in, showing a marked swing away from the Liberals in England, there was no Irish despondency. Tim Healy, the member for Cork and, together with John Dillon, one of Parnell's two most able lieutenants, declared the results 'a mere temporary set back'.[13] The general feeling was that a Conservative government could hardly last and that every effort must be concentrated on another great battle in a few months' time.[14]

Both inside and outside Parliament Irishmen went out of their way to emphasize that they were prepared to accept Home Rule as a full and final settlement of the national question. What then exactly did Home Rule mean?

Like the three subsequent Home Rule Bills which were to follow it over the course of the next thirty-five years, the first Home Rule Bill offered Ireland no more than a domestic legislature and executive for Irish affairs only, with such legislature and executive itself expressly subject to the supremacy of the British Parliament. In addition to this latter overall constitutional limitation, all matters affecting peace or war, foreign affairs or even customs and excise were specifically excluded from the Irish Parliament's powers.* Ireland was to have no army or navy of her own and even control of the police was reserved to the Imperial Parliament for a certain period. Unionist opponents of the bill who were worried that Ireland might nevertheless at some future date raise a body of Volunteers through her own legislature were immediately reassured that this would be a specific occasion for the Imperial Parliament to assert its supremacy. What the Imperial Parliament had granted, it was proclaimed by the bill's promoters, the Imperial Parliament could also take away.

This was a puny position compared with the aspirations of the United Irishmen or the Fenians or even the Young Irelanders of 1848. Much of the Unionist criticism of the bill was in fact based on the argument that it was so inadequate a fulfilment of the Irish national demands that Irishmen could not possibly accept it as a final settlement. Joseph Chamberlain taunted Gladstone and Parnell simultaneously by recalling a speech of Parnell's in which he had said he would never be satisfied until Ireland took her full

* It was to enjoy virtually the same status as is today enjoyed by the Government of Northern Ireland.

place among the nations of the world. 'How can Ireland,' asked Chamberlain, 'take her place among the nations of the world when her mouth is closed on every international question? Ireland is to have no part in the arrangement of Commercial Treaties by which her interests may be seriously affected ... and Irishmen under this scheme are to be content to be sent to battle and to death for matters in which Irish members are to have no voice in discussing or determining. I say that Ireland under this scheme is asked to occupy a position of degradation.'[15] Lord Wolmer said he could not believe that a proud nation like Ireland 'would accept a back-seat like that';[16] while Lord Randolph Churchill declared that if he were an Irishman he 'would be deeply wounded and affronted'.[17]

And yet Irishman after Irishman got up in the House of Commons and solemnly declared that subject to such minor modifications as he hoped to gain in committee he did accept this bill in principle as a final settlement. 'We look upon the provisions of this bill,' said Parnell, 'as a final settlement of this question and I believe that the Irish people have accepted it as such a settlement. ... Not a single dissentient voice has been raised against the bill by any Irishman ... holding national opinions.'[18] J. F. X. O'Brien, who less than twenty years previously had been sentenced to be hanged, drawn and quartered for his attack on Ballyknockane barracks, County Cork, in the Fenian rising, assured the House that the bill would be 'loyally accepted as a settlement by the vast majority of the Irish people at home and abroad and will put an end to the strife of centuries'.[19] Another Irish member who had been a Fenian as a very young man, William O'Brien, the editor of *United Ireland*, was even more impressive by being more realistic. They did not pretend for an instant, he said, that the bill would satisfy every man of Irish race. O'Donovan Rossa, for instance, didn't like it and they did not altogether hope to conquer his objection. 'We do not even promise,' he said, 'that by any incantation you can eradicate the feelings [which were] the growth of many a sad year and many a sad century.' But he did think that the Irish people had never been so united or unanimous as in acceptance of the bill.[20] Ireland itself, both through the voice of the Church and of the Irish popular press, bore him out. O'Brien's own fiery paper *United Ireland* raised its circulation some thirty per cent in one week by presenting its readers with a coloured portrait of Gladstone.[21]

Many Unionists maintained that what was said in Parliament by the Irish party was simply a tactical device and that the Gladstonians were being deceived into allowing the thin end of the wedge of separation. Even those who were prepared to accept that the Irish party were acting in good faith expected to see its members swept aside in any Irish Parliament as part of a great wave of national disappointment with absurdly exaggerated hopes.[22] But experienced Irish politicians like Parnell, O'Brien and Healy would never have said the sort of things they were saying in the Commons if there had been any danger of that. The whole success of the Parnellite movement was based on its acute sense of what would or would not go down well in Ireland. In any case, such a supposition quite misread the history of the development of Irish nationalism. The really remarkable thing was not so much that the majority of the Irish people could now accept so little in the way of a national demand, but that they had again been sufficiently well-organized to make any coherent national demand at all.

For, unlike O'Connell's Repeal, the attraction of Home Rule did not lie principally in any economic panacea it seemed to offer, but in a pure if unambitious demand for national self-respect. As far as economic conditions were concerned, the Imperial Government itself had long ago begun reforms. A major breach in the injustice of the land system had been made by the Land Act of 1881 with its concession of the principle of protection from eviction and fair rents. Fair rents were actually being applied in practice by the Land Court. It was true that in times of bad harvest, such as those which once again visited Ireland in the mid-eighties, the inflexibility of the rents adjusted by the Land Courts could and did lead to hardship and exposed some tenants once again to the horrors of eviction; and undoubtedly it was believed that under an Irish Parliament such things would all be much easier. But it had been proved already that such battles could be fought out successfully by a combination of action on the land itself and action in the British Parliament. Equally, the principle of land purchase by which the State bought out the landlords and the tenant was enabled to buy the land from the State by a series of annual mortgage payments, though not yet operating to any large extent, had been established and was being slowly extended. This meant that 'national independence' was no longer an indispensable prerequisite if the tenant farmer was to obtain ownership of the land. Nationalism was thus to a considerable extent deprived of the force which had given it its vague dynamic. Left to itself it amounted to nothing very remarkable – a reasoned if not impassioned demand that Irish identity should to a limited extent be recognized in some political form.

Unionists were unable to realize what had happened. For decades they had consistently underestimated the demands of the common people of Ireland. Now they exaggerated them. For the greater part of the Union's history English Unionists had been content to know little about Ireland, dismissing its persistent calls for special attention as either irritating or mischievous. Similar ignorance now dominated their excessive attention to Home Rule. Appalled by the Fenians, Land League agitators and American-based dynamiters who had been the superficial product of the country's long neglect, they saw in Irish nationalism little else. For the thirty years in which Home Rule remained the Irish national demand, the majority of Unionists allowed themselves to be hypnotized by almost nameless fears of what would happen if Home Rule were granted. Predictions of inevitable calamity and disaster multiplied each time the subject came under debate.

Certainly it was understandable that, for many people, the Irish 'national' position should seem menacing. Irish politicians who had so often used wild, green-flag oratory about freedom in the past were themselves largely to blame for this. It needed a knowledge of the balance of political forces between the party and its American supporters, and an appreciation of the need actually to work up emotive feeling for Home Rule in Ireland, to fathom the currents of Irish political language. In the circumstances it was largely a question of personal political temperament whether an Englishman decided that Home Rule was likely to be the final goal of Irish nationalism or the beginning of something which would lead to the 'separation condemned by all parties'.

Joseph Chamberlain in 1884, while still a radical, had understandably confessed himself bewildered by the term Irish nationalist as then in use. 'I should like to know clearly what this word means', he wrote to a friend. He could not, he said, regard the Irish people as having the separate rights of an absolutely independent community any more than he could the people of Scotland or Wales ... 'or to take still more extreme instances, of Sussex, or of London'. Rather than agree to separation he would 'govern Ireland by force to the end of the chapter. But if nationalism means home rule I have no objection to grant it in principle, and am only anxious to find out what it means.'[23] Curiously, having found out that it did not mean separation, his fears of separation assumed precedence and he opposed it in principle and practice to the end at least of his own chapter.

Even accepting the good faith of the Irish, there was certainly a logical argument to be made that separation might be the final result. Parnell himself had said that no man 'could set a boundary to the march of a nation'. There was no knowing what might happen in future generations. In the light of our own knowledge of subsequent colonial and commonwealth development the possibility that Home Rule might eventually have led to separation can by no means be discounted. Chamberlain and other Unionists had a valid constitutional point when they met reassurances about the reserve supremacy of the Imperial Parliament with the objection that such supremacy was at that time still retained by the British Parliament over Canada, but that no one would ever realistically think of trying to assert it.[24]

Nevertheless, it is difficult now not to regard the failure to grant Home Rule in 1886 and for the next thirty years as a tragedy for both the Irish and the British peoples. Given the undoubted acceptance of Home Rule at the time by the great majority of Irishmen as a satisfaction of national demands, and given the continuing extension over the next thirty years of social and administrative reforms which did at times, in the Tory phrase, almost kill even the demand for Home Rule by kindness, it now seems probable that extreme separatist nationalism – so totally unrepresentative at the time – would certainly have been killed, and that Home Rule would have kept Ireland a part of the United Kingdom rather than have taken her or the greater part of her outside it. All a historian can definitely say, however, is that, whether or not Home Rule would in the end have led to separation, the refusal to grant it over the next thirty years certainly did so.

4

The Orange Card

For thirty years the political definition of Irish nationality, for the vast majority of Irishmen, remained that given by Home Rulers in the course of the Home Rule debates. One Irish member, Sir Thomas Esmonde, had expressed it neatly when he described the Irish as being 'a distinct though not a separate nationality'.[1] Gladstone himself had given as accurate a version as any:

'We stand,' he wrote, 'face to face with what is termed Irish nationality. Irish nationality vents itself in the demand for local autonomy, or separate and complete self-government in Irish, not in Imperial affairs. Is this an evil in itself? Is it a thing that we should view with horror or apprehension? ... I hold that there is such a thing as local patriotism, which, in itself, is not bad but good.' He cited the instances of Scotsmen and Welshmen, both 'full of local patriotism'. Misfortune and calamity had wedded the Irishman even more profoundly to his country's soil than the English, Welsh or Scotch, 'but it does not follow that because his local patriotism is keen, he is incapable of imperial patriotism ...'[2]

The numbers of Irishmen who were to fight under the British colours in the Boer and First World Wars were to confirm his point.

But there were two complications in this view of Irish nationalism as formulated in the Home Rule era. Two groups of Irishmen, both minorities, were left outside it. One was that tiny minority stemming from the old Fenian tradition who still felt that only complete separation from Britain and an independent republic was an adequate satisfaction for Irish national pride. This group was, at this time, virtually of no significance. Many old Fenians had become wholly absorbed by the now more successful parliamentary tradition, and though the Irish Republican Brotherhood continued to exist as a secret society, it was by the last decade of the nineteenth century a minute and isolated organization. That it could ever again be in a position to influence Irish affairs at all, let alone decisively, seemed then, to the overwhelming majority of Irishmen, unthinkable.

The other minority, which like the IRB was also to influence future events decisively, was then already of far greater significance. This was composed of the million or so Protestants of Ireland, slightly under half of whom lived in the north-east corner of Ulster.

To understand fully the action by which the Ulster Protestants were soon to change the course of Irish history it is indispensable momentarily to look back three centuries.

The ancestors of these twentieth-century Irishmen had been, in 1609, strangers to Ireland, brought over mainly from Scotland as settlers, on favourable terms, of lands confiscated from the Catholic Gaelic tribes which had owned them.* The newcomers were Protestants. But though the Chiefs of the Gaelic tribes, the Earls of Tyrone and Tyrconnell, had fled the country, the people of the tribes remained to a large extent surrounding the new occupiers. In such a situation, two salient considerations dominated the Protestants' everyday lives and everyday thinking: they were on their own and they were surrounded by enemies. This sense of isolation, combined with an originally rational fear that their Catholic neighbours would try to regain their lands and dispossess them, became as much a part of the Protestant Ulster heritage as the land itself. Ingrained in the ordinary Protestant Ulster mind was the thought that the Catholic represented a material threat to him. Ingrained, too, became the belief that when a crisis threatened the safest way of driving such a threat away was to drive the Catholic away physically, much as the armed warriors whom the earls had left behind had been driven by law, at the time of the Plantation, into Connaught.

The reasoning behind such thinking was long kept alive by history. The 1641 native rebellion in Ulster, a violent attempt by the Catholic Irish to recover their lands, seemed to provide full vindication of Protestant fears. Half a century later a Catholic monarch, James II, came to the throne of England and Ireland and actually carried out legally that same threat of dispossession which Protestants had hitherto successfully survived. Before, however, an attempt could be made to put the new laws into force, the English Revolution took place and dethroned James II, who made his last stand in Ireland. James's defeats at the battles of the Boyne and Aughrim saved the Ulster Protestant inheritance, and the sense of salvation imprinted itself so indelibly in the Ulster Protestant memory that it is common to this day to see crude portraits of William of Orange, the Protestant saviour, and the slogan 'Remember 1690' chalked up on the walls of Belfast. Celebrations of this famous victory on 12 July,† and similar ritualistic recollections of the siege of Derry when London apprentices shut the gates in the face of the advancing troops of the Catholic Earl of Antrim, became themselves bastions against a continuing sense of insecurity.

* See *The Most Distressful Country*, p. 12. Before this Plantation of Ulster, and before the Reformation, there had been intermittent small-scale Scottish settlement of this part of Ireland by clans from across the intervening water, but their religion was, of course, Catholic.

† 1 July, old-style calendar.

For nearly a century after the defeat of James II the fear of Protestants that Catholics would try to regain their lands remained in the background. It had indeed become an ineradicable part of Ulster Protestant tradition, but the rigour of the penal laws against the Catholics, particularly those which prevented Catholics from buying land, inheriting it, or even renting it as a commercial proposition, removed the old fear at least from the realm of immediate reality. But throughout the eighteenth century the other half of the Ulster Protestant personality was strangely accentuated: namely, its awareness of its isolated identity in Ireland. The penal laws themselves did not only contain the Catholics. They also set apart the Ulster Protestants from most of the rest of the Protestants of Ireland by inflicting certain religious tests and restrictions on them as Presbyterians, the sect to which the vast majority of Ulster Protestants belonged. This Presbyterian religion conditioned a state of mind different from that of other Irish Protestants, for its rejection of bishops and respect for the opinions of the meeting-house gave Ulster Protestants a radical attitude to politics ahead of their times, and even a potentially republican as opposed to a monarchical outlook.

Though most of the tenants of Protestant Ulster, descendants of the original planters, customarily held land on terms which gave them – centuries before Gladstone's Land Acts – a security of tenure provided they paid their rent, together with compensation for their improvements, rents had been high. Their own secret agrarian associations which they formed to protect their interests against landlords had not always been able to prevent distress and hardship. Thanks, however, to a higher standard of living than in the rest of Ireland, due to the Ulster custom, Ulster Protestants had often had the money to emigrate. Emigration from Presbyterian Ulster to America had been a feature of eighteenth-century Ireland and had contributed to some of the most fiery republican spirits of the American independence movement.

Much of the same radical Ulster Protestant spirit had manifested itself in Ireland in the Volunteer movement of the late 1770s and early 1780s, and in the movement which evolved from that to try to obtain a reform of the newly 'independent' Grattan's Parliament.* The stronghold of the Irish parlia- mentary reform movement had been in the North, and it was of course in Belfast that the first Society of United Irishmen had been formed in 1791 to try and secure reform by bringing Irishmen of all denominations together to act as Irishmen. Desirable, however, as was the objective of parliamentary reform to all Ulster Protestants, the methods proposed were for a special reason then particularly inappropriate. For with the relaxation of the penal laws as they affected land, Catholics had once again moved back into the North. Because of the lower standard of living to which Catholics were long accustomed, they were bidding up the price of land to levels which Ulster Protestant tenants found ruinous. This was a new version of the old threat,

* See *The Most Distressful Country*, p. 32.

and many Protestants reacted in the old style. Clashes between organized Protestant Peep o' Day Boys and reciprocally organized Catholic Defenders had been the result, culminating in the famous Battle of the Diamond and the formation of the Orange Society in 1795. Verbal and written threats, frequently carried out, to burn out Catholic families and drive them 'to Hell or Connaught' made their appearance – as indeed they have continued to do whenever Protestants have felt that Catholics in Ulster were getting above themselves, well into the second half of the twentieth century.

When the United Irishmen had eventually tried to organize themselves in arms for reform, the fact that most of the Ulster Protestants were by historical temperament more anti-Catholic than they were anti-government made it relatively easy for the government to break the revolt at least as far as its manifestation in Ulster was concerned. The only two counties of Ulster which rose at all in 1798 were, significantly, those of Antrim and Down, which had been outside the area of settlement in the early seventeenth century, having been already more gradually permeated by Scots over a longer period and therefore less traumatically involved in the classic Catholic–Protestant confrontation of the area. But here, too, Protestant United Irish Societies – full of strong anti-Catholic feeling from the start, as Tone had found – came out in their true Orange colours and were soon as identified with the government cause as they had been with the republican.

It would be a mistake to deduce from this that the Ulster Protestants' new-found loyalty to the government was the really characteristic feature of their new attitude. This was not so. What still moulded the Ulster Protestant Irish personality was its radical self-sufficiency. Anti-Catholic feeling, charged certainly with nearly two centuries of emotion but still predominantly of the traditional economic type, finally determined their attitude in 1798, but even today when 'loyalism' has long been the hallmark of Ulster it is only so because loyalism has long suited the interests of Ulster Protestants. It is no paradox that many a 'loyalist' today in Ulster is proud to claim that he had an ancestor out for an Irish Republic in 1798.

Environment had conditioned Ulster Protestants from the first to be self-protective and self-reliant in a potentially hostile situation. What motivated them was always their self-interest. Thus in 1800, loyal as most of them had in the end been in the crisis, they were opposed to the idea of the Union because they doubted whether a Union Parliament could maintain as strict an ascendancy over the Catholics as Protestants could themselves. Then, with the Union, new forces of self-interest developed to bind them to it fiercely.

One of the most astonishing social phenomena in the history of the Union was the growth in the course of it, both in population and prosperity, of the City of Belfast. A Belfast population of twenty thousand at the time of the Union had expanded more than ten times that number by the late

1880s to some 230,000. The population of Dublin in the same period only doubled. At the same time Belfast, also in contrast with Dublin, became one of the most thriving industrial cities of the United Kingdom. As a modern Irish historian has put it, Belfast, instead of being the solitary Irish industrial city, became an outpost of industrial Britain.[3]

This was principally due to the overwhelmingly successful development of the linen industry, which, unlike wool, had not been suppressed by the English Parliament in the late seventeenth century since there had been no English linen industry which it had threatened as a competitor. Linen, then a cottage industry in Ireland, had flourished, particularly in Ulster, partly because of the custom of tenant right which gave the farmer a security conducive to its practice, and partly because of an influx of skilled French Protestant refugees who settled near Belfast at the end of the seventeenth century and taught new techniques of spinning, weaving and bleaching. When at the beginning of the nineteenth century the industrial revolution began to gather momentum, North-East Ulster was the only area in Ireland in a position to take advantage of it.

Around 1800, with the development of new machines and new processes, cotton also temporarily took root and flourished in and around Belfast, and though it succumbed to competition from Lancashire after about twenty years its short period of success was of the utmost importance for the future, for it not only attracted labour into Belfast but also served as a model for the technical reorganization of the linen industry. Linen expanded rapidly as the industrial revolution gathered pace with the faster transport facilities provided by rail and steamship, and the Ulster linen industry finally consolidated its position as one of the major industries of the United Kingdom when, during the cotton famine caused by the American civil war, it was able to step into the gap as an alternative.

From the 1850s onwards another highly successful industry was started in Belfast, thanks primarily to the genius of one man, Edward Harland, who came as manager to a small shipyard on Queen's Island, Belfast, in 1853. Harland's revolutionary designs for iron and steel ships gave Belfast an international reputation for shipbuilding, and a flow of rewarding contracts for passenger and naval vessels, which by the end of the century had made shipbuilding as important in its own right as the flourishing linen trade.

Thus, by the time of the first Home Rule Bill, the Ulster Protestants felt wedded to the United Kingdom by something much stronger than mere traditional opposition to Catholic Ireland. Their livelihood was wholly bound up with the United Kingdom's prosperity, and any proposal which seemed to tamper with their bonds with it seemed also to tamper with that prosperity and that livelihood. The apprehension was particularly strong when the proposal did in fact come from the traditional source of all apprehension: Catholic Ireland.

The Orange Society had had some ups and downs in the course of the century, but was relatively flourishing by the early 1880s. It was now to become the nucleus round which the new mood of defensive militant Protestant self-interest consolidated.

The Orange Lodges had always operated on two levels. The first was that of a fairly crude Protestant working-class self-protection society operating in the linen mills and shipyards, the direct descendant of the Peep o' Day Boys with their tough anti-Catholic approach of the end of the eighteenth century. However, just as in the late 1790s the gentry had taken over leadership of the Orange Society in order to make its power respectable, so at later crises of Irish history the society had always been able to show a constitution expressed in unexceptionable terms about brotherly love, toleration and loyalty to the Crown, and to display an impressive string of eminent and respectable landed gentry as its higher functionaries. A Royal Commission had once drawn attention to this dichotomy, commenting that 'the educated and refined classes may possibly make such an organization to be compatible with brotherly love and toleration to those who differ from them, but the uneducated and unrefined, who act from feeling and impulse, and not from reflection, cannot be expected to restrain the passions excited by the lessons of their own dominancy and superiority over their fellow subjects whom they look upon as their conquered foes. In practice it is not as it is in the letter of its constitution ...'*⁴

Because of this double edge, the Orange Society was always a potentially significant political element in the Ulster situation.

Banned by the government in 1836 after a curious conspiracy in which it had become part of a British political plot to set the Duke of Cambridge on the throne of the United Kingdom, it had been reconstituted in August 1845 at a meeting in the town of Enniskillen, with the Earl of Enniskillen himself in the chair. This was at the height of the last phase of O'Connell's Repeal campaign and the Orangemen were then particularly protesting against what they regarded as the thin end of the wedge of separation in the government's grant of a subsidy to the Roman Catholic seminary at Maynooth. Believing as they did that the Papacy was pursuing a systematic policy 'aiming at the subjugation of all nations beneath the sway and tyranny of the Roman pontiff', they resolved to combine under the old name, but, theoretically at least, without the old secret signs and passwords 'to preserve inviolate the Legislative Union, and the blessings of civil and religious liberty'.⁵ Three years later, at the time of Smith O'Brien's foray into Tipperary, the government made a special arrangement with the Orangemen by which they should be allowed to buy arms even though an arms ban was then in force. Money for the purpose was actually handed over to

* Even the formal records of the society at this time showed regular expulsions for 'marrying a Papist'.

the Grand Master of the Orange Lodge, the Earl of Enniskillen, by the Viceroy's Master of the Horse, but O'Brien's half-hearted venture collapsed before anything could come of the project.[6] A tentative link between the Orangemen and the establishment, qualified by the Orangemen's fear that the establishment might sell them out, had become a part of Irish historical tradition.

It had been in 1868 with the prospect of Disestablishment for the Protestant Church that the true shape of things to come was first clearly outlined. For months militant clergymen in Ireland had been using the sort of fanatical language which was to become commonplace in the North over the next fifty years and more. 'We will fight,' declared the Reverend Thomas Ellis of Newbliss in County Monaghan, 'as men alone can fight who have the Bible in one hand and the sword in the other; we will fight – nay, if needs be we will die as our fathers died before us ... and this will be our dying cry, echoed and re-echoed from earth to heaven and from one end of Ulster to the other: "No Popery, no surrender".'[7] Such a mood was not of course confined to the North but to be found among Protestants all over Ireland, and a Reverend Ferrers of Rathmines, Dublin, also proclaimed that 'if the Church Establishment be destroyed ... there shall not be peace in Ireland'.[8]

A central Protestant Defence Association founded at Hillsborough, County Down, Ulster, in October 1867, held its first meeting in Dublin in February 1868, attended by 50 peers, 20 honourables, 46 baronets and knights, 36 members of Parliament, 127 deputy lieutenants and lords-lieutenant, 17 privy councillors, 360 JPs and more than 500 others.[9] A resolution was passed to the effect that 'the Protestants of Ireland, from their social position, wealth, intelligence and loyalty are entitled to as ample consideration and protection of their interests as any other class of Her Majesty's subjects in the realm and ... that in all legislation affecting their property, liberty or religion Ireland shall be dealt with not as a separate country but as an integral part of the United Kingdom'.[10]

A special Ulster Defence Association was also formed. But the relationship between the movement's aristocratic element and the Orangemen was uneasy, even though the Earl of Enniskillen, the Orange Lodge's Grand Master, had taken part in the Dublin meeting. The radical streak in the Orange Society's activity was represented by William Johnston of Ballykilbeg House, the Grand Master of County Down, who, in March 1868, was sentenced to a month's imprisonment for marching, in defiance of the Party Processions Act, from Newtonards to Bangor at the head of a crowd of twenty to thirty thousand with beating drums, orange flags and a band playing the 'Protestant Boys' and other provocative tunes.

Though educated opinion in Ulster disliked the Act under which Johnston had been sentenced, it did not condemn the sentence itself. And the Protestant

Defence Association, whose meetings were at this time, as the *Freeman's Journal* put it, 'as plentiful as blackberries'[11] with at least twenty-five branch associations all over Ireland, was to go out of its way to dissociate itself from the Orange Society altogether, even though the Earl of Enniskillen was a pillar of both organizations.[12]

Nevertheless, it was with the radical Orangemen that the real vitality of the movement lay, and when Johnston was released from prison in April special trains were run to Belfast for the celebrations, and the Reverend Drew declared that the government 'might trample on their hearts if they dared, but they never should crush or trample on the Orangemen of Ireland'.[13] At another celebration meeting the following month the resentment felt by rank and file Orangemen for the upper-class conservatives was particularly marked. Such conservatives, said Johnston, liked their votes very much but they disliked the name of Orangemen. They had used the Orangemen for thirty years and it was 'now time to put their members of Parliament through their catechism'.[14] In June 1868 the Grand Lodge of the Institution further reiterated the determination of Orangemen and Protestants that they would 'never surrender their civil and religious rights' purchased by the blood and treasure of their ancestors.[15] And when in July the Earl of Enniskillen, concerned to keep the Orange and conservative elements together, called a meeting in his ancestral town, he issued a Nelson-like summons 'expecting that every Protestant from 14 to 60, whether he be an Orangeman or not, will be at his post in Enniskillen to protest against meditated attacks'.[16]

But all the brave words which had seemed to create such a belligerent mood and atmosphere came to nothing when in due course Gladstone, having fought and won an election on the question of Disestablishment of the Irish Church, proceeded, early in 1869, to pass the Act through Parliament. As late as February 1869 one Ulster clergyman was boasting that he would put his house, glebe, church and schools under the protection of two thousand Orangemen against all comers, even including Her Majesty's Home Secretary.[17] But the general tone was one of impotence and bitterness. A speaker at one Protestant Defence Association commented with some foresight that the government 'should beware lest they made Protestant Fenians'.[18] And a manifesto issued by the Grand Orange Lodge, sensing correctly that even more fundamental changes than Church Disestablishment would one day be in store, laid down that as it was by virtue of the third article of the Act of Union that the Imperial Parliament was constituted and invested with legal authority, so 'upon the cancelling of that Act their functions as a Parliament would be extinguished'.[19] In other words, Protestant Ulstermen might not only one day have to look after themselves but would have the self-proclaimed constitutional right to do so.

This was inaccurate constitutional doctrine since the British Constitution recognizes only one unalterable legislative principle, namely that Parliament can always legislate to supersede earlier legislation. But it was to become a sincerely and widely held point of view that must be appreciated if later Ulster attitudes are to be understood.

For the time being, however, the impression left by the crisis was the dangerous one that all the talk of the Ulstermen and other Irish Protestants was mere bombast.

'Many in their ignorance,' Johnston had said in the course of the crisis, 'had talked of an Orange revival, but Orangeism never was dead and was undying.'[20] This was true in so far as the society permanently kept alive the rather aggressive Protestant solidarity of the labourers and dock workers of North-East Ulster. But it was outside events and the interests of more important parties alone which gave the society political significance. Thus it was not again until the great Land League crisis of 1881 and the signs of government 'weakness' in the Kilmainham Treaty that the Orange Society once more began to assume a prominence it had lacked throughout the seventies.

In July 1882 the society obtained an important new recruit in a wealthy Protestant landlord of County Cavan, a major in the militia and a Tory Member of Parliament for his county, Edward Saunderson. He had become an Orangeman, he announced, because the state of the country for the past two years – the years of the Land League – had been 'simply unbearable'. Having asked himself whether there was any organization capable of dealing with this condition of anarchy and rebellion, he had decided that there was only one 'not afraid to face and cope with it and that was the Orange organization'. But he had also come to the conclusion that the organization could be much improved by more discipline. It needed training in the use of the arms which many of them possessed and they should adopt a uniform. Then: '... If England in a moment of infatuation, determined to establish Home Rule ... they would take up arms and ask the reason why ...'.[21]

The following year Lord Arthur Hill, Orange Grand Master of County Down, was also asserting that tens of thousands of loyal Irishmen 'with stout hearts and strong arms were ready to defend to the death if necessary' their principles, calling for the combination of all Protestant Unionists whether originally Liberal or Conservative in one political party.[22]

Early in 1884, with the prospect of the extended franchise making a Home Rule Bill possible, Saunderson proclaimed that 'every Protestant was as ready to fight today as his ancestors were two hundred years ago', and boasted that the Orange Institution could concentrate fifty thousand men at any given point in Ulster at the shortest possible notice. He was in contact with foreign armament firms obtaining quotations for rifles with which to supply an Orange army.[23] To a crowd of twenty thousand Orangemen celebrating the anniversary of the Boyne on 12 July 1884, some with their drums stained with the blood of their wrists after the fury with which they had been beating their traditional tattoo, he declared that the organization had made more progress in the past three or four years than the most sanguine Orangemen would have thought possible.[24] But perhaps because Saunderson was such a jaunty likeable Irishman, so wealthy, a favourite in London drawing-rooms and, after all, a major only in the militia, with little real experience of soldiering, no one in the sophisticated world of British politics took his threats of action very seriously. It was not until after the General Election of 1885 which gave the balance of power to the Irish party in the House of Commons that a new significance was given to such militaristic vocabulary by support from a source which had hitherto treated it with little respect.

As late as 16 November 1885 Lord Randolph Churchill, the young Tory radical, had been writing of the 'foul Ulster Tories who have always ruined our party'.[25] During the election of 1885 the Orangemen had delivered their most violent and successful attacks against their fellow conservatives in Ulster, suspecting a betrayal to Parnell. The prospect of the Conservatives trimming with Catholic Irish nationalism had long been the Orangemen's bogey. But this was now largely dispelled by the political evolution in London, when Gladstone, faced with the results of the election, finally came out for Home Rule and the Conservatives nailed their colours then and for the next thirty-five years to the anti-Home Rule mast.

At the prospect of a Home Rule Bill the tension in Ulster and among Irish Protestants generally had risen immediately. On 1 December 1885 at a great Orange soirée in Dublin William Johnston stated plainly: '... the day that any Government brings into the House of Commons a Bill to separate Ireland from England and to dissolve the legislative Union, the Orange Volunteers would be mustered in Ulster under able and experienced officers, and if the bill proceeded further and received the Royal Assent there would be at once a civil war in Ulster ...'.[26] It was hardly surprising that Lord Randolph Churchill for the Conservatives now decided that 'the Orange card was the one to play'.[27] The Loyal and Patriotic Union, formed in Ireland in the summer of 1885, began to spread branches into England. In January 1886, the Ulster Loyalist anti-Repeal Union was formed and at its first meeting, symbolically at Dungannon, on 1 February 1886, one Orangeman called for an appeal to Germany if that to England should fall on deaf ears.[28]

At the New Year Churchill had met Saunderson and discussed the situation, and a month later, a few days before proceeding to Belfast for an organized campaign against Home Rule, he made a significant speech in his own constituency at Paddington. He declared that England could not leave the Protestants of Ireland in the lurch and that there were hundreds and thousands of English hearts – 'aye, and English hands' – that would stand by them.[29] He also made an astonishing statement, the arrogance of which was to underlay much of the English Conservative philosophy towards

Ireland for the next thirty-five years. 'The Protestants of Ireland,' said Churchill, 'on such an occasion as this, and in a national crisis such as this, are the only nation which is known to the English people in Ireland.'[30]

In February he crossed to Belfast and reassured the Ulstermen that 'in the dark hour there will not be wanting to you those of position and influence in England who are willing to cast their lot with you – whatever it may be'.[31] Ulster, he said a little later, 'would fight, and Ulster would be right'.

Appearances seemed to bear him out. The *Belfast News-Letter* declared that though the Loyalists did not want civil war they were not afraid to resort to it 'rather than submit to be ruled by boycotters and moonlighters exercising legislative functions in an Irish Parliament which would be the laughing stock of the civilized world'.[32] Advertisements appeared in the paper, asking for twenty thousand rifles and for competent men 'who must not be in receipt of pensions to instruct in military drill'.[33] As the second reading of the Home Rule Bill was argued out in the Commons, reports began to come in of enrolments of Orange volunteers between eighteen and sixty, and of drilling with and without arms, from various parts of North-East Ulster.[34] On 8 May 1886 Major Saunderson declared to a large and enthusiastic meeting of the Loyal and Patriotic Union in Dublin that 'there could only be one appeal left, and that was an appeal which they unquestionably intended to make and that appeal was to their own strong right arms'.[35] There was talk of Lord Wolseley and a thousand British officers putting themselves at the service of the Orangemen; of Lord Charles Beresford saying he would resign from the Navy rather than lead it against Ulster; of a supposed Ulster army of two army corps, an active one of thirty-eight thousand men, and a reserve of twenty-eight thousand. There was even a proposal for an Ulster convention and a solemn covenant.[36]

Home Rulers continued to dismiss all this as, in the last resort, 'all bunkum and bounce', as one Irish member put it. '... They have no intention whatever of fighting,' he said.[37] And he was echoed everywhere on the government benches. Labouchère described the advertisement for Snider rifles in the Ulster papers as 'a game of brag'. The whole thing, he said, was 'arrant humbug'.[38] They had not fought over Disestablishment and they would not fight now. 'A manufactured thing, a good deal of bluster and a good deal of bunkum,' Sir Charles Russell called it all.[39] T. D. Sullivan, the Irish member for College Green, also taunted the Ulstermen with their behaviour at the time of Disestablishment and went on to call their historical bluff. 'Their talk,' he said, 'about the battle of the Boyne was as great a fraud as their talk about Ulster.... Why, the Irish Protestants at the Battle of the Boyne represented only one eighth of King William's Army, and as an Irishman he was almost ashamed to say they were the least effective part of it.'[40]

It was as well perhaps that Home Rulers should enjoy the joke while it lasted. They were making the classical political mistake of thinking that reason rather than power would eventually decide the issue. In fact, the Home Rule Bill was rejected on its second reading on 8 June 1886 before the seriousness of such preparations could be put to the test. Certainly they never reached anything like the magnitude or level of organization that was to be achieved twenty-five years later. But what was important for the future was not just the precedent, but the firm establishment in the Home Rule mind of the conviction that this was all *only* bluff. The belief became part of standard Home Rule dogma.

This confidence was not based only on wishful thinking. Honourable men, it was felt, would see that the Ulster case did not stand up to rational scrutiny, and that all reasonable safeguards which Ulstermen or other Irish Protestants might require had been met in the proposals of the Home Rule Bill. Gladstone in introducing the bill devoted far more attention to what seemed to him a greater problem than that of Ulster, namely the decision whether or not to retain Irish members in the imperial legislature, which he had finally resolved in the negative. On Ulster he merely mentioned that a number of suggestions had been made, including one for the exclusion of part of Ulster from the operation of Home Rule, none of which had seemed to warrant inclusion in the bill, though he offered to keep an open mind on them in committee.[41] The confidence with which he was able to approach the problem undoubtedly derived partly from the fact that, as a result of the election, the Nationalists were actually in a majority of one – seventeen seats as opposed to sixteen – for the nine counties of Ulster: Antrim, Armagh, Down, Derry, Tyrone, Fermanagh, Donegal, Cavan and Monaghan. Given a belief in the elementary working principles of democracy it was unthinkable that certain minority objections in these counties should be allowed to wreck the proposal for the whole of Ireland. As one Liberal Ulsterman declared, it was virtually impossible 'to draw a plan of even a section of a county in the whole of Ulster in which section there would not be comprised persons of all the religions of Ireland'.[42] Statistics indeed seemed to make nonsense of the idea that Ulster should have any special say. The percentages of population over the entire province were fifty-two per cent Protestant and forty-nine per cent Catholic. In the counties of Antrim and in parts of Down and Armagh there was a concentration of Protestants which outnumbered Catholics there in the proportion of five and a half to two. Over the rest of Ulster, however, Catholics actually outnumbered Protestants by two to one.[43]

It was therefore not surprising that Lord Randolph Churchill in making his famous remark about the Orange card should, while hoping that it would prove the ace of trumps, have also expressed a fear that it might turn out to be the two.*[44] As regards any special treatment for Ulster, Saunderson him-

---

* It may be noted that Lord Randolph was only echoing, however unconsciously, a magistrate of the 1790s, who had also referred to the Orangemen as 'a rather difficult card to play' (Lecky, *History of Ireland in the Eighteenth Century*, vol. iii, p. 437).

self, speaking proudly as an Irishman, indignantly rejected the idea. 'We are prepared to stand or fall,' he declared, 'for weal or woe, with every loyal man who lives in Ireland.'[45] Except in fact for Joseph Chamberlain, who first seriously put forward a proposal for local autonomy for part of Ulster in a letter to *The Times* on 14 May 1886, no one on either side of the House entertained a partition of Ireland as a serious possibility at all.

Parnell himself made the most effective case against a separate legislature for Ulster. It would not be giving 'protection' to Irish Protestants for there would be as many as 400,000 Protestants left outside. Moreover, since in Ulster there was actually a majority for the Nationalists, the first action of any Ulster Parliament would be to unite with the Dublin Parliament. On the other hand, if a special Parliament were created simply for the concentration of Protestants in North-East Ulster alone it would entail abandoning to an even greater extent those Irish Protestants on whose behalf the exclusion was invoked, for seven-twelfths of all Irish Protestants lived outside the area.[46] He went on, in handsome terms, to express his positive objections as an Irish nationalist to any such measure. 'We cannot,' he said, 'give up a single Irishman. We want the patriotism, the talents and the work of every Irishman to ensure that this great experiment shall be a successful one. The best system of government should be the resultant of what forces are in that country.... The class of Protestants will form a most valuable element in the Irish legislature of the future, constituting, as they will, a strong minority, and exercising ... a moderating influence in making laws.... We want all creeds and classes in Ireland.... We cannot consent to look upon a single Irishman as not belonging to us.'[47]

To encourage Irish Protestants to respond to such an appeal significant concessions had been made in the framing of the bill. Care had been taken to ensure for them greater representation than their numbers alone warranted, in acknowledgement of their special position and influence. The Irish Parliament was to consist of two 'orders' which would normally sit together as one chamber. The upper order would consist of twenty-eight representative Irish peers, together with seventy-five members with a special property qualification, elected only by voters with higher property qualifications than normal. The two Houses could on the demand of either, vote and sit separately, and in this case either could put a veto on legislation initiated by the other for a limited period. In other words the Irish Protestants, including the Protestant Ulstermen – for theirs would be primarily the interests represented in the upper order – would not only be guaranteed an inbuilt influence in the single chamber Parliament but would also have a suspensory power if the majority in that single chamber initiated any legislation which seemed to threaten their freedom or interests. Assuming that the same attitude of cooperative goodwill towards constitutional safeguards were to prevail in the Irish as in the Westminster Parliament and the same disposition to make them work sensibly, these were as fair safeguards as any Irish Protestant could reasonably expect, who was prepared to accept the democratically expressed will of the majority. But the men of Ulster were not primarily concerned with democratic reasoning, nor in the long run with the interests of other Irish Protestants. They were thinking, as Irish history had trained them to think, in terms of their own interests, and they were convinced that these demanded that there should be no Home Rule for Ireland. The real questions were whether they would have the strength and determination to defy the British constitution if the time ever came when the Crown in Parliament were to grant Home Rule; and how far the British Conservative Party would be prepared to go in helping the Ulstermen in that defiance.

5

Parnell's Fall

Home Rule had really only acquired a true dynamic force in the mid-eighties under Parnell. It was easy for this to fade again in face of rebuff or the distraction of other matters. History written from a later separatist premise has sometimes implied that the eventual Irish disillusionment with Home Rule arose from the inadequacy of the national demand Home Rule made. But from 1886 to the passing of a Home Rule Act in 1914 few, apart from the usual tiny minority of Fenians, ever suggested that Home Rule was an inadequate national demand. All the public emphasis was the other way: that it was totally adequate. The real truth was that even for such a limited national demand, there was not, when things turned difficult, the enthusiasm to make it a cause of overriding, compelling urgency.

Certainly, the Irish Parliamentary Party and their full-time professional and amateur adherents had nailed their colours unequivocally to the Home Rule mast. And the people followed and voted for it because it was the only political avenue there was. But it became a cause of routine orthodoxy, not of burning enthusiasm. After all, there was no real prospect of Home Rule's success for nearly two decades after the failure of Gladstone's second bill, and yet Ireland was quieter during most of that time than ever before in her history; such disturbances as occurred centred as usual around the land and not around the national issue at all.

In fact, so unexciting did the political avenue become that even intellectual interest in nationalism began to turn more and more down non-political avenues altogether – into a study and attempted revival of Gaelic, the 'national' language, and Gaelic sports, into an interest in being Irish and culturally different for its own sake, as an escape from the monolithic advance of European materialist culture. In the Irish language, in Irish literature and a new Irish theatre many sought an 'Irishness' which as a personal characteristic would give them more dignity than any political creed. Of course, even this new development was the activity of a minority, just as political 'Irishness' had been. Most people, as throughout Irish history, remained interested only in their material relationship with the land. This, however, was becoming tolerable at last.

When the House of Commons rejected Gladstone's first Home Rule Bill on its second reading, the Land War itself was by no means over, though in retrospect it is possible to see that the path of development down which the Land Act of 1881 had set the land system was irreversible. There remained, however, technical problems which were to cause severe recurrences of disorder and repression, though never on such a scale as had marked the days of the Land League. Though the principle, at least, of security of tenure had been won, it was soon to be replaced as the chief agrarian issue by that of actual ownership. The peasant wanted to become not just the secure tenant, but the owner of the soil. The financial terms on which he was to do so under land-purchase arrangements, including whether or not such sale through land-purchase arrangements was to be made a compulsory obligation on the landlord, were to become a new source of agrarian dispute in Ireland. Even after a further Land Purchase Act of 1886, only 73,868 holdings altogether out of a total of something like 500,000 had come under land-purchase arrangements since the idea had been first introduced. And it was not until the Land Purchase Act of 1903, to be followed by another even more comprehensive, in 1909, that really large-scale transfers of ownership from tenant to landlord took place.

Meanwhile, however, many difficulties of the old rent-paying tenant–landlord relationship survived to give trouble. Though the Land Act of 1881 had been a success in its most important aspect – the control of rents – there was one major flaw in it as a solution to the land problem, quite apart from the arrears detail which had had to be cleared up after Kilmainham. This flaw in the rent-fixing arrangements under the Act was that they made no allowance for bad harvests and for the consequent variable ability of tenants to pay even the new fixed rents. The years immediately after the Land Act saw good harvests, but when prices turned down again in the mid-eighties tenants were once again faced with the age-old dilemma of being unable to pay their rents in bad times, and thus vulnerable to the most terrible fate which could threaten the Irish peasant: eviction.

By the time this further renewal of the land crisis developed, Parnell's political mind was concentrated on the Home Rule issue, which was in a state of deadlock. After the heroic failure of the bill he had fallen back on one of his chief political tactics, which was to do nothing when there seemed nothing very obvious to do. It was also a time in his life when personal considerations, centring round his clandestine life with his English mistress in the south of England, pulled strongly against his involvement in day-to-day Irish matters. Captain O'Shea, husband of Parnell's mistress, whatever his attitude to the liaison may have been in the past, and whatever his reason may now have been, had decided to try to break it up and was putting strong pressure on his wife to leave Parnell.[1]

A political consideration was that, since on the Home Rule front Parnell had achieved the remarkable success of bringing one of the two political parties respectably on to his side, he was unwilling to involve himself in a land situation to any degree, which by its lack of respectability might prejudice that alliance. He therefore took a guarded and equivocal attitude to the land war, which in this second phase was run almost entirely by John Dillon and Parnell's own one-time acolyte, the journalist William O'Brien.

Dillon and O'Brien's offensive weapon, which epitomized this phase of the land war, was the so-called Plan of Campaign, an ingenious device by which tenants on estates where evictions were being carried out calculated what they could afford to pay in rent, offered this to the landlord, and if it was refused paid the money into a fund which was then used to defend and protect those threatened by eviction. The stir which this bitter and violent campaign, lasting several years, caused in the life of the country and on the British political scene was out of proportion to the actual number of holdings involved, which were only 116. Of these the landlords on sixty gave in at once, and on twenty-four more after a struggle; on fifteen they held out and won, while on the remaining seventeen the disputes were still unsettled by 1893.[2] But the political impact was considerable. The campaign was resisted by the new Conservative Chief Secretary for Ireland, Arthur Balfour, with unexpected toughness and severity, and Dillon, O'Brien and their henchmen, who often included parish priests, more than once landed in prison where they enjoyed no special privileges as political prisoners and were even forced to wear convict clothes.

As usual the land war had a two-way significance as regards Irish nationalism. On the one hand it showed how the everyday issue of the land, a social issue, took precedence in Irishmen's minds over the political national issue. No one, after all, took to violence or incurred prison sentences in protest against the rejection of Home Rule. On the other hand the bitterness of each phase of the land war consolidated emotional feeling against the government and indirectly strengthened general 'national' feelings. The Plan of Campaign was organized by the party organization, the National League, whose overall demand for Home Rule was strengthened by the bitterness aroused.

In such circumstances Home Rule might indeed have continued the dynamic it had developed in 1886 but for other special factors which intervened. One was the conscious Conservative policy of 'killing Home Rule by kindness', that is to say, combining coercive toughness against agrarian disorders with real concessions such as further Land Purchase Acts (in 1891 and 1896) and – a truly revolutionary measure for Ireland – the Local Government Act of 1898. This for the first time gave the Irish people a direct share in their own administration, taking local government power out of the hands of the old property-controlled grand juries and placing it in the hands of elective county councils. And though such measures did not in the end succeed in killing Home Rule they certainly did much to sap its immediate vitality. But a surprise event did more than Conservative policy to cause Home Rule to fade as a dynamic issue. This was the loss to the Irish Parliamentary Party by his death in 1891 of Charles Stewart Parnell, as the result of a most dramatic development.

Parnell's love affair with Katharine O'Shea had been going on since before the days of the Kilmainham Treaty. Their relationship had undoubtedly by the late eighties acquired in all but name that depth and significance of a true marriage which Parnell himself liked to claim for it. She had borne him two more children after the first child which had died in infancy soon after his release from Kilmainham, and in their letters the two old-established lovers liked to address each other as husband and wife. The only trouble with this 'marriage' of Parnell was that his wife was married to someone else for eight of the nine years it lasted, and that, since early in 1886 at any rate, her legal husband had been trying to get her to give her lover up. It was very typical of Parnell, and illustrative of that natural haughtiness which he often turned to such effective use in politics, that neither of these facts seems to have worried him unduly and he therefore assumed that they need worry no one else. It seems certain, admittedly, that Katharine O'Shea convinced Parnell early on that O'Shea was a complaisant husband and her marriage with him one in name only. A complicating factor was the need to keep the situation concealed from an old rich aunt of Mrs O'Shea's, a Mrs Benjamin Wood, who intended to leave her a fortune. It is possible that Katharine O'Shea may have successfully concealed from Parnell for some time after 1886 the fact that Captain O'Shea was by then insisting on the affair being broken up. But even if Parnell could have pleaded the total complaisance of Captain O'Shea it was a situation unlikely to commend itself to the moral outlook of either Liberal nonconformist England or of Catholic Ireland.

Early in 1886 O'Shea seems to have got wind of charges then being prepared in certain Conservative quarters and subsequently to be ventilated in *The Times* newspaper, to the effect that Parnell had written a clandestine letter of sympathy to the Phoenix Park murderers after that gruesome event in 1882,* assuring them that his denunciation of them had been merely for show. Thereafter, O'Shea developed something of a frenzy in his efforts to get his wife and Parnell to separate. This seems to substantiate the contention that his chief objection to the affair was fear of the loss of the Wood fortune, for if he already dreaded Mrs Wood getting wind of her favourite niece's intimate association with Parnell – and we know he did – how much more disastrous would have been the consequences if she had discovered that such an intimate association was with an accessory after the fact to a particularly appalling political murder?

* See above, p. 87.

In 1889 the rich aunt, Mrs Wood, died. Later that year O'Shea brought proceedings for divorce. He cited only the period from 1886, thus making Parnell look particularly guilty, however much complaisance may or may not have been an earlier feature of the affair, for letters produced in court proved clearly that ever since that date O'Shea had been trying to persuade his wife to leave Parnell.

Parnell's personal standing with the British and Irish public had been particularly high when the divorce action broke; his fall now was to be all the greater. Only a year before he had been personally cleared of the Phoenix Park charges by a specially-appointed Government Commission. The allegedly incriminating letter, which had been reproduced in *The Times,* was found to have been forged by a nationalist journalist, Richard Pigott, a man at one time of some consequence in near-Fenian quarters but whom personal insolvency had increasingly obliged to exploit nationalism for financial advantage.

Right up to the hearing of the divorce case Parnell seems to have been confident that its revelations could do him no harm, and during the year that had elapsed between the serving of the divorce papers and the action's hearing he had continually reassured his colleagues and associates that it would not affect his political career. His confidence seems to have been based at least partly on his conviction of the utter moral propriety of his own behaviour. Partly, however, it was also based on the belief that O'Shea could be bought off, for Mrs Wood had duly bequeathed Mrs O'Shea the expected fortune. But the Wood family had disputed the will and at the last minute neither Mrs O'Shea nor Parnell could lay their hands on the necessary £20,000 which O'Shea seems to have been demanding.

The humiliating details of deception and dissimulation by Parnell – false names and other ruses traditional in such triangular situations – duly emerged in the courts. Parnell to the end maintained a defiant confidence that by character and political strength he could brazen the thing through. In this he proved wrong and received the only major political setback of his life, though if he had lived it is not inconceivable that he would have been proved right in the end.

For a moment, even so, it seemed that his strength might triumph. Immediately after the result of the divorce case the Irish party passed a unanimous vote of confidence in Parnell's leadership. But then something happened to turn the name of Mrs O'Shea into more than a mere cause of scandal in Irish history. Gladstone, though he personally had almost certainly known of the liaison between Mrs O'Shea and Parnell for many years, was made aware of such strong feeling of revulsion over the divorce details from his nonconformist supporters in the country that he issued a statement of the most profound importance. Parnell's continued leadership of the Irish Parliamentary Party, he said, was likely to render his own leadership of the Liberal

Party 'almost a nullity'. In other words, the Irish must choose between Parnell's continued leadership of the Irish party and the party's continued alliance with Gladstone in the cause of Home Rule.

Frightened by this the party, after a long and agonizing debate full of mutual invective in Committee Room 15 of the House of Commons, went back on its original unanimous decision and voted 45–29 against Parnell's continued leadership. Though Parnell refused to accept this result, nominal leadership of the majority of the party now passed to Justin McCarthy, a pleasant but uncommanding figure more at ease in literature than politics. The most effective character on the anti-Parnell side had been Tim Healy. Healy it was who in reply to a Parnellite supporter's interjection that Gladstone seemed to be the master of the party, called out viciously in front of Parnell, 'Who is to be the mistress of the party?'

Blows were nearly struck in Committee Room 15 and certainly were struck in the succession of bitter by-election battles that soon followed in Ireland between Parnellite and anti-Parnellite nationalists. Much of the newly mobilized national energy of the Home Rule movement now drained away into this dismal and vindictive quarrel between the two halves of the great national party which Parnell had brought so high.

Having, in his day, fought the House of Commons to a standstill on behalf of Ireland, Parnell was suddenly now at bay in his own country, taking on the greater part of his own party and the enormously powerful political influence, previously on his side, of the Catholic Church. His principal tactic had been, from the first, one of breath-taking arrogance, but of the sort that might have been expected of him, and well designed to appeal again to his earlier allies, the 'hillside' men and so-called 'ribbon-Fenians'. He seized on that aspect of Gladstone's statement which could be expected to divert attention from his own personal behaviour and indignantly challenged on behalf of Ireland the right of any English politician to lay down to Irishmen who should or should not be their leader, simultaneously vilifying any Irishmen who might slavishly acquiesce in such dictation. At the same time, he magnificently confused the issue by suddenly purporting to reveal that when he had stayed at Gladstone's home at Hawarden in Cheshire some months earlier and had discussed with the Grand Old Man the terms of the next Home Rule Bill which a Liberal government would introduce when next returned to power, these had turned out to be humiliating to Ireland and a retreat on the provisions of the 1886 bill.

The obvious retort to this – and one that was made by Healy and co. – was to ask why such an important fact had not been revealed before, and Gladstone himself issued a denial of the conversations as recounted by Parnell. But drawing once again on the full force of his political strength, Parnell swept such objections and all references to his personal conduct aside, and continued to try and fight on the ground of his own choosing, namely, whether or not the Liberal alliance should be supported if the price was to be English dictatorship on terms detrimental to a good Home Rule Bill. It was a political manoeuvre and *tour de force* of astonishing daring but of no avail. Making the laborious journey to Ireland via Euston and Holyhead from Brighton where he lived with the former Katharine O'Shea, now his legal wife, he campaigned week after week in support of his own candidates in three consecutive by-elections, all of which he decisively lost. At one of them lime was thrown in his eyes. He fought on more savagely than ever.

On Sunday, 27 September 1891, he spoke at a meeting in pouring rain in County Galway, bareheaded and with one arm, crippled by rheumatism, in a sling. The change of clothes which Katharine Parnell had packed for him was somehow mislaid and he sat about for several hours in his wet suit. He then went to Dublin where he spent a few days before leaving for England on Wednesday, 30 September, saying he would be back on 'Saturday week'. He was a few hours out in his forecast. He died at Brighton with his wife by his side on 10 October, and his body was brought into Kingstown harbour on Sunday morning, 11 October, and buried in Glasnevin cemetery. The chances of Home Rule for the next twenty years were buried with him.

The split in the party caused by the O'Shea divorce was damaging enough while Parnell was still alive. But he was at least a political giant, a man who, so long as he remained upon the scene, might have achieved anything. With his sudden death, which shocked both friends and enemies equally, as if all recognized the profound change in the quality of political life it heralded, the dispute between them degenerated into a squalid and sterile internecine warfare that lasted the better part of ten years. Most of the energies which needed to be devoted to the Home Rule cause, if it was to be pursued successfully in the extremely difficult English political situation of the day, were turned inwards in this self-consuming Irish quarrel. And the dynamic of the relatively new nationalist movement which had survived the rejection of the first Home Rule Bill with such self-confidence failed to develop properly under the effects of such an apparently insatiable cancer.

The period that followed the death of Parnell in 1891 is often described as a political vacuum. In one sense this is accurate. Politically, there had been only two giants in Ireland in the nineteenth century: O'Connell and Parnell. Now Parnell was gone, and it was not so much the split in the party that was the cause of the vacuum after his death as the fact that there was no man on either side of the split to make Home Rule the vital issue Parnell could have continued to make it.

What is unsatisfactory about the vacuum description is the argument for which it has sometimes been made the premise: namely, that the Parliamentary Party was itself now a meaningless and vacuous institution and its final demise inevitable. This was by no means so. Home Rule remained the only viable national ideal for the vast majority of the Irish people, and the party's collapse, when it came many years later, was in fact quite sudden and, until 1916, not even seriously expected. It was the men who proved inadequate — not the cause.

6

Second Home Rule Bill:
Orangemen at Play

The level to which political passions in Ireland descended after the Parnell split may be gauged from a sermon preached at Roundwood, County Wicklow, by the parish priest just before the General Election of 1892.

'Parnellism,' he told his flock, 'is a simple love of adultery and all those who profess Parnellism profess to love and admire adultery. They are an adulterous set, their leaders are open and avowed adulterers, and therefore I say to you, as parish priest, beware of these Parnellites when they enter your house, you that have wives and daughters, for they will do all they can to commit these adulteries, for their cause is not patriotism – it is adultery – and they back Parnellism because it gratifies their adultery.'[1]

At the election only nine 'Parnellite' nationalists were elected (under the leadership of John Redmond), against seventy-one 'anti-Parnellites'. But the disarray of the Home Rule party was to be far greater than these figures suggest. For among the anti-Parnellites themselves personal rivalries, jealousies and animosities soon brought about a further inward dispersal of political energies. Among the anti-Parnellites there were to be Healyites, Dillonites and O'Brienites, all at first precariously kept together under the compromise leadership of the literary figure Justin McCarthy.

Faction fighting at Irish fairs had been a perennial feature of Irish national life. Soon this was proceeding on a national scale. The internal political partisanship it bred was felt more keenly than the national cause itself. This correspondingly began to go by default, though that it could do so was in itself evidence of a lack of coherent nationalism widely felt. There was almost certainly more truth than most nationalists would have admitted in the words of the Irish peer Lord Muskerry, who, speaking in 1893 from the experience of seventeen years' residence among tenant farmers in the south-west of Ireland, contended that they had no particular desire for Home Rule. 'Why should they,' he added, 'under the present system of land confiscation?' Discounting the pejorative bias in his definition of the land purchase revolution there was some sense in the remark.

Yet so long as Gladstone himself was alive and leader of the Liberal Party, it was impossible for Home Rule to become a wholly remote issue. He personally was totally committed to it in a way no other Liberal leader was ever to be again, and when he formed his last government in August 1892 at the age of eighty-three it was the major issue with which he concerned himself.

His second Home Rule Bill was similar in its limitations on Irish sovereignty to that of 1886. In a special preamble it declared the Westminster Parliament to be supreme; decisions on foreign affairs, trade, customs and excise and all ability to form military or naval forces were specifically removed from the proposed domestic Irish Government's powers. This time there were to be two separate chambers in the Parliament, each with a veto over the other. One chamber, the Legislative Council, created to help protect minority Protestant rights, was to be elected from a special 'constituency', as Gladstone called it, composed of electors with a special property qualification, and was to consist of 48 members. The other chamber, elected by the normal electorate, was to be the Legislative Assembly, consisting of 103 members from the usual constituencies. The chief difference between this bill and that of 1886 was that this time Irish members, to the number of 80, were to be retained at Westminster, partly as an outward manifestation of the supremacy of the Imperial Parliament, and partly as a means of allowing the Irish some say in imperial affairs.

All the old arguments for and against Home Rule were put forward on both sides. The Unionists said that the safeguard for the Protestant minority allegedly contained in the Legislative Council was quite inadequate. Though the special 'constituency' to elect it was to consist of only one in six of the total electorate, the qualification for this – a £20 rating value – was only half that of the common juror and his verdicts were often of a notoriously 'national' tinge. One Unionist claimed that the Legislative Council would in fact be composed of that very class of tenant farmer who was 'most under the influence of the Roman Catholic clergy'. It would, he claimed, be 'a priests' house'.[2]

But, as before, the chief argument against the bill was that it represented the thin end of the wedge of separation. As in 1886, the Unionists used the very feebleness of the bill's appeal to Irish national aspirations as an argument against any likelihood of it proving a permanent settlement. 'You told them,' said the Conservative leader Balfour, 'that they are a nation and that they deserve the treatment of a nation, and now you put them off with a constitution which does not only not make them a nation, but which puts them immeasurably below the smallest self-governing colony in this empire. How can you expect that they ... are really content with the measure of Home Rule you put before them?'[3]

The Irish, however, as in 1886, again insisted that though they might wish for changes in certain details, they regarded the satisfaction of national demands in the bill as adequate and demanded no more. Thomas Sexton, one of the ablest of the anti-Parnellites, delivered a eulogy of Gladstone, saying that he had secured beyond all change the gratitude of the Irish people. The first Home Rule Bill, he said, 'had been accepted by the Irish party and by the Irish people and their race throughout the world as the basis of a permanent settlement', and the present bill was 'on the whole a better plan than that of 1886 ...'. 'The supremacy of the Imperial Parliament,' he conceded, 'exists and cannot be altered.'⁴ Michael Davitt, who now sat in Parliament for Cork N.E., confirmed this view: 'The overwhelming majority of the Irish people and the Irish race abroad, as well as at home, accepted the Bill of 1886 as a satisfactory settlement of the Irish question and would have acted loyally upon that acceptance if the bill had become law. I assert the same of this bill now before the House. I go further and say that thirteen million of the Irish race, scattered round this world, will accept the bill as a pact of peace between Ireland and the Empire to be honourably upheld on both sides.' And later in his speech he called the bill 'an honourable and lasting compact between the people of Ireland and Great Britain'.⁵

Redmond, for the nine Parnellites, was expected to be more intransigent on the national issue. But he, too, made clear, on the first reading of the bill, that its severe limitations to what might be thought normal national aspirations were accepted by the Irish people. He went so far as to state categorically his willingness 'to accept a measure of this kind, based on the validity of the Act of Union and acknowledging the supremacy of the Imperial Parliament ...' adding, 'We have never asked for the curtailment of the Imperial Parliament under a Home Rule scheme.'⁶ On the second reading Redmond said candidly that he did not expect the bill, if passed, to be 'absolutely final or immutable', but thought that the constitutional principle involved would be a success and, because a success, would involve some development.

The leader of the anti-Parnellite group, Justin McCarthy, reinforced the solemnity of his own acceptance of the bill in similarly realistic terms. 'Although,' he said, on the second reading, 'no generation can pretend to bind all future generations – for the time may come when the whole constitution of these countries may be changed – all we say is this, that so far as our foresight will enable us to look into the future, we do believe that the measure when duly improved in committee, will be, for all events for our time, a final settlement of the Irish question.'⁷ And on the third reading, after the committee stage, he was if anything even more emphatic: 'I do not believe,' he said, '... that there will ever be the slightest desire on the part of the Irish people to break away from the principle of this great settlement.'⁸

Some Unionists undoubtedly were genuinely convinced that such statements were made only for the benefit of an English audience. But every Irish politician knew that for remarks made in the House of Commons he was answerable not so much to Westminster as to Ireland itself. No Irish politician would have dared give such categorical assurances on such an emotive issue if they had not substantially represented the Irish public opinion of the day.

On the third reading Redmond, for the small group of Parnellites, was less enthusiastic than he had been at first. He was deeply disappointed by alterations to financial provisions of the bill which had been made in committee. 'As the bill now stands ...' he said, 'no man in his senses can any longer regard it either as a full, a final or a satisfactory settlement of the Irish National Question. The word "provisional" has, so to speak, been stamped over every page of the bill' and he drew attention to the fact that a gathering of his own party in Dublin had come to the same conclusion.' However, the gathering of his own party, the National League, had voted overwhelmingly for support of the third reading and the small extent to which even their limited dissatisfaction was representative of public opinion can be partly gauged from the position of their Independent Home Rule Fund at the time. This stood at only £2,516 in August 1893 and was increasing at the rate of about £12 a fortnight at the time of the bill's rejection.[10]

John Dillon, by virtue of his vigorous activity in the land war, in both its Land League and Plan of Campaign phases, had at least as much right to speak for belligerent nationalism as Redmond. He maintained a diametrically opposite view on the question of the bill's finality: '... this bill,' he said in answer to Redmond, 'so far from settling nothing, is a great Charter of liberty to the people of Ireland, and they will accept it in that sense'. Finality, he said, was an impossible thing to accept with any law but '... if by finality we are to mean, as I think we ought to mean, that the people of Ireland ... would accept it, if passed into law, in good faith as a settlement of the National claims of Ireland, I say I believe they would.... We accept the supremacy of this [the Imperial] Parliament, and I am not aware that any considerable section of the Irish people wish to deny it."[11]

Not only the branches of the anti-Parnellite organisation, the National Federation, bore him out. The *Freeman's Journal* expressed its confirmation of this point of view most fulsomely.

'Beyond all question,' it wrote, 'the bill will give to Ireland the substance of all that her patriots fought for through the long centuries.'[12]

This was of course a travesty of the truth. Who could possibly imagine that Tone, Lord Edward Fitzgerald, Emmet, Davis, O'Connell, Mitchel, Stephens, Allen, Larkin and O'Brien would have accepted the supremacy of the Westminster Parliament as a satisfactory final settlement of the Irish National Question? Yet the writer not only confidently assumed that the statement was reasonable but also correctly, that almost everyone else would think so too. A woolly imprecision still remained one of Irish nationalism's salient characteristics.

Meanwhile, other 'patriotic' Irishmen, the Protestant minority with their special concentration in the north-east corner of Ulster, were anything but content with this 'national' status envisaged for them.

The mobilization of Ulster opinion had this time been organized on a far more impressive scale than in 1886. In the spring of 1892, even before Gladstone had taken office again, but when it seemed probable that he would soon do so, an 'Ulster Unionist Convention', consisting of delegates elected from the electoral rolls of every district in the province, was summoned to Belfast. The convention met in a special wooden pavilion constructed in three weeks on the plains beside the Botanical Gardens, Belfast, on Friday, 17 June 1892. It was to be a landmark in Ulster history. The main streets were decked with flags and bunting; hotels and all other available accommodation were booked up days beforehand, and crowds poured into the city by every train and steamer.[13]

Four thousand of the twelve thousand delegates who attended were tenant farmers, and most of the rest businessmen. Few came from the landed classes, who were nevertheless well represented among the four hundred or so leading Unionists on the platform. The whole convention met under the chairmanship of the Duke of Abercorn. Above the platform were the arms of Great Britain and the words of the Poet Laureate:

> One with Great Britain, heart and soul
> One life, one flag, one fleet, one throne.

All around the walls of the pavilion hung numerous shields and appropriate mottoes, including an unfortunate quotation from the Gladstonian Liberal Lord Spencer, dating from before his leader's conversion to Home Rule. This ran: 'We feel like the Americans when the integrity of their country was threatened, and if necessary we must shed blood to maintain the strength and salvation of the country.'

A number of resolutions were passed by the convention. The first asserted Ulster's status as an integral portion of the United Kingdom and declared that the convention met 'to protest in the most unequivocal manner against the passage of any measure that would rob us of our inheritance in the Imperial Parliament, under the protection of which our capital has been invested and our homes and rights safeguarded'.

A second resolution expressed a determination to have nothing to do with a Parliament 'certain to be controlled by men responsible for the crime and outrage of the Land League, the dishonesty of the Plan of Campaign and the cruelties of boycotting, many of whom have shown themselves the ready instruments of clerical domination'.

A third resolution had a more positive inference. The attempt, it declared, to subject Ulster to a Parliament run by such men would 'inevitably result in disorder, violence and bloodshed such as have not been experienced in this century' and the convention resolved to take no part in the election of or the proceedings of such a Parliament, which they would repudiate. When the Duke of Abercorn, with upraised arm, declared 'We will not have Home Rule', the whole audience sprang to their feet and cheered for several minutes. But the greatest cheers of all were reserved for another speaker who in trumpet tones pronounced, 'As a last resource we will be prepared to defend ourselves.' At this, in the words of *The Times*' man on the spot, 'the feelings of the spectators appeared to lose all control'. It was not surprising that after attending such an impressive and enthusiastic gathering he should conclude emphatically that these were 'men to be reckoned with'.[14]

Their political opponents took them less seriously. Shortly before the convention Colonel Saunderson, the parliamentary leader of the Ulstermen, whose activities had earned him a place in Mme Tussaud's as long ago as 1888,[15] invited the Gladstonian Liberal, Sir William Harcourt, over to Belfast to see for himself the stuff of which the Ulstermen were really made. Harcourt had declined in bantering tones.

I understand [he wrote] that your June review is rather in the nature of a preliminary review with a regard to future contingencies than an immediate call to arms with a view to instant hostilities. ... When your hypothetical insurrection is a little more advanced and war is actually declared, I may perhaps take advantage of your offer and solicit a place as spectator on your staff. I do not know if your plan of campaign contemplates a march upon London against the Crown and Parliament; if so, I might meet you half-way at Derby, which was the place where the Liberals of the last century encountered the 'loyal and patriotic' Highlanders who disapproved of the 'Act of Settlement' and resolved to resist it. ... I presume that might be the point where the rebel army would effect its junction with the ducal contingent from Chatsworth under the command of the Lord-Lieutenant of the county ...[16]

The Duke of Devonshire, as a prominent southern Irish land-owner, though unable to be present at the convention had expressed his total sympathy with its objects. But it was to be many years yet before the combination of the Ulstermen with the English upper classes and Conservative Party were to turn this sort of joke, so typical of the Liberals' attitude for so long, against them.

As Gladstone went ahead with his bill the Protestant Ulstermen exercised their verbal licence to the full. Their forefathers, proclaimed Colonel Saunderson in December 1892, held the walls of Derry; they would hold the gates. Their opponents wished them to leave those gates ajar; but they would have no Home Rule of any kind or any description. They rejected the policy of Home Rule not simply as Protestants but as Irishmen....[17] And in January 1893, at a great meeting in Belfast under the auspices of the Ulster Convention League, the Grand Master of the Belfast Orangemen, Dr Cane, while thanking God that they still had the House of Lords, reminded his audience that they also still had their own right arms and that if ejected from the Union 'they would carve out for themselves their new destiny'.[18] It was, he said, going to be quite different from the Church Disestablishment crisis, for on that issue Protestants had been divided and now they were united.

In Parliament, too, from the beginning the Ulster Unionists stated their position without equivocation. In the debate on the queen's speech in the House of Lords, the Marquess of Londonderry made it clear that he thought the men of Ulster would be justified in shedding blood 'to resist the disloyal Catholic yoke'.[19] Saunderson's own harangue in the Commons on the occasion of the bill's first reading contains an almost prophetic note.

'You have,' he said – conveniently forgetting his allies in the House of Lords for the sake of rhetorical effect – 'the power, I admit, to pass your Home Rule Bill and to create this Dublin Parliament and this government, but you have not the power to make us obey it.' The statement was greeted with a laugh, from the Home Rule benches. 'Allow me to tell them,' Saunderson cried, 'that before the Army of Great Britain is employed to shoot down the Irish loyalists you must have a British majority at your back.' What would happen, he asked, if Dillon, Healy and O'Brien started 'issuing orders, perhaps to Lord Wolseley, to march with the Army of the Curragh to shoot down Ulstermen? It requires,' concluded Saunderson, 'an imagination far greater than mine to conceive such a possibility.'[20]

Saunderson's implication that a purely British majority exclusive of Ireland, and not just an overall United Kingdom majority, was necessary for Home Rule before it could be constitutionally acceptable was to become an important part of anti-Home Rule doctrine. But it was a curious one for Unionists to employ whose chief constitutional tenet was after all that Ireland was indistinguishably merged in the Union.

As the bill proceeded through its various stages in the House of Commons the temperature in Belfast continued to rise. The appeal by a Derry Justice of the Peace to the men of Belfast 'to strike the note at the proper time and unfurl the flag, and call upon their fellow Loyalists to arm'[21] was hardly necessary. In Belfast, William Johnston holding up an open Bible received from a vast audience a vociferous and solemn pledge against Home Rule Saunderson himself initiated an Ulster Defence Union and began to receive both arms and many offers of armed support from England. A general officer wrote to *The Times* demanding that the position of army officers should be made clear in the event of a conflict of loyalties in any possible civil war. One retired cavalry officer told Saunderson that he would advise his three sons to resign their commissions at once in such an event. Further shapes of things to come were outlined when Balfour, the Conservative leader, visited Belfast to watch a march past of some eighty thousand Ulster Loyalists. In words which were to be echoed with even greater force by another Conservative leader nearly twenty years later, Balfour declaimed:

'I do not come here to preach any doctrines of passive obedience or non-resistance. You have had to fight for your liberties before. [A Voice: 'And will again!' - cheers.] I pray God you may never have to fight for them again. I do not believe you will ever have to fight for them, but I admit that the tyranny of majorities may be as bad as the tyranny of Kings and that the stupidity of majorities may be even greater than the stupidity of Kings ... and I do not think any rational or sober man will say that what is justifiable against a tyrannical King may not under certain circumstances be justifiable against a tyrannical majority.'[22]

It would be hard to formulate a more succinct derogation of the whole principle underlying parliamentary democracy.

The Ulster Defence Union had made plans for an Ulster Assembly of six hundred delegates to be elected from among its own Unionist members. These six hundred were then to elect a council of forty to which would be added Ulster members of Parliament and Ulster peers as *ex officio* members making something very like a provisional government.[23]

'If,' word had gone out from the Orangemen of Belfast, 'If, which God forbid, we are forbidden to advance in the way of legislative union, then we most earnestly and solemnly desired to do as our fathers did, and, with trust in the God who inspired men to battle for truth and light, it will be our duty to take the path of self-reliance and insist on their right to carve out the future for ourselves.'[24] And the Orangemen resolved that they would resist an Irish Parliament and its new executive 'by every means in our power ... we will not recognize their officers, nor obey their laws, nor pay the taxes which they may pretend to impose ... come weal, come woe, we will stand by the Legislative Union if we have to fight over again the Battle of the Boyne.'[25]

What made it easier to laugh off rather than take too seriously this theoretically ugly situation was the knowledge that, though the bill was likely to pass in the House of Commons, it was certain to be rejected in the House of Lords. The contingency for which such theoretical preparations were being made was itself theoretical and remote. The statement made the previous year by a Belfast Unionist to the effect that Mr Gladstone had no more power to pass Home Rule than he had to install waterworks on the moon was not altogether a ludicrous one.[26]

The 1893 Home Rule Bill eventually occupied more parliamentary time than any other bill in the history of the century - eighty-two days altogether compared with forty-seven for the Reform Bill. Four hundred and thirty-nine speeches were made for it in the Commons and nine hundred and thirty-eight against. It passed the House of Commons on its third reading in the early morning of 2 September by a majority of 34. Everyone knew that the Lords would reject it, which they did after four nights' debate in the early morning of 9 September by 419 votes to 41. The margin in favour in the Commons itself had been far too small for Gladstone to feel confident enough to go to the country on the issue, and he did not dissolve Parliament. Soon afterwards, however, he retired from the Liberal leadership, giving place to Lord Rosebery whose dislike for Home Rule in the prevailing political situation was barely concealed. Gladstone did not die until 19 May 1898. By then Home Rule as a real prospect as opposed to a political slogan had already disappeared from view for the foreseeable future. But on the occasion of Gladstone's death John Dillon paid a well-deserved tribute to that great Englishman who while he 'loved his own people as much as any Englishman that ever lived ... acquired that wider and greater gift, the power of understanding and sympathizing with other peoples'.[27] It was a dimension of patriotism which had escaped and was to continue to escape every other major English statesman who concerned himself with Ireland. For the absence of it in future England was to pay dearly.

7

Nationalists at Ease

The relative complacency with which news of the Lords' rejection of the Home Rule Bill was received in Ireland epitomized the lack of urgency which was soon a characteristic of the Home Rule movement. One might perhaps have expected some prepared, even menacing, reaction to this blow at national aspirations, a display of resentment at least analogous to that of the Ulstermen when they regarded *their* rights as threatened. Some Irish speakers in the Home Rule debate had indeed hinted darkly at the violence that might follow if Ireland's wishes were thwarted. But absolutely nothing of the sort occurred. The branches of the National Federation sent in their congratulations to their parliamentary representatives and to Gladstone and his Liberals on their performances.[1] The *Freeman's Journal* reminded its readers that defeat in the Lords had been the forerunner of every great measure of reform that had ever taken place. It raised a laugh by singling out from the enormous hostile majority of peers Lord Hadley, who had returned to London after two and a half years shooting big game beyond the Zambesi to pass judgement on the Irish people.[2] Hopes were pinned, fairly unrealistically, on the results of the next General Election.

This took place in the summer of 1895 and, in the words of Gladstone's disciple John Morley, a third Home Rule Bill was 'expressly, deliberately before the electors in the very forefront of our programme'.[3] The result was an overwhelming Conservative victory and the Conservatives were to remain in office for ten years. Yet while accepting that 'Home Rule in 1895 had lost the enormous headway it made between 1886 and 1892' the *Freeman's Journal* still saw 'no grounds for despondency', and in an even self-congratulatory tone noted from the election results that Ireland itself was 'as much for Home Rule in 1895 as in 1892, and even more so'.[4]

The same note of papery optimism was to be sustained in the face of discouraging realities for many years, imparting a certain artificiality to the concept of the cause itself. The blunt truth had been stated by Redmond, who himself much later was to pay for forgetting its implications. They were, he said, in 1894, 'face to face with the ruin of the Home Rule cause ... any measure of autonomy must be hung up till the English cared to give it'.[5]

With no alternative but to accept this state of affairs Irish politicians increasingly talked as if the real state of affairs were somehow different. All that was needed, said William O'Brien in 1895, was for Redmond to re-unite with the Irish party and 'the Irish party would use their victory tomorrow not for the purpose of trampling over or upon any of their fellow countrymen but for the purpose of pressing all good and honest Irish nationalists into one solid phalanx under the old flag to prove to England that the spirit of Irish nationality might be conciliated but never could be conquered or subdued'.[6]

The anniversary of the centenary of the rebellion of 1798 at the very nadir of the parliamentary party's fortunes in 1898 proved further what flights of fancy could do with Home Rule even if politicians themselves remained earthbound.

Arrangements for the centenary were in fact made by an Executive Committee brought into being by the IRB, which flickered into apparently innocuous life for the occasion. President of the committee was the aged literary Fenian John O'Leary, long considered harmless enough to be allowed to live in Ireland, as indeed was now the old chief himself, James Stephens, whose permission to return to Ireland had been obtained from the government by Parnell himself shortly before his death.[7] Stephens, however, who was to survive Parnell by ten years, was only allowed to return on condition that he took no part in public life, and it was the incumbent 'President of the Irish Republic' in the person of F. J. Allan who figured on the Executive Committee of the '98 Centenary Celebrations with O'Leary. Clubs with evocative names were formed to help: Wolfe Tone clubs in many cases, but others were named after Father Murphy, Oliver Bond, Lord Edward Fitzgerald, Napper Tandy, the Sheares brothers, Michael Dwyer and other heroes of a hundred years before.

The Nationalist Parliamentary Party, both Parnellites and anti-Parnellites as they still were, were soon in on the performance. The spirit of their participation was typified early by J. Jordan, the MP for Fermanagh, S., who declared at Belfast in June: 'Let them ungrudgingly celebrate the centenary of '98, and, inspired with the principles of the heroes of that time, let them too with constitutional weapons in their hands perform deeds of daring for the full enfranchisement of their native land.'[8] He was greeted with loud cheers. John Dillon said that 'every advance ... made in asserting the liberty of Ireland or of any other nationality has been a triumph for the principles of the United Irishmen'.[9]

But to claim that most of the humble and bewildered peasants of a hundred years before had died asserting the liberty of Ireland or the purity of Irish nationality was an unjustifiable stretch of the historical imagination. Further, to equate the cause with which the United Irishmen tried to inspire the peasantry with the Parliamentary Party's own sophisticated brand of limited nationality known as Home Rule was little better than a historical confidence trick. It was one which the party practised shamelessly.

J. F. X. O'Brien, the victor of Ballyknockane barracks in 1867, declared to Irishmen in London in June 1898 that the struggle for Irish liberty which was carried on in the present generation was the same struggle in which the men of '98 were engaged, and it was their duty to carry on the struggle in the best way they could as long as life remained to them.[10]

The respectable *Freeman's Journal* equally blandly declared that wherever a croppy's grave was known, faithful hands would 'strew it with the flowers of an Irish summer', and eulogized Wolfe Tone as 'the grandest of Ireland's heroes'.[11]

In Dublin a great demonstration took place in memory of Tone himself. The day was virtually regarded as a bank holiday. Many establishments, as the *Freeman's Journal* reported, gave their employees 'the opportunity of fulfilling what to them was a patriotic duty'.[12] Dillon, the anti-Parnellite Party's Chairman, was present together with Redmond, leader of the Parnellite group, and eleven other MPs. Green banners were on display, one carrying the slogan 'Remember '98, '48, '65, '67'. The Dublin Trades Association all took part in the procession – coal labourers, book-binders, poulterers, gentlemen's bootmakers, etc. – and the pawnbrokers' assistants in particular 'made a very good turn out'. John O'Leary presided over the laying of a foundation stone for a memorial in St Stephen's Green, recalling that he himself had been in the dock thirty-three years before. The poet Yeats made a surprisingly cliché-ridden speech about the inextinguishable fire of patriotism rising like smoke from the breasts of the peasantry. Later, together with Maud Gonne, a beautiful Protestant upper-class Irish girl who had identified herself with extreme nationalist politics, and F. J. Allan of the IRB, Dillon, Redmond and other national and municipal figures, Yeats attended the Lord Mayor's banquet.

At Sligo William O'Brien cried: 'Let us prove by our lives and our actions that the fight of the men of '98 is not over yet. Let us show the world once more that the core and essence of the Irish question is this – that the relations between this country and our English rulers are the relations of civil war just as real as if it were carried on with firearms.' His words were greeted with loud cheers.

Dillon, speaking on Oulart Hill, claimed to sound a realistic note. 'Times have changed,' he warned, 'and the pikes which your forefathers used in the battle of Oulart ... would now be of little avail in your hands.... Why,' he added, 'they could drop shells here from the sea on us under modern conditions!' But his conclusion that they must not forget the principles of the men of '98 and that 'a free Ireland, a free nation, the mistress of her own destinies is the only complete and true monument to the memory of these men' combined oddly with the realities of those Home Rule Bills he was sincerely able to regard as a final settlement of the Irish national question.

This sort of double talk was eventually to rebound on the party in several ways. In the first place it enabled the party to deceive itself and by unending self-indulgence in such pseudo-heroics to believe that it embraced as much national vigour as it supposed. Secondly, it sickened those who saw through the intellectual dishonesty and thus sent some of the Nationalist Party's supporters off in search of other leaders. Thirdly, while reviving talk of the principles of the United Irishmen and the Fenians as clichés, it gave them renewed currency without being able to ensure that they would always remain mere clichés.

At the end of August 1898 there appeared a small item of news to the effect that a man named H. H. Wilson had been released from Portland Gaol. This man whose release had been granted as part of a centenary amnesty had been serving a life sentence for his role in an unsuccessful dynamiting campaign organized from America in the early 1880s. He was a small, rather insignificant figure, prematurely aged at forty by the harshness of a prison life which had driven at least one of his fellow conspirators mad but which he had endured with spirit unbroken. He must have seemed at the time a very minor figure in the mythological hierarchy then being evoked. He was soon to emigrate to America again. Yet he was to constitute one of the few tenuous links eventually binding the centenary proceedings to reality. Even his real name was not then known for Wilson was a pseudonym he had adopted for his dynamiting operations fifteen years before. As Thomas J. Clarke he was to be the first signatory on the proclamation of an Irish Republic in 1916.

In 1900 the party became technically re-united under the new chairmanship of John Redmond. But personal quarrels between the leading figures continued, and the reunion was of small immediate benefit to the cause of Home Rule because, as Redmond himself had said, this was now entirely dependent on the English political scene. The Conservatives who returned to office for a second consecutive term in 1900 were unaffected by the reunion, while the Liberals after the death of Gladstone came swiftly to regard Home Rule much more as an embarrassing electoral liability than a noble cause.

In Ireland, 'national aspirations' – in so far as preoccupation with the Land Purchase revolution left time for any – lived a life of the imagination, partly within the otherwise increasingly sterile clichés of the Home Rule cause and partly in new forms altogether.

8

Growth of National Consciousness

Although Home Rule so soon became politically impracticable and remote, the idea itself had produced an atmosphere in which national consciousness in its own right began to grow. The movement which came generally to be known as the Irish Ireland movement or Irish revival is often regarded as a reaction from the apathy caused by the party's political ineffectualness after the Parnell split. But it would be truer to say that it coincided in the first place with the first waves of enthusiasm for the Home Rule movement and later continued to flourish on its own account as the political aim lacked lustre and receded.

Arthur Griffith himself, at this time an obscure young compositor but in thirty years to become first President of an 'Irish Free State', was one of the very few young men of this period eventually to look for actual political alternatives to Home Rule, but his national consciousness stemmed originally from the Home Rule movement when Home Rule seemed a close probability.

Already at the time of the introduction of the second Home Rule Bill he was writing newspaper articles on 'Notable Graves Round Dublin', and joining Celtic literary societies with his friend William Rooney.[1]

Earlier still, a Gaelic Athletic Association had been founded by a prosperous civil service crammer named Michael Cusack, under the patronage of Archbishop Croke of Cashel. It was the Archbishop himself who had defined the association's aims as being to remedy 'a parlous state of national pastimes and the consequent decline in national virility' and to replace tennis, croquet, cricket, polo, 'and other foreign and fantastic field sports' by Gaelic football and hurley. The association had actually held its first meeting at Thurles in County Tipperary in November 1884, before even the introduction of the first Home Rule Bill. By 1889 it had achieved a membership of over fifty thousand,[2] spreading a simple pride in Irish-consciousness for its own sake over large areas of the countryside.

It was also two years before Parnell's death - when in fact Parnell was at the height of his reputation - that a young poet, W. B. Yeats, born of a

Protestant family in County Sligo, made an accurate analysis of something else then happening in Ireland. 'A true literary consciousness – national to the centre – seems gradually to be forming...' he wrote. 'We are preparing likely enough for a new literary movement like that of '48 that will show itself in the first lull in politics.'[3]

Yeats was referring to a series of books, revealing the largely forgotten wealth of Irish historic legend and folk tales, that had begun to make an appearance. The earliest and perhaps most important of all these was by a Unionist discoverer of legendary Irish history, Standish O'Grady, who had published his *History of Ireland: Heroic Period 1* as long ago as 1878. A two-volume collection of folk tales was published in 1887 by Lady Wilde, mother of Oscar, who in her youth had been a fierce poetess of Duffy's paper *The Nation* under her pen-name Speranza. Her mood now was gentle and nostalgic for an Irish culture that seemed, with the language itself, to be dying away. Yeats himself published in 1888 his own collection of such tales and was about to give a remarkable impetus to the new movement he foresaw.

His father was an Irish artist, a Protestant, who had lived off and on in London, and was permanently settled there by the end of the eighties. But Yeats himself had spent many holidays with his grandparents and an uncle in County Sligo. There his inquiring imaginative nature found a new world in the ancient outlook of the common people. He was particularly fascinated by their relationship with the 'dim kingdom' of ghosts and fairies. Even among the fisherfolk of Howth, County Dublin, where his father had had a house for a time, Yeats had found stories to excite him. In Sligo, short-cuts to the dim kingdom were all about him. Though he had become a friend of the old literary Fenian John O'Leary and had even in 1888 assisted in a publication of Young Ireland verse, his political nationalism was always perfunctory rather than deeply felt. Spiritual Irish nationalism was what engaged him. Poetically idealistic, and apprehensive before the growing shadow of vulgarity and commercialism which he saw as the advancing shape of the modern world, he delved enthusiastically for something better into '...that great Celtic phantasmagoria whose meaning no man has discovered and no angel revealed'.[4]* Others were soon to take the plunge with him and find many other things besides ghosts and fairies, including ancient heroes.

It may seem improbable that such an esoteric venture could have made a contribution to the development of Irish nationalism. Yeats looked not to Tone and Emmet for inspiration, but to a little bright-eyed old man named Paddy Flynn living in a one-man cabin in Sligo, whose stories – remote

* The real pioneer of this romantic therapeutic view of Celtic legend had been the English poet Matthew Arnold, whose Oxford lectures 'On the Study of Celtic Literature' were published in 1867. For a first-class account of the origins of the whole Celtic historical and literary revival and its political implications see the first two chapters of William Thompson, *The Imagination of an Insurrection* (New York, 1967).

indeed from the green flag and the stones of Westminster – would begin with words like:

'One night a middle-aged man, who had lived all his life far from the noise of cabwheels, a young girl, a relative of his, who was reported to be enough of a seer to catch a glimpse of unaccountable lights moving over the fields among the cattle, and myself were walking along a far western sandy shore.'[5] Such stories Yeats published in an English magazine edited by W. E. Henley, the *National Observer*, and these were in 1893 collected into a volume called *The Celtic Twilight*. 'Perhaps,' he wrote of Paddy Flynn in the introduction, 'the Gaelic people shall by his like bring back again the ancient simplicity and amplitude of imagination.'[6] It is in this early stirring of Gaelic imagination that Yeats is historically important.

The cultural personality of the ordinary Irish people – in so far as it was any longer different from that of the English – had remained submerged beneath the outer veneer of respectable Irish life for much of the nineteenth century. It was almost as if invisible penal laws had been in effect, acting this time not against the popular religion but against the popular culture of the country. To most of the Irish gentry the Irish peasant, when he had not been a dangerous nuisance, was a joke. One important aspect of the literary renaissance and the much wider Irish Ireland movement of which it became a part was that it took the Irish peasant and his family seriously as people. And though this was done in a deliberately apolitical manner it inevitably helped to produce a climate in which an Irishman could feel new self-respect for being Irish.

It is easy to forget how much of what the world now finds the special charm and delight of Irish personality had to be pointed out to the world in the nineties by Yeats and the literary friends with whom he was soon working. Hitherto, for intelligent people the Irish peasant had been chiefly characterized by the Punch cartoon or the stage Irishman with his 'Begorrahs' and sly unreliability and fondness for liquor. And though there was often more truth in the stage Irishman than many Irishmen were prepared to admit – Yeats's Sligo man after all was called Paddy and died of drink[7] – yet the inaccuracy of the caricature lay in what was left out: the seriousness and innocence of a different way of life, inherited through many centuries from the ancient Gaelic world and preserved by isolation in poverty much as Gaelic clothing and butter and even people had sometimes been preserved in Irish bogs.

In 1890 a first book had appeared by another collector of folk tales who was soon to exercise a far greater influence on thought and style in Ireland than Yeats. This book was *Beside the Fire*, by Douglas Hyde, whom Yeats had met years before in the late 1870s when Hyde was a student at Trinity and even then a member of the 'Society for the Preservation of the Irish Language'. Yeats had been struck by the peasant quality of the dark young man's face, with his vague serious eyes and high cheekbones, and had found himself wondering how he had managed to get into Trinity.[8] In fact Hyde was the fairly well-to-do son of a Protestant clergyman of County Roscommon where in his youth Irish had been widely spoken and where he had learnt it fluently from the peasantry among whom he had grown up. His easy access to and delight in both spoken and written Gaelic tradition was of immense value now in helping to bring that tradition to life. He even wrote songs and poems in Irish himself and, according to Yeats, while Hyde was still a quite unknown student in Dublin, his songs were being sung by mowers and reapers from Kerry to Donegal.[9]

Hyde had sent Yeats what Yeats regarded as the best story for his own collection, *Fairy and Folk Tales*, published in 1888. Now Hyde's *Beside the Fire* and his *Love Songs of Connacht*, published in 1893, shed a new illumination on the Gaelic world. Half a century later it was to these two volumes of Hyde's that at least one Irishman who had been young at that time looked back as marking a new epoch.[10]

In 1892 Yeats, who had returned to live in Ireland, founded with Hyde the National Literary Society. At one of its early meetings – before Gladstone's second Home Rule Bill had been introduced – Hyde delivered what was to become a famous lecture under the title of 'The Necessity of De-Anglicizing Ireland'. Despite its title it was intended to be a wholly non-political lecture. Hyde addressed its appeal to all Irishmen – to 'everyone, Unionist or Nationalist, who wishes to see the Irish nation produce its best'.[11] But though his appeal to Unionists was sincerely meant – an equivalent to Davis's 'Gentlemen, you have a country' appeal to the Dublin historical society over fifty years earlier – he was, in the context of the time, even less likely to be sympathetically received by Unionists than Davis. It is a measure of Hyde's essential political naïvety that he can seriously have supposed that in a lecture employing phrases like, 'this awful idea of complete Anglicization',[12] he could attract the Unionist gentry of the day. His strictures against 'West Britonism', that half-culture, neither Irish nor English, which dominated Ireland, extended to almost every aspect of everyday life: music – where the song of the harp was to replace 'Ta-ra-ra-boom-de-ay'; anglicized surnames and Christian names, among which Patrick was to be replaced by Padraig and Charles by Cahal; and even clothing. Deploring 'English second-hand trousers', Hyde recommended in their place the clean worsted stockings and knee breeches of the past, and a more universal use of wholesome Irish tweed.[13] Only in the work of the Gaelic Athletic Association did he find any cause for self-congratulation in Ireland, remarking that the GAA had done more for Ireland in the past five years than all the speeches of politicians.[14] He even went so far in his enthusiasm to recommend that the 'warm green-striped jerseys' of the association should replace altogether in common usage the 'torn collars and ugly neckties hanging away' of the average

134

male.[15] Cranky and even slightly absurd as some of this sounds today, its tone was to be taken up eagerly by a small but enthusiastic minority, making possible the Gaelic League founded in the following year and the whole movement which followed. That such ideas were now capable of capturing the idealism of young people in Ireland was the point of significance.

Hyde's severest strictures were reserved for those Irishmen indifferent to 'the loss of our language', by which he meant Irish. Even before the Parnell split Hyde had been criticizing the Nationalist Party for 'attempting to create a nation on the one hand and allowing to be destroyed the very thing that would best differentiate and define that nation'.[16]

When, fifty years earlier, Davis, as part of a political movement, had tried to inculcate an interest in things Irish, one salient fact of Irish life had been very different. Half the population had still spoken Gaelic as its first language. But since then the population had been almost halved by starvation and emigration and the use of Irish had been rapidly dying out. As a normal feature of everyday life it was now confined largely to the western and north-western seaboards, with some pockets on the southern coast, though a few old men and women could still be found even round Dublin and in the central counties to testify to its comparatively recent decay elsewhere. Perhaps the most significant feature of the language situation was that even where it was remembered and could be spoken the Irish peasantry themselves discountenanced it as something to be ashamed of. English was the language by which you got on in life. Hyde himself was once talking in Irish to a girl in County Sligo when her brother came in and started sneering at her for speaking Irish, at which she immediately broke into English.[17] On another occasion he had evidence of an even more unconscious rejection of the language. After talking some time in Irish to a Mayo boy who kept answering him in English he said:

'Nach labhrann tu Gaedlig?' ('Don't you speak Irish?')

To which the boy had replied:

'Isn't it Irish I'm speaking?'

Hyde said, no, it was not Irish but English he was speaking.

'Well, then,' said the boy, 'that's how I spoke it ever.'[18]

The story was also told of a couple of earnest Gaelic Leaguers who had been painstakingly teaching their parlourmaid Irish and only discovered when she left to get married that she had been brought up in an Irish-speaking district but preferred English because it was more respectable.[19]

Hyde was, of course, no pioneer in his interest in the language. Even in the mid-eighteenth century Irish Protestant gentlemen had been proud to associate themselves with their country's Gaelic past and traditions. Ever since the middle of the nineteenth century, when those few people who cared had realized that the Irish language and the quality of mind that went with it was vanishing, there had been clubs and societies for studying and

preserving it. Smith O'Brien before his death in 1864 had lent his support
to one of these. But at the beginning of the nineties, with Home Rule still
apparently a real possibility, and with a new respect for the Gaelic mind
quickening under Yeats's and others' interest, the climate for the foundation
of a new society to propagate the language was particularly favourable. As
early as 1891 the Professor of Irish in the Catholic priests' training college
at Maynooth, Father Eugene O'Growney, who published a popular Irish
grammar, had been corresponding not only with Hyde but also with a civil
servant from Ulster, John MacNeill – soon dutifully calling himself Eoin –
over their common enthusiasm for Irish. In July 1893, originally as a result
of a suggestion from MacNeill, the three founded the Gaelic League with
the declared object of preserving the national language of Ireland and extending its use as a spoken language. Hyde became the Gaelic League's President.
He was to remain, like Yeats, essentially not a politically-minded man, but
one for whom a cultural rather than political Irish nationalism seemed to
open the way to a whole new spiritual emancipation. But he was to generate
a warm and popular affectionate enthusiasm both for himself and his ideas,
which were to permeate much of middle-class Ireland, and girls were before
long to appear at Gaelic League festivals with his Irish *nom de plume* –
An Craoibhin Aobhinn ('the pleasant little branch') – inscribed on the bands
of their hats, almost as if he were some democratic politician.

Though the Gaelic League took some years to spread widely over Ireland
and was always confined largely in its activity to the towns, it was to play
a most significant part in widening and strengthening the Irish consciousness
of many a middle-class and lower-middle-class Irishman. It had 58 branches
by 1898; 200 by 1901; 600 by 1903; and 900 by 1906, with a total membership of 100,000.[20] By that time it could claim to have enforced the teaching
of Irish in three thousand schools and to have enlisted the enthusiasm of
some quarter of a million Irish men and women in learning Irish. With its
language classes, its monthly and weekly magazines, its summer schools,
music and poetry festivals and prizes, it was not unreasonable to describe
it, as one contemporary observer did, as 'the only National University that
Ireland possesses'. (The official National University of Ireland was not
founded until 1909 and the Gaelic League could rightly claim to have played
an important part in bringing this into being.)

The Gaelic League became the urban counterpart of the Gaelic Athletic
Association. And though non-political in motive it could not help having
an oblique political influence. Those to whom it appealed were primarily
Nationalist party voters whatever they may have thought of the Nationalist
party politicians, and the League gave backing to that vote by teaching that
Irishness was in itself something to be proud of rather than provincially
ashamed of.

A whole respectable way of looking at Ireland was in fact created by the

Gaelic League. Snobbishness was a powerful political factor in the Ireland of the turn of the century. It prospered particularly in the small county towns where real distinctions of wealth and birth were so small that only a competition in snobbishness could seem to provide them.[21] The Gaelic League and the Irish Ireland movement in general now attacked the conventional small-time snob, the 'seonin' (shoneen) or sycophant who tried to demonstrate his personal superiority by apeing the manners and attitudes of his English-oriented 'betters'. The League countered such snobbery with a new version by which it became respectable and praiseworthy to aspire to different Irish-standards. Occasionally it even managed to get the best of both worlds, as when the League magazine, *An Claideamh Soluis*, wrote: 'We condemn English-made evening dress, but evening dress of Irish manufacture is just as Irish as a Donegal cycling suit. Some people think we cannot be Irish unless we always wear tweeds and only occasionally wear collars.'[22]

Much of the later mass support for the Sinn Fein movement, to which the success of the Gaelic League indirectly contributed, can be explained by the opportunity it extended to a snobbishly afflicted middle and lower-middle class independently to assert a new social self-respect.

As the Irish Ireland movement grew in popularity it attracted many different individual prophets, often crying alone in what was still something of a national wilderness, often warring with each other or with the Gaelic League, but always sharing a freshness and independence of mind in looking beyond stale political cliché, to new things Irish.

One of the most original and astringent of these new voices was that of an Irish journalist, D. P. Moran, who published his views in a new weekly paper, the *Leader*, which he edited from 1900. The gist of Moran's purposefully shocking argument was that it was now very doubtful if there was such a thing as an Irish nation at all, and that if there was to be one – as he thought there should be – drastic action along the lines of the Gaelic League's principles, only more so, was immediately necessary. 'There are,' he wrote, 'certainly some traits to be found in Ireland which stamp her as a distinct race even yet, but they characterize her torpor and decay rather than her development.'[23] If her energies were to be revived Ireland must start by becoming bilingual, for the language was the great basic link with nationality. She could move on from there towards the separation of national personality which must be her goal. If she was not prepared to do this then she might just as well accept what was already almost a historical *fait accompli*, namely that she was English, or at least West British. Anywhere between these two positions was humbug, and humbug rather than England was Moran's enemy.

What had passed for national sentiment for so long Moran dismissed with devastating scorn and historical perception. The wave of emotive public opinion which had backed the Land League he saw correctly as being inspired chiefly by materialism. From whom, he asked, could one get any rational expression of that nationality about which all talked so loudly? Irish nationality had been 'stuck on a flag of green' and Irishmen had pursued this instead of the different Gaelic civilization which had once been the only true meaning of nationality in Ireland. Irishmen had gone in for clatter and claptrap which they miscalled nationality, playing the fool throughout the century like a lot of hysterical old women. The nineteenth century, he said, had been mostly a century of humbug. 'We are sick of "Irish National" make-believes and frauds.' Turning from the general to the particular he castigated the Irish Parliamentary Party – each section of which had for ten years been calling themselves 'Nationalists' while accusing the others of being 'West British'. 'It began gradually to dawn upon the average mind,' he wrote, 'that, as there was practically no difference between A and B but a cry Irish Nationality, Irish Nationality must be made of a very cloudy substance indeed.'[24]

While Irish parliamentary politics flowed unevenly but monotonously on in the foreground of Irish life, Irish opinion was being subtly conditioned by these other forces in the background. There was nothing particularly coherent about such conditioning except that it was concerned with something different from what had gone on before, and with Irishness. But inasmuch as attention and energies were being focused on something different, and Irish, at a time when the Irish Parliamentary Party remained doggedly fixed on the same old goal of Home Rule, a potential detachment from the party was growing all the time beneath the surface.

In 1897 Yeats, together with the forty-four-year-old widow of an ex-Governor of Ceylon, Lady Gregory, who lived at Coole Park in Co. Galway, and a thirty-eight-year-old wealthy eccentric neighbour of hers, Edward Martyn, had founded the Irish National Theatre which was soon to make the name of the Abbey Theatre, Dublin, famous all over the world. Moran early dismissed all such activities with cynical contempt. 'The birth of the Celtic note,' he wrote in 1899, 'caused a little stir among minor literary circles in London, but much less in Ireland itself, where the "Irish national" demand for *The Mirror of Life, The Police Gazette* and publications of a like kind, showed no signs of weakening.'[25]

Easy as it was to disparage the literary renaissance and even the new Irish theatre as untypical fringe activity, they had many repercussions on a wide range of Irish opinion. Lady Gregory's researches among the Sligo peasantry had revealed particularly a living tradition not only of ghosts and fairies but of the ancient Gaelic heroes. Thus, hearing from a centenarian how the hero Cuchulain fought with and slew his own son, she received in

138

parenthesis a physical description of his love, Grania, as if the narrator had actually known her: 'Grania was very small, only four feet.'[26] And together with these living traditions she had found among the Gaelic-speaking peasantry an ancient love of country stemming from far beyond the days of the green flag. Indeed, she went so far as to write, 'Love of country is, I think, the real passion.'[27] Her popularizations of the legends of Cuchulain and other heroes, though they met with the disapproval of some scholars, did much to make available to anyone who might want to adopt it a new Gaelic warrior pride.

By unleashing Cuchulain and Finn and other Gaelic warrior chiefs from the mists of heroic mythology, Lady Gregory's and Yeats's and Hyde's primary objectives were those of literature and art. But the national myth had had to subsist so long on noble failures like Tone and Emmet that these new figures from the Gaelic past, combining in their remoteness even more convincingly god-like attributes with superior military prowess, proved irresistible to those looking to the national myth for intoxication. When Lady Gregory collaborated with Yeats on his play *Caitlin ni Houlihan* for the Abbey they created a model for an entire renewal of patriotic Irish thought. This story about Humbert's landing at Killala in 1798 ended with a famous line after an old woman, Caitlin ni Houlihan, tragic and symbolic figure of Ireland, had called at a peasant's cottage to summon him to join the rebels. Just after she had left, the peasant's brother came in and, on being asked if he had seen an old woman going away down the path, gave the reply: 'I did not, but I saw a young girl and she had the walk of a Queen.' When many years later Yeats was to ask himself, 'Did that play of mine send out Certain men the English shot?' the answer was 'Yes' – perhaps more obliquely than Yeats would have liked to think, but 'Yes' all the same.[28]

> Know that I would accounted be
> True brother of a company:
> That sang, to sweeten Ireland's wrong,

he had written. And so he should be accounted.

Paradoxically, as part of his motivation in the literary renaissance, Yeats quite soon engaged in a battle against the claims of conventional patriotism and on behalf of true art. 'All the past,' he complained later, 'had been turned into a melodrama with Ireland for blameless hero; and poet, novelist and historian had but one object: that we should hiss the villain.'[29] The trouble was of course, as he admitted, that there really had been victim and villain however different in form. His battle against clichés old and new was eventually to prove a losing one, and in the first decade of the twentieth century he drifted further and further away from the renaissance's nationalist implications. A personal complication for him, apart from his friendship with O'Leary, was the romantic attachment he had formed for Maud Gonne, the beautiful daughter of an Irish Unionist colonel, with whom he had collaborated in the '98 centenary celebration. Converted to an ardent nationalism by O'Leary, Maud Gonne had been confirmed in it by the relief work she carried out with passionate zeal among the distressed and often still starving peasantry of the west of Ireland in the nineties. In her honour Yeats dutifully maintained a patriotic and even political involvement, at least until painfully released by her marriage to an active member of the IRB, John MacBride, in 1903. But the primary object of his own energies was always aesthetic: that new kind of Ireland which he optimistically discerned in May 1899 as rising up amid the wreck of the old 'and in which the national life was finding a new utterance'.[30]

Moran, for all his gibes at Yeats, had the same aspiration. Having made the point that the Irish people did not hate England – 'the genius of our country is far more prone to love than hate' – Moran concluded in 1899: 'The prospect of such a new Ireland rising up out of the foundations of the old, with love and not hate as its inspiration, has already sent a great thrill through the land.'[31]

However imperfectly such aspirations from different quarters might be realized, the significant point was that new thoughts and emotions were thrilling certain people in Ireland, and the most thrilling thing about them was that they were new. Beside this excitement the political stalemate in which Home Rule found itself seemed less important.

Of course, the Irish Ireland movement and the Gaelic League themselves appeared to have limitations to many. A powerful school of Irish academics poured scorn on the whole idea of reviving the language. Trinity College, where this school was centred, had turned down Hyde for its Professorship of Irish two years after the foundation of the Gaelic League on the grounds that he knew only 'baboon Irish'.[32] John Mahaffy, the Vice-Provost of Trinity, vigorously though unsuccessfully tried to prevent Irish being incorporated into secondary school education in 1901, while even John Dillon himself opposed it as a compulsory subject for the new National University of Ireland in 1909.[33]

Even for its supporters the Gaelic League cannot always have been wholly inspiring. George Moore, the novelist, grandson of the independent-minded Member of Parliament for County Mayo in the days of the Pope's Brass Band, found himself caught up in the new movement for a time. He has left one memorable portrait of Hyde through the droop of whose moustache, he says, 'the Irish frothed like porter, and when he returned to English it was easy to see why he wanted to change the language of Ireland'.[34]

Moreover, the Gaelic League and the Irish Ireland movement, though influential, were all minority movements. To the great majority of the people of Ireland during these years the prospects and terms of land purchase in the countryside and the hard living conditions in the towns were the dominating considerations of everyday life. But for all their faults and limitations they were minority movements whose character slipped, often unnoticeably, into the national ethos. As a result, when in 1911 Home Rule once again became a practical possibility, the sensitiveness of Irish national opinion, though it had developed virtually no new political demands, was much greater than a quarter of a century before.

Many individual and often unconnected voices helped to produce this change in the Irish national mood. Some were even Unionists who, by their moderate and reasonable paternalist approach to the encouragement of Irish self-reliance and a share in administration, inevitably made Home Rule seem all the more reasonable and in the long run irresistible. The Local Government Act of 1898 itself contributed to this effect, establishing elected County Councils in Ireland, and thus taking the administration of local affairs out of the hands of the property-qualified grand juries and the local gentry. And the initiative for the great Land Purchase Act of 1903 (the Wyndham Act, so-called after the Irish Chief Secretary of the day) came first from a group of Unionist landowners headed by a Colonel Shawe Taylor and the Earl of Dunraven.

One particular Unionist had encouraged in agriculture something of an Irish Ireland outlook almost approaching the philosophy of D. P. Moran. This was Sir Horace Plunkett, an Irish Protestant landowner and farmer who had spent some years ranching in the United States. In 1889 he had begun an Irish cooperative movement in agriculture known as the Irish Agricultural Organization Society, which by 1903 had eight hundred branches with a membership of eighty thousand representing some 400,000 persons.[35] Its secretary was a Protestant Nationalist, an Irish poet and painter called George Russell (his *nom de plume* was 'AE') who, apart from running the Society efficiently, blurred the spiritual, political and economic interests of Ireland into something like a mystical quest for what he called the 'national soul'.

Plunkett in 1895 had taken the initiative from which eventually the Dunraven Land Conference and other changes of climate in Ireland were to spring. He wrote a letter to the Irish press suggesting that a committee should be formed during the parliamentary recess of Irish Members of Parliament of both sides and all shades of political opinion who might have the interests of Ireland at heart. 'We Unionists,' he wrote, 'without abating one jot of our Unionism, and Nationalists, without abating one jot of their Nationalism, can each show our faith in the cause for which we have fought so bitterly and so long, by sinking our party differences for our country's good, and leaving our respective policies for the justification of time . . .'

This was strange talk of 'our country's good' from a Conservative of the late nineteenth century. And more orthodox Unionists certainly looked at it askance. After all, this collaboration of Irishmen of all classes and creeds for Ireland's sake was the very goal which the United Irishmen and the nationalists of the 1840s had always striven for.

Significantly, the majority of the parliamentary nationalists did not now like it either. For it set up a sort of Unionism as an alternative goal to the pure formula of Home Rule in which the party had a vested interest. The party similarly disliked Sir Horace Plunkett's Irish Agricultural Organization Society. Town shopkeepers and suppliers of farmers' credit in the party felt themselves threatened by the commercial rivalry of the cooperative societies and agricultural banks. The Nationalist Party, a quarter of a century earlier under Parnell, had been the radical force in Ireland. Now it was in many respects an alternative Irish Establishment to the Vice-Regal Lodge and Dublin Castle. And it is in the nature of all establishments that they can be toppled.

When Plunkett's campaign led in 1902 to the creation by the government for the first time of an Irish Department of Agriculture, with a partly elected Council of Agriculture to decide agricultural policy for different Irish localities, he regarded this as a new moral force in Ireland and talked of the 'reconstruction of Irish life' and 'organized self-help' like the Irish Ire-landers.[36] Redmond, who when split from the rest of the party had taken part in Plunkett's Recess Committee, now turned unashamedly against him. He described Plunkett with almost incredible unfairness as having an 'undisguised contempt for the Irish race'.[37] What rankled was the suggestion that anything but Home Rule might be the answer to Ireland's problems. But with Home Rule politically in the doldrums it was inevitable that national feeling, if it had any vitality at all, should switch much of that vitality into some of the many various channels now available. The party became increasingly aware that an enthusiasm of which it should have had the monopoly was going elsewhere. 'An effort must be made,' wrote John Dillon to Redmond in 1906, 'to put some life into the movement. At present it is very much asleep, and Sinn Feiners, Gaelic League etc. etc. are making great play.'[38]

This reference to 'Sinn Feiners' was to a small section of the new national mood which had actually switched into an alternative political organization altogether.

9

Arthur Griffith
and Sinn Fein

An essay written by Douglas Hyde just before the turn of the century described 'a blackness on the sun of Ireland' – a dark cloud, like a great crow choking and smothering the people of Ireland, breathing poison from its beak, sucking away the courage of the people and putting fog and cold into their hearts. This crow was the English mind and 'the Englishing of Ireland'. It was to be slain by a bow whose arrow was the Irish language, its archer the Gaelic League. The Irish people would then 'stand without chains on body or mind, free in the presence of God...'.[1]

In the essay, Hyde translated some Irish verse which expressed an ancient tradition constant in Irish folk legend through centuries of sorrow and misfortune:

> There is a change coming, a big change
> And riches and store will be nothing worth,
> He will rise up that was small eyed,
> And he that was big will fall down.
>
> The time will come, and it's not far from us,
> When strength won't be on the side of authority or law,
> And the neck will bend that was not bent,
> When that time comes it will come heavily ...

The essay was called 'The Return of the Fenians'.

But in recalling this legend of Finn and his warriors coming down from the North to destroy the enemies of Ireland, Hyde did not mean to appeal to the ideals of 1865 and 1867. He was using it as an allegorical summons to spiritual renewal through the language and ennobling standards of ancient Gaeldom. With such open abandon did he express his theme, concluding with a final cry of '...And the time is not far off', that clearly no possibility of a political interpretation can have entered his mind. That it should have been possible thus to talk of Fenians, without apparently suggesting any attempt to revive the republican separatist spirit of thirty years before, shows how remote that spirit itself had then become. Inevitably attempts were soon made to revive it together with other legends from the glorious past.

Irish history was then quite untaught both in the so-called National Board Schools and in private education. For those who in the new Irish Ireland climate suddenly began to discover their history, all periods, even quite recent ones, easily became mythological. Among the many individuals who in the nineties discovered Irish history in this manner were two middle-class young women of Protestant stock from Ulster, Alice Milligan and Anna Johnston (the latter writing under the name of 'Ethna Carberry'). In 1896 they started a monthly magazine in Belfast called the *Shan Van Vocht*, the name of the legendary old woman who was Ireland. 'Ireland dear,' wrote Alice Milligan in an ode for 6 October, the anniversary of Parnell's death, and dedicated 'to the memory of the dead and the cause that shall not die',

> Ireland dear! through the length of my childhood lonely,
> Throughout the toilsome hours of my schooling days,
> No mention of thee was made unto me, save only
> By speakers in heedless scorn or in harsh dispraise ...

In this childhood which she had spent in an Orange district of Ulster, Alice Milligan had often been brought in from play of an evening by a nurse's threat that if she stayed out the Fenians would get her:

> An army of Papists grim
> With a green flag o'er them,
> Red-coats and black police
> Flying before them.
>
> But God (who our nurse declared
> Guards British dominions)
> Sent down a deep fall of snow
> And scattered the Fenians.

The child had dropped asleep romantically sympathizing with the rebels and

> Wondering if God,
> If they prayed to Him
> Would give them good weather.

Anna Johnston, Alice Milligan's literary colleague, also dreamt of the Fenians, romanticizing them in the same golden terms as Cuchulain, Conor MacNessa, Finn and the other heroes of ancient legend. She wrote a poem about the *Erin's Hope*, the boat-load of square-toed Irish Americans who in reality had sailed belatedly across the Atlantic to join the fiasco of '67, unable to find a welcome the whole length of the Irish west coast.

> A sail! a sail upon the sea – a sail against the sun!
> A sail, wind-filled from out the West! our waiting time is done;
> Since sword and spear and shield are here to free our hapless One!

The distinction between myth and reality had always been vague in Irish history. But from this sort of thing it was to be a short step to living out mythology in the present.

The Irish Republican Brotherhood, clinging to the antique dogma of the 1860s that only physical force could help Ireland, was by the mid-1890s virtually moribund. Such vitality as the IRB had preserved after its reorganization in 1873 under Charles Kickham had been deflected to other fields than those of violent national revolution. Some Fenians had gone into the Parliamentary movement; others had diverted their energies into the Land League activity of the late seventies and early eighties. Still others, clinging almost desperately to violent action as an instrument of policy, had joined the Invincibles, the secret society which had killed Lord Frederick Cavendish in Phoenix Park. During the 1880s the IRB's one notable activity had been an attempt to secure control of the newly-founded Gaelic Athletic Association. Inasmuch as this was successful however, it led to a temporary but sharp decline in the GAA's membership, for the clergy, who were far more influential than the IRB, discouraged membership which fell in consequence from 52,000 in 1889 to 5,446 in 1892. But when the Brotherhood's influence on the direction of the GAA waned, membership revived, and Archbishop Croke was in 1895 again able to give it his support.[2]

The effectiveness of the Parliamentary Party under Parnell, and the apparent near-success, at least until mid-1893, of Home Rule as the national goal, made the Brotherhood seem more and more of a museum piece. Its continued existence was known to the police and watched though not taken seriously by anyone as a threat to the constitution. As if to stress the museum quality, John O'Leary and James Stephens himself were to be found harmlessly on view in Dublin. A Supreme Council of the IRB remained technically in being however, a nominal apparatus of radical extremists, fanatically devoted to a safely theoretical cause.

This reserve of individuals had played some part in Parnell's last campaign of 1891 when, deprived suddenly of his usual sources of support, he had turned back to 'the hillside men'. But the IRB's cause – that of the green flag to be carried to victory through shot and shell over the British Army – necessarily remained a near-theological rather than a practical issue, something to be argued about rather than engaged in.

That a revival of interest in such theology should form part of the generally awakening interest in things Irish was inevitable. But one young man whose interest had been thus aroused, John MacBride, whose family came from Ulster, though he had been born in County Mayo, was soon disillusioned by what he found in the IRB. Such energy as there was in the organization in the early nineties seems, by his own account at any rate, to have been supplied largely by himself. '... The older men were doing then what they are doing now,' he wrote in 1902 to John Devoy, the old Fenian who ran

Clan-na-Gael, the Irish extremist organization in America. 'Sitting on their backsides and criticizing and abusing one another.'[3]

The IRB's link with Clan-na-Gael and with that organization's financial resources in the States was the one feature that gave it any continuing significance. But that the cause of 'physical force' in Ireland, for which it stood, should ever again become a serious practical consideration seemed at this time beyond the bounds of possibility. Even in 1898 when under Fred Allan the IRB stirred itself into some activity to organize the centenary celebrations of that year, the qualities it revealed had not been very impressive. John Daly, a recently released Fenian, wrote to Devoy that summer: 'I would like to tell you something about how Mr Fred is running things on this side, but ... I must let it stand over.... I can't or won't play in with the chaps that run or work the rings.... And in truth I think it's nearly all rings now and rot and humbug...'[4]

By 1896 John MacBride had left Ireland to seek a living for himself in South Africa. Besides being a member of the IRB he had also been a member of the Celtic Literary Society, the members of which had contacts with Alice Milligan and Anna Johnston of Belfast, in whose monthly they published verse and articles. In the Celtic Literary Society MacBride had become a friend of the nationally minded compositor and journalist named Arthur Griffith, and early in 1897 he had persuaded Griffith to come out to the Transvaal to join him.

There Griffith, after working for a short time as a journalist, took a job as a machine supervisor in a gold mining company in Johannesburg and with MacBride helped to organize the Irish '98 centenary celebrations in that town. When Griffith gave up his job and returned to Dublin later in the year, he decided with his other friend from the Celtic Literary Society, William Rooney, to found a newspaper.[5] The characteristic note which this paper struck immediately was very much in line with the sort of republican ideology Griffith had learned from MacBride. It took the name of Mitchel's paper the United Irishman, and the leader in the first issue of 4 March 1899 proclaimed its acceptance of 'the Nationalism of '98, '48, and '67'.

Both Griffith and Rooney were soon to become sworn members of the Irish Republican Brotherhood and their paper at first largely reflected its ideals in the context of the new Irish Ireland climate. It was only gradually in the years to come that Griffith evolved a different political position from that of the IRB.

The United Irishman, written at first almost entirely by Rooney and Griffith, set itself up as a watchdog of iconoclastic militant nationalism. It was not only the Parliamentary Party that was attacked – either directly, or by implication with the use of quotations from Mitchel, Meagher, Davis and James Fintan Lalor. The Gaelic League itself was assailed for preaching that nationality was 'not a thing of rights, arms, freedom, franchises and brotherhood' but a thing of 'singing and lute-playing, of mystic prose and thrice mystic poesy' and for its insistence on 'no politics'.⁶ Yeats, who had been saying that he believed the work of Ireland was to lift up its voice for spirituality, ideality and simplicity in the English-speaking world, was told by the *United Irishman* that *it* believed nothing of the kind. 'The work of Ireland', it declared, 'is to uplift itself.'⁷ Anyone reading the early issues would reasonably have supposed that the paper was preaching a thinly disguised Fenianism. 'Not a local legislature – not a return to "our ancient constitution" – not a golden link . . .' ran a prominently displayed quotation from Mitchel, 'but an Irish Republic One and Indivisible.' One early issue contained an article on the continuity throughout history of the Fenian spirit ('Fenianism is the Irish incarnation of . . . Delenda est Carthago. Read Britannia for Carthago . . .') and there were occasional snippets of news about old Fenians, particularly about the attempts of the released dynamiter Clarke to settle down in regular employment.⁸

But though letters and articles striking an old-fashioned military and insurrectionary note continued to appear in the *United Irishman* for several years, a potential development from the old cliché-ridden attitudes began to emerge in 1899 with increasingly insistent proposals from correspondents, taken up with interest by the editor, for some new 'National Organization' to coordinate the activities of those who thought as the *United Irishman* did. There were a number of small 'national' societies in existence, most of them remnants of groups that had come into being to help celebrate the rebellion of 1798, though many of these had quickly disintegrated.⁹ Societies with names like the Robert Emmet '98 Club, the Oliver Bond Young Men's Club and the Old Guard Union were, together with Rooney and Griffith's old Celtic Literary Society, all at home in the *United Irishman*'s pages. A tentative plan for some new comprehensive organization was first formulated in the *United Irishman* of 16 September 1899 by a correspondent, George Morton Griffith, a nationalist who was no relation of the paper's editor. Because constitutionalism was so deeply ingrained in the public's attitude, his argument ran, any such new party would have to sit in Parliament, but should do so, sworn to support Irish revolutionary principles and backed by an extreme party at home, which would be organizing and advising people for armed revolt. 'An Irish Party in Parliament,' the letter continued, 'need not necessarily be "Constitutional" except in so far as it was politic for them to be so.'

Arthur Griffith, who in an earlier issue had specifically declared that 'the era of constitutional possibilities for Irish nationality ended on the day Charles Stewart Parnell died',¹⁰ merely called for the names and addresses of those who were interested in forming any new organization. And in the following week other correspondents continued to press for some sort of amalgamation of existing societies.

'What we want now,' wrote one of them, 'is a policy and an organization which will take practical steps to preserve our Irish nationality, foster our industries, protect our commerce and keep our people at home. If we wait for these things until the present warring parliamentarians have made Ireland a Nation, the country will be either a grass farm or a desert.'[11]

In the end the organization came before the policy and outside events gave the impetus for its foundation.

In the Transvaal in 1899 the Boer farmers were up in arms against the British Empire. Griffith's friend John MacBride, who had remained there, now helped to form and became second-in-command of a small 'Irish Brigade' of men of Irish origin in the Transvaal – mainly Americans – pledged to fight for the Boers.*[12] Opinion in Ireland, as in much of Liberal Britain, was strongly pro-Boer. On 10 October 1899 an Irish Transvaal Committee was formed in the offices of the Celtic Literary Society at 32 Lower Abbey Street, Dublin, with Maud Gonne in the chair, and a resolution sending congratulations to MacBride was seconded by Griffith. A green flag, gold-fringed with a harp in the centre inscribed 'Our Land – Our People – Our Language', was also sent, and before the end of the year was waving over the Irish Brigade camp among the Boers besieging Ladysmith.[13]

A short-term policy for this embryo 'national organization' represented by the Transvaal Committee was immediately available: a campaign against recruitment for the British forces. It issued a poster carrying such slogans as: 'Enlisting in the English Army is Treason to Ireland', and 'Remember '98. Remember the Famine. Think of the ruined homes, of the Emigrant Ships'.[14]

Much of the committee's activity met with superficial popular support. In November 1899, when Griffith and Maud Gonne visited Cork on behalf of the committee, the horses were removed from their carriage by the crowd who themselves dragged them in triumph from the railway station to the Victoria Hotel.[15] In December, Dublin Castle, aggravated by the temporary success of the anti-recruiting campaign, banned a Sunday meeting of the Transvaal Committee, which decided to go ahead with it. A horse-drawn brake containing Maud Gonne, Arthur Griffith and the Chairman of Dublin's tiny Irish Socialist Republican Party, an ex-British Army man himself, named James Connolly, drove into Beresford Square, Dublin, in defiance of the ban. A riot took place and James Connolly was later arrested and given a fine of £2 – paid by Maud Gonne – for driving a licensed vehicle, 'he not being a licensed driver'.[16] Griffith was sent sprawling by mounted police, who attempted to capture a child's Boer flag from the brake. At one time he was

---

* The Commander was a Colonel Blake, a former US army officer. The figure for the Brigade's numbers (1,000) in the *United Irishman* of 7 October 1899 is certainly an exaggeration. See below, p. 148.

seen waving both the flag and a police sword before hurling both into the crowd.[17]

A Frenchman who was in Dublin at the time of the early Boer victories wrote: 'The crowds would thrill with excitement, and men, radiant with delight, would stop in the streets to express to utter strangers the pleasure that the news gave them.'[18] But such reactions should probably be understood more as an Irish conditioned emotional endorsement of standard Liberal views on the war than as a reasoned expression of hatred for England. Irish regiments in the British Army served with honour in the war on many occasions. The Inniskillings, the Connaught Rangers and the Dublin Fusiliers all fought the Boers with particular distinction and the latter suffered heavy casualties. English music-hall songs, 'Bravo, Dublin Fusiliers' and 'What do you think of the Irish now?' duly signalized the fact. One of the actions in which MacBride's pro-Boer Irish Brigade took part was at Nikolson's Nek, a Boer victory where considerable numbers of the Royal Irish Fusiliers were among the captured.[19]

The pro-Boer Irish Brigade itself, of which MacBride himself took charge after its commanding officer had been wounded, played, by comparison with these Irishmen in the British Army, a totally insignificant part in the war. It existed only for one year, from September 1899 to September 1900, when it was disbanded by the Boers and the men gave themselves up to the Portuguese frontier post at Kamati.[20] They had fought in about twenty battles altogether, including Colenso, Spion Kop and Ladysmith, but had suffered no more than a total of eighty casualties of whom only seventeen had been killed.[21] Irish casualties among the British forces ran into thousands. Mac-Bride, who personally seems to have fought with gallantry and was thrown from his horse by a shellburst at Colenso, and slightly wounded at the battle of the Tugela river, later estimated his brigade's casualties at some thirty per cent of the total force.[22] This suggests that this 'Irish Brigade' in contrast with that of the British Army, which was a full brigade in the military meaning of the term, did not number much more than three thundred men altogether, although the *United Irishman* had at different times suggested that it consisted of between 1,000 and 1,700.[23] A second pro-Boer Irish brigade formed under the command of a 'Colonel' Lynch, who had originally gone to South Africa as a correspondent for the American magazine *Collier's Weekly*, was composed largely of Afrikaners, Germans and Frenchmen, built round a small nucleus of Irish. It was disbanded after three months and saw no fighting.*[24] Lynch later became a Nationalist member of Parliament.

Irish public opinion itself, for all the readiness of a respectable Dublin crowd to cheer Boer victories or a Dublin mob to riot in favour of the

* A Captain O'Donnell on the staff of de Wet, the Boer commander, is quoted in *United Irishmen*, 30 August 1902, as saying that the Irishmen involved on the Boer side numbered '500 and double that number of Irish-Afrikanders'.

Transvaal Committee, was by no means so clear-cut as appearances suggested. When in April 1900 Queen Victoria visited Dublin, the 'Famine Queen', as Maud Gonne described her in an issue of the *United Irishman*, seized by the police the week before, she received a friendly reception. The *United Irishman* itself had to admit that she was 'frantically cheered' in some quarters though it maintained that this was only done 'by those who look to her for their bread and butter'.[25] Where elsewhere there were silent people on the pavement there were 'cheering toadies in hired windows'. The Transvaal Committee tried to organize a demonstration that evening protesting that 'the loyalist pageant in the streets today in no wise reflects the sentiment of the people of Dublin'. A charge by Irish policemen dispersed it before its torchbearers could leave the building. Connolly was brought to the ground and Griffith struck by a baton.

The complex state of Irish public opinion on the national issue presented Griffith with a more serious obstacle than any police baton. He had already been given a devastating proof of the unpopularity of the simple neo-Fenian conclusions he and his friends drew from the Boer War situation. In February 1900 a parliamentary by-election had come up in the constituency of South Mayo where MacBride had been born. The Transvaal Committee nominated MacBride as an independent nationalist candidate against the orthodox candidate of the Parliamentary Party. John O'Leary and the recently released Fenian John Daly sat with Griffith on MacBride's election committee. In the *United Irishman* Griffith published a stirring version of 'The Wearing of the Green'.

> From land to land throughout the world the news is going round
> That Ireland's flag triumphant waves on high o'er English ground.
> In far-off Africa today the English fly dismayed
> Before the flag of green and gold borne by MacBride's brigade ...
>
> With guns and bayonets in their hands, their Irish flag on high
> As down they swept on England's ranks out rang their battle-cry:
> 'Revenge! Remember '98! and how our fathers died!
> We'll pay the English back today,' cried fearless John MacBride.
>
> They'll raise the flag of Emmet, Tone, and Mitchel up once more
> And lead us in the fight to drive the tyrant from our shore ...[26]

When the election result was announced it was found that MacBride had been defeated by the Parliamentary Party's candidate by a majority of over five to one in a campaign in which only twenty-five per cent of the electorate voted. The figures were: O'Donnell 2,401; MacBride 427.[27]

As the theme of the need for some new national organization was raised again in the columns of the *United Irishman* one correspondent, while himself enthusiastic, added a further realistic note:

Are the people of Ireland ready [he asked] to help in establishing such a confederation as that proposed? I fear not. ... In the very neighbourhood in which I reside poor men and women are to be found to whom it would be dangerous to say a word derogatory of England's invincibility. They have relatives among the Fusiliers etc. who are at present fighting in South Africa, and they are proud of the fact.[28]

But Griffith, hard-working, courageous, often oblivious of personal discomfort and uninterested in his material advancement, tenacious and single-minded almost to a fault, was not a man to be deterred from what he had decided was the right path, by lack of popularity. On 30 September 1900, with the Irish Transvaal Committee as a nucleus, he formed in its rooms in Lower Abbey Street an organization called Cumann na Gaedheal to unite a number of existing open national societies. This in turn was to be the nucleus of his later party known as Sinn Fein.

No clear agreed policy for the new organization was as yet evolved. The objects of Cumann na Gaedheal were listed as (a) diffusing a knowledge of Ireland's resources and supporting Irish industries; (b) the study and teaching of Irish history, language, music and art; (c) the encouragement of Irish national games and characteristics; (d) the discountenancing of everything leading to the Anglicization of Ireland. Membership was open to all who pledged themselves 'to aid to the best of their ability in restoring Ireland to her former position of sovereign independence'. But what precisely was meant by that – the sovereign independence of Grattan's Parliament under a Crown shared with England, or something more revolutionary after the style of 1798 – was not specified. Meanwhile, an article in the current issue of the *United Irishman* on the 'Use of the Pike and Bayonet in Warfare' drew attention to the uselessness of the pike.[29]

When the first Convention of the new organization was announced for 25 November 1900 – the anniversary of the execution of the Manchester martyrs – it was stressed by Griffith that it was in fact 'no new affair.... It is merely a combination of a number of existing National bodies working heretofore locally on the broad principles enunciated by Tone and Davis.'[30] He then made plain that he was not just indulging in the traditional vague lip service to such heroes now claimed by virtually all Irish patriots. Cumann na Gaedheal, he wrote, 'come to insist on the difference between the ideals of '98, '48 and '67 and those which in our time are sought to be identified with them'.[31] John MacBride, who had just returned from South Africa, expressed a wish to join the new organization, and when the Convention met was elected Vice-President. John O'Leary was President. Rooney and Griffith took an active part in the proceedings.

Not surprisingly the new organization made little impact. It had little specifically to offer. Articles about some curiously unspecified future war continued to appear in the *United Irishman*, in one of which an offensive–defensive war was envisaged of attacks on the enemy in Ireland by exceedingly mobile forces who would live off the land. And where a gesture could be made Cumann na Gaedheal made it. It attended the funeral of James Stephens when he died at last in Dublin on 29 March 1901. But then so did the Lord Mayor – though he trimmed by not coming 'in state' – and even the Irish Parliamentary Party passed a resolution of regret – 'for American consumption' commented Griffith's paper sourly.[32] It was true that political gestures had been two a penny in Ireland for years. What Cumann na Gaedheal in particular wanted was not political gestures but political ideas. Before it could develop any, Griffith's friend and collaborator, William Rooney, died suddenly at the age of twenty-seven. It is an indication of how undeveloped Griffith's own political ideas were at this stage that he could write later, in describing the setback entailed by this relatively obscure young man's death, that 'for a time it seemed as if the blow would be a fatal one'.[33] Among those who attended Rooney's funeral was another relatively obscure young man of literary bent, an executive of the Gaelic League called P. H. Pearse, who occasionally contributed to the *United Irishman*.[34]

All the movement really amounted to at this early stage was an untypical but articulate dissatisfaction with the incompleteness and inadequacy of Home Rule as an expression of Irish nationalism. As Rooney had said: 'Home Rule might be an improvement on this state of affairs but it would not be nationhood.'[35] The chief difficulty Griffith and his contributors and the thirty thousand odd Irishmen who subscribed to the *United Irishman* had to contend with, was that for the vast majority of their countrymen Home Rule meant nationhood enough.[36]

Griffith first worked away at basic principles, trying to establish a suitable national anthem ('A Nation Once Again', 'Let Erin Remember ...', 'God Save Ireland'), trying to define who was an Irishman and who was not. A long discussion took place in the *United Irishman* between those who said that only 'Gaels' were true Irishmen and those who maintained with Davis that 'Irish' and not 'Gael' was the key word. Supporters of the latter view quoted Davis's verse:

> Yet start not, Irish-born man,
> If you're to Ireland true,
> We heed not race, nor creed, nor clan,
> We've hearts and hands for you.[37]

On the other hand, one correspondent even maintained that a large body of the non-Gaelic population of Ireland would have to be deported from the new Ireland, though he recognized that individuals of the settler race might in exceptional cases be admitted if they had proved themselves 'in touch with the Gael'.[38] He could hardly do anything else. Tone, Mitchel, Parnell and others of his heroes all fell into this category.

Griffith, in his editorial judgement on the matter, was more consistent and logical. Again, he could hardly afford not to be, for though he was himself 'Gaelic' in the sense that he was Catholic, his grandfather had been a convert to the religion and he came from a family of Ulster Protestant farmers.[39] Griffith now defined an Irishman as one who accepts Ireland as his country and is ready to do a man's part for her; 'such a man, whatever his creed, is our brother and the Gael of a hundred generations who accepts the Empire is our enemy, did he belong to our creed a thousand times.'[40]

Griffith, while priggish almost to the point of absurdity on occasion about lapses from severe Irish Ireland standards, and resenting strongly, for instance, the guying of an Irish peasant on stage as a man in a battered hat or the singing of 'Phil the Fluter's Ball' at a concert, was free of a racial view of Irish nationality even in his attitude to the language.*

'Ireland is truly no longer the Gaelic Nation of the fifth or the twelfth or even the eighteenth century ...', he wrote. 'The Gael is gone, the Dane is gone, the Norman is gone, and the Irishman is here.... And he turns to the language of the Gaels, not because the Gael spoke it, but because it was moulded and formed in Ireland, and is therefore fitter for an Irishman than any other.'[41]

There was little tendency to shirk the essentially synthetic nature of the work ahead. 'We are nation-makers,' a *United Irishman* correspondent had written.[42] But how practically was the nation to be made when the bulk of the nation did not think nationally in this extreme sense at all, and when even those who did think nationally were concerned mainly for cultural and spiritual renewal and not political nationhood?

Griffith remained a member of the IRB, and in the early part of 1902 the *United Irishman* still had no newer policy to offer than a 'National Brigade' and a plea for drilling in Cumann na Gaedheal.[43] Meanwhile, it vigorously supported the work of the Gaelic League in the language revival and encouraged Irish industry, recalling the self-reliance preached by Young Ireland and embodied twenty years before in the motto of the Cork exhibition as Sinn Fein (Ourselves Alone).[44]

However, on 26 October 1902 at the third annual convention of Cumann na Gaedheal a practical policy which had been periodically advocated before in Irish history was officially adopted as the national organization's programme. It was contained in a resolution of Griffith's which ran: 'That we call upon our countrymen abroad [Irish Americans] to withhold all assistance from the promoters of a useless, degrading and demoralizing policy until such time as the members of the Irish Parliamentary Party substitute

* He was less free from bigotry on other matters, giving evidence of anti-semitic feeling more than once in the *United Irishman*. See, e.g., the issues of 9 September 1899 and 23 September 1899. When in 1900 his prediction that the Boer capital of Pretoria would never fall proved false he ascribed its capitulation without a shot to 'masonic influences' (Lyons, *Griffith*, p. 43).

for it the policy of the Hungarian deputies and refusing to attend the British Parliament or to recognize its right to legislate for Ireland, remain at home to help in promoting Ireland's interest and to aid in guarding its national rights.'[45] 'The "Hungarian Policy".' added Griffith, 'is the policy for Ireland to pursue, so long as she is unable to meet and defeat England on the battlefield.'[46]

There was nothing new in such a tactic, though it had not been revived for some time. The proposal that Irish Members of Parliament should withdraw from Westminster and sit in Ireland with other representatives as a National Parliament had first been made in *The Nation* of 19 November 1842.* The idea had been elaborated by O'Connell as a proposed Council of Three Hundred, inevitably hedged about with devices for circumventing the Convention Act, which then made any such activity in Ireland illegal. A general analogy between Ireland and the European nationalist movements developing under the Austrian Empire had also been made by Davis and the Young Irelanders in the 1840s. After the Fenian rising of 1867 the nationalist paper *The Irishman* had expressly recommended imitation by the Parliamentary party of the action of the Hungarian Deputies of 1861 in withdrawing from the Imperial Parliament and returning home.† Parnell and Michael Davitt had discussed such a course of action in 1877.‡ But then as now, when Griffith put it forward, the policy failed totally to recommend itself to the only people in a position to carry it out: the Parliamentary Party itself. In such circumstances it was bound to remain a rather academic proposal and, though it met with a welcome from supporters of Cumann na Gaedheal, little was heard of it again for almost another year after November 1902. The leadership of Cumann na Gaedheal remained theoretically Fenian with John O'Leary still President, and Thomas Clarke (then settled in New York), John Daly, Maud Gonne and John MacBride as Vice Presidents.§ Articles enjoining the patriotic citizen to practise route marching and drill continued to appear in the *United Irishman* well into 1903.

The executive of Cumann na Gaedheal to which Griffith had been elected met every Saturday and Griffith himself was invariably present. Apart from its routine work in trying to keep alive the spirit of the various affiliated clubs and 'national' societies, it also tried to discourage recruitment for the British forces and the police by counselling local authorities not to give jobs to men who had served in them.[47] Occasionally it ventured more boldly still into the field of public affairs. In April 1903 it passed a resolution calling on all public bodies in Ireland which professed to be National to reject with

* See *The Most Distressful Country*, p. 199.
† See above, p. 58.
‡ See above, p. 75.
§ Maud Gonne and John MacBride married in February 1903. The marriage was not a success and MacBride was reported to be drinking heavily later that same year. They eventually separated. (See Yeats, *Correspondence* (London, 1954), pp. 412–14.)

contempt any proposal to welcome King Edward VII to Ireland when he paid his proposed visit in the summer. 'To the Irish Nationalist,' wrote Griffith, 'the King is as foreign as the Akond of Swat, but, unlike that potentate, he claims to be the sovereign of this country.'[48]

Next month the Cumann na Gaedheal executive decided to call a conference to stimulate protest against the king's visit, and on 20 May 1903 a 'National Council to uphold National self-respect' on the occasion issued a letter calling for public support. As well as Griffith and the Fenian John Daly, Yeats and Lady Gregory's eccentric neighbour from County Galway, Edward Martyn, were among the signatories.[49]

This National Council met for the first time in Dublin on 6 June 1903 and held a public meeting on 2 July. Edward Martyn, a wealthy unmarried middle-aged landlord, who collected impressionists and had been opposed even to Home Rule as late as 1887, was in the chair.[50] A resolution of protest against the passing of loyal addresses to the king was passed, and a fortnight later as a result of the campaign the Dublin Corporation decided by a very small majority not to vote one.

This was about the limit of the National Council's achievement for the time being. The king and queen's visit to Ireland turned out to be an outstanding success, in marked contrast with their reception as Prince and Princess of Wales eighteen years before in 1885. They visited Dublin, where they walked in the streets, Belfast, Derry, Galway, the west coast and the Catholic seminary at Maynooth. 'No sovereign,' wrote the Nationalist *Cork Examiner*, 'visiting our shores, ever met with anything like the hearty good will, the honest, unaffected welcome extended by the people of all classes – in every part of the country.... This fortnight ... has made history, has provided materials for nation building....'[51]

It was to be a long time before any idea of nation-building other than one based on the concept of King and Country was to receive popular support in Ireland. The National Council, together with Cumann na Gaedheal, which still maintained a separate existence, was out of tune with the national mood. A few days after the royal departure, it published its Constitution, the first principle of which was that it should consist only of members opposed to British rule in Ireland. It elaborated a rather vague progressive political programme, including the abolition of slums, but there was no mention of the 'Hungarian policy'.[52]

However, in the New Year, 1904, a series of articles by Griffith began to appear in the *United Irishman*, entitled 'The Resurrection of Hungary'. At often tedious length and with some dubious historical interpretation they recounted the steps by which the Hungarians forty years earlier, using methods analogous to the Irish revival on a cultural level, and by political withdrawal of their representatives from the Imperial Parliament to their native land, had won for themselves the concession of a dual monarchy.

What was really most interesting about these articles was not what they taught so remorselessly about the history of the remote Hungarians, but an excursion which they began to take in the twenty-seventh article of the series into the history of Ireland itself. For Griffith thereby began to divert his readers' attention to a political model nearer home: the Protestant national movement of the late eighteenth century.

Again, in considerable detail he recounted how the patriots of that era had won 'legislative independence' for Ireland by forming themselves into Volunteer companies which put extra-parliamentary pressure on the government. Meeting in Dungannon, Griffith reminded his readers, the Volunteers had declared that 'the claim of any body of men other than the King, Lords and Commons of Ireland to make laws to bind this kingdom is unconstitutional, illegal and a grievance'.[53] Sweeping aside the entirely different historical conditions of the eighteenth century, Griffith now proclaimed the Volunteers' goal as the political objective for twentieth-century Ireland. 'We must retrace our steps,' he wrote, 'and take our stand on the Compact of 1782.' The tactic to be employed was that of the Hungarian deputies, or, as Griffith now conceded, again coming rather belatedly nearer home for his example, that proposed by O'Connell in his idea for a Council of Three Hundred. Griffith recommended that an Irish Parliament should be called consisting of the 103 members at present chosen for Westminster, with the addition of elected delegates from the County Councils, Corporations and Rural District Councils. A second or upper house with a discretionary power to delay legislation should be nominated from recognized bodies devoted to science, the arts, agriculture and industry. Griffith also adopted O'Connell's idea of independent civil arbitration courts to supersede the normal processes of law. Summing up his own personal position carefully, he declared: 'We hold that the subsistence of the connection between this country and Great Britain in any form is not for our country's good, but we recognize the existence of a large mass of our countrymen who believe ... that provided the countries retain each their independence, and exist co-equal in power, the rule of a common sovereign is admissible.'[54]

Here at last was some new thinking for the present – if based on an old style. An alternative both to Fenianism and the Parliamentary Party was being proposed. And when letters of support for the new policy began to come in to the *United Irishman*, recommending that Griffith himself should play the leader of such a new movement, he declared that he personally could not accept the link with the Crown without being untrue to his convictions. He took his stand, he said, with Tone, Mitchel and Emmet. Another member of the Brotherhood, his old friend John MacBride, actually expressed his scepticism of the proposed policy, pointing out that it would fail to appeal widely to the average Irishman who was only too willing to fit into the established order as it was. 'It is the ambition of every small farmer,' he wrote, 'to have a son in the clergy or in the police and sometimes both. . . . Today,' concluded the Major, 'the protest would end in smoke unless armed men were prepared to back it.'[55]

Griffith's articles, 'The Resurrection of Hungary',[56] reproduced as a pamphlet, sold something under thirty thousand copies in three months, most of these presumably to the converted since this was about the figure for the circulation of the *United Irishman*.[57] 'It would be pleasant,' wrote a contemporary later who had been one of Griffith's earliest supporters and a contributor to the *United Irishman*, 'to record that Mr Griffith's pamphlet sounded a trumpet-call which awakened a slumbering Ireland. . . . Nothing of the sort happened.'[58]

Although one man who knew Griffith at this time has written that behind all his composure and seriousness there was 'a very real jollity',[59] it is difficult to resist the impression from Griffith's writing that he was sometimes narrow-minded and lacking in humour and that his one great characteristic was his relentless doggedness. At the time of the appearance of the Hungarian articles he was engaged in a quarrel with Yeats from which he emerges poorly as a puritanical critic of J. M. Synge's play *The Shadow of the Glen*, and he was later strongly to disapprove of *The Playboy of the Western World*. Yeats, fast growing disillusioned with the political side of the Irish revival, had already accused Griffith of that 'obscurantism' of the politician 'who would reject every idea which is not of immediate service to his cause'.[60] But it is this very obscurantism, a determination to persist in working out and maintaining an alternative ideal for Irish nationalism to that so successfully promoted by the Parliamentary Party, that gave him ultimately his historical importance. And already, slowly, barely perceptibly, there were some signs that he was influencing opinion if not events.

The National Council put up a few candidates at selected local elections. They had a little limited success, but more important was the reflection of their recently proclaimed policy in a meeting of the General Council of County Councils, consisting of delegates from all the elected county councils of Ireland, which met in Dublin in January 1905. This, said Griffith, was the most pregnant gathering of representative Irishmen since the Irish Volunteers had met in the church of Dungannon, and certainly in their resolution calling for a Home Rule Parliament they echoed almost exactly the words of that meeting of 1782, adding that 'the claim of any other body of men to make laws for or govern Ireland is illegal, unconstitutional and a grievance intolerable to the people of the country'.[61]

From May 1905 Griffith's new policy generally began to be called the 'Sinn Fein' rather than the 'Hungarian' policy. The suggestion for the new name had been made to him by a young woman named Mary Butler, late in 1904, though the words had long been fairly commonly used as a motto for Irish self-reliance and had in fact been the early motto of the Gaelic League.[62] The first National Council Convention met on Tuesday, 28 November 1905, under the slogan Sinn Fein and with Edward Martyn in the chair. It seemed later to a supporter, looking back on the occasion, to have been a forlorn affair.[63]

Indeed contemplating now this relatively obscure and slightly cranky organization, with its eccentric president, Edward Martyn, who retained his position until 1908 when he retired to devote himself wholly to literature, and the dogged but rather gauche journalist, Arthur Griffith, who was its tireless overseer, it seems almost incredible that within seventeen years the course of Irish history should have been irrevocably altered in its name. Within seventeen years the journalist was to be president of an Irish Free State, with its own flag, its own army and as full a control of all its internal and external affairs as the Dominion of Canada. To almost no one at the time could such an achievement have seemed remotely possible, except possibly to Griffith himself.

It has been stated by an early supporter of Sinn Fein that Griffith did not expect to see Sinn Fein enjoy a political success with the electorate in his own lifetime,[64] but this underrates that rather blinkered persistence which was partly responsible for Sinn Fein's ultimate success. 'I have no doubt,' he wrote in October 1906 in his new paper, *Sinn Fein*, which replaced the *United Irishman* that year, 'of the acceptance of the Sinn Fein policy as the policy of all Ireland in the near future, and no doubt of its ultimate triumph'.[65] Yet, for all his confidence, that triumph was to come about in a way which even he cannot possibly have foreseen.

The actual political significance of Sinn Fein in these early days can best be gauged if it is seen as a minority of a minority – the political offshoot of an Irish-Ireland movement which had itself preferred to turn its back on politics. Even some Irish Irelanders treated it as a joke, like Moran with his reference in *The Leader* to Griffith's 'green Hungarian Band' and 'Mr Martyn's excellent troupe of broad comedians'.[66] Its impact in the open political arena was negligible. Apart from its minor successes in local elections for the Dublin Corporation it achieved nothing which could be seen openly as a threat to the Parliamentary Party. It contested only one by-election in the entire period, early in 1908, when it reached what was to seem for years the zenith of its success.

The political situation was then particularly favourable to Sinn Fein. The impotence of the Nationalist Party at Westminster had been recently clearly demonstrated anew. For after the General Election of 1906 the Liberals found themselves with such a large majority that they could safely ignore the Irish demand for Home Rule altogether. They had gone into the election with a wary assurance that they would not grant Home Rule without further reference to the electorate, and they proposed if returned to power

only to introduce a bill for devolution or decentralization of some administrative powers from Westminster to Dublin. Redmond had tacitly accepted
this procedure for Home Rule by instalments.[67] It was an election pledge
which the Liberals were scrupulous in observing when they found themselves
returned to power with an enormous majority. Tepidness towards Home
Rule had seemed to pay off with the electorate.

There can be little doubt that, on the tactical level, even for the Irish party,
the instalment procedure towards Home Rule was an intelligent one, for each
new step forward made the next both easier to ask for and easier to concede.
But Home Rule nationalism was by now an emotive issue or it was nothing,
for social and economic changes were already proceeding on their own
account with the Land Purchase Acts. If the national issue was to be raised
at all it had to be raised sufficiently emotively to satisfy a minimum national
self-respect. It now seemed for a moment as if the Parliamentary Party had
lost sight of this fact.

The Liberals' Devolution Bill when it came provided for a so-called Irish
Council of 106 members, 82 of whom would be elected and the rest nominated by the government. This Council was to have no law-making or tax-
raising ability whatever. Its sole function was to take over administrative
control for Ireland of eight of the forty-five government departments, the
most important of which were those of Education, Local Government, Public
Works, Agriculture and the Board created by Balfour for helping with the
backward districts of Ireland and known as the Congested Districts Board.
It offered a small sop to Irish national feeling only in so far as it proposed
to hive off into Irish control some of the administrative functions of the
unpopular Dublin Castle.

Augustine Birrell, the Liberal Chief Secretary for Ireland, introducing
the bill went out of his way to belittle its scope in an unashamed effort to
appease English critics of Home Rule. He virtually took credit for the fact
that the bill did not contain 'a touch or a trace, a hint or a suggestion of
any new legislative power or authority ...' and the Government Front
Bench actually cheered their opponent Balfour when he conceded that the
bill could not lead to a larger policy.[68]

Redmond, though naturally in these circumstances approaching the bill
warily, seemed tentatively favourable at first. He admitted that the one
important question to decide was the effect it would have on the prospects
for Home Rule and that this must be decided by a National Convention of
the party organization, which was now called the United Irish League. His
own personal answer was inclined to be 'that its enactment would be an aid
and not a hindrance to Home Rule'.[69]

The National Party newspaper, the *Freeman's Journal*, and the *Cork
Examiner*, expressed a similar view at first.[70] But it soon became clear that

the party was underestimating the sense of disappointment in the constituencies. The branches of the United Irish League preparing for the Party Convention gave the bill a very bad reception.[71] When Griffith, for Sinn Fein, described it as an insult, he was more in tune with public opinion in Ireland than at any time since the Boer War. He called for an implementation of the Sinn Fein policy by a withdrawal from Westminster. At a private meeting of Nationalist Members of Parliament a small group of five actually put forward a resolution to this effect, though they were quickly voted down and three of them eventually resigned from the party.

Faced by the evident strength of feeling at the United Irish League Convention the Parliamentary Party rapidly retracted its tentative welcome for the bill. A resolution expressing Griffith's view that the bill was an insult was unsuccessful, but a unanimous resolution was passed that the party should reject it. The Government was left with no alternative but to drop it.[72]

That the Parliamentary Party had been to some extent losing its grip on its supporters had been noticed by John Dillon, a less complacent political observer than most within the party, almost a year before.* But he tended to put the trouble down to organizational difficulties and particularly shortage of funds. He had little real fear of Griffith himself.[73]

'I have always been of the opinion,' he had written to Redmond in September 1906, 'that this Sinn Fein business is a very serious matter and it has been spreading pretty rapidly for the past year. But if the party and movement keep on right lines it will not become very formidable, because it has no one with any brains to lead it.'[74]

Now the party had shown signs of wavering from 'right lines' over the Irish Council Bill and, though it had been quickly put back on them, the voice of Sinn Fein had at least been clearly heard in the moment of shocked silence. It was in this favourable climate that Sinn Fein was enabled early in 1908 to challenge the party outright in a by-election at North Leitrim. The sitting Nationalist Party member, a young man named Charles Dolan, an effective orator if a bit long-winded,[75] had been one of the small group in the party which had proposed withdrawal from Westminster. He resigned and now offered himself for re-election in his constituency as a Sinn Fein candidate. It was a straightforward fight with the new party candidate.

Dolan and Sinn Fein were overwhelmingly defeated, winning just over a quarter of the total poll. It is a measure of the political insignificance of Sinn Fein hitherto that this was regarded by Griffith as something of a triumph. Tim Healy agreed with him that it meant a new political era was beginning.[76] They were both wrong in the short term. But in the sense that a more serious alternative to the party than Fenianism was now on the political map they were right.

* See above, p. 141

In 1909, however, the year after the North Leitrim by-election, political developments at Westminster began to take a favourable turn for the Irish Nationalist Party, with the prospect of a head-on clash between the Commons and the House of Lords, and the need of the Liberals for Irish Nationalist support. After the election of 1910, holding the balance between the two great English parties in the Commons, the Nationalists were once again in a position to force the Liberals to commit themselves to a new Home Rule Bill. And though the powers of the House of Lords had to be dealt with first, this was in any case an essential preliminary to the passing of a Home Rule Bill. Suddenly it seemed as if the prospects for Home Rule and the Nationalist Party had never been so bright and Ireland warmed to both.

Griffith, who recognized frankly that in this developing situation such support as had been slowly coming Sinn Fein's way was slipping back to the party, accepted what he called a 'self-denying ordinance' in order to give Redmond a fair chance and full freedom to secure Home Rule by his own methods. If, however, the Parliamentary Party were to fail, he said, 'Sinn Fein must be ready to form the rallying centre of a disappointed nation.'[7] As to the goal of Home Rule itself, Griffith and Sinn Fein accepted it, not – as the party and the majority of the country were prepared to do – as a final settlement of the national question but as a stepping-stone to national independence under a Dual Monarchy of the 1782 pattern. 'Sinn Feiners,' Griffith said in 1912, 'desired as much as any other section to see Home Rule established – not as a national settlement but because it might be used to Ireland's advantage.'[8] And on this basis of giving Redmond a free hand Sinn Fein virtually stood down and ceased from political activity.[9]

Of far greater importance all along than Sinn Fein's practical impact had been its position as a rallying point for all radical, dissatisfied and potentially disappointed individual nationalists in Ireland. The hybrid nature of its support with an overlap of poets, eccentrics, members of the Irish Republican Brotherhood, politically-minded Gaelic Leaguers and frustrated parliamentarians had been the movement's chief characteristic. Many lone wolves with a romantic or dogmatic or otherwise obsessional love of Ireland that had been born of Irish history, but frustrated in the present, gravitated towards Sinn Fein. And as with every movement that attracts rebels there were those who put into their love of Ireland obscure psychological motivations of their own.

Among the more extreme of such figures were some drawn from what would normally have been thought of as the Protestant ascendancy. Maud Gonne was one of these. Another woman from the same upper-class background was Constance Gore-Booth, born of a land-owning Protestant family that had lived for centuries in County Sligo. After breaking away from her family in fairly traditional style by going to art school first in London and then in Paris, she had married an attractive Polish Count named Markievicz and returned to live in Ireland at the beginning of the century. She had already met Yeats when he had visited the Gore-Booth family house, Lissadell, in County Sligo. There a Master of the Sligo Hunt had once described her as the equal of any good rider, man or woman, he had ever known,[80] and Yeats himself was to write of her:

> When long ago I saw her ride
> Under Ben Bulben to the meet
> The beauty of her countryside
> With all youth's lonely wildness stirred ...

Her intellect was not great and her artistic talent was no better than second rate, but it was this spirit of the hunting-field, and a lonely wildness that endured beyond all the physical ravages of time, which she was to carry into Irish nationalist politics.

Constance Markievicz had contributed money to that Irish theatre which Yeats and Lady Gregory founded at the Abbey. Her own and her husband's interest in painting had led her into Irish Ireland circles principally through George Russell, the painter and poet 'A.E.' who worked for Sir Horace Plunkett. But she was still attending fashionable receptions at Dublin Castle as late as 1904.[81] It was not until 1908 when she was in her fortieth year that she plunged suddenly into Irish nationalism, having accidentally found a copy of Griffith's *Sinn Fein* lying about a hall in which she was rehearsing some amateur theatricals.[82] She read an article about Robert Emmet who until then she had vaguely thought a Fenian.[83] She now made up for lost time with a vengeance. She joined Maud Gonne's national women's organization Daughters of Ireland (Inghinidhe nah Eireann) and before the end of 1908 was earning her own mention in Griffith's paper *Sinn Fein* for her nationalist activity.[84] At the fifth annual convention of what was now called the Sinn Fein Organization in 1909 she was elected to its council.[85] 'Ahland' was the manner in which, in her upper-class accent, Constance Markievicz always pronounced her country's name, but it was Caitlin ni Houlihan she now followed for the rest of her life with a dedication which ironically was eventually to earn her Yeats's bitter condemnation.[86]

Another wayward individual Protestant early drawn towards Sinn Fein, though he spent much of his life out of Ireland altogether, was a tall bearded figure from the glens of Antrim named Roger Casement. Casement had won some renown in the consular service for a devastating report published in 1904 on Belgian atrocities in the Congo. He, too, was to sacrifice himself in the cause of Caitlin ni Houlihan, to whom he had long been in thrall. It was, he said, soon after the Congo report was published in 1904, his sensitiveness to oppression as an Irishman that had made him take up the cause of the Congo native so insistently.[87] Early in 1905 he contributed an article to Griffith's *United Irishman* about his father who had helped the

Hungarian patriot, Kossuth.[88] Later the same year he was recommending in a private letter that the Irish Parliamentary Party, instead of hanging uselessly about Westminster, should come back to Ireland and form a National Executive with prime minister, ministers, etc. and 'create a confident reliant National mind in the country'.[89] But of course he recognized that there was not the slightest likelihood of such a thing happening. And before returning to consular service, this time in South America, in the autumn of 1906, he expressed admiration for Griffith in what otherwise seemed to him a bleak outlook for Irish national consciousness.[90]

Casement liked to insist that his address while abroad on consular service was not 'British Consulate' but 'Consulate of Great Britain and Ireland';[91] and he turned his mind frequently to the prospects which a nationalist Ireland might hope to have in the field of foreign relations. 'I am trying,' he had written in August 1905 to a young man he was befriending, 'to get some representative Irishmen interested in "foreign policy" and if we can succeed in getting a commercial agency into existence it will be a beginning. France will be our first field of effort ...'[92] Two years later, in 1907, in a letter to the same young man, he was saying that he wanted to see Ireland have her own team in the Olympic Games.[93]

This young man was a fellow Ulsterman, named Bulmer Hobson, whom Casement had first met at a Gaelic League festival in Antrim in 1904, and with whose prospects and material welfare he was to concern himself intermittently for the rest of his life. Hobson had come under the influence, while still at school, of Alice Milligan and Anna Johnston and their monthly magazine, the *Shan Van Vocht*. He had early declared his support for Griffith and had on his own account started up a number of nationalist-minded organizations, together with another young Ulsterman from the Falls Road area of Belfast, Denis McCullough.

Both McCullough and Hobson became sworn members of the IRB and represented in it a new wave which tried to reanimate the organization. This, in John MacBride's long absence abroad, had sunk back into inactivity under the dead hand of the older and longer-established members.[94] Together in 1905 they founded so-called Dungannon clubs, named after the meeting place of the Volunteers of 1778, and soon engaged as a full-time organizer for these another young man, Sean MacDermott, from County Leitrim, who had been earning his living in Belfast as a bar-tender and tram conductor.[95] All these young men found a natural rallying point in Griffith's activity in Dublin, culminating in the organization which became Sinn Fein.

In fact, for the greater part of the first decade of the century Griffith, though he himself left the IRB in 1906, acted far more than the IRB as a rallying point for active republican thinking, as well as for those more inclined towards his own slowly evolving ideas. In the early days the *United Irishman* had received substantial subsidies to enable it to keep going from

John Devoy's republican Clan-na-Gael in America,[96] and John MacBride had written to Devoy at that time: 'The *United Irishman* at present supplies the place of organizers in Ireland and is at least equal to a dozen.'[97] The Fenian representation on Cumann na Gaedheal and the National Council was always strong, and Hobson who for a short time in 1905 edited a new paper called *The Republic* was proud to declare himself simultaneously a Sinn Feiner.[98] Another young republican, an organizer for the IRB named Sean T. O'Kelly, one day to be President of the first internationally recognized Irish Republic, worked as Honorary Secretary on the National Council's executive in 1907.[99]

In the North Leitrim by-election in 1908 the principal organizer on behalf of the Sinn Fein candidate, Dolan, was the young man whom Hobson and McCullough had brought into the IRB and made an organizer of the Dungannon clubs, Sean MacDermott.[100] After the by-election defeat MacDermott continued to be described as a 'Sinn Fein organizer', and as such he lectured at a National Council meeting attended by the old dynamiter Tom Clarke, recently returned from America to live in Ireland.[101]

Clarke, Griffith's paper announced, had set up in business as a tobacconist and was acting as an agent for a special Irish stamp, sales of which were to help finance a new project for a Sinn Fein daily paper to replace the weekly.[102] Many other names besides MacDermott's and Clarke's, all to play vital parts in the near future of Ireland – Cosgrave, Cathal Brugha, the brothers Patrick and Willie Pearse, the O'Rahilly – are to be found associated with Sinn Fein activity at this time. A rather imprecise association of men, whose dedication to a fuller independence than Home Rule seemed more important than their differences about what exactly that independence was to be, or how it was to be achieved, was in being under the name Sinn Fein. It was an imprecision which was never wholly sorted out and which ultimately was to prove disastrous.

In 1909, as Griffith withdrew into political inactivity to give Redmond a chance with Home Rule, the republican elements associated with Sinn Fein expressed themselves as more and more dissatisfied. By August 1909 Hobson 'was considering whether or not he should throw the whole thing up'.[103] Another young Ulster IRB man, named Patrick McCartan, a former medical student and friend of Hobson and McCullough, was writing to Devoy in the States in March 1910 that 'things here' are in a queer mess and nobody knows what to make of it all ... the Executive, the Resident Executive and other humbugs will be gravely elected by the frequenters of the club where the children will be taught to break Ireland's chains with their song.... McCullough, Countess Markievicz talk of the advisability of all clearing out of it and leaving them to go their own way.' Others on the executive, he said, including the IRB man Sean T. O'Kelly, 'all trimmed when they attended the meetings.... So you see there is not much hope.'[104]

What was interesting was the tacit admission that the only source of hope for republicans, if there was to be any, was Griffith and his organization. In 1911 an IRB paper, *Irish Freedom*, edited by Bulmer Hobson, was started in order to preach a traditionally outspoken and active line. But the IRB was not in itself strong or even confident enough to make a political impact on its own; it needed some other organization to work through. Griffith's, which had seemed so promising, was now in the light of his own new position disappointing. But if not round Griffith, where could they rally effectively? For the time being there seemed no answer.

Meanwhile, for the average citizen the IRB was popularly thought to have become defunct years ago. Both it and Sinn Fein's momentary flash in the pan seemed irrelevant. All eyes in Ireland were turned on Westminster where at last, after nearly twenty years, the people's representatives seemed set to win Home Rule. After such a long time in which Home Rule had been remote, it came suddenly into very sharp focus and in the new atmosphere of Irish-consciousness seemed all the more worth winning.

10

Asquith and the Third Home Rule Bill

The Liberal Party approached Home Rule in 1910 in a quite different spirit from that in which it had launched the first Home Rule Bill in 1886 and the second in 1893. The idealistic sense of crusade with which Gladstone had invested the issue had largely disappeared. Home Rule had become more a question of political arithmetic: 272 Unionists opposed by 272 Liberals, in a House of Commons which also contained 42 Labour and 82 Irish Nationalists, equalled Home Rule.* It was as crude as that. The fact does much to explain a certain lack of total determination in pressing the issue home, which finally proved fatal to it. The Liberals, subconsciously at least, were prepared for some compromise from the start.

Though Irish Home Rule had continued after 1893 to be theoretically one of the party's basic philosophical tenets, a policy of disengagement from any practical concern with it had been deliberately adopted in 1899, ironically by Gladstone's son Herbert, then the Liberal Chief Whip.[1] He had taken careful soundings of the party on his appointment to that post and found a general disposition to regard Home Rule as an electoral handicap. An official policy of 'stand and wait' was formulated, giving, as Herbert Gladstone put it, 'plenty of scope for individual divergencies. The flag might be nailed by some, while others might to some extent dissociate themselves from the question.'[2] The party had gone into the election of 1900 publicly declaring that it would 'let that question sleep awhile'.[3]

But after the Liberal defeat of 1900 the difficulty of papering over differences on a matter so close to the party's soul had become evident. The internal debate was fought out in the open in a manner that permanently sapped some of the Liberals' vigour on the whole issue. Positions within the party ranged across a wide spectrum. Rosebery, the former leader who had succeeded Gladstone as prime minister for a short time, now emerged from retirement to call for 'a clean slate' in Liberal policies and an abandonment of 'the fly-blown phylacteries of the past', by which he meant principally Home Rule. The new leader, Campbell Bannerman, a strong

* The figures are those for the second of the 1910 elections.

Home Ruler, equated Rosebery's clean slate with 'a white sheet' and declared that Liberal policy should be based on principles and not on electoral expediency.[4] Somewhere in the middle, but inclining more to the anti-Home Rule position of Lord Rosebery, had been Henry Herbert Asquith, the ambitious son of a small Yorkshire woollen manufacturer, and member for East Fife since 1886. Gifted with an effortless intellectual mastery of most subjects to which he turned his mind, Asquith had attained the post of Home Secretary in Gladstone's last government. By 1910 he was fifty-eight, in the prime of life for a politician.

As far back as September 1901 Asquith had publicly declared that Liberals should never again take office if they were dependent on the Irish members for a majority in the House of Commons.[5] In February 1902 he actually became a vice-president of Lord Rosebery's Liberal League, founded to promote the ex-premier's anti-Home Rule views, and he explained to his constituency chairman in East Fife that since the Home Rule policy had proved a failure the Liberals must dissociate themselves from all obligation to a third Home Rule Bill if returned to office.[6] In rather typical fashion he added that the party did still have an obligation to find ways of reconciling Ireland to the British Empire and of relieving the pressure of business on the Imperial Parliament at Westminster, but that these goals could only be arrived at 'by methods which carry with them, step by step, the sanction and sympathy of British opinion'.[7] It was this cautious 'step by step' principle that finally became the agreed Liberal policy for the 1906 election, with the reluctant acquiescence of the leader, Campbell Bannerman.

'If we are to get a majority in the next House of Commons,' Asquith had written to Herbert Gladstone shortly before that election, 'it can only be by making it perfectly clear to the electors that ... it will be no part of the policy of the new Liberal government to introduce a Home Rule Bill in the new parliament.'[8]

And it was on this understanding that the Liberals had gone before the electorate and triumphed. The abortive Irish Council Bill of 1907 was the only step taken towards Irish Home Rule during the four years' Liberal government that followed.* In 1908 Campbell Bannerman died and Asquith became prime minister. And when, after two successive general elections in 1910 with almost identical results, the Liberals were left dependent for their parliamentary majority on the Irish, it was ironically Asquith who introduced to the House of Commons the third Home Rule Bill in April 1912.

But if not really a Home Ruler by conviction, Asquith was by temperament, ambition and intellectual aptitude a politician of great skill and intelligence. A living embodiment of the principle that politics is both the art of the possible and the art of the unavoidable, he took in his stride the

* See above, pp. 158–9.

realization that with the Liberals dependent on Irish support for a majority in the House of Commons the time had come for some substantial measure of Home Rule. 'Solvitur ambulando', or 'taking it on the curve', as he himself put it on two different occasions, was the cardinal principle of his political technique. Applied to the issue of Home Rule this inevitably meant a shallower level of commitment than that of the Irish nationalist who saw in Home Rule the final resolution of seven centuries of discord. But having satisfied himself that there was no possibility of a workable compromise on Home Rule to be obtained by agreement with the Conservatives, Asquith was prepared to assume towards the issue an uncompromising dedication, at least until such time as the need for compromise might or might not enforce itself.[9]

In one essential respect Asquith was in a much stronger position to carry Home Rule than Gladstone had ever been. The power of the House of Lords permanently to veto any bill had been removed the year before. This vital constitutional change, first demanded by the need to pass the Liberal 'People's Budget' of 1909 and now enshrined in the Parliament Act of 1911, had been the result of two years' mounting constitutional crisis involving two general elections in 1910. Throughout the crisis, Irish support for the Liberals in the House of Commons had been the decisive factor, and the implications for Home Rule of the abolition of the Lords' veto had never been far from Irish nationalists' minds. Though the two elections of 1910 had been fought by the Liberals on the specific issues of the Budget and the Lords' veto, Asquith, as part of a political bargain with the Irish, had to give them a clear public commitment to Home Rule, and he did this at the Albert Hall on 10 December 1909. Liberal policy, he there declared, was 'a policy which, while explicitly safeguarding the supremacy and indefectible authority of the Imperial Parliament, will set up in Ireland a system of full self-government in regard to purely Irish affairs'.[10] He had kept further pronouncements on the subject to the minimum in the course of the two elections, and 1911 had been occupied chiefly with the passage of the Parliament Bill.

But now in 1912 the Irish Nationalists were to be finally rewarded for their two-year-long support. As a result of the Parliament Act any bill rejected by the House of Lords could, if passed through the Commons again in two more consecutive sessions, automatically qualify for the royal assent and become law regardless of the Lords. Theoretically there was now nothing to stop the Liberals, with their Irish-based majority in the Commons, from passing a Home Rule Bill.

It was this very seeming inevitability that was to put such desperate vigour into the anti-Home Rule cause. A sense of unfairly imposed impotence dominated the opposition. If Asquith, the Liberals and the Irish Nationalists were theoretically in an unassailable position, the anti-Home Rulers became determined that it should not be theory alone that counted. Two important political factors lent them dynamism and strength. One was the urgent need for the Conservative Party to unite firmly on a good electoral issue after their embarrassing internal divisions over tariff reform. The other was the extent of the organization already in being in North-East Ulster dedicated to practical opposition to Home Rule at all costs.

Organized practical opposition to Home Rule from Ulster already had a long history. Naturally, the peaks of such organization had been achieved at moments when the danger seemed the greatest, that is to say, at the time of the two abortive Home Rule Bills of 1886 and 1893. Once those specific dangers were past, there had been a tendency for activity to lapse and intense emotion to wane, though the Orange Lodges ensured the permanence of at least a nucleus organization. However, in the first decade of the twentieth century a more subtle danger had appeared for the die-hard Unionists of Ulster, which had led to the construction of a permanent defensive organization on a more sophisticated political basis than that merely of the Orange Lodges. This danger was the appearance among Unionists themselves of a movement favouring the 'devolution' of at least some statutory powers to an Irish body, a proposal which looked to die-hard Unionists very much like a proposal for Home Rule by instalments.

This 'devolution' idea took shape under the aegis of the Irish Reform Association, a body sponsored by the Earl of Dunraven, a liberal-minded Unionist landlord who in 1903 had played a prominent part in negotiations leading to the great Land Purchase Act of that year. The Reform Association's plans eventually came to nothing, but the crisis to which they gave rise in 1904 sounded the alarm for all orthodox Unionists.

Through a misunderstanding the Under-Secretary of the day, Sir Anthony Macdonell, a Catholic whose brother was a member of the Nationalist Party, involved Dublin Castle more deeply and more sympathetically with the Reform Association's plans for devolution than the Chief Secretary, George Wyndham, intended. When this became apparent there was an explosion of wrath in the Unionist Party and though Wyndham publicly dissociated himself from the project he was eventually compelled to resign. The whole incident touched a most sensitive nerve in the Ulster Unionist temperament, already alerted by such conciliatory measures as the Local Government Act of 1898, the increasingly generous land-purchase arrangements and other aspects of 'killing Home Rule by kindness'. A suspicion was excited of 'softness towards Irish nationalism on the part of the adminstration', and the fear aroused that Ulster Unionists might be taken in the rear while facing the orthodox Home Rule enemy in front.

Within two days of the breaking of the devolution crisis of 1904, two Ulster Unionist Members of Parliament had declared it 'an opportune moment to revive on a war footing for active work the various Ulster Defence Associations'.[11] The practical consequence was the establishment in March

1905 of an Ulster Unionist Council. 'Consistent and continuous political action' was to be the watchword.[12] Thus when, in 1911, after the passing of the Parliament Act, the real crisis and the real enemy had to be faced in circumstances of grim finality, the Protestants of Ulster were prepared and an effective organization was in being and active.

It was an organization incomparably more professional than anything that had been seen in 1886 or 1893. In November 1910, even before the results of the second election of that year were known, the Ulster Unionist Council had opened an armament fund.[13] Colonel Saunderson, the colourful leader of the Ulster Unionists in the two previous crises, had died in 1906. His place had been taken for a few years by the English Conservative Walter Long, MP for Dublin South. But in the first General Election of 1910 Long had been returned for a London seat and the Ulster Unionists had to look round for another leader. Their choice fell on the senior Member for Dublin University, a Southern Irishman who enjoyed wide renown as the leading advocate of his day and who had been Solicitor General in the last Conservative government. His name was Sir Edward Carson.

Carson was fifty-five in 1910, and though something of a hypochondriac was then at the peak of those powers which had brought him such success and wealth at the bar. Courage, single-mindedness, clear-sightedness and determination, but above all an unquestionable and unflinching honesty of purpose, were his salient characteristics. Descended on both sides of his family from Protestant settlers who had first come to Ireland two centuries before, he was an Irishman whose devotion to the country of his birth was as great as his devotion to its union with the rest of the British Isles. 'It's only for Ireland that I'm in politics,' he said on one occasion, and on another: 'It's only for the sake of the Union that I am in politics.'[14] The two were indistinguishable in his mind and formed a single emotion. 'Heaven knows,' he said a few weeks after his wife died in 1913, 'my one affection left me is my love for Ireland.'[15]

He believed in order and discipline and firm government, and thought that administration of such things by the British Parliament through Dublin Castle was in the best interests of his country. But he was no blind reactionary. While a student at Trinity College, Dublin, he had spoken in the Historical Society's debates in favour of women's rights and the abolition of capital punishment.[16] And when nearly twenty years later he allowed his name to go forward as a candidate to represent his old college in Parliament objections were raised to him on the grounds that he was tainted with liberalism.[17] When he was finally elected it was as a Liberal Unionist.

Carson's work at the bar in Ireland, where he made his name and had been Crown Prosecutor before moving to England, had confirmed in him a natural distaste for the lawlessness and disorder with which all attempts to change the social and political *status quo* in Ireland were inevitably associated. On circuit in the eighties at the height of the Plan of Campaign* he had shown some personal courage in expressing his disdain for the mob at Mitchelstown on a day when three people were killed there by the RIC. Yet he did not allow his dislike of his country's popular movements to warp his attitude towards the people themselves. 'We welcome,' he once declared, curiously echoing something Parnell had once said, 'aye and we love, every individual Irishman, even though opposed to us."[18] Though a Protestant he was a staunch defender, in an Irish rather than a Protestant way, of Catholic claims for university education. 'Honourable Members in their hearts,' he said on one occasion in the House of Commons, 'are afraid of something or other connected with the Catholic religion which they will not suggest and which they will not explain. I ask, what is this fear of a Catholic University? ... Do you think that the Catholics of Ireland will be worse off with the enlightenment of a university education than they are now when they are deprived of it?"[19]

It was only because Carson believed passionately that Irishmen would be worse off with Home Rule that he so steadfastly opposed it. When, in his speech against Home Rule in a debate in the Commons in February 1911, he said that he had first most earnestly and thoroughly considered whether it might be of any benefit to Ireland, it was impossible not to believe that he spoke the truth.[20] The worst that can be said of him as an Irishman is that, unlike Parnell, he over-readily identified Ireland with the interest of his own class.

Carson was incapable of taking up something he did not intend to go through with. Hints during 1910 of certain Conservative inclinations to compromise on Home Rule had exasperated him and, though they came to nothing, it was a possible failure of determination that he saw as the principal menace to the anti-Home Rule cause. 'I wish I could be in Ulster,' he wrote to Lady Londonderry in January 1911, '... to know whether men are desperately in earnest and prepared to make great sacrifices.'[21] And later that year, appalled by the Conservative leadership's attitude of resignation towards the Parliament Bill, he wrote to James Craig, Member of Parliament for East Down and the most active member of the Ulster Unionist Council: 'What I am very anxious about is to satisfy myself that the people over there really mean to resist. I am not for a mere game of bluff, and, unless men are prepared to make great sacrifices which they clearly understand, the talk of resistance is no use.'[22] In this respect Craig was his man.

Son of a self-made whisky millionaire, James Craig had been a founder member of the Belfast Stock Exchange as a young man and had then fought with gallantry and been wounded and taken prisoner in the Boer War. Affection for his home background in Ulster and for the Empire which he had helped to see through the testing time of the war provided the simple emotional inspiration for this solid upright man of independent means when he decided to enter politics in 1903. It was a vision not in any way complicated, as was that of Carson, the Southern Irishman, by thoughts for the rest of Ireland. Now that the testing time had come for Ulster itself, as Craig saw it, he devoted all his energies and considerable cool organizing ability to what he saw as Ulster's cause, and filled the role of Carson's principal lieutenant.

It was Craig who arranged the first big Ulster demonstration of the new anti-Home Rule epoch at his own home of Craigavon just outside Belfast on 23 September 1911, six months before the bill was introduced. Here, after a wet morning, the sun suddenly came out and Carson spoke to an awed crowd of some fifty thousand Orangemen and Unionists assembled on the lawns in front of the house. It was his first big speech to the Protestants of Ulster as their leader in the new crisis and he began as he intended to go on.

'I now enter into compact with you,' he declared, 'and with the help of God you and I joined together ... will yet defeat the most nefarious conspiracy that has ever been hatched against a free people.'

He proceeded to outline how to do this:

'We must be prepared, in the event of a Home Rule Bill passing, with such measures as will carry on for ourselves the government of those districts of which we have control. We must be prepared ... the morning Home Rule passes, ourselves to become responsible for the government of the Protestant Province of Ulster.'[23]

His audience had also begun as they intended to go on. At least one of the contingents of Orangemen who had marched the two miles out from Belfast to Craigavon that day in columns of four, particularly impressed people by their order and discipline. They had already been practising drill.

It was soon discovered that an authorization to drill could be obtained quite legally from a JP, provided the object was to help maintain the rights and liberties of the United Kingdom's constitution.[24] From the beginning of 1912 more and more licences for drilling were applied for and by the time of the next great Ulster demonstration at Balmoral, a suburb of Belfast, on 9 April 1912, two days before the Home Rule Bill was introduced, there was a distinctly military flavour to the proceedings. Over 100,000 men, it was reckoned, marched past a saluting base in columns while a Union Jack, said to be the largest ever made, flew from a ninety-foot flagstaff in the centre of the grounds. Carson must have been deeply reassured by what he saw. His one fear was still that people would think they did not mean business. His own mind, he wrote privately, was implacably made up for 'very drastic action in Ulster'.[25] At a private dinner a fortnight before the Balmoral demonstration he had been introduced by Craig to Lord Roberts, who, though retired, was the senior Field Marshal of the British Army. 'I hope,' wrote Carson significantly, 'something will come of it.'[26]

At the same time, the most significant feature of the whole Balmoral demonstration was the presence on the saluting base of the new leader of the Conservative opposition in the House of Commons, himself a Scot of Ulster descent, Andrew Bonar Law. 'There will not be wanting help from across the Channel when the hour of battle comes,' Law had said on arrival in Ulster the day before, and, as an Ulster Scot, he had spoken of the possible need for Ulster to be prepared to face a Bannockburn or Flodden.[27] At Balmoral itself he reassured his vast audience that the Conservative Party regarded their cause as the cause not of Ulster alone but of the Empire. The Conservatives, he declared, 'would do all that men could do to defeat a conspiracy as treacherous as had ever been formed against the life of a great nation'.[28] From this moment onwards there could be little doubt that the Conservatives intended to identify themselves at least as much as twenty years before with the extra-parliamentary force gathering in Ulster. Bonar Law said himself that they were 'even more in earnest than before'.[29]

Two days later, on 11 April 1912, Asquith introduced the new Home Rule Bill in the House of Commons.

The principle of Home Rule had already been much debated since the new Parliament's inauguration in 1911. For although the first major business to concern this Parliament had been the veto of the House of Lords and the passage of the Parliament Bill, it had been impossible to argue about that without at the same time discussing the first immediate result which the removal of the veto was likely to lead to: namely, Home Rule for Ireland. Even in the Debate on the king's speech in February 1911 which had not mentioned Ireland at all, one Unionist member had threatened civil war if a Home Rule Bill were to go through.[30] Another Unionist member in the same debate, asserting that Ulster could not be coerced, had cried prophetically: 'Try it. Call out the British troops to compel Ulster and see what happens!'[31]

To understand the intensity of passion and fury which the prospect of Home Rule for Ireland unleashed among Conservatives during the years 1911–14 it is necessary first to realize that the pattern of the British Constitution which is taken for granted in the second half of the twentieth century was not yet quite consolidated. Indeed, it was the events of these years which finally consolidated that pattern. What is assumed today to be part of the essential working of the constitution was then in the hazier area of doubt and imprecision which characterizes all formative periods. One essential element in today's constitution, the supremacy of the Commons over the Lords, was after all, in 1911, still being debated, and only introduced as a new feature at the end of that year. Even the role of the monarch seemed less firmly circumscribed than it is today. Nothing in fact illustrates better the slightly different constitutional climate of that time than that it should have been possible for one of the leading legal figures of the day, Carson himself, to make the following bitter joke and consider it nothing but a joke.

'Apparently,' he wrote in the middle of 1912, after reading an article in the *Spectator* which maintained that the royal assent to a bill was a formal, automatic affair, 'if the King was asked to sign a bill for the abolition of the monarchy he must as a constitutional sovereign obey!'[32]

This would not be questioned today, but such a possibility seemed then preposterous to Conservatives like Carson who could write of the king: 'I am told he is saturated with the idea of "constitutionalism" which he translates into doing everything his PM tells him. What a good King!'[33]

However, even such a disappointingly constitutional sovereign as George v was to try to assert himself before the crisis was out.

Only if this subtly different constitutional climate of the day is appreciated can the indignation of the Conservatives, and their feeling that the normal limits of constitutional action had been virtually suspended, be fairly understood. By modern constitutional conventions Asquith's political behaviour, if adroit, was scrupulously correct. At the same time, to some people it was questionable; to others, actually 'a conspiracy'. Asquith in his own political interest had used his Irish support to remove the Lords' veto. He had then paid the price for such support in the form of a Home Rule Bill which had not been the main issue of either election but against which the Lords were now impotent. This was the substance of the charge against the government.

'They have sold the Constitution,' Bonar Law told his Ulster audience. 'They have sold themselves and they thought they could sell you, but you were not theirs to sell. Under such circumstances, in order to try to force this calamity upon you ... it would not be by government at all, it would be by tyranny, naked and unashamed, and tyranny not the less real because the tyrants have usurped their power not by force, but by fraud.'[34] When later in the summer Bonar Law addressed a giant Unionist meeting at Blenheim in England he deliberately paraphrased Balfour's famous words of twenty years before, which he had carefully studied, about the tyranny of parliamentary majorities being as bad as the tyranny of kings.* 'There are things stronger than parliamentary majorities,' was the way he now put it, adding, 'I can imagine no length of resistance to which Ulster will go, in which I shall not be ready to support them ...'[35] Law had already told the king himself at a dinner at Buckingham Palace in the course of a conversation which made the king blush: 'They may say your assent is a purely formal act and the prerogative of veto dead. That was true as long as there was a buffer between you and the House of Commons, but they have destroyed that buffer and it is true no longer.'[36]

Both in the preliminary discussion of Home Rule during the passage of the Parliament Bill, and in the early debates on the new Home Rule Bill itself, argument concentrated less than on the two previous occasions on the old question of real Irish intentions and the danger of ultimate separation. In

* See above, p. 124.

the first stages there was some repetition of the familiar quotations from Parnell and other Nationalists still members of the House, suggesting that there were no final bounds to the measure of Irish freedom to which nationalists aspired. And though many were prepared to treat such remarks as the necessary exaggerations of a bygone political age, Carson made a neat point when he complained: 'We are always being told we must trust the Irish Nationalist members. But on what ground? Upon the ground that we ought not to believe a single word they ever said.'[37] On the other hand, whatever they might have said in the past, Redmond, Dillon, O'Brien and co. had now publicly committed their careers to a nationalism which fully accepted the overriding supremacy of the Imperial Parliament. In his very first speech in the new Parliament of 1911 Redmond, as Irish leader, had once again declared that a Home Rule incorporating this principle would be a final settlement and had pledged his countrymen to accept it as such.[38]

In general, many fundamental changes had taken place in the Irish situation in the previous twenty years, and both sides tried to argue from them to their advantage. Perhaps the most powerful new argument was that used by Carson when he said that there was now hardly a single special Irish grievance left for an Irish Parliament to deal with, as they had all been dealt with by the Imperial Parliament.[39]

Inasmuch as the vast majority of Irishmen were now owners of their farms, that there was since 1909 a Catholic University and since 1898 representative local government, there was undoubtedly much truth in this. But typically, coming from a man of Carson's class, such a view left out of account all the emotional residue of earlier suffering and the consequent really very modest demand for some national self-respect under the name of limited Home Rule.

The transformation of the atmosphere of Ireland could equally well be used to argue, as Winston Churchill did, that it was now very much safer to give Ireland Home Rule. The Irish question, said Churchill, no longer presented itself in the same 'fierce and tragic guise.... Rebellion, murder and dynamite, these have vanished from Ireland.'[40] At the same time, the success of self-government conferred on South Africa seemed to augur well for Ireland.

The practical workings of the 1898 Local Government Act were cited as evidence by both sides. A Unionist complained that 'even in the appointment of doctors the test has been one not of fitness for the post, but one of religion or being a good nationalist', to which Redmond's brother, Willie, replied indignantly that the proportion of local jobs given to Protestants in Catholic areas was very much fairer than the proportion of jobs given to Catholics in Protestant areas.[41] However, the weight of argument soon shifted away from the desirability of Home Rule for the greater part of Ireland. This, reluctantly, came to be virtually accepted as inevitable. The argument concentrated on whether or not, in the special circumstances in which the Home Rule Bill had been introduced, it was allowable to override the objections of 'Ulster'.

The bill itself was in general principle much the same as the two previous Home Rule Bills. It set up an Irish legislature with an Irish executive for purely domestic Irish affairs, while reserving for the Imperial Parliament all matters affecting the Crown, peace and war, the army, navy, international treaties, the imposition of most taxation in the first instance, and even, for a period of six years, control of the Royal Irish Constabulary – though control of the Dublin Metropolitan Police was to pass to the Irish immediately. The total supremacy of the Imperial Parliament over such an Irish Parliament was clearly stated and repeatedly emphasized by Asquith.

'We maintain,' he declared, '... unimpaired, and beyond the reach of challenge or question, the supremacy, absolute and sovereign, of the Imperial Parliament.'[42]

There were those Unionists who maintained that such legalistic supremacy would mean nothing. Balfour said it was like Kings of England continuing to call themselves Kings of France for several hundred years after they had been driven out of that country.[43] It was pointed out that such power existed equally over the Parliaments of the Dominions though no one would ever dream of trying to exercise it. But this was not on the whole a much debated issue, for the simple reason that the supremacy of the Imperial Parliament was something the Irish had no difficulty in accepting.

Redmond's support for the bill in Parliament was immediately echoed and confirmed by almost all Irishmen not only in Ireland but all over the world. The *Freeman's Journal* – the Nationalist Party paper – finding this Home Rule Bill 'the greatest, boldest and most generous of the three', forecast Irish reaction correctly when it declared that 'Ireland under this Bill, trusted and liberated, armed with all the powers necessary to the full development of her aspirations and her resources, will warmly reciprocate so splendid an invitation for final reconciliation between her and the people of England.'*[44] Unanimous resolutions congratulating Redmond and the party poured in from branches of the United Irish League (the Party organization), from Irish local authorities and from prominent Irish Nationalists in all parts of the United States and Australia, including Patrick Egan, former Treasurer of the Land League. Although in the general chorus of approval there were criticisms of some financial details of the bill, no voice was raised, except by the tiny Sinn Fein and Republican minority in Ireland and the extremists in America, to criticize the principle of the Imperial Parliament's supremacy or

* Items in the bill singled out for favourable comparison with earlier bills were: the use of the term 'parliament' rather than 'legislature', as previously; immediate control of the Judicial Bench and the Dublin Police; and the provision of a financial subsidy instead of, as previously, the demand for a financial contribution.

to say that in terms of the aspirations of Irish nationalism the bill was inadequate. A vast National Convention in Dublin passed a unanimous resolution welcoming the bill 'as an honest and generous attempt to settle the long and disastrous quarrel between the British and Irish nations'.[45] And when in January 1913 the bill passed its third reading by a Commons majority of 110, tar barrels and bonfires blazed in celebration of the Home Rule 'Triumph' all over Ireland and innumerable bands pumped out the strains of 'A Nation Once Again'.

But already there were unmistakable indications that such rejoicing was premature. Victory over the bill's Unionist opponents in Parliament was not what mattered so much as the possible action such opponents might take outside Parliament to prevent the bill becoming law under the procedures of the Parliament Act.

The chief rational argument with which anti-Home Rulers backed their increasingly menacing protest was that Home Rule had never been properly submitted to the electorate at the second election of 1910. It was true that the Liberals had done much at the time to avoid mentioning what was still thought of as a potentially embarrassing political issue. Only some 84 of the 272 successful Liberal candidates in England, Scotland and Wales had actually mentioned Home Rule at all in their election addresses, and these 84 did not include, significantly, the Prime Minister, the Chancellor of the Exchequer, the First Lord of the Admiralty, the Home Secretary, or the Chief Secretary for Ireland.[46] Asquith, fighting on the Lords' veto and wanting to keep Home Rule as much in the background as possible, had presented it, when compelled to refer to it at all, rather as a technical adjustment to the administrative arrangements for the United Kingdom than a concession to Irish national feeling. He had noticeably refrained from re-asserting the Liberals' commitment to it until a good number of the election results of December 1910 were declared.* However, it was also true, as Ramsay Macdonald among many other supporters of the government pointed out, that if the Liberals had not presented Home Rule as an issue at the election the Conservatives certainly had.[47] Almost every Conservative candidate had been at pains to stress that if the Liberals won on their main issue of the Lords veto, the way would then be open for them to pass Home Rule without further hindrance. 'He who gives a vote for the Parliament Bill,' the renowned constitutional lawyer Dicey had declared, 'most assuredly gives a vote for Home Rule for Ireland.' Though the Liberals could reasonably be censured for political cowardice, it could not reasonably be said that the British public had been unaware of the Home Rule question during the election. Reason, however, was fast fading into the background, and emotion was increasingly the spur to action.

The expressions 'Ulster' and 'coercing Ulster' had already assumed such

* Election results were then declared over a period of some weeks.

emotive force that it is necessary now to remind oneself of the facts behind them. The nine counties of Ulster contained, according to the 1911 census, 886,000 Protestants of all sects, and 690,000 Catholics. Though it is roughly reasonable to regard the Protestants as Unionists and the Catholics as Home Rulers, this was not literally quite so. A more accurate idea of the Ulster population's feelings can be obtained from election figures. On the basis of the second General Election of 1910 these gave a total of 103,367 Unionist votes and 94,073 Home Rule votes over the whole province. Looked at by other democratic standards: five of the nine Ulster counties had Nationalist Home Rule majorities and the other four Unionist majorities; while the distribution of Ulster's elected representatives in the House of Commons was, immediately after the 1910 election, sixteen Home Rulers to seventeen Unionists, but, after a by-election in Londonderry South early in 1913, seventeen Home Rulers to sixteen Unionists. There was thus actually a technical democratic majority of one in favour of Home Rule over the whole of Ulster. None of these figures seem to assert any very obvious right to special treatment by the Unionists of Ulster, given the fact that Ulster was itself only a minority of the whole unit of Ireland. (In the rest of Ireland by the 1911 census there were some 250,000 Protestants to 3,000,000 Catholics.)

But since democracy can never provide precise mathematical justice, an essential part of its successful functioning is the spirit in which it deals with those minorities which it inevitably overrides. In the British Constitution an unwritten safeguard is provided for minorities in parliamentary con-stituencies since each representative represents as well as he can, compatibly with his own conscience, those who compose the minority against him equally with those who vote for him. It could be argued that, in the Irish situation, regard for minorities had to be abnormally acute just because religious differences made it difficult for this spirit to be applied in the normal way. If a substantial minority cared principally for its Protestant religion it might reasonably be doubted whether the conscience of a predominantly Catholic Parliament and Executive could be rigorously exercised in its favour.

There were, it is true, special safeguards built into the Third Home Rule Bill to give the Protestants of Ulster disproportionate consideration. Apart from the overriding supremacy of the imperial legislature there was to be an Upper House or Senate whose members would be nominated, and over-representation of Ulster in the Lower House together with a provision by which both Houses should sit and vote together if there were a dispute be-tween the two. None of these safeguards, however, could provide the sort of absolute certainty Ulster Protestants wanted. They did not want reassurance. They simply did not want to be in a situation in which they needed re-assurance. They did not want any new arrangement at all. The political mentality of the Protestant Irishmen of the North had been conditioned long ago by a self-perpetuating fear and mistrust of Catholics. And such mistrust had been consciously activated by Conservative political interests for the past quarter of a century. Moreover, even if there were no genuine grounds at all for the Protestant's religious and economic fears, there would always be a psychological loss involved for Ulster Protestants in a Home Rule Ireland – the loss of that status identified by Lecky when he wrote of the penal law era, that 'the most worthless Protestant, even if he had nothing else to boast of, at least found it pleasing to think that he was a member of a dominant race'.[48]

There was an almost indistinguishable overlap of the irrational and the rational, of emotion and reason in the Ulster Protestant attitude. One of the reasoned arguments much used in support of the basic emotion was that if special treatment in the form of Home Rule was justified for Catholic Ireland, which was after all a minority of the United Kingdom, then Ulster Protestants who were a minority of Ireland were equally justified in seeking special treatment. But this argument could soon be reduced to an absurdity of democratic Chinese boxes. For there was also a Catholic minority within the Protestant minority within the Catholic majority. In any democracy which is to function effectively there must come an arbitrary point at which minorities must accept a majority decision they dislike. Since five of the nine counties had a Nationalist majority, and four of them a Protestant one, a possible arbitrary dividing point might reasonably be said to have existed there. This would have left the five counties of Donegal, Monaghan, Cavan, Tyrone and Fermanagh to go to a Home Rule Ireland and the other four to be allowed to remain within the United Kingdom as the majority of their inhabitants demanded.

Given the fact that the vast majority of Irish nationalists were in any case prepared to accept considerable qualifications to their 'nationalism', involving identification on many points with the rest of the United Kingdom, such a solution was, at that time, in terms of logic and reason, probably the best and most equitable that could have been devised. But logic and reason were not the prime movers on either side of the Irish situation. It was not only Ulster Protestants but Catholic Nationalists whose fundamental attitude was emotive: Home Rule itself was for the Irish nationalist a strange compromise between reason and emotion. William O'Brien, who now sat in the House of Commons at the head of a small group of independent Home Rule MPs had conveyed well the confused nature of such a compromise in his moving speech on the first reading of the Home Rule Bill. The Bill involved, he had said, 'a certain degree of renunciation, by Irish nationalists of the old school, of those dreams, perhaps only dreams, but dreams that came in the youth of some of us as the blood in our veins'. And he asked, reasonably, for a parallel sacrifice on the part of Unionists.

If much of the emotive dream was being sacrificed in the permanent limita-

tions of the Home Rule Bill, a bare minimum had to be retained if any illusion of that dream's fulfilment were to survive. The dream had been about
Ireland as a country, and the indispensable part of that dream, even for
Home Rulers, was that the country should still be Ireland as a whole. Thus,
though in a purely reasonable and logical atmosphere the exclusion of the
four counties of Derry, Down, Armagh and Antrim from the operation of
the Home Rule Bill might have seemed an intelligent solution, anyone who
really understood the nationalist element in Home Rule or comprehended the
emotive sacrifice of which O'Brien had spoken could have seen that to
exclude any part of Ireland permanently was simply not an acceptable
possibility.

Gladstone might well have understood this. Unfortunately, neither for
Asquith nor for the rest of the Liberal Cabinet was understanding of, or
identification with, the deep feelings behind Home Rule an important
motivation. Home Rule for them was merely a reasonable political necessity.
They worked within the framework of reason. Therefore, presented from
the start with 'Ulster's' obstruction to the whole principle of the bill, they
moved gradually towards the logical point of compromise, regardless of
the fact that it could never be acceptable to their Irish nationalist allies. This
point of compromise involved the exclusion of some part of Ulster, presumably at least the four predominantly Protestant counties of Derry, Down,
Antrim and Armagh.

Winston Churchill, First Lord of the Admiralty, perhaps because of the
identification of his father with the Ulster Unionist cause in 1886, had been
in favour of some such compromise even before the framing of the 1912
Bill. Lloyd George had backed him, but they had been over-ruled by Asquith
and the rest of the Cabinet. It was not in the nature of Asquith's political
skill to compromise before he had to. And yet Asquith's own pre-disposi-
tion to compromise on Home Rule was so long established that his position
was weak from the start. It was a fair enough gibe when F. E. Smith, the
brilliant Conservative Front Bench lawyer, said that it had always been
Asquith's policy to drop Home Rule whenever he had had the chance of
carrying it independently of the Irish. 'His haste in dropping it,' Smith added,
'is only equalled by the celerity with which he takes it up again as soon as he
sees he cannot live as a Minister without the votes of the Irish party.'[49]

He was probably relieved to hear Bonar Law himself, as early as the first
reading of the bill, hint at a reasonable point of compromise with a reference
to Ulster 'or if you do not like to hear it called Ulster, of the north-east
corner'.

In fact the broad lines of some eventual 'reasonable' solution were soon
being aired. On 2 May 1912 W. G. Agar-Robartes, the Liberal Member for
St Austell, on the second reading of the bill said that he thought there was
only one solution to the problem and that was to leave Down, Derry, Antrim

and Armagh out of the Home Rule scheme.[50] Just over a month later he introduced an amendment along these lines. The government opposed it, but the debate was useful to them in revealing something of the opposition's hand. For Bonar Law spoke in favour of the amendment and so did Carson though he declared that he could not make it his terms for Home Rule. He could not, he said, in the first place leave out Tyrone and Fermanagh from any such exclusion, and secondly he personally had to insist that he thought Home Rule would be disastrous for the rest of Ireland. But what the debate at least indicated was that Bonar Law would settle for exclusion on some terms. Since Carson's strength in Ulster, though increasingly effectively organized, was ultimately dependent on his support from Bonar Law and the Conservatives, this meant that he too would probably in the long run be prepared to settle for exclusion. He had even enumerated his minimum terms: the six counties of Derry, Down, Antrim, Armagh, Tyrone and Fermanagh. The government knew now at least that there was a safety valve.

Meanwhile Carson, ably assisted by Craig, set about further strengthening his practical position in Ulster. He was still worried that people in England did not seem to care in the same way as the people of Ulster cared, and a dramatic campaign to convey the depth and intensity of Ulster feeling was planned for the autumn of 1912. This centred round a 'Solemn League and Covenant' to resist Home Rule to be inaugurated in Belfast Town Hall, on 28 September, which was declared 'Ulster Day'. For ten days beforehand meetings were held all over Ulster, at which men paraded with wooden dummy rifles to fife and drum while Carson, F. E. Smith and other prominent Unionist orators addressed them, carrying unanimously time and time again the single resolution: 'We will not have Home Rule!'

On 28 September itself, in Belfast all shipyards and factories were closed and the day was devoted to the formal solemn ceremony of the signing of the covenant. After religious services in the churches, in which the hymn 'O God Our Help In Ages Past' epitomized the air of crisis, a procession headed by Carson and the faded yellow silk banner said to have been William III's at the battle of the Boyne marched through the streets to Belfast Town Hall, escorted by a guard of honour of 2,500 men in bowler hats, carrying walking sticks.[51] At the Town Hall Carson himself, with a silver pen, was the first to sign the pledge to refuse to recognize any Home Rule Parliament's authority. For the rest of that day tens of thousands streamed into the hall to desks arranged down a third of a mile of corridors to add their signatures. Many signed in their own blood. Within a few days it was found that 218,206 Ulstermen altogether had signed the Covenant while 228,991 women had signed a parallel declaration supporting them.

'Lions led by asses' was how the Liberal press had jeered at what it called the 'brayings of civil war' two years before.[52] But though there were still many English Liberals and Irish Nationalists who comforted themselves that

Carson was bluffing, Carson was not bluffing. Ulster Day and the Covenant made clear the area on which he was in deadly earnest. 'We will not have Home Rule' was the essence of the message. The unspoken accent was on the 'We'.

On New Year's Day 1913, Carson, in the House of Commons, moved an amendment to the Home Rule Bill to exclude all nine counties of Ulster and he was supported by Bonar Law. Though government supporters tended to dismiss the amendment as a 'wrecking amendment' designed merely to make things difficult for the bill as a whole, it was an important debate inasmuch as it once again suggested that both English parties were prepared to compromise in the long run. Bonar Law for his part declared that if Asquith were first to submit the Home Rule Bill to the electors and the electors were to approve, then he would no longer stand in its way.[53] And though the Ulstermen dissociated themselves from this viewpoint it proved that the Conservatives attached importance to seeming reasonable. Churchill, for the government, now declared: 'We shall not be found wanting if an opportunity occurs to grasp the prize of a settlement by consent and agreement. We recognize that such a settlement would involve real sacrifices from both parties.'[54] A fortnight later Asquith on the bill's third reading said: '... if we could meet the case, so far as it is founded on justice, *or even apprehension*, of those counties without doing injustice to Ireland as a whole we should be most glad and delighted to do so'.[55] And though he went on to say that exclusion of those four counties would violate the principles of democratic government, he had nevertheless opened up the possibility of *some* acceptable formula involving those counties.

Craig himself defined the Ulster position clearly. 'We all know,' he said, '... the vast majority of our fellow countrymen who are Nationalists in the South and West of Ireland will have Home Rule if this Bill becomes law, and we shall not have power to stop it. All we propose to do is to prevent Home Rule becoming law in our own part of the country.'[56]

To which William O'Brien replied that the nationalists were prepared to go to almost any lengths to meet the Ulstermen, 'with one exception – that is, the partition of our country'.[57]

The lines of battle were becoming clear.

11

Ulster Volunteers

The Ulstermen were taking no chances. In January 1913 the Ulster Unionist Council decided to raise an Ulster Volunteer Force of one hundred thousand men between the ages of seventeen and sixty-five. Organization of this force on a county basis through the machinery of the Orange Lodges and the Unionist clubs was soon proceeding fast. Drilling took place in Orange Halls usually with dummy wooden rifles ('one and eightpence in pitch pine, and one and sixpence in spruce' according to one advertisement),[1] but at the same time genuine rifles were beginning to appear from England, purchased by wealthy supporters of the movement.

By June 1913 recruiting for the Ulster Volunteer Force was ahead of expectations, and in that month Carson's private dinner with Lord Roberts of eighteen months before finally bore fruit. Roberts obtained for the Ulster Volunteer Force the services, as its commander, of a retired English General of the Indian army, Sir George Richardson. When Richardson arrived in Belfast in July to take up his post he found he had already fifty thousand men at his disposal. An efficient Headquarters Staff was organized, headed by another ex-Indian Army officer, Colonel Hacket Pain. It employed among others Captain Wilfrid Spender, who had recently secured his release from His Majesty's service, having been the youngest and one of the most brilliant staff officers in the British Army. At a review of fifteen thousand well-trained Volunteers at the Balmoral grounds near Belfast in September, Richardson took the salute with F. E. Smith acting as his galloper. 'Does anyone suppose,' Smith had asked in the House of Commons earlier that year, 'that any of us enjoy the prospect of playing a part for which so many of us are not obviously suited? I myself am a middle-aged lawyer, more at home, and I may perhaps add, more highly remunerated, in the law courts than I am likely to be on the parade ground.'[2]

Three days before, Carson had written to Bonar Law from Craigavon, saying that things were shaping towards a desire to settle on terms for the exclusion of Ulster. 'A difficulty arises, as to defining Ulster,' he wrote. 'My own view is that the whole of Ulster should be excluded but the minimum would be the six plantation counties, and for that a good case could be made.... Everything here,' he added, 'is going on splendidly ...'[3]

Meanwhile, Nationalists with what today seems unbelievable complacency treated the Ulster Volunteer Force as a joke. The *Freeman's Journal* much enjoyed itself in June 1913 when some 1,800 rifles labelled electrical plant were seized on arrival at Belfast. The paper headlined its story 'The Orange Farce' and 'Playing At Rebellion'.[4] Redmond himself was convinced that Carson was bluffing.

If Carson had been defying a government uncompromisingly determined to pass its own Home Rule Bill as it stood and to enforce without question what would then become the law of the land, it might have been reasonable to dismiss Carson's actions as bluff. But his position was by no means so isolated. In the first place, it was already clear that the Protestant Ulstermen were no longer trying to deny Home Rule to most of Ireland and were prepared to settle on the basis of some sort of Ulster exclusion. Second, there had been unmistakable signs that the government were prepared to be less than adamant. All Carson had to do was to remain adamant himself. The real bluff was the government's, and Carson was calling it. Redmond, it could be argued, should have been doing the same.

Redmond, however, does not seem to have become seriously alarmed about the way things were going until September 1913 when, while resting at Parnell's old shooting lodge of Aughavanagh in the Wicklow mountains, he read in *The Times* a most singular letter from a recently retired member of the Liberal Cabinet, Lord Loreburn.[5] Loreburn had been Asquith's Lord Chancellor until a year before, had helped draft the Home Rule Bill and had hitherto been one of its most uncompromising supporters. Now he wrote to *The Times* that in view of the Ulstermen's preparations ministers should be 'willing to consider proposals for accommodation', and he urged a conference to find a means of settlement by consent.

Lord Loreburn was not the only august personage who had been doing such thinking. The king, deeply concerned by the distressing constitutional prospect before him and unable altogether to suppress a personal sympathy for the Protestant Ulster point of view, had been taking the initiative to bring the two British parties together. As a result of conversations between Churchill and Bonar Law when both were staying at Balmoral in September 1913, two secret meetings took place a few weeks later between Asquith and Bonar Law. In the course of these they discussed their respective positions with remarkable frankness.[6]

By this time Redmond had been thoroughly alerted not only by reports of the Churchill–Law conversations, but also by a speech by Churchill himself at Dundee on 9 October 1913 in which he declared that Ulster's claim for special consideration, if put forward with sincerity, could not be ignored by the government. Clearly the aspect of the Home Rule Bill that concerned the satisfaction of Irish national aspirations was being lost to view. Redmond replied a few days later that 'Irish nationalists can never

be assenting parties to the mutilation of the Irish nation; Ireland is a unit. . . .
The two nation theory is to us an abomination and a blasphemy."[7]

Signs of anxiety and restlessness began to appear in Ireland itself. The
Bishop of Raphoe wrote to Redmond of 'a growing apprehension on the
part of a good many Catholics and Nationalists in the North of Ireland. . . .
If anything special is attempted for Ulster by the Government you will have
a most troublesome business in hand . . .'[8]

On 17 November 1913 Redmond received Asquith's account of his meeting with Bonar Law. Law, Asquith said, had proposed 'the total and permanent exclusion of Ulster from the bill – Ulster to mean an area to be
settled by agreement and discussion'.[9] Asquith – or so he told Redmond –
had flatly rejected this and suggested administrative autonomy for Ulster
within Home Rule, a solution which at this stage was the furthermost limit
of Irish Nationalist concession, preserving as it did the integrity of Ireland
but conferring what was sometimes known as Home Rule within Home Rule.
Law had turned this down. The conversation had been reported to the
cabinet and in the course of cabinet discussion Lloyd George had proposed
the exclusion of an area of Ulster (to be specified) for a period of five years
after which, unless the Westminster Parliament decided otherwise, the area
would be brought automatically into the jurisdiction of an Irish Parliament.
But quite apart from any objections Carson might have to this, Asquith had
told the cabinet that he did not think many English Home Rulers let alone
the Irish could accept this. To Redmond, Asquith had confided that the
government believed the Ulstermen to have something like five thousand
rifles and that anything up to thirty per cent resignations among army
officers must be expected, if the army were ordered to put down insurrection
in Ulster.[10]

Asquith had not been altogether frank with Redmond. There had in fact
been two meetings with Bonar Law, and Asquith seems only to have informed Redmond of the second. Perhaps this was because at the first meeting
Asquith had said to Law, when each leader was discussing his own recalci-
trant wing, that though people usually spoke of the Liberals as being
dependent on the Irish it was really the other way round.[11] The Nationalists,
said Asquith, were powerless without the support of the Liberal Party, and
if he or the government decided on any course which commanded the support of their own party, the Nationalists would have no choice but to accept
it. This must have been encouraging to Law, indicating that in the long run
the Liberals were not altogether averse to leaving the Irish in the lurch. If
the Irish had known of the remark, they might have been able to make
more effective plans on their own account accordingly.

It was at the second meeting between Bonar Law and Asquith that the
proposal for some form of exclusion for some part of Ulster was discussed
in detail. But at this point Asquith's version of what was said differs rather

from Bonar Law's, and both differ from the version Asquith gave Redmond. Law thought that Asquith had said he would definitely propose to the cabinet the exclusion of either four or six counties – probably six – on the basis that only a plebiscite by the area excluded could bring them under an Irish Parliament. According to Law, Asquith said he thought he could carry his cabinet and his own party with him on this.[12] In Asquith's own notes of this conversation, though the substance of the proposal was the same, namely the exclusion of six Ulster counties with a plebiscite alone capable of bringing them into a Home Rule Ireland, he committed himself to no more than saying he would report the substance of this proposal to the cabinet, and, if they approved, sound out the Nationalist leaders.[13] He did, however, tell Bonar Law that 'I might probably be able to carry my own cabinet and party with me, in any form of settlement that in the end I pressed upon them.'[14] Needless to say, Asquith gave Redmond no inkling either of this last remark or of his preparedness to consider what amounted to the permanent exclusion from the Home Rule Bill of six Irish counties.[15]

Over the next few months Redmond made it increasingly clear that he could not accept any form of permanent exclusion of 'Ulster', and insisted that any offer at all should first come from the Conservatives. However, he received a number of indications that he was in an increasingly weakening position. In an interview with Lloyd George on 25 November he was told that, though the cabinet agreed that for tactical reasons no proposals should be made 'for the present', nevertheless, 'under certain circumstances, if no offer were made', Churchill, Haldane, Sir Edward Grey and possibly he, Lloyd George himself, might resign.[16] Asquith seemed to give Redmond some temporary reassurance when he told him on 2 February 1914 that he and his cabinet colleagues were all firmly opposed to the exclusion even temporarily of any part of Ulster.[17] It would, said Asquith, be 'most disastrous' for Ireland; he himself favoured concessions in the form of some local autonomy for Ulster within Home Rule, with the addition of a right of appeal by the majority of Ulster members in the Irish Parliament direct to the Imperial Parliament.[18] However, by March 1914 Asquith had succeeded in persuading a most reluctant Redmond to agree that the government should initiate proposals for Ulster after all. In spite of what Asquith had said about even temporary exclusion being disastrous, the offer was to be a form of exclusion.

The proposal was that any Irish county should have the right to opt itself out of the Home Rule Act by plebiscite for a period of six years. After six years, if the Imperial Parliament had not in the meantime made other provision, such county should come under Home Rule. This was basically the same proposal which Lloyd George had made to the cabinet a few months earlier, and which Asquith had then described as very doubtful because of its probable unacceptability to the Irish and even many English

Home Rulers. The point about the six-year period was that it would enable another General Election to be held, the result of which could determine that the opted-out county continued to remain out. Redmond's reluctant consent was obtained on the firm understanding that this should be the very last concession the Nationalists would be asked to make, and that if the offer was rejected by the opposition then the government would pass the bill as it stood.

In thus accepting, even as a possibility the principle of permanent exclusion, Redmond can now be seen to have made a disastrous move. A number of painful but just tolerable concessions had been open to him, and he had already shown himself prepared to make them. Unfortunately, none of these, which included additional representation for Ulster Protestants in a Home Rule Parliament, and 'Home Rule within Home Rule', were relevant since there could be no question of their satisfying Ulster Protestants. It was only in fact within the notion of 'exclusion' that any conceivable area of agreement lay. But if the Nationalists were to remain true to their principle of one Ireland, there was virtually no possibility of agreement in this area at all.

The one inalienable nationalist principle Redmond had laid down was that Ireland must remain a single unit. It was just possible to reconcile with this principle some temporary exclusion which could provide a psychological breathing space for the more apprehensive Ulster counties, after which they would automatically be included under the new Irish Parliament. But the period of six years now envisaged allowed a British General Election to intervene, after which new Westminster legislation might alter the arrangement altogether. To reconcile this concession with the 'one Ireland' principle it was necessary to convince onself that after six years' exclusion Ulster Protestants would find themselves so attracted by the shining example of a Dublin Parliament that there could be no prospect of a newly-elected Westminster Parliament wanting to continue the exclusion. It could also be argued that even if further continuation of exclusion were to be legislated for it could not, in the nature of the British constitution, ever be permanent; but to regard the 'one Ireland' principle as safeguarded by such a hypothetical possibility of unity in the remote future came close to the absurd.* After so long, no finalization of an Irish national demand, however moderate, could afford to be absurd. Redmond had allowed the opening of a tiny but fatal breach in his whole position.

Quite apart from nationalist theory, the 'one Ireland' principle was a very practical down-to-earth consideration for hundreds of thousands of Catholic

* This, of course, is what the various governments of the twenty-six counties have done since 1921. Because they, in their minds, regard Ireland as one country, they regard the nationalist principle of one Ireland as at least theoretically maintained. They have not therefore countenanced further direct action of the sort that brought them to power.

Nationalists living in those Ulster counties which might be excluded. It says much for Redmond's political personality that, with the help of the leader of the Ulster Nationalists, Joe Devlin, he should have been able to get them to agree to a proposal involving any exclusion at all, even temporary. But he was under no illusion about the extent to which he was straining loyalties. The strain was increased to the very limit by an additional painful twist. Whereas the original proposal, to which Devlin had got his supporters to agree, was for a three-year exclusion, Redmond had finally had to accept a cabinet demand that the proposed period of temporary exclusion should be extended to six years. It is hardly surprising that in finally giving his consent to Asquith's proposal Redmond should have insisted that this must be the Nationalists' last concession.[19]

But once the government had thus breached their own position Carson was on strong ground. Some months previously he had got the southern Unionists to agree, with considerable reluctance, that he should settle for the best possible terms he could get for Ulster alone. And although there were inevitable difficulties for Bonar Law with his extreme right wing over this abandonment of the southern Unionists, the Conservative Party's effectiveness depended not on its extreme right wing but on the alliance between Law and Carson. Now that the government and Redmond had bowed before their threat sufficiently to offer them the principle of exclusion of four Ulster counties, they could feel confident of obtaining better terms still.

On 9 March 1914, under the processes of the new Parliament Act, the second reading of the Home Rule Bill took place for the second time round, having suffered its first rejection in the House of Lords. Carson dismissed the government's offer with contempt.

'We do not want,' he said, 'sentence of death with a stay of execution for six years.'

Incomprehensibly, no one pointed out that the whole point of the six years was that it gave a new British Parliament a chance to review its situation and thus grant a virtually permanent reprieve. A few days later, on 19 March, Carson stalked indignantly out of the House altogether and left for Belfast. People speculated on whether or not he had gone to proclaim the Ulster Provisional Government.

The British Government had pledged themselves to Redmond that this would be their last offer to Ulster. Now they were obliged to see that the Home Rule Bill when passed should be enforced as law. The firmness of their resolve was about to be put to the test.

12

The Liberal Nerve
Begins to Fail

Would the government 'coerce' Ulster? This was the usual form in which
the question was put. Over and over again Conservative spokesmen in the
House of Commons and elsewhere asked the government if they seriously
thought of using British troops to 'coerce' Ulster. Even Liberals came to
accept the term as convenient jargon. But it was an emotive term, putting
the prospect of government action into a false pejorative light.

In the first place, the implication was that the province of Ulster was
solidly against Home Rule. But a narrow majority of its parliamentary
representatives were actually for it. And even among the voters themselves
in the most Protestant parts of Ulster – those four counties to which the
government was prepared to offer exclusion – there was a sizeable proportion of Home Rulers to Unionists.* Then again: the term 'coercion' in Irish
history had hitherto been a highly respectable one, meaning special legislation to enforce the rule of law. But now that the very people who had
continually called for it in the past were being required to obey the law,
coercion had become a term of abuse. If the Home Rule Bill, under the
processes of the Parliament Act, passed through three successive sessions
of the House of Commons, and received the royal assent, it would become
the law of the land. Any attempt to refuse to recognize the authority of the
Irish Parliament which the law set up would have been a disturbance of law
and order. Only if force were to be used to suppress the Ulster Unionist
Council and the Ulster Volunteer Force before they had broken the law
could reasonable exception be taken to coercion, and even so there is always
an area in which authority is entitled to assert itself in order to prevent a
breach of law. 'Coercion of Ulster' meant virtually no more than the maintenance of law and order.

In fact it was not illegal to drill or even, up to December 1913, to import
arms (provided certain technical import regulations were complied with).
It might have been said with accuracy that some of the public speeches of
Carson, Craig and other Ulster leaders were an incitement to disobey the

* About 5:8 on votes cast, but unopposed returns increased the unionist proportion.

law in certain circumstances, and at one stage their prosecution was considered. But Redmond and the other leaders of the Irish Nationalist Party were against such prosecution. It was distasteful for them that the final recognition of Irish nationalism by a British Government, which had so often used legal restraint to suppress nationalists in the past, should itself be marked by the prosecution of fellow Irishmen. Moreover, there was nothing that Carson and the others had said in this vein that had not been said with equal force by Bonar Law and other Conservative leaders.

We now know that the preparations of the Ulster Volunteer Force to make the law of the land unenforceable were, by March 1914, so well advanced that the government would have been wholly justified in striking against the entire organization at this stage. As early as July 1913 the staff of the Ulster Volunteer Force had been seriously considering advice that it should not wait for the Home Rule Bill to become law before acting. An unsigned paper in the Unionist Council records the belief that the British Army, though hating its duty, would probably fight a Provisional Government of Ulster.[1] 'They, the Government,' this paper continued, 'will probably wait as long as they dare in the hope of things quietening down, and at the last suddenly move 20,000 to 30,000 men into Ulster – secure railways, bridges, etc., and reinforce weak police posts. If they are allowed to do this (and with the help of the Navy they could certainly do it in two days) I do not see how you can hope to get your men out and concentrate them in suitable positions. *Must you give up the enormous advantage of the first move?*'

Certainly by March 1914 the Ulster Volunteer Force, consisting by now of the 100,000 figure originally envisaged, had got itself on to a war footing. With the help of a British movement for the support of Ulster, founded the year before and now vigorously activated by the eminent proconsular figure of Lord Milner,* a number of half-pay and reserve officers from the British Army were recruited to take command of some of the regiments of the Ulster Volunteer Force.[2] This, with its highly efficient transport and communications corps, medical corps, intelligence corps and a Special Section with its own uniform, already had the makings of a real army. It had no artillery, but did have six machine guns, and although it was short of rifles – of which Asquith's estimate of five thousand at this stage may not have been far wrong – plans were already laid to remedy this defect in a most spectacular manner. Finally, some time early in 1914, a 'No. 1 Scheme' of action was adopted involving, along the lines of the advice given, 'a sudden, complete and paralysing blow' to be struck simultaneously at all railway communications by which troop or police reinforcements might be brought into Ulster, all telegraph and telephone lines and all depots of artillery, ammunition and other military equipment.[3]

But perhaps the Ulster Volunteer Force's most effective asset of all was

* Elgar and Kipling were among Milner's supporters in London.

the state of mind of much of the officer class of the British Army. The attitude which the army might take if called upon to act against Ulster Unionists in support of a law passed to appease Irish nationalism had long been a subject of speculation and debate. The improbability of the army obeying orders to shoot down Ulster 'loyalists' had been raised as a spectre as long ago as the earlier Home Rule debate of 1886. Ever since 1910 the question had never been far from the public mind.

The British Army was, of course, theoretically quite detached from politics. Yet the officer class was of an undeniably Conservative cast of mind, and as individuals most officers had undoubted sympathies with the Protestant Ulster point of view. Was it right, people asked, and if right feasible, to put such a strain on the professional officer's devotion to duty as to ask him, in the peculiarly new situation that emerged from the combination of the Parliament Act and the Home Rule Bill, to act against all his individual instincts? It is, of course, exactly the ability to do this, to obey legal orders to the exclusion of all personal feeling, that underlies the whole philosophy of a reputable officer corps and of all professional military mystique. The curious spectacle was now to be witnessed of those very people who normally set such store by the self-denying spirit of discipline in the call of duty, making excuses for a different line of behaviour when it suited their own interests to do so.

The king himself had posed the question to his Prime Minister in September 1913 when he had asked Asquith:

'Will it be wise, will it be fair to the Sovereign as head of the Army, to subject the discipline, and indeed the loyalty of his troops, to such a strain?'

It might have been replied without *lèse-majesté* that the only meaning words like discipline or loyalty had at all lay in their demand for submission to all personal strain within the limits of the law. This is certainly the meaning the sovereign and other senior officers had been accustomed to give them when personal feelings imposed a strain on the rank and file. Any Irish soldier employed, say, on enforcing an eviction in Ireland, who had pleaded personal feelings for absenting himself from duty, would have received short shrift.

One senior officer in particular now had no qualms whatever about suiting his concept of military honour to his own individual beliefs. This was no less than the Director of Military Operations at the War Office himself, Sir Henry Wilson, an Irishman from a well-to-do family that had lived in County Longford for more than two hundred years, and who was implacably opposed to Irish nationalism. In the circumstances a professional military man in such a responsible position might have been expected to do everything in his power to ease the strain on the army and ensure that it should keep its professional role strictly separate from its private feelings. International tension was gathering and it was more essential than ever in the national interest to keep the army an integrated disciplined force. But the feelings of sympathy for Ulster which Wilson shared with most army officers were too much for him. These were undoubtedly sincere and deep, and it never seems to have occurred to him that in intriguing, as he now did continually with both the leaders of the Conservative opposition and the Ulster leaders to try and deprive the government of the army's assistance in maintaining the law in Ulster once the Home Rule Bill had passed, he was doing anything but what was right.

The troops on whom the government would have to depend if necessary for the enforcement of the law in Ulster consisted of two infantry divisions and two cavalry brigades. A substantial part of these forces were quartered in the old military camp at the Curragh, a large grassy plain in County Kildare, in the centre of Ireland. On 14 March 1914 Churchill, challenging Carson's rejection of the government's offer, denounced in a public speech at Bradford the so-called Ulster Provisional Government as 'a self-elected body, composed of persons who, to put it plainly, are engaged in a treasonable conspiracy', and declared that the moment had come to 'go forward together and put these grave matters to the proof'.[4] On the same day the army council sent to the commander-in-chief in Dublin, Sir Arthur Paget, instructions for the tightening up of security on barracks, arms depots and government stores in the North which it declared were particularly liable to attack. Conceivably, intelligence of the UVF's 'No. 1 scheme' for pre-emptive action had come its way. Four days later, on 18 March, Paget came to London in answer to a summons to give details of his plans. On 20 March he returned to Ireland with amplified orders for the disposal of forces to meet an Ulster threat. It seems virtually certain that, although these further orders involved the movement of troops to certain key points such as rail junctions, they were solely of a precautionary nature and that no 'plot' as was alleged by Conservatives existed to deny Ulstermen the expression of their legal democratic rights.[5] Movements of warships to Northern Ireland waters were to coincide with the troop movements.

Sir Arthur Paget, who brought these orders back to Ireland early on the morning of 20 March, had waived aside an offer to have them put in writing, and this fact was partly to determine what followed. Paget was an expansive, not particularly clever, officer of the old school of sociable army men, fond of hunting and gardening and much given to reminiscing at table about his campaigns in Africa and Burma. Immediately on his return to Dublin he coloured his explanation to his senior officers of what was about to happen with his own vivid imaginings. 'The whole place would be in a blaze tomorrow' was a phrase of his which one eye-witness of that early morning conference remembered.[6]

Nothing could have been better calculated suddenly to inflame the anxieties of officers who for months past had been concerned about their likely role in any future development of the Ulster crisis. What made things much worse was Paget's clumsy handling of an even more important aspect of the situation. While at the War Office in London the day before, he himself had brought up the possibility that some of his officers might be unwilling to participate in action against 'Ulster'.[7] What was he to do about this? It seems an odd question for any self-respecting commander to have posed about his senior officers. But it is an indication of the abnormal atmosphere of the time that it was not regarded as unreasonable, and Paget was given a matter-of-fact answer. Officers domiciled in Ulster, he was told, might be exempted from taking part in operations there and allowed temporarily 'to disappear'. Any other officer unwilling to serve would be dismissed the service.[8] Though these instructions had been given him at his request for his own guidance he made the foolish mistake, on arrival in Dublin, of immediately placing before those officers not domiciled in Ulster the alternatives of either agreeing to serve there in the forthcoming movements which would set the whole place 'in a blaze' or being dismissed the service. He asked them to make their choice. When General Sir Hubert Gough, Commander of the Cavalry Brigade at the Curragh, notified Paget that he and fifty-nine of his other officers chose, in these circumstances, the alternative of dismissal from the service, the incident popularly known as 'The Mutiny at the Curragh' had begun.*

It was, of course, no mutiny in the strict sense of the word, for Gough and his colleagues had disobeyed no orders: they had merely been asked to make their choice by their commanding officer and had done so.[9] Yet the effect was exactly the same as if there had been a mutiny, for the entire reliability of the British Army in Ireland was now in question. In fact the 'mutiny' was far worse than the action of Gough and the fifty-nine other officers indicated. For, on the alternatives being placed before officers of the infantry regiments in Ireland, the majority had also at first immediately expressed their preference for dismissal. Only the impeccable example of the officer commanding the fifth division, Sir Charles Fergusson, finally persuaded them to refrain from making their attitude public and eventually, often 'with a bad grace', to re-think their position.[10] Nor was the unreliability of the officers confined to Ireland. When General Gough was summoned to London to explain himself, General Douglas Haig, the Commander-in-Chief at Aldershot, also came up to the War Office to warn his administrative superiors of the strong feeling among the officers of his command in favour of Gough.[11] He told the government that the only way to quieten unrest in the army was to issue an unequivocal statement to the effect that the army

* The number of officers involved in this section of the incident is often given as fifty-seven, as this was the figure cited in an official telegram, afterwards published in a White Paper from Paget to Seely, the Secretary of State for War.

would not be used to coerce Ulster, a line of argument in which Sir Henry Wilson enthusiastically supported him. The resignation of every officer in the Aldershot command could be expected, Haig warned, if Gough were punished.[12] A junior officer named Archibald Wavell, who found himself disturbed by much of this as improper, heard in the War Office of the possibility of 'wholesale resignations in the army', including that of Wilson, unless a pledge were given that the army would not be used against Ulster.[13]

To all intents and purposes the government had a major army mutiny on their hands. In a disastrous attempt to make out that things were not as bad as they were, they virtually condoned it. There was talk of 'misunderstanding', of a misinterpretation of the type of action intended against 'Ulster'. Gough was actually able to return to Ireland 'reinstated' in his command, carrying a document from the Chief of the Imperial General Staff which guaranteed him that the troops under his command would not be 'called upon to enforce the present Home Rule Bill on Ulster' and that he could assure his officers to that effect.[14] He was naturally welcomed back to the Curragh by his officers as a conquering hero.

The paragraphs in this document explicitly guaranteeing Gough that the army would not be called upon to enforce the Home Rule Bill on Ulster had in fact been added subsequently to the cabinet's approval of the rest of the document, by the Secretary of State for War, Seely, and the Chief of the Imperial General Staff, Lord French, acting on their own initiative. When this amplified text became known it spelt out the extent of the government's climb-down far too embarrassingly, and both Seely and French had to resign, while Asquith himself took over the office of Secretary of State for War along with the premiership. But the original document that Asquith and the Cabinet had approved was, with its accepted reinstatement of Gough and its reference to the resignations arising from 'misunderstanding' alone, quite enough to justify Gough's triumphal return from such a stand. Asquith repudiated in the House of Commons the guarantee not to use the army to enforce a Home Rule Bill in the name of maintaining law and order, but the personal guarantee to Gough was never specifically withdrawn, and he continued to hold it in a solicitor's office in Dublin. The government's humiliation, for all Asquith's face-saving gestures, had been sufficient for Gough never to have to make use of it.

The net result of the incident was that the army was shown to be too unreliable for Asquith ever to risk getting so close to mutiny again by putting 'these grave matters to the proof'. From this moment onwards Redmond's defeat on the issue of one Ireland was assured. Politically, the deadlock continued, but the one sure means of resolving it, the eventual use of force to prevent the Ulster Volunteer Force interfering with the rule of law when the Home Rule Act was passed, was no longer available, and both Carson and Asquith knew it. Carson's future negotiating position was virtually impregnable. As if to emphasize their 'Ulster' triumph, a month later, on 25 April 1914, long-laid plans for a mass importation of arms for the Ulster Volunteer Force came to fruition. A highly efficient mobilization of the force round the ports of Larne and Bangor physically prevented His Majesty's police and customs officers in the areas from interfering with the operation, while 24,600 rifles and some three million rounds of ammunition, secretly purchased in Germany by a former army officer named Crawford, were landed and dispersed throughout Ulster with total success.*

Certain bitter lessons from all this were beginning to be learned in the rest of Ireland.

Looking back many years later, one of the strangest phenomena of the time is the virtual paralysis with which Redmond and the Nationalist Party seem to have been afflicted when faced with such unmistakable evidence of the government's increasing reluctance and inability to support them. Redmond in particular seemed to accept with little more than wistful disappointment the series of *faits accomplis* with which he was presented and his own increasing impotence in the situation.

Partly this was due to his own political personality. Long years in Parliament had made of him an exemplary House of Commons man, unprepared as Parnell had been to make use of Parliament rather than be used by it. He no longer found it so easy to look beyond Parliament to Ireland as Parnell and O'Connell had both done. He seemed to feel himself almost as much a prisoner of the parliamentary deadlock as Asquith himself. For all the warnings that had already been given him of uneasiness in Ireland about the increasing concessions, he seems to have been slow to appreciate that new political forces were capable of arising there. And when the strength of these began to develop, though they were not basically hostile to him, they caught him by surprise.

But a quite different reason for the party's virtual impotence at the time was the fact that attention in Ireland was by no means solely focused on Home Rule. A separate and more down-to-earth issue altogether, in the form of labour troubles in Dublin, held the scene almost equally with the constitutional issue of Home Rule. Amazing as it now seems, when John Dillon in Dublin wrote to T. P. O'Connor in England at the time of the crucial Bonar Law–Asquith conversations in the autumn of 1913, he could say that 'the Ulster question and the cabinet appear dim and distant and of minor importance'.[15] His mind was dominated by the bitter labour dispute which since August 1913 had seen some twenty thousand of the desperately

---

* For this exact figure of rifles see Stewart, *Ulster Crisis*, pp. 244–9. The *total* number of rifles in the possession of the Ulster Volunteer Force by July 1914 was a little over forty thousand. At the time of the Second Home Rule Bill in 1893 Crawford had had a plan to kidnap Gladstone from the front at Brighton and take him to a lonely Pacific island.

poor workers of Dublin locked out by employers, most of these employers being – and the fact is not insignificant for the future – ardent Home Rulers.

The labour troubles in Ireland were the climax to years of activity in the trade union field by a wild and dynamic organizing genius named James Larkin. Born in 1876 in the Liverpool slums, the son of a poor Irish emigrant family, Larkin had worked in the docks there, had become an active socialist and been elected General Organizer for the National Union of Dock Labourers. Extending his work first to Belfast in 1907 and then to Dublin in 1908, he had organized the dockers and carters there, become involved in many successful and some unsuccessful strikes and disputes all over Ireland, and in December 1908 founded the Irish Transport and General Workers' Union. He became its General Secretary and in his preface to the new union's first rule book castigated the 'soulless, sordid money-grubbing propensities of the Irish capitalist class', and with talk of 'the land of Ireland for the people of Ireland' held out hopes that all Irish men, women and children might one day 'become entitled to the fullness of the earth and the abundance thereof'.[16] He made enemies not only among capitalists, but also among rival trade unionists, as well as many politicians of the United Irish League, and the supporters of Sinn Fein, whose founder Arthur Griffith denounced him futilely as the representative of English trade unionism in Ireland.[17] All sensed in him, rightly, an independent, restless force dangerous to all carefully prescribed modes of thinking. His one concern, manically displayed through a powerful ego, was to organize effectively for their own welfare the wretched urban working classes of Ireland. Now that the tenant farmer increasingly flourished as an owner-occupier under the operation of the Land Purchase Acts, this urban poor had inherited something of the role of the national down-trodden.

The poverty and squalor of much of Dublin in the early years of the twentieth century appalled all who encountered it. A government report issued in 1914 assessed that of a Dublin population of 304,000, some 194,000, or about sixty-three per cent, could be reckoned 'working classes'. The majority of these working classes lived in tenement houses, almost half of them with no more than one room to each family.[18] Thirty-seven per cent of the entire working class of Dublin lived at a density of more than six persons to a room; fourteen per cent in houses declared 'unfit for human habitation'.[19] The only water supply for houses that sometimes contained as many as ninety people was often a single tap in the outside yard, where were also usually two lavatories, often used by passers-by coming in off the street. Human excreta lay scattered about the yards and in some cases in the passages of the houses. 'We cannot conceive,' wrote the committee who presented this report, 'how any self-respecting male or female could be expected to use accommodation such as we have seen.'[20] Of the non-tenement houses in which the rest of the working-class population lived, they wrote that some 'scarcely deserve the name of house, and could be more aptly described as shelters'.[21] They usually had no lavatory of their own. The death rate in Dublin was higher than in any other large centre of population of the United Kingdom, largely due to the tuberculosis which flourished in such conditions.[22] In all the principal towns of Ireland, in fact, the death rate was much in excess of that in the great towns of the rest of the United Kingdom, being highest of all in Wexford, Galway and Cork.[23]

The report on Dublin housing reproached the Dublin Corporation for 'a want of firmness in the enforcement of the ordinary Public Health Laws with regard to housing', and it also pointed out that three members of the corporation, Aldermen O'Reilly and Corrigan and Councillor Crozier, owned substantial blocks of tenement houses and actually received rebates of tax on them though some of the property was classed as unfit for human habitation.[24] Again, in looking for underlying reasons why some of the Dublin working class were soon to diverge politically from the policies of the Nationalist Party, it may not be insignificant that the Corporation at this time was solidly Nationalist, and Messrs O'Reilly, Corrigan and Crozier were enthusiastic supporters of Home Rule.

It was against a background of such conditions that Larkin had been more or less successfully building and giving strength to an organized labour movement in Ireland. Though his aim, like that of any labour leader, was to raise the workers' standard of living, particularly that of the unskilled workers whose rates of pay in Ireland were well below the average of those in England, his main battle concerned the actual organization of his union and the need to establish a firm foothold for it in the leading areas of employment. His attempt was equally firmly combated by the employers – mostly Home Rule Nationalists who, with the introduction of the Home Rule Bill, were anticipating political mastership in their own house.

Larkin, lion-hearted and personally erratic, was assisted in his work by two remarkable lieutenants of different character from himself. One was a clever and less heroic but well-balanced young tailor named William O'Brien (no connection of the Nationalist MP), who supplied the movement with much of the level-headedness and administrative efficiency which Larkin lacked. The other was James Connolly, born of a poor Irish family in Edinburgh in 1868.

Connolly's father had been an Edinburgh Corporation manure carter without any prospects except continuing poverty and the fear of losing his job. At the age of fourteen his son, the young James Connolly, had enlisted in the British Army, in the King's Liverpool Regiment, and remained in it for nearly seven years.[25] He spent almost all this time stationed in Ireland, and though it is a period about which he was afterwards reticent, it was also the period of the eighties when the land agitation was at its height and clearly helped to crystallize in his mind that identification of Irish national feelings with the interests of the working class which was always to the forefront of his thinking.

Connolly was personally made in a heroic mould, like Larkin, but was thoughtful as well as a man of action, pondering deeply from an early age the intolerable conditions of the nineteenth-century working class. He had soon been drawn towards Marxism and the socialist groups then proliferating in Britain. After his army service he had returned to Scotland and worked for the Scottish Socialist Federation and the Independent Labour Party with which it was affiliated. Supporting himself and a young family by casual labour, and for a time rather unsuccessfully as a cobbler, he was desperately poor, and in 1895 answered an advertisement for a post as paid organizer to a 'Dublin Socialist Club'. The following year in Dublin he himself helped to found the Irish Socialist Republican Party, the first manifesto of which appeared under a slogan of Desmoulins', 'The great appear great because we are on our knees', and which called for the establishment of an Irish Socialist Republic 'based upon the public ownership by the Irish people of the land and instruments of production, distribution and exchange'.[26] Once again as in Fenian times the heroic national ideal of an Irish Republic was being tinged with notions of international socialism.

The essentially twin nature of Connolly's political thinking, as simultaneously nationalist and socialist, was already clear. He was under no illusions about pure emotional nationalism. Writing in Alice Milligan's paper, *Shan Van Vocht*, he declared: 'If you remove the English army tomorrow and hoist the green flag over Dublin, unless you set about the organization of the socialist republic, your efforts would be in vain.... England would still rule you to your ruin, even while your lips offered hypocritical homage at the shrine of that freedom whose cause you betrayed.'[27] In a way it was a modern version of what Fintan Lalor (whom he had read thoroughly) had taught, with the urban working class increasingly replacing the now quite prosperous farmer. The implications for Irish nationalism were the same: that it had small substance unless the welfare of the people were bound up with it.

But though Connolly had contacts with all the other fringe groups active in Ireland at the turn of the century and figured prominently in at least one incident in the days of the Irish Transvaal Committee,* the Irish Socialist Republican Party did not flourish, and in 1903 Connolly emigrated with his family to America where he stayed seven years. On his return in 1910, practical rather than theoretical developments in the Irish labour movement were under way under the inexorable pressure of Larkin's personality. Connolly, whose return had been largely made possible by Larkin and O'Brien, threw in his lot with them. In 1911 he was appointed Belfast organizer of the Irish Transport Workers' Union.

* See above, p. 147.

Subsequent dramatic events, together with bitter internecine disputes in the Irish labour movement, have had the effect of making Connolly seem the major labour figure in twentieth-century Irish history. He was certainly a thinker of greater magnitude than Larkin, and as an individual more personally sympathetic. But the fact that Connolly was to be cut off in his prime and win an Irish martyr's crown in 1916, while Larkin, accidentally missing the heroics, was to live on to 1948 through years of Irish disillusion, political quarrelling, and personal identification with Soviet Communism, should not blind one historically to the other fact that it was Larkin who first effectively brought the old incoherent national emotions into Irish twentieth-century labour relations. He reactivated to some extent in the urban scene that incoherent national extremism which the Land Purchase Acts and the other successes of the Nationalist Parliamentary Party had laid to rest in the countryside. The lasting significant effect of this was to be extremely limited, but as a very small minority influence it was to play some part in events in which the actions of only a very small minority were to count decisively.

In the *Irish Worker*, a paper which Larkin had founded in 1911 and which had a regular circulation figure some ten times higher than Griffith's *Sinn Fein*, Larkin regularly attacked the nationalist failings of the Parliamentary Party, describing them as 'hypocrites, trading under the cloak of religion and hiding under the mantle of Nationality'.[28] In a public speech in Dublin in May 1913 he had spoken of his union's plans in words that conjured up the days of the United Irishmen and the Fenians: 'We are going to make this a year to be spoken of in the days to come. In a few days we are going to start a new campaign in which Sergeants, Captains and Commanders will require a discipline of a very high order.... There is a great dawn for Ireland.'[29] He cited Emmet and Tone as worthy models for the Dublin workers.[30] And when, in August 1913, threatened by a Larkin-organized strike on the Dublin trams, the tramway owner William Martin Murphy, a millionaire former Nationalist MP, started dismissing union members and thus provoked a strike which in turn provoked a general lock-out by the employers, Larkin defied the police to prevent him from holding a banned meeting in O'Connell Street with the following words:

'I am going into O'Connell Street on Sunday. I am going there, alive or dead, and I depend on you to carry me out if I am dead.... Remember the old song about the meeting by the river, with pikes on your shoulders by the rising of the moon. I would ask you to meet me at the old spot in O'Connell Street and you men come on ...'[31]

By that Sunday a warrant was out for Larkin's arrest, but after hiding in the house of Constance Markievicz he appeared disguised in a beard on the balcony of the Imperial Hotel and was, after a few words, carried out, alive, by the police. A street riot followed in which the police used their batons with considerable brutality, injuring some four hundred people and killing at least one. A lecturer at University College named Thomas MacDonagh, who was also a poet, was present that day and saw sometimes three policemen attack a single individual. He saw them baton an old woman with a shawl over her head and attack a small man who had lost his hat and who had to fly for refuge inside the railings of the Metropole Hotel. 'There was continual rapping of batons on people's heads ... you could hear from the cries and shrieks that the same thing was happening opposite the Metropole and opposite the Post Office.'[32]

Since this brutality on 31 August 1913 has its place in subsequent national mythology it needs to be remembered that the individual policemen involved had names like MacGrath, Murphy, Ryan, McCarthy, O'Connor and O'Rorke.[33] But the riot did have a traumatic effect on the atmosphere of Dublin. Violence now became more and more part of the everyday order of things as the strike and lock-out continued and clashes took place between 'scab' workers protected by police and union pickets. Eventually, after repeated talk of the need for the workers to form a self-defensive force on their own, a so-called 'Irish Citizen Army' was officially formed on 23 November 1913.

The idea had first been vaguely mooted by Larkin himself as long ago as 1908,[34] but since during the early months of the lock-out Larkin was mostly either in gaol or in England trying to rally support from British labour, responsibility for the Citizen Army's organization largely fell on Connolly, as Larkin's deputy at Liberty Hall, the Union's Dublin headquarters. The Citizen Army's title expressed aspirations rather than reality, for it consisted only of a few hundred workers who were drilled periodically with hurley-sticks and wooden shafts on the recreation ground Larkin had purchased for the union at Croydon Park, Dublin. The drilling took place under the supervision of an unlikely figure, Captain Jack White, son of a much-honoured British general, who had won particular fame for his relief of Ladysmith during the Boer War. White, an ardent enthusiast for Home Rule, had been one of the originators of the Citizen Army scheme, referring to it at first as a Civic Guard. By its very name and existence the Citizen Army attracted many wayward aspirations beyond its practical purpose of a strikers' defence force. This was evidenced by a telegram which Sir Roger Casement, one of the many individuals increasingly anxious over the fate of Home Rule, sent to one of the inaugural meetings early in November 1913. He supported the 'drilling scheme' as a step towards the foundation of a corps of national volunteers.

Larkin himself continued to identify the cause of the workers with the national cause of Ireland. A government inquiry – in which the employers had been legally represented by the Independent Nationalist Member of Parliament, Tim Healy – failed to bring the two parties together. Eventually,

200

at the end of January 1914, beaten by lack of funds and the failure to raise
sufficient support from the rest of the United Kingdom's Trade Union and
Labour movement, Larkin had to acquiesce in a return to work under terms
which secured no gains for the union and were even humiliating to it, though
the employers' declared aim of breaking the union remained equally un-
achieved. But in spite of what amounted to a defeat, Larkin's voice was raised
in increasingly powerful national strains.

When in March 1914 the offer was made to Carson of the exclusion of
some Ulster counties, the Parliamentary Committee of the Irish Trades
Union Congress, of which Larkin was Chairman, recorded its 'emphatic
protest' against the partition as 'a national disgrace'.[35] And speaking at the
Congress he declared: 'I claim we have an opportunity given us of achieving
much in the near future of our beloved country, to work for, and if needs
be to die, to win back, in the words of Erin's greatest living poet, for Caitlin
ni Houlihan her four beautiful fields.'[36] And as the government's weakness
before Carson became clearer and clearer Larkin wrote in the *Irish Worker*
in July 1914: 'We can only say that if the workers of Ireland stand idly by
whilst they are being betrayed, they get what they want and only that. Our
fathers died that we might be free men. Are we going to allow their sacrifices
to be as naught? Or are we going to follow in their footsteps at the Rising of
the Moon?'[37]

By that time similar feelings of exasperation in other classes in Ireland,
less drastically expressed, had made themselves felt and Redmond had had
to take account of them.

13

Volunteers and Home Rule

Within the loose conglomeration of extreme national thinkers who had gravitated round Arthur Griffith's Sinn Fein, there was of course little surprise at the way in which Redmond and the Nationalist Party were apparently being entrapped into betrayal even of their own limited nationalist principles by the deadlock in English politics. Whether or not, like Griffith and his closer followers, the extremists stood for total Irish independence under the Crown, or whether, like the members of the Irish Republican Brotherhood, they stood for total Irish independence in the form of a republic, they had always seen Home Rule as, at best, only a means to an end. They inevitably became increasingly restless now as even the prospect of Home Rule began to recede before Asquith's appeasement of Ulster. But, more significant for the future, wider sections of public opinion, still resolutely pro-Redmond, were becoming restless too, and thus for the first time for over thirty years gave the fringe elements of extreme nationalism an access to, and a meaningful contact with, ordinary mass Irish opinion.

Griffith himself, though he had accepted an inactive role for Sinn Fein while the Home Rule Bill was before Parliament, thus dismaying many IRB and other extremists who regarded him as a rallying point, took a strong stand immediately the prospect of a compromise involving partition became clear. He wrote in his paper *Sinn Fein* on 21 February 1914, before Redmond had agreed to Asquith's county-option offer to Carson: 'The Irish leader who would connive in the name of Home Rule at the acceptance of any measure which alienated for a day – for an hour – for one moment of time – a square inch of the soil of Ireland would act the part of a traitor and would deserve a traitor's fate.'[1]

The mass rank-and-file supporters of the Parliamentary Party would not have used such strong language. They remained faithful to Redmond as a man doing his best for Ireland in extremely difficult circumstances. Yet they had already by that date joined with Griffith and other even more extreme national elements to form an organization which expressed alarm about the fate of the Home Rule Bill and a determination to stand fast in the face of further pressure for concessions. This was a body designed to counterbalance the Ulster Volunteers. It was called the Irish National Volunteers and was formally founded in Dublin on 25 November 1913 as an organization quite unconnected with the Parliamentary Party as such, though party supporters joined it. By the end of 1913 the Irish National Volunteers had achieved only a moderate membership of some ten thousand. But the partition offer to Carson in March 1914, and his rejection of it, followed by the Curragh incident and its implications, led to a very rapid rise in membership of the Volunteers during the next few months so that, by May, it was reckoned that over a hundred thousand men had been enrolled.[*2] This was actually a slightly higher figure than the estimated strength of the Ulster Volunteer Force at this time, though as military bodies there was otherwise little comparison between the two. The Irish Volunteers, while often drilling enthusiastically under former British Army instructors, had very few arms and achieved nothing like the same degree of military organization or efficiency as the Protestant Ulstermen.

The way in which the Irish Volunteers had come into being itself indicated a new tentative merging of separate patterns within Irish nationalist opinion. The first moves towards the formation of such a body had been made locally at Athlone in the centre of Ireland in October 1913.

This fact is even today little known, because the men who made these initial moves had no connection with those others who, some weeks later, first organized the movement on a national scale and later still won for themselves places in the national mythology. But the fact remains that several weeks before the official foundation of the national Volunteer movement, the idea of forming a nucleus of Volunteers to defend if necessary the Home Rule Bill in the same way as Carson's Ulstermen were preparing to attack it, had already been discussed and acted on in Athlone.

On 11 October a general parade of 'about a thousand' men, calling themselves the Midland Volunteer Force,[†] was held at Fair Green, Athlone, under a Mr Paddy Downing, who supervised the arrangements from a spirited charger.[3] A local newspaper commented reasonably that the only surprising thing was that no such action had been taken before.[4] A more ambitious parade with bugles, drums and fifes but no other weapons than sticks was held on 22 October 1913 when it was estimated, possibly optimistically, that five thousand men, including many British Army reservists, paraded in twenty companies with company commanders and a General Officer Commanding.[5] On a route march through the town afterwards there

---

* The police estimate of the Irish Volunteer numbers as given in Parliament by the Secretary of State for Ireland, Augustus Birrell, was eighty thousand but this was almost certainly an underestimate. (Hansard, H.C. Debates, 5th series, vol. 63, col. 764.)

† A contemptuous reference to the Midland Volunteer Force, implying that they were a figment of imagination, was made by Michael O'Rahilly (The O'Rahilly) in his *The Secret History of the Volunteers* (Dublin, 1915). See F. X. Martin (ed.), *The Irish Volunteers 1913–1915* (Dublin, 1965), p. 76.

was much singing of patriotic songs and simultaneous cheering of Redmond and the men of '98, '48 and '67. A prospectus issued by the Organizing Committee, whose chairman was an Athlone man named M. D. Hayes, opened: 'As Loyal Irishmen to our King and Country, the objects of the Midland Volunteer Force must enlist your sympathy and approval.'⁶ And when a Westmeath Warrant Officer in the British Army wrote from India in the following month asking to be enrolled in the force, the secretary, himself a Catholic Ulsterman, elaborated: 'We are simply banded together to give encouragement and help if necessary to the Catholics of Ulster in their struggle against the gross tyranny and intolerance of the rabid Orange-ism of the north-east corner of Ulster.'⁷

It is clear, however, that the organizers of the Midland Volunteer Force had no great organizing ability, for in spite of their expressed hopes that the movement would spread to other Midland and Western towns, it developed no substance until quite different men began to develop the idea from Dublin some weeks later. The prime movers among these were Eoin MacNeill, the professor who had founded the non-political Gaelic League twenty years before, Bulmer Hobson, the active young man who had recently done so much to rejuvenate the Irish Republican Brotherhood, and Michael O'Rahilly, well-to-do heir of a Kerry clan and known as The O'Rahilly, who had been an enthusiastic nationally-minded Gaelic Leaguer for many years but was not a member of the IRB.

The O'Rahilly was then running the Gaelic League magazine *An Claid-eamh Soluis* and, having recently decided to re-style it, had asked MacNeill to write an editorial for the first issue of the new series. He suggested that it should be on some wider subject than mere Gaelic pursuits. MacNeill complied with an article entitled 'The North Began' in which he advocated that Home Rulers should imitate the example which Carson's Volunteers were setting them from the four Ulster Counties of Derry, Down, Antrim and Armagh.⁸

'There is nothing', MacNeill wrote, 'to prevent the other twenty-eight counties from calling into existence citizen forces to hold Ireland for the Empire. It was precisely with this object that the Volunteers of 1782 were enrolled, and they became the instrument of establishing Irish self-govern-ment...'⁹

Hobson had spotted the article and immediately went first to The O'Rahilly, and then with him to MacNeill to ask him if he would head a com-mittee to bring such an organization into being. MacNeill agreed and Hobson, with the help of his young friends in the Irish Republican Brotherhood, then successfully set about organizing such a committee which formally in-augurated the Irish Volunteers under MacNeill's presidency just over three weeks later. Though a report of the meeting did not seem to warrant inclusion on the main news page of the Nationalist Party's newspaper it was, as reported on another page, a success and some three thousand people joined the Volunteers at once.

Hobson and other young members of the secret IRB like Sean MacDermott had done much to give the Volunteer organization its initial momentum, but its importance as they themselves appreciated derived from the non-extremist support it attracted. Two well-known followers of Redmond became officers of the committee, while many other party loyalists, untroubled by their new association with men of more extreme views like Griffith or Casement, gave it immediate encouragement and support. Of the thirty men who formally constituted the Provisional Committee twelve were – unknown, of course, to most people – members of the IRB, while three of the others were later to join it.[10] Of the four officers of the Provisional Committee who signed an appeal to the public on behalf of the Volunteers in December 1913 none were IRB members. The document ended with an appeal 'to every Irishman who believes in a self-respecting, self-reliant Ireland to do his part in equipping the first National Army of Defence established in Ireland since the great days of Grattan'.[11] The Gaelic title of the Volunteers was Oglaigh na hEireann, Army of Ireland, and the uniform cap badge was to bear the letters FF, standing for Fianna Fail, the mythical warrior band of Fionn Mac Cumhail. 'Are we to rest inactive,' the opening manifesto asked, 'in the hope that the course of politics in Great Britain may save us from the degradation openly threatened against us. . . . In a crisis of this kind, the duty of safe-guarding our own rights is our duty first and foremost. They have rights who dare maintain them.'[12] The manifesto had been written by MacNeill. The wonder only was that Redmond himself had not already undertaken some such Irish move to give himself manoeuvrability in his increasingly constricted political situation in England.

In spite of the fact that a number of prominent Redmond supporters were identified with the Volunteers from the start, the attitude of the official party and Redmond himself to the new organization had been ambivalent, not to say apprehensive.

'Redmond does not like this thing,' wrote an Irish MP close to the leader to whom a loyal party man in Cork had written for guidance. 'Neither,' he added, 'does Devlin, but they are loath to move at present. . . . Dillon is much more against it. It could not be controlled, and if the army met some day and demanded an Irish Republic where would our Home Rule leaders be?'[13]

This hypothesis must have seemed far-fetched at the time, particularly as MacNeill went out of his way to stress to Redmond that he had always been one of his supporters and pledged himself against any use of the Volunteer movement to weaken the party.[14] But certainly the Volunteers were an indication to Redmond that not only was he falling into an increasingly isolated position in the English political deadlock, but also that there was a danger of the situation in Ireland partly slipping out of his control too.

Dillon, not so sure as some of his colleagues that the movement would 'fizzle out', told Redmond, 'We must watch it.'[15] As they watched, it became clear that, with the situation at Westminster and in Ulster deteriorating, it was not fizzling out at all. There was only one thing for the party to do: itself to take control of the Volunteers.

This was not inherently difficult. Most of the rank-and-file Volunteers by the early summer of 1914 were Redmond's supporters anyway. It was true that some of the resolutions and messages of support that streamed in for him from all over Ireland carried anxious undertones as the spectre of partition emerged. But these were loyally expressed, as in a resolution from Clonakilty which approved and endorsed all the party's actions, simply singling out especially its stand of 'no more concessions'.[16] There was no doubt that the country, gritting its teeth, was solidly behind Redmond. It was a foregone conclusion that having once decided to get control of the Volunteers he would easily be able to do so. But the manner in which he eventually did so antagonized the original committee and caused difficult self-searching among its extremist members. For, exasperated by several weeks of inconclusive negotiations with MacNeill, who was not a particularly efficient man and did not keep his colleagues fully informed, Redmond on 9 June 1914 simply presented the committee with an ultimatum to co-opt an equal number of his own nominated representatives on to the committee of the Volunteers.

It was under the influence of Hobson himself that the majority of the committee finally agreed to accept Redmond's demand. Hobson argued sensibly that any split would be disastrous to the whole concept of national unity embodied in the Volunteers, and that in any case if there were a split Redmond would command by far the largest section of the one hundred thousand odd members.[17]

Hobson's attitude involved him in bitter recriminations with his IRB colleagues. Tom Clarke, who otherwise greatly admired his ability, gave him 'a very unpleasant time indeed'.[18] He was accused of 'selling-out', and dismissed from any connection with the paper *Irish Freedom*.[19] John Devoy in America, who was appalled by the development, also dismissed Hobson as a correspondent for the Clan-na-Gael paper, the *Irish American*.[20] With his income gone, Hobson actually thought for a time of leaving the national movement to its own devices and even getting out of Ireland altogether.[21] But largely thanks to Casement's intervention on his behalf, Devoy reinstated him, and Hobson returned to the inner councils of the IRB only to clash once again with his colleagues in a much graver crisis two years later.

There can be little doubt that quite apart from the realities of the situation which were all in favour of Redmond, to keep the Volunteer movement intact was the best policy for those members of the IRB who hoped to use it from within for their own purposes. For the first time since the days of the

Land League the extreme republican element in Irish nationalist politics was in association, if under cover, with a large body of Irish public opinion. It was an elementary tactical consideration for the IRB to preserve that link at all costs.

Even in recent years, with the rejuvenation of the IRB by the activities of men like Hobson, MacDermott and the father figure of Tom Clarke recently returned from America, there had been little focus for their enthusiasm once they had become disillusioned with Griffith's Sinn Fein. Hobson, that 'Napoleon', as his patron, Roger Casement, had once dubbed him, had done what he could.[22] Helped by the new-found national enthusiasm of Constance Markievicz he had founded in 1909 a nationally-minded boy scout movement called Fianna Eireann. The paper *Irish Freedom* started in 1911, which appeared first under Patrick McCartan's and then Hobson's editorship, had boldly and publicly preached the IRB's traditional republican creed, but to little apparent effect. Of the Fianna Eireann, it declaimed: 'The Fianna have not begun one day too soon to prepare for the final struggle ... come it will, and that before the boys of the Fianna are full grown men.'[23] And again a few months later an editorial declared: 'The work we have to accomplish is to establish an independent Irish Republic here in this country.'[24] But there was nothing to indicate that such rhetoric was in any different category from that with which Ireland had long been familiar, and the paper had a small circulation. The note of bombast sounded by Major John MacBride on, of all occasions, the Battle of Sydney Street in East London, was of typical unreality. Noting scathingly that two armed men with revolvers had been able to hold up 1,500 soldiers armed with magazine rifles and a Gatling gun for twelve hours, MacBride commented: 'The whole business should put heart into the younger generation of Irishmen', and, asked what lesson he learned from the event, he replied: 'As to that it is the lesson I learned on the battlefields of South Africa – that the English army is of very little account as a fighting force.'[25]

Irish Freedom consistently carried with approval remarks such as that 'no National Movement could ever be successful if it could not rely on the ultimate backing of the sword', and that 'the only thing which would fire the imagination of the young people was the ideal of an Irish republic, the means to it, physical force'.[26] But the uncomfortable fact of Irish life remained, as it had done ever since the republican creed had been first propounded in the 1790s, that the idea of an Irish republic to be achieved by physical force did not fire the imagination of many young people at all, however much some believed that it should.

One new voice making itself heard in the columns of *Irish Freedom*, while not actually adding anything new to the old creed, at least succeeded in imparting to it a new note of dedication and passion. This was Patrick Pearse, Gaelic League poet and schoolmaster, son of a Birmingham stone-mason and an Irish mother, who since 1908 had been running a nationally minded school for boys called St Enda's at Rathfarnham on the outskirts of Dublin. The boys were partly taught in Irish and the rooms in the school had the names of Irish heroes round the walls; Emmet even had a room to himself. Pearse was not yet a member of the IRB but had many friends who were. Beginning a series in *Irish Freedom* entitled 'From a Hermitage' in June 1913, he wrote: 'This generation of Irishmen will be called upon in the near future to make a very passionate assertion of nationality. The form in which the assertion shall be made must depend on many things, more especially on the passage or non-passage of the present Home Rule Bill.'[27]

One immediate limited national task which the re-animated IRB had set itself was to erect the Wolfe Tone Memorial for which John O'Leary had laid the foundation stone in St Stephen's Green as long ago as the anniversary celebrations in 1898, but which had never been completed. Tom Clarke became president of the new executive committee of which Sean MacDermott was secretary. But it was Pearse who, at a ceremony at Tone's grave in June 1913, delivered a strikingly unequivocal oration:

'We have come here,' he said, 'not merely to salute this noble dust and pay our homage to the noble spirit of Tone. We have come to renew our adhesion to the faith of Tone; to express once more our full acceptance of the gospel of Irish Nationalism which he was the first to formulate in worthy terms ... his voice resounds throughout Ireland calling to us from this grave when we wander astray following other voices that ring less true ...' And he concluded: 'When men come to a graveside they pray; and each of us prays here in his heart. But we do not pray for Tone – men who die that their people may be free have no need of prayer. We pray for Ireland that she may be free, and for ourselves that we may free her. My brothers, were it not an unspeakable privilege if to our generation it should be granted to accomplish that which Tone's generation, so much worthier than ours, failed to accomplish! To complete the work of Tone.... And let us make no mistake as to what Tone sought to do. We need not re-state our programme; Tone has stated it for us: "To break the connection with England, the never-failing source of all our political evils ..."'

A very small crowd accompanied Pearse and Clarke to Bodenstown.

The tiny Irish Republican Brotherhood and their friends were well aware of their isolation. 'Ten years ago,' declared *Irish Freedom* in October 1913, 'the Parliamentary Party was losing its grip on the country.... Today the Parliamentary Party controls more thoroughly than ever the daily press and the public mind in Ireland.'[28] And earlier the same year an American correspondent had written to John Devoy of Clan-na-Gael, the IRB's counterpart in America: 'The dark side of the prospect here and overseas is not so much what Lloyd George, Redmond and Ryan propose, but the fact that there and here the Irish people accept and applaud their betrayal of everything

national they once professed to advocate. It is not so much the apostasy of
the platform demagogues as that of the people that disgusts ...' He added
hopefully that he didn't believe that at heart the Irish people had lost 'the
old manly spirit of '98, '48 and '67 but publicly they give no sign that it still
lives'.[29]

Given the historical facts of '98, '48 and '67 it was hardly surprising that the
spirit should be difficult to find in 1913, for it was something mythical that
was being sought rather than something which had actually existed. The
task of Irish republicans, though they seldom recognized this, consisted in
having to turn myth into reality. It was to be Patrick Pearse's own special
contribution to Irish nationalism that by acknowledging unashamedly the
mythical and even mystical nature of the Republic he paradoxically brought
it closer to reality.

But it was not until after the foundation of the Volunteers that Pearse or
any other of the new aspiring extremists had a framework within which to
become effective. Until that date both he and more down-to-earth republicans
had had to admit that they were an unrepresentative handful working in an
Irish void. The two-thousand-odd members of the Irish Republican Brotherhood, which was the total for the entire United Kingdom at the time,[30] had
to content themselves with manipulating influence inside extra-political
bodies like the Gaelic Athletic Association, making the occasional individual convert to their own doctrines, and, on the initiative of Hobson in 1913
who appreciated the opportunities opened up by Carson's example, taking
part in a small amount of secret ritualistic drilling.[31] In any case, it was only
the younger men in the organization, together with the recently returned
Clarke, who were at all active. The older and controlling members of the
Supreme Council, men like Fred Allen, 'almost stifled all activities' and were
even opposed to the publication of *Irish Freedom* and reluctant to give it
IRB funds.[32] One example of the conversion of one individual recruit to
republican doctrines serves to illustrate how insignificant and ineffective a
force the Irish Republican Brotherhood had long been even as a propagandist
in its own cause. In June 1911, to protest against the visit to Ireland of
George V in the year of his coronation, public meetings were held by a
specially organized committee of extreme nationalists in which some members of the IRB were prominent. The campaign did not prevent the royal
visit from being a popular success, but at one of the Dublin meetings a young
teacher of mathematics and Irish, Eamon de Valera, found himself listening
for the first time to advocacy of an Irish Republic. The idea had not come his
way before. He went home approving of it but thinking it had little chance of
success.[33] He joined the Irish Volunteers on the night of its inauguration on
25 November 1913.

The ineffectual isolation of the IRB was revolutionized by the foundation
of the Volunteers. A quite new perspective for IRB men and other extreme

nationalists now opened up. Pearse himself, speaking at the inaugural meeting, declared, 'The history of the last hundred years in Ireland might be described as a hopeless attempt of a mob to realize itself as a nation. Today we have an opportunity of rectifying the mistakes of the past. We go back therefore to the policy of the Volunteers [of 1778] . . .'[34] Before the month was out he was moving unashamedly beyond the constitutional aims of eighteenth-century nationalism into those realms of national mysticism which he was to make peculiarly his own.

'I have come to the conclusion,' he wrote, 'that the Gaelic League, as the Gaelic League, is a spent force; and I am glad of it. . . . The vital work to be done in the new Ireland will be done not so much by the Gaelic League itself as by men and movements that have sprung from the Gaelic League or have received from the Gaelic League a new baptism and a new life of grace. . . . [The Gaelic League] was a prophet and more than a prophet. But it was not the Messiah. . . . I am not sure that there will be any personal and visible Messiah in this redemption: the people itself will perhaps be its own Messiah, the people labouring, scourged, crowned with thorns, agonizing and dying to rise again immortal and impassible.' He concluded this article: '. . . We must accustom ourselves to the thought of arms, to the use of arms. We may make mistakes in the beginning and shoot the wrong people; but bloodshed is a cleansing and a sanctifying thing, and the nation which regards it as the final horror has lost its manhood. There are many things more horrible than bloodshed, and slavery is one of them.'[35]

This must have seemed very unreal stuff to any average rank-and-file members of the Volunteers who may have read it. Even the IRB members were thinking in more mundane terms of using the organization as a cover for their own activities. By April 1914 they had been able to convince John Devoy of Clan-na-Gael that this was seriously feasible and sums from Clan-na-Gael were being taken back for the Volunteers by IRB visitors to America.[36]

'You may have some doubts as to our personnel,' Devoy was told by The O'Rahilly (who though not an IRB member was close to the IRB's councils). 'Dismiss them. The men at the wheel are straight thinkers and include all the advanced and sincere men who are interested in nationality. . . . The objects of the men who are running this movement are exactly the same as yours.'[37]

Not all the 'advanced' men were nearly so sanguine. Thomas Ashe, an IRB man, wrote to Devoy a few weeks later that though MacDermott and others were 'doing their utmost to keep them [the Volunteers] straight' their chances were not good because of the preponderating majority of Redmondite supporters in the movement. And he quoted a letter he had had from a correspondent to the effect that 'They [the Volunteers] comprise outside a few good men, all the frauds that ever lived in this blessed country and you know how numerous they are'.[38] However, Tom Clarke was able to write in May to Devoy, ''Tis good to be alive in Ireland in these times', drawing attention incidentally to difficulties the Volunteers were experiencing from another quarter altogether, namely the Larkinite Citizen Army. These, he wrote, had been largely inspired 'by a disgruntled fellow named O'Casey ... '.[39] But, he concluded, 'Liberty Hall is now a negligible quantity here'. He added that Mrs Clarke had just presented a new badge to the women's organization of the Volunteers the Cuman na Mban. It consisted of orange and green on the wings with white in the centre. It was a quite novel symbol, the significance of which had to be explained before they adopted it unanimously.

Yet Clarke's confidence in the IRB's ability to maintain its influence with the Volunteer movement was severely shaken by Redmond's take-over. Hobson undoubtedly kept the cooler head for he saw that without Redmond the Volunteers were nothing.

The notion is sometimes held that it was the IRB who secured such arms as the Irish Volunteers were able to obtain by August 1914 and indeed, given their under-cover role and ulterior motives, one might have expected this to be so. But it was not so. Before the foundation of the Volunteers the IRB using Clan-na-Gael funds had purchased a few rifles for such drilling as took place under Hobson's influence. Considering that there was then no ban on the importation of arms into Ireland and that advertisements appeared in *Irish Freedom* from gunsmiths offering Mauser magazine rifles in perfect order from 30s and Lee Enfield magazine rifles in perfect order at £2 17s 6d, this represented no very great achievement.[40] Indeed, given the basic IRB belief in the need for an ultimate resort to arms, and given Clan-na-Gael financial resources, one might have expected a stock of rifles to be laid up at least against some such eventuality as the formation of a Volunteer corps. But virtually nothing of this sort was done.

After the foundation of the Volunteers an arms sub-committee was set up and The O'Rahilly was charged by this committee to inquire into the possibility of purchasing arms from the Continent.[41] But this did not lead to the positive results one might have expected from the IRB's theoretical professional revolutionary role behind the scenes. The government had not made things easier by banning in December 1913, soon after the Volunteers had come into existence, the import of arms into Ireland, but it is with just such a situation that professional revolutionaries claim to be able to deal. The truth seems to be that the IRB at this stage was still a very amateurish organization.

The real initiative in procuring arms for the Volunteers came from a quite different group of people, and these may certainly be labelled enthusiastic amateurs.[42] They were a collection of individual Anglo-Irish Home Rulers, drawn largely from the upper and upper-middle classes and mainly resident in London. Their contact with the Volunteers in Ireland was Sir

* O'Casey was Sean O'Casey, the playwright.

Roger Casement, the distinguished consular official who was a friend and patron of Bulmer Hobson and was on the Volunteer Provisional Committee. But neither the Committee nor Hobson were responsible for the first steps in getting the Volunteers their one sizable batch of arms. The initiative was Casement's own, and the operative factor his friendship with the sixty-seven year-old widow of the famous English historian, J. R. Green, then living in Westminster.[43]

Alice Stopford Green had long lived in London but had been born in Ireland where, a daughter of the Protestant Archdeacon of Meath, she had spent the first twenty-five years of her life. Her studies of Irish history, made while helping her husband with his researches, had led her to a quasi-mystical view of Irish nationality. She saw in its full realization the payment of a sort of debt to history and to the memory of the Irish dead. In fact her wish to see this realization in the near future had sometimes led her in her writings to perceive it prematurely in the past.[44]

Mrs Green had been corresponding since 1904 with Casement when he had first written to her on behalf of the Congo Reform Association.[45] Neither she nor Casement was a revolutionary, as were, at least in intent, the young men of the IRB. But both shared a sympathy for a more profound concept of Irish Nationality than that to which the Parliamentary Nationalist party, with its pragmatic political outlook, gave currency. And like Casement, Alice Stopford Green was in principle a supporter of Griffith's Sinn Fein, though she found the Ireland of those days a depressing place to live in.[46] By 1913 she and Casement were addressing each other in correspondence in affectionate mock-heroic terms such as 'My dear Woman of the Three Books' or 'My dear Knight of the Island', and in the warm but rarefied atmosphere of this relationship there now prospered a most romantic conspiracy.

The other participants were all friends and acquaintances of Mrs Green. They consisted of the Hon. Mary Spring Rice, daughter of Lord Monteagle and cousin of an English Privy Councillor then British Ambassador in Washington; Erskine Childers, an English Liberal born in Ireland who had volunteered for the British Army in the Boer War and been Clerk to the House of Commons for fifteen years, and his American wife, Mary; Conor O'Brien, a Sinn Fein supporter who was a cousin of Mary Spring Rice and a grandson of the Smith O'Brien of 1848; and Darrell Figgis, a young writer and literary journalist who lived in London but spent the winter months on the isle of Achill off the west coast of Ireland and was also a supporter of Sinn Fein. The one thing all these people had in common was a passionate belief that Ireland should be in a position to defend her constitutional rights against every threat in the probable event of the Home Rule Bill becoming law. The decision to purchase arms was made in London, and the money to finance it was largely raised there.

Early in May 1914 Casement had gone to London with MacNeill to open the first phase of negotiations with Redmond over his participation in the Volunteer movement. They had found Redmond determined to get complete control of the movement and at the same time mistrustful of some of the Volunteer Provisional Committee, notably of Patrick Pearse.[47] Lunching next day at Mrs Stopford Green's house at 30 Grosvenor Road, Westminster, where the young writer Darrell Figgis was also a guest, they discussed the situation and reasoned that the best way in which they could counter-balance Redmond's otherwise inevitable dominance of the Volunteer movement was by independently securing the arms the Volunteers were longing for. They were being forced to drill with wooden rifles, and broom handles. Figgis, who had known something of The O'Rahilly's preliminary inquiries, suddenly offered to go at once to the Continent and buy them.

'That's talking!' cried Casement, walking across the room from the window where he had been staring out at the Thames, and now placing his hand on the table in a rather characteristic melodramatic gesture.[48]

The decision was taken. The arrangements were to be made known to as few people as possible.

Just over a fortnight later Figgis went to Hamburg with Erskine Childers, who was a more ardent Home Ruler than most Liberals, in advocating not just the Home Rule Bill but full Dominion status for Ireland. He now offered his twenty-eight-ton white yacht, the *Asgard*, for the arms shipment.[49] He was an experienced seaman who as long ago as 1903 had written an excellent spy novel about sailing off the German North Sea coast, called *The Riddle of the Sands*. In Hamburg Childers and Figgis agreed to purchase 1,500 single-shot Mauser rifles and some 45,000 rounds of ammunition from a German firm.

Arrangements for the secret landing of this cargo in Ireland were necessarily complex and depended on the careful synchronization of an elaborate time-table. Details of the purchase were made known in June 1913 to Hobson who, keeping the knowledge very much to himself, assumed responsibility for the landing procedure. His plan, agreed with Casement and Childers in Dublin at the end of June, was that half the guns and ammunition should be brought into Howth harbour at twelve noon on Sunday, 26 July.[50] The remainder were to be brought the same day by another yacht, Conor O'Brien's *Kelpie*, to be landed at Kilcoole in County Wicklow. (Because both O'Brien's nationalism and his yacht were well known and therefore might be suspect, his cargo was to be transferred at sea before landing to another yacht belonging to a Dublin surgeon.) It was a hazardous plan, for the *Kelpie* and the *Asgard* had to sail for the Continent on 29 June and 2 July respectively, and from then on until the date of the Irish rendezvous were virtually out of touch with Hobson. Neither yacht had engines or radio. Each had first to keep a precise rendezvous on 12 July with Figgis who was bringing the cargo by tug from Hamburg to the Roetigen lightship in the North Sea on that date. The eventual arrival of the cargo precisely to synchronize with the landing arrangements in Ireland was also essential. For ever since the gun-running by the Ulster Volunteers at Larne three months before, the authorities had been keenly on the look-out for further such operations both North and South, but particularly South.

In the end the whole affair was a dazzling success, as brilliant a feat in its small amateur way as the much larger and more professional gun-running at Larne three months before. The rendezvous at the Roetigen lightship and the transfer of arms from Figgis's tug to the two yachts took place like clock-work, though Mary Spring Rice, who, with the two Childers, a young British Army man named Shepherd and two Donegal fishermen, formed the crew of the *Asgard*, found herself wondering if they would ever get their nine hundred rifles stowed into the tiny yacht.[51] Together with the heavy am-munition boxes these filled the saloon and the cabin and blocked the passage and the companion hatch. The possible effects of such extra weight in the event of bad weather caused anxiety. But Childers's one thought was to take everything; in the end he had to jettison only three ammunition boxes which had been kept on deck because there was no room for them below. In the *Kelpie* too, which had loaded up just before the *Asgard*, the rifles were stacked so high in the saloon that there was barely room to crawl over the bundles and nowhere to sit. In fact the reason why Childers in the *Asgard* found himself with rather more than half the total of 1,500 to carry was that the *Kelpie* could take no more than 600.

It was as well that Childers was an expert seaman. Thirty-six hours before the rendezvous at Howth the *Asgard* hit the worst storm in the Irish Sea since 1882. It was as well too that he was a man of both dash and resolution. For it had been agreed with Hobson that if the coast was clear at Howth a motorboat should emerge from the mouth of Howth harbour before the appointed time as a signal that all was well. The *Asgard* cruised up and down that Sunday morning just outside Howth waiting for the signal for two hours. No motorboat appeared. Childers finally decided to go in all the same. The *Asgard* sailed into Howth harbour at the very moment that the vanguard of a thousand Volunteers, mobilized by Hobson to land the arms, appeared at the other end of the jetty.

Hobson's stage management of the reception arrangements had been brilliant.[38] He had let only very few people into the secret of what was afoot, among them Tom Clarke, and some of his young friends in the IRB, such as Sean MacDermott. At the end of the previous month he had arranged for the Volunteers to undertake a series of weekly Sunday route marches to different destinations round Dublin. These had attracted some attention from the police at first, but after two or three weeks had come to be accepted as routine. The march out to Howth on Sunday, 26 July, therefore, attracted no particular attention and few even among the Volunteers – who included Arthur Griffith – knew the object of the exercise. A contingent of the youth movement, the Fianna, under a young man named Sean Heuston, accompanied the column. A number of taxis ostensibly taking young men and their girls to the coastal resort for the day had set out ahead under the leadership of a young IRB member, Charles Burgess, usually known in the Irish version of his name as Cathal Brugha.

The unloading of the *Asgard* was accomplished in about half an hour, and those rifles which had not been dispatched in the taxis with the ammunition were carried back towards Dublin rather unmilitarily – some on right shoulders, some on left – but in triumph, by the Volunteers.[53] Coastguards had spotted the landing but, overwhelmingly outnumbered, had not interfered. The police had, however, notified Dublin Castle. At Clontarf on the way back the Volunteers found themselves confronted and halted by a body of police reinforced by a military detachment of the King's Own Scottish Borderers.

The Assistant Police Commissioner in charge, named Harrell, was there on his own initiative. It was a delicate situation, for although in the light of the arms ban of the previous year the actual landing had been illegal, the legal position about forcibly removing the arms once landed from those in possession of them was less clear. The Ulster Volunteers were after all parading freely with arms through the streets of Belfast at this time and no attempt was being made by the law to interfere with them.

It was in fact afterwards found by a Royal Commission that Harrell in trying to disarm the Volunteers had acted with technical illegality.[54] In any case, some uncertainty was clearly apparent in Harrell's behaviour at the time. For after a first attempt by the police to take the Volunteers' rifles a fracas developed and Harrell let himself become involved in an argument with Figgis and the poet Thomas MacDonagh, under cover of which most of the Volunteers managed to slip away with their rifles across the fields. Only nineteen rifles were lost. But that was not the end of the incident.

By about half past four in the afternoon, both Volunteers, triumphant with their rifles, and the police, largely thwarted in their attempt to disarm them, had dispersed. Only the detachment of the King's Own Scottish Borderers remained at Clontarf for another hour or so: a hundred men in all carrying a hundred rounds of ammunition per man.[55] During the argument between Harrell and Figgis and MacDonagh they had been given the order to load, and had never subsequently been ordered to unload. While now waiting for orders to move off they were surrounded by a jeering and hooting bunch of civilians, angry with them for the part they had played in the incident.

A small crowd, continuing to scoff and jeer, eventually followed the soldiers back the three miles or so into Dublin, and there were moments en route when the rear ranks made lunges at the crowd with their bayonets. In Dublin the Sunday evening crowds following them through the streets began to grow. As the soldiers, making for their barracks, turned off O'Connell

Street on to one of the Quays by the Liffey named Bachelor's Walk – the site of a tram terminus and a particularly busy place of congregation on Sunday evenings – stones, bottles and other missiles were thrown. The senior officer present, who had not been at Clontarf but had come out to join the returning column, ordered the rearguard to wheel and face the crowd. He did not know that the men's rifles were already loaded.

Detailing five or six men to load and be ready to fire he then stepped out and raised his hand for silence so that he could address the crowd. Immediately a shot rang out, and this was followed by a volley. A man of forty-six, a woman of fifty and a boy of eighteen were killed, the latter by a shot fired through a simultaneous bayonet wound. Thirty-eight people were wounded, fifteen of them seriously, and one of these later died.

Appalling as the incident was, the emotive shock it caused in Ireland carried a special significance. It seemed almost that the southern Irish were being massacred for trying to assert their rights to Home Rule. In fact, what had happened was that for a few moments a tired, frustrated and exasperated local soldiery, jeered at for two hours and recently subject to a bombardment of stones and bottles, had too easily surrendered to a vague impression that there had been an order to fire. No soldier fired more than two rounds.[56] Within a fortnight a government commission concluded that the action of the police and troops had been 'tainted with illegality' and specifically censured the troops for lack of control and discipline. This does not exactly square with a picture of tyrannical repressive government.

Yet the significance of Bachelor's Walk was that it connected easily in the Irish mind with other bloody events which had been repressive in the past, and which had themselves been worked into a national myth. A relatively small single incident, it was not the only thing at the time to evoke the national myth. Below the surface of mass opinion the whole political situation, suggesting an English compromise at the expense of Ireland, was beginning to work on the emotive undertones of Irish history which ran through every Irishman.

'Bachelor's Walk' came as a climax to a period of extreme political tension. For there had been absolutely no progress with the attempt to solve the deadlock over 'Ulster'. The Government's offer 'to Carson – made with Redmond's and the majority of the Irish people's reluctant consent – still stood, giving the option to any Irish county that so wished to opt itself out of the jurisdiction of an Irish Home Rule Parliament for a period of six years. After this, unless the Westminster Parliament were in the meantime to legislate otherwise, it would automatically fall back within the Irish Parliament's jurisdiction. But if the offer still stood, it also still stood rejected. Carson's minimum terms – which he had not yet had to formulate precisely – were the total exclusion from an Irish Parliament for ever of the six Ulster counties of Derry, Antrim, Armagh, Down, Tyrone and Fermanagh. On this there could be no meeting point, for Redmond had already stretched the One-Ireland principle to the then endurable limit, if not beyond it.

In fact the deadlock was far worse than it had ever been before. For in a last-minute desperate effort to solve it the king had persuaded Asquith and the Conservative, Ulster and Irish Nationalist leaders to agree to attend a conference at Buckingham Palace. This sat from 21–24 July. Though the personal atmosphere of the conference was civilized it broke down at once over the area of Ulster to be excluded. On this no agreement could be reached. The even more difficult question of the extent of time for which any such area was to be excluded was never even discussed.

Two days later the arms for the southern Volunteers sailed into Howth in the *Asgard* and their successful arrival was followed by the traumatic news of Bachelor's Walk.* Under the mechanism of the Parliament Act the Home Rule Bill would shortly have to come up to be passed into law. In the North, more determined and efficiently organized to resist a Home Rule Act than ever, the Ulster Volunteer Force waited.

In this highly critical situation, events elsewhere were to rescue the government from their dilemma of having committed themselves to an agreed 'final settlement' of the Irish question while yet being unwilling to carry it out. On the same day, 24 July, on which Asquith informed the Commons of the breakdown of the Buckingham Palace Conference, he also had to tell them of the Austrian ultimatum to Serbia. The greatest international crisis in European history began to overshadow even the complexities of Ireland.

* The other consignment of arms transported in Conor O'Brien's yacht *Kelpie* was delayed because of a broken maintail in the yacht *Chotah*, to which it was to be transferred off the coast of County Wicklow. The six hundred rifles were eventually successfully landed without incident at Kilcoole, County Wicklow on the night of 1 August 1914.

14

Volunteers and the European War

The political deadlock in which the outbreak of war found the Irish problem had been virtually unchanged for months. But the atmosphere pervading it now changed almost overnight.

Towards the end of June the government had introduced, with Redmond's agreement, via the House of Lords, an Amending Bill to the Home Rule Bill. This incorporated the offer of county option for Ulster which Carson had already rejected when outlined by Asquith just before the Curragh crisis. But the offer had to be formally rejected if conciliation were to be seen to be done, and the Lords was the place where the government might most conveniently learn the worst at once. The Lords in fact amended the Amending Bill to exclude positively all nine counties of Ulster until such time as, voting in one block by plebiscite, they might vote themselves into the jurisdiction of an Irish Parliament. Given the small but unmistakable majority of Protestant inhabitants over Catholic, this proposal meant that all nine counties would be excluded from an Irish Parliament for any foreseeable future and virtually for ever. It was thus not conceivably acceptable to Redmond.

However, the willingness to compromise had to be placed fully on record, and, with this ominous prologue already performed, the Amending Bill was now due to come to the House of Commons. An indication of the terms on which the Conservatives and Carson might finally be induced to settle was revealed to Redmond through private intermediaries on 2 July.[1] The proposal was the positive exclusion of a geographical area of Ulster consisting of Antrim, Down, Derry, Tyrone, North and Mid Armagh, North Fermanagh and Derry City until such time as this area might vote itself under the rule of a Home Rule Parliament. Though this was, of course, a considerable improvement on the Lords' intransigent stand, releasing not only the three predominantly Catholic counties of Donegal, Cavan and Monaghan but also some Catholics in Armagh and Fermanagh, it still meant that substantial numbers of nationalists would be voted out of the Irish Parliament virtually for ever.

There was, of course, no guarantee that Carson and Bonar Law would be able to get their own followers to agree to such terms, but from a nationalist point of view they were in fact better than the form of partition which, some years later, Ireland had to settle for. Redmond might even have been able to improve on them marginally in negotiation. This can, however, be no valid argument for suggesting that in the context of that time Redmond should therefore have settled for them.

It would have been impossible for him to do so. The exclusion of Tyrone, where Catholics were in a small minority over Protestants, for any time at all, and the exclusion even of the predominantly Protestant parts of Ulster virtually for ever, stretched the already overstretched principle of One Ireland beyond endurance.

The failure of the Buckingham Palace Conference merely formalized this deadlock. But in terms of the parliamentary time-table the Amending Bill was still due to be offered in the House of Commons. In accordance with Redmond's agreement with Asquith, since the Tories were rejecting the offered conciliation, the Home Rule Bill was to go through as it stood, under the Parliament Act. As a very last concession and after persuasion by Asquith, Redmond and Dillon reluctantly agreed to let the county option proposal in the Amending Bill be put forward *without* the six-year time limit.[2]

But in the end the Amending Bill never came up in the House of Commons at all. In the six days before Redmond's final concession and the date due for the bill's introduction the European crisis deteriorated sharply. Moreover, the intervening episode in Ireland of the Howth gun-running and the shooting on Bachelor's Walk inevitably made Redmond's hold over his party in the light of this latest concession more difficult, though his ability to hold it was not in question. But for comfort's sake the bill was postponed for two days, due finally to be introduced on the afternoon of Thursday, 30 July 1914.

That very morning Asquith was sitting in the cabinet room with a map of Ulster, polishing up his speech for the afternoon, when a telephone call came from 'of all people in the world' Bonar Law to suggest a meeting with Carson in Law's house, Pembroke Lodge, Kensington. Law had sent his car for him. The Prime Minister got in, half wondering if he were being kidnapped by a section of the Ulster Volunteers.[3] Nothing so desperate was in store for him, though the meeting was not without drama.

Law and Carson proposed that in the interests of a united national front in the European crisis the introduction of the Amending Bill should be postponed to avoid the bitterness of public controversy. After consultation with his cabinet colleagues and Redmond, Asquith accepted this in principle. The procedure they agreed on among themselves was that Home Rule should become law and be placed on the statute book, but simultaneously with a Suspensory Act which would prevent it coming into force until a

new Amending Bill could be introduced later. For an invaluable moment
at least, a sudden calm settled over the wholly unsolved Irish problem.

When Grey, the Foreign Secretary, spoke to the House of Commons in
sombre terms on 3 August 1914 he was able to say that 'the one bright spot
in the very dreadful situation is Ireland. The position in Ireland – and this I
should like to be clearly understood abroad – is not a consideration among
the things we have to take into account now.'

Redmond then took a political gamble. 3 August was a Monday and
he had not been in touch with his colleagues Dillon and Devlin in Ireland
since the previous Friday, though he had clearly given the question of
what he should say some thought over the weekend. The Prime Minister's
wife, Margot Asquith, even wrote to him on the Saturday evening appealing
to him to offer the Volunteers to the government, and, though he would not
normally have taken much notice of such advice, it seems to have fitted in
with the way in which his mind was moving.[4] He may even have read a
letter from Darrell Figgis who had played such an important part in the
arming of the Volunteers to date, which appeared in the *Freeman's Journal*
of Saturday, 1 August, suggesting that the government should give arms to
the Volunteers for the defence of Ireland.[5] At any rate, while Gray was
speaking in the House, Redmond consulted one Irish member, John Hayden,
about whether he should speak in this sense and received an encouraging
reply. Another member, however, T. P. O'Connor, to whom he also spoke,
thought that the bitter feeling over Bachelor's Walk made support for such
a line in Ireland too problematical.[6] However, Redmond took the chance.

He knew that his authority in Ireland was immense. He was determined to
do all he could to get the Home Rule Act on to the statute book in spite of
the outbreak of war. The essence of the Irish nationalism for which he and
the vast majority of the Irish people stood was that, individual as it was, it
was a part of a wider family relationship with the rest of Great Britain. That
family was now threatened with one of the greatest crises in her history and
Redmond, re-emphasizing Ireland's individual claim to be a self-respecting
member of that family, spoke for her as such.

'... In past times,' he said, 'when this Empire has been engaged in these
terrible enterprises, it is true ... the sympathy of the Nationalists of Ireland,
for reasons to be found deep down in the centuries of history, has been
estranged from this country. Allow me to say, sir, that what has occurred in
recent years has altered the situation completely. I must not touch and I
may be trusted not to touch on any controversial topic; but this I may be
allowed to say, that a wider knowledge of the real facts of Irish history has,
I think, altered the views of the democracy of this country towards the Irish
question, and today I honestly believe that the democracy of Ireland will
turn with the utmost anxiety and sympathy to this country in every trial
and every danger that may overtake it.'[7]

He told the government that they could take their troops out of Ireland tomorrow and that the coasts of Ireland would be defended by Irishmen of the Irish Volunteers, in conjunction he hoped with the Ulster Volunteers of the North.

The speech was welcomed with such relief and enthusiasm in the House of Commons that the references to the workings of Irish history may not have received the attention they deserved.

Outside the House of Commons it was a gamble which, in the short term and in the light of the calculations on which it had been taken, came off triumphantly. Except inevitably for the very small minority, consisting of IRB men, supporters of Sinn Fein and some of the other extreme nationalists in the original committee of the Volunteers, Redmond's attitude as expressed in the House of Commons speech was welcomed and applauded with enthusiasm throughout Ireland. But that it had been a risk was something Redmond himself was well aware of. Only two days before, he had received a letter from Colonel Maurice Moore, the Inspector General of the Volunteers and a staunch supporter of Redmond's, which said that should there be any hesitation on the part of the government in getting the king to sign the Home Rule Bill then Irish reservists should be told not to join up.[8] On returning to his room in the House of Commons after his speech on the 3rd, Redmond actually found a telegram awaiting him from the Volunteers in Derry which ran: 'Army and Naval Reserve met, decided refuse join colours until assured that King will sign Home Rule Bill.'[9]

Colonel Moore's letter had argued: 'This is the only pressure we can exert against a combination of the two English parties ...'[10] Redmond had merely decided to make the pressure a moral one rather than aggressively direct. Part of his calculation had been that a generous gesture of goodwill from Irish nationalists would prove more effective than any threat in enabling Asquith to get Home Rule onto the statute book. And certainly many Tories were deeply impressed by his attitude[11].

The element in his calculation which reckoned that Irish opinion would support him was confirmed at once. Colonel Maurice Moore sent immediate congratulations from Dublin. For over a week messages of endorsement and support continued to flow in to Redmond from individuals, local government bodies and local organizations of the Volunteers all over Ireland.[12]

On the main part of Redmond's calculation, that he could bring Asquith to place Home Rule on the statute book, there were to be some unpleasant moments when it seemed as if Asquith might be prevaricating. The Prime Minister had, in the war situation, many grave considerations that might reasonably be pleaded as more urgent. The opposition leaders, Law and Carson, while agreeing in the interests of national unity not actively to oppose the placing of Home Rule on the statute book, refused to acquiesce in it in any way, even given the assurance of an accompanying Suspensory

Act. Without Redmond's constant pressure and insistence that if Home Rule were not passed Ireland would once again become as grave an element in the situation as ever before, Asquith might well have found it more convenient to continue to evade the issue. But Redmond had plenty of evidence to support him. Already by the beginning of September Colonel Maurice Moore, the Volunteers' Inspector General, was complaining that the government had not taken a single step to help the Volunteers implement Redmond's offer. They had been offered neither rifles, money, officers nor any plans whatever for integration in the defence system.

Ten days later a correspondent wrote to the *Freeman's Journal*: 'Irishmen are beginning to have grave doubts.... A generous enthusiasm has been met by neglect. And another opportunity, greater perhaps than any before it, of treating Ireland with confidence and respect has been rejected.'[13]

However, Redmond had kept something in reserve. He had hitherto restrained his natural inclinations to encourage Irish recruiting until the *quid pro quo* he had bargained for was forthcoming. And within a week of the *Freeman's Journal*'s bitter comment the situation was transformed by Asquith's decision to put the Home Rule Act on the statute book immediately. Although the entire Conservative opposition walked out of the House of Commons in protest, on 18 September 1914 the Home Rule Act received the royal assent. It was accompanied by an act simultaneously suspending it for twelve months or until the end of the war, whichever were the longer period – and in the light of the then recently won Battle of the Marne there seemed indications, as the *Freeman's Journal* put it, that the war would 'last for a much less time' than twelve months.[14]

The net effect of the passing of the Home Rule Act was simply to shelve the problems of Ulster to be argued about again when peace returned. Yet it seemed a great landmark at the time. Even in retrospect it must be accounted as psychologically a great political victory for Redmond, for it meant that when Ulster did come to be argued about all over again, Redmond and the Nationalists would be theoretically in possession. Concessions from them would seem more remarkable concessions, and at the same time the enthusiastic participation of Ireland in the war effort would have conditioned English opinion even more favourably towards Irish sensibilities.

At the time, the passing of the Home Rule Act was indeed regarded as a major triumph at Westminster and in Ireland. After returning from the House of Lords to hear the Clerk of the Crown proclaim the royal assent, one Nationalist member produced a miniature green flag with a golden harp in the centre and carried it aloft into the Chamber. Cheers were followed by the singing of 'God Save the King' in which people in the gallery joined. At the end of it a Labour member cried out: 'God Save Ireland!' to which Redmond replied: 'God Save England too!'[15] For a few moments, forgetting the awkward realities that lay concealed by the Suspensory Act and the projected Amending Bill, it seemed a fitting climax to Redmond's long and selfless parliamentary career of thirty-four years.

All Ireland joined in the sense of triumph. Though Dublin itself received the news relatively quietly, in most parts of the country there were bonfires, street illuminations and bands playing 'A Nation Once Again' and 'God Save Ireland', while local bodies of Volunteers paraded proudly with their rifles. In Wexford tar barrels blazed on, among other places, Vinegar Hill. In the celebrations at Charleville, County Cork, it was noted that for the first time in living memory the words 'God Save the King' were heard on a Nationalist platform, and as the speaker uttered them a great outburst of cheering arose from the assembled multitude.[16] The *Freeman's Journal* itself, which saw 'the opening of an era of freedom, happiness and prosperity such as Ireland has not experienced for more than a hundred years', carried a banner headline crying IRELAND'S DAY OF TRIUMPH across all seven columns of its centre page.[17] On the opposite page there was a drawing of the old Irish Parliament House headed AT LAST! OUR OWN AGAIN! accompanied by sketches of Emmet, Napper Tandy, Lord Edward Fitzgerald, Grattan, Wolfe Tone, James Stephens, Butt, Davitt, O'Connell and Parnell, as if every thread that had ever appeared in the complex pattern of Irish nationalism had somehow been happily tied up at last. Indeed, that day's leader commented: 'Yesterday the charter of Ireland's freedom was signed.'[18]

Nor were the grounds for such feeling purely emotional. The very fact that Carson and the Tories had preferred to walk out of the House of Commons rather than witness the event seemed some proof that a real change had taken place. Hitherto in Irish history it had been the Irish who walked out of the House of Commons frustrated, either because they were ordered to, or because it was the only gesture left to them in a situation in which they were politically impotent. Now it seemed to be the Tories who were demonstrating their impotence.

In retrospect all this can easily be seen to have been an illusion. Within a few months the Tories were part of the government and Carson himself a member of the cabinet. Within a few years Redmond's triumph had turned to ashes. But things looked very different from Ireland at the time. Even though there were in the background disturbing features which made many feel that all might still not be well, it was the sense of Home Rule triumph which dominated the foreground.

Some ill omens might have been discerned in the very words with which Asquith, hoping vainly to avoid a scene in the House of Commons as the Home Rule Bill passed onto the statute book, sought to ingratiate himself with Carson and Bonar Law. He agreed that 'it might be said that the Ulstermen had been put at a disadvantage by the loyal and patriotic action they had undertaken' and continued: 'I say, speaking again on behalf of the Government, that, in our view, under the conditions which now exist ...

that employment of force, any kind of force, for what you call the coercion of Ulster is an absolutely unthinkable thing ... that is a thing we would never countenance or consent to.'[19] This did not augur well for the future of a united Ireland. Ever since the affair at the Curragh such an admission had been implicit in the situation, but it had never been made openly and voluntarily by the government before.

A further disappointment was the government's neglect of Redmond's offer of the Volunteers for the defence of Ireland. No move at all had yet been made or was ever to be made by the War Office to incorporate them in the defence forces. But with Home Rule on the statute book Redmond generously accepted the government's part of the deal as fairly completed, and proceeded to embark in Ireland on a recruiting campaign for the British Army. He had already, the day before the royal assent, issued a manifesto urging full cooperation by Ireland with the war effort. It was, he said, the most serious war in the Empire's history, 'a just war provoked by the intolerable military despotism of Germany.... It is a war for high ideals of human government and international relations, and Ireland would be false to her history, and to every consideration of honour, good faith, and self-interest, did she not willingly bear her share in its burdens and its sacrifices.'[20]

He returned to Ireland at the end of the week and on Sunday, 20 September 1914, while motoring to his house, Parnell's old shooting lodge of Aughavanagh in County Wicklow, happened to hear that a parade of East Wicklow Volunteers was being held at Woodenbridge on the way. He stopped and made them a short impromptu address. He was not going to make a speech, he said. But the words he did use were to have a far-reaching result.

This war, he said, was 'undertaken in defence of the highest principles of religion and morality and right, and it would be a disgrace for ever to our country, and a reproach to her manhood, and a denial of the lessons of her history, if young Ireland confined her efforts to remain at home to defend the shores of Ireland from an unlikely invasion, and shrunk from the duty of proving on the field of battle that gallantry and courage which has distinguished our race all through its history'.[21] He urged the Volunteers to go on drilling so that they could eventually account themselves as men in the firing line wherever that might be.

Although, as when he spoke in the House of Commons six weeks earlier, he had virtually consulted no one before speaking, he had gauged the mood of Irish opinion exactly. What he said was wholly in line with what the majority of the people of Ireland were thinking, and the recruiting figures from Ireland were soon to show it. Dillon, who was less enthusiastic about the war than Redmond in terms of international policy, though not in terms of Ireland's identification with the rest of Britain, made no objection at the time to this speech as he had made none to the earlier one, and indeed he was to support it and elaborate it on public platforms over the months to come. The only people who did object were a small caucus of the Volunteers comprised mostly, as one might have expected, of the IRB men, Sinn Fein supporters and other advanced nationalists who still wanted to think traditionally of England's war being Ireland's opportunity. Twenty members of the committee, including most of those who had given the Volunteer movement its original impetus, resigned. Under Eoin MacNeill they formed a new splinter body of Volunteers. The vast majority of the rank and file stayed in the main organization with Redmond.

Out of a total of some 188,000 Volunteers altogether at the time of the division, only some 13,500 had over four weeks later declared their allegiance for MacNeill.[22] The secessionists, who were widely regarded as a clique of almost unknown cranks (MacNeill was the only name among them widely known at all), were immediately popularly dubbed the 'Sinn Fein' Volunteers. Their official title was the 'Irish Volunteers', while the main body under Redmond continued to be known as the Irish National Volunteers, or simply National Volunteers to make the distinction clearer.

It so happened that in the face of this impertinent challenge Redmond was able to display immediate confirmation of the very wide support he commanded in Ireland over the attitude he had expressed at Woodenbridge. Asquith himself had come to Dublin that week to help celebrate the passing of the Home Rule Act, and a public meeting took place on the day after the MacNeill breakaway before a packed audience of three thousand people in the Round Room of the Mansion House with another one thousand overflowing into the supper room. Both Asquith and Redmond received long standing ovations, while five hundred Volunteers, who had marched through O'Connell Street to the Mansion House with rifles and bayonets, proudly acted as marshals at the meeting. When Redmond claimed that in proportion to population Ireland had a larger quota serving in the firing line than any other part of the United Kingdom (and the large number of Irish regiments already figuring in the casualty lists bore him out), he was particularly loudly cheered.[23] John Dillon seconded the vote of thanks to Asquith in words that showed no misgivings about Redmond's recruiting appeal. 'We have now got an opportunity,' said Dillon, 'and we shall avail ourselves of the opportunity of proving to the people of Great Britain and of Britain's Empire that the friendship of Ireland is worth the price.... England will learn and learn in her hour of need that Ireland never broke faith in her history.' He promised that Ireland would be 'united in our determination to prove ourselves brave and efficient friends to the British Empire and to England in this struggle'.[24] He too was cheered to the echo.

In fact, only in Dublin itself was the split in the Volunteers even of minor significance at the time. Slightly under one-third of the five Volunteer battalions there went with MacNeill into the Irish Volunteers.[25] But in the county of Dublin as a whole, only 210 out of a total of 3,719 Volunteers opted for MacNeill and the proportion was similar for other parts of the country.[26] Resolutions supporting Redmond and his attitude and repudiating the minority poured in, usually unanimously, from all over Ireland.[27] Even where a special effort was made by an individual Volunteer of outstandingly strong convictions to persuade his colleagues to join MacNeill the results were not far different. At a drill meeting at Larkill, Eamonn Ceannt, a member of the IRB, addressed the Volunteers in this strain but only managed to persuade fifteen out of seventy to go with him.*[28]

The impression has often been given that Redmond's pro-recruiting speech at Woodenbridge left the minority Irish Volunteers as the only active group in Irish nationalist opinion. This is a travesty of fact and of the whole character of Irish nationalist history. The vast majority of Irish nationalist opinion – those whose nationalism found expression in the idea of Home Rule – remained as nationalist and active as before, behind Redmond's policy of support for the Imperial war effort. The long-term result of this was inevitably that the cream of the Volunteer movement was eventually drawn off into the British Army, and the majority Volunteer movement at home gradually lost its vitality. Even by the early autumn of 1914, at the time of the split, many of the best of the Volunteer drill instructors, who had mainly been ex-British Army men on the Reserve, had been recalled as reservists. Other enthusiastic Volunteers were naturally among the first to leave to enlist in the British Army. But for a time even at home the Redmond National Volunteers remained strong and active, certainly putting the activities of the small body of obscure secessionists into the shade for the time being, and demonstrating that Redmond's attitude had in no way bewildered or confused the majority of nationalists.

A new Committee of the National Volunteers was immediately elected, with Redmond as President and Colonel Maurice Moore Inspector-General in 'Supreme Command of the Military Council'.[29] At a vast review of these Volunteers at Wexford on 4 October 1914, when long lines of National Volunteers, very many of them fully armed and in uniform, stretched for some miles into the countryside to welcome Redmond on his arrival by road into the town, he told them confidently not to worry about any future Amending Bill to the Home Rule Act but to trust the party as they had trusted it four years before.[30] Also on the same Sunday the indomitable Republican Mac-Bride addressed the Volunteers of the Colley and Carlingford districts in County Cork. But when he made a reference to the Irish party leaders as the 'so-called leaders' and described them as 'recruiting sergeants for the British

---

* The mathematics professor, Eamon de Valera, managed to persuade a majority of his company to follow him into the Irish Volunteers under MacNeill, but these 'thirty or forty' men soon dwindled to 'seven' at subsequent parades. Lord Longford and T. P. O'Neill, *Eamon de Valera* (London, 1970), p. 23.

Empire', the bulk of the audience rose in their seats, gave three cheers for Redmond, and marched out of the hall leaving only about a dozen behind.[31] On the same day in Limerick, while some 1,200 of the National Volunteers held a route march and review, what was described as 'the Sinn Fein' company could only muster 150 men.[32]

On the following Sunday, 11 October, Redmond held a review at Waterford of four thousand armed Volunteers, many in uniform and with their 'bayonets glinting in the sun', while there were other parades the same day at Athy and Naas and manoeuvres in the north of County Dublin.[33] It was also the twenty-third anniversary of Parnell's death, and some eight hundred National Volunteers, almost all armed, had acted as a guard of honour at the cemetery. A small group of MacNeill's Irish Volunteers had been to the cemetery earlier with rifles and in uniform, but their claim to speak for Ireland was further disputed when they found themselves in embarrassing disagreement even with Larkin's Citizen Army which had also paraded with rifles and in uniform at Parnell's grave. Larkin, who found himself prevented by the Irish Volunteers from speaking at an Irish Volunteer meeting in Parnell Square, though he insisted that he had been invited to do so, held a rival meeting at which he called out derisively in the direction of MacNeill's men: 'Nice rebels they are – they're not fit to run an ice-cream shop!'[34] It was a turbulent day for Larkin altogether, for later that afternoon some five hundred National Volunteers tried to march through his meeting and found their way barred by Citizen Army men flourishing swords and bayonets.[35]

In fact, for some weeks it looked as if the split in the Volunteers, far from weakening Redmond and the bulk of the Volunteer body, had given them new power and energy. 'The Volunteers are at last getting down to business ...' wrote the *Freeman's Journal* on 15 October. 'The departure has ended the reign of the do-nothings and made for the men of action.' A well-produced weekly paper, the *National Volunteer*, was started. The National Committee of the Volunteers, meeting at their offices in 24 Parnell Square, reaffirmed their objects as being 'to train, equip, and arm a Volunteer force for the defence of Ireland and the advancement and presentation of Irish rights and the maintenance of Irish self-government'.[36] On the following Sunday Redmond held another review, this time of some five thousand Volunteers at Kilkenny, which the local reporter described as 'a Citizen Army sprung into existence to safeguard Irish rights'.[37] Many of the Volunteer companies were in uniform and carried rifles and bayonets; the cheering crowds which welcomed Redmond beneath triumphal arches waved Irish flags, and numerous bands played national airs. 'The Union of 1800 is dead ...' declared Redmond in his speech. 'A new era has arisen in the history of our country ... we have won at last a free Constitution.'[38] The same afternoon Joe Devlin was presenting colours to the First Derry Regiment of National Volunteers in Derry, describing them as part of that 'Irish National

Army which had come into being to help the Irish party win Home Rule and help them maintain it once it had been won'.[39]

In this phase of Irish history it is necessary to free one's mind not only of the knowledge of what was to happen in Ireland in 1916 and after, but also of the knowledge of how the Great War was to develop. The confidence and enthusiasm with which Redmond and the vast majority of Irish nationalists in the National Volunteers could view the future in these late months of 1914, and even well into 1915, must be seen in the light of the European war as it then appeared. No one then knew that the war was going to last four years. No one could fully imagine the scale of the slaughter or the magnitude of the cataclysm in which Europe was involved. It was even still quite reasonable to think that the war might soon be over. What had hitherto been a war of rapid movement was only beginning to settle into the bloody stalemate of the trenches, and no one yet knew that it was a stalemate. As Sunday after Sunday reviews of several thousand armed National Volunteers were held in different parts of Ireland to be addressed by the Nationalist Party leaders[40] their political position seemed logical and vigorously optimistic.

Dillon in November made crystal clear the purpose for which the Volunteers were in existence when he said: 'If the army does not enforce the new law [i.e. Home Rule] which gives liberty to Ireland – the army which was only too willing to enforce the old bad law at the slightest hint from the government – Ireland will enforce it herself.'[41] And Redmond himself in December 1914, addressing some ten thousand National Volunteers on parade with arms on Limerick racecourse with the national flag of the gold harp on the green background flying above them, declared: 'The discipline and the unity of the Irish Party ... and the National Organization ... were never as necessary as they will be in the interval between now and the assembling of the Irish Parliament.'[42]

The logic of the position was straightforward: Home Rule, which was the form of nationalism the vast majority of the Irish people wanted, was law; it was law as it stood without any amendment and law for the whole of Ireland. This law was merely suspended either for twelve months, or if the war was by then not over, for a further period to be fixed by the king in Council, but in no case lasting longer than the end of the war. Thus once the initial twelve months were up, as Redmond himself put it in the middle of 1915, a Home Rule Parliament could come into existence before the end of the war but could not be delayed one hour longer.[43] When, in September 1915, this original twelve months did expire, the suspension of Home Rule was continued only for another six months or until the end of the war if that were to come sooner.

An as yet unspecified Amending Bill to the law was also provided for, but this it was hoped would be a matter for mutual agreement between all parties after discussion. Meanwhile, the Volunteers were a physical guarantee both that the law would be enforced and that, in the amendment to be agreed, nothing unacceptable to Irish national opinion such as the permanent partition of Ireland could be introduced. The Nationalist MP John Hayden, speaking for his leader to a parade of National Volunteers in Westmeath in March 1915, spelt this out:

'We desire to say,' he declared, 'when the Amending Bill comes forward that if it be unsatisfactory, and if we wish to reject it, we have behind us not only the sense and feeling of the people, but that we have also behind us a determined, united and disciplined body of Irishmen who are prepared to back us up at any hazard. If that is done, then I say you need not be afraid of anything in connection with this Amending Bill.'[44]

Redmond himself was optimistic that agreement on the terms of the Amending Bill would be achieved. But he, too, stressed that if an unacceptable Amending Bill should be forthcoming, possibly from a Conservative government, then the National Volunteer Force, 'if such a contingency should arise, will stand at the back of the civil organization and see that no successful attempt is made to filch from us the rights we have won'.[45]

And the party newspaper, the *Freeman's Journal*, urging an improvement in the arming and organization of the National Volunteers, wrote in a leading article:

'The National Volunteers will be the great rampart of defence against any attempt to defeat or delay Home Rule or to impair the guarantees of national autonomy contained in the Act to which the King has appended his sign manual.... Now is the time to take steps to make the National Army an effective weapon in the hands of the Nation's leaders ...'[46]

But apart from this sanction what grounds were there for optimism? What made Redmond suppose that there could be any more agreement over North-East Ulster in a future Amending Bill than there had been in the total deadlock reached in July 1914? It was an essential part of his whole policy that in addition to the new physical sanction of the National Volunteer Force there was simultaneously a moral sanction which had entirely altered the situation since July 1914. This was the moral sanction built up by nationalist Ireland's participation in the war.

Redmond had fought hard, often in the teeth of War Office and regular Army Unionist dislike of southern Irish nationalists, to give a specifically Irish National flavour to Ireland's contribution to recruiting. There had been a tendency at first to disperse southern Irishmen, who wanted to enlist, into English regiments rather than let them concentrate in their own units. This was in marked contrast to the treatment given to the Ulster Volunteer Force who were at once allowed to form their own Ulster Division of the British Army with distinctive badges and emblems. But eventually, thanks to Redmond's pressure, there was formed, in addition to the regular 10th Irish Division stationed at the Curragh, a third Irish Division (the 16th) with headquarters in Cork and Tipperary. Nevertheless, its commanding officer, General Sir Lawrence Parsons, a Unionist Irishman, though proud of his family's opposition to the Union in 1800 and its support of Catholic emancipation, was reluctant to allow the use of specific Irish badges and pedantically adamant against Redmond's wish to refer to the Division under the nostalgic Irish title of 'the Irish Brigade'.[47] These influences had acted as a slight brake on Irish recruiting fervour after the initial enthusiasm of the first few weeks of the war. Nor had some of the speeches made in favour of recruiting in the North by die-hard Unionists there helped recruiting in the rest of Ireland. Carson promised those whom he encouraged to enlist that he would see that those Ulster Volunteers left behind would be effectively reorganized and kept in being. 'I promise you,' he said, 'that they will be strong enough and bold and courageous enough to keep the old flag flying while you are away. We are not going to abate one jot or tittle of our opposition to Home Rule, and when you come back, you who go to the Front to serve your King and Country, you will come back just as determined as you will find us at home.'[48]

General Richardson, commander of the Ulster Volunteer Force, based his appeal for recruits unashamedly on Protestant Ulster's obligation to a British Army which, in the Curragh episode, 'came to the help of Ulster in the day of trouble and they would do so again'.[49]

But in spite of such provocation, and thanks both to Redmond's persistence over the Irish division and to the undoubted extent to which his own feeling about the duty of Irish nationalists to engage in the imperial war effort was genuinely reflected in the Irish nation, the recruiting figures were by the autumn of 1915 such that even the dour anti-nationalist Lord Kitchener had to describe them as 'magnificent'.[50] By that date there were already in the British Army 132,454 Irishmen, of whom 79,511 were Catholics and 52,943 were Protestants. Of these only some 22,000 had been serving when war broke out and a further 30,000 had been called up as reservists. Since the outbreak of war, altogether 81,408 Irishmen had volunteered as recruits, 27,412 of these being Ulster Volunteers and 27,054 being National Volunteers. The appalling casualty lists teemed with the names of great Irish regiments: Royal Irish Fusiliers, Munster Fusiliers, Dublin Fusiliers, Inniskilling Fusiliers, Royal Irish Rifles, the Leinster Regiment, the Irish Guards and Connaught Rangers. Irishmen had won seventeen VCs in the first thirteen months of the war. The first of the three great Irish Divisions, the 10th, was fighting with great gallantry at Gallipoli (though typically the War Office was reluctant to have the Irish identified by nationality in its despatches).

All of this had undoubtedly made a deep impression on reasonable Unionist opinion, and Redmond's, Dillon's and the rest of the leadership's assumption that this in itself would alter the old Unionist attitude when it came to an Amending Bill to accommodate Ulster seemed logical and reasonable. The Unionist paper, the *Birmingham Post*, wrote at the end of October 1915 that there was no doubt that the population of Ireland as a whole was 'heart and soul with England and their allies in this war' and concluded: 'Not that she has not sent more, but that she has sent, and freely sent, so many men is the most recent miracle of Ireland.'[61]

In such a climate the party's confidence remained high. John Dillon declared at a big review of National Volunteers in Belfast in March 1915 that men like the Irish VC Michael O'Leary were 'fighting for Ireland and for Ireland's rights as truly as any Irish Brigade ever fought on the fields of Flanders in the past. It is their deeds that will stand to us in the struggle that may yet be before us when we have ... to take up the threads of Irish politics when the war is over.'[52] And after a vast review of 27,000 National Volunteers from all parts of Ireland, almost all armed and many with rifles and even bayonets, held in Phoenix Park on Easter Sunday 1915, Dillon told the Convention that followed: 'We look forward to the day when we have to resume those arguments about the Amending Bill and when the National Volunteers may be again summoned to the capital, and shall march not 20,000 but 50,000 or 100,000 all armed and drilled and disciplined through the streets of Dublin. Then I think it will become manifest ... that Ireland free and indivisible must be conceded. That is my idea of the object of the National Volunteers.'[53]

'Given,' declared Redmond that summer of 1915, 'Given these two things – Ireland doing her duty to herself in the war and Ireland doing her duty to herself in keeping her political and military organizations intact ... there is nothing more certain in this world than that as soon as the war ends Ireland will enter into the enjoyment of her inheritance.'[54]

But there was in this twin moral and physical sanction a fatal flaw already beginning to be revealed but which, in the nature of the way in which things unfold in time, could still not be seen quite clearly. The very enthusiasm with which national Ireland asserted her moral claim by sending recruits to the British Army automatically weakened her physical sanction by depleting the strength of the National Volunteers. Supplying an élite for one purpose she deprived herself of an élite for the other. And simultaneously the moral fervour at home was directed rather to the fight overseas than into the state of preparedness at home. For a relatively short period of time the physical drain could have been tolerable. But the removal of the British Army reservists on the outbreak of war had deprived the Volunteers of almost all their best training instructors. By early 1915 the drain was beginning to tell. National Volunteer parades began to appear noticeably thinned by the departure for the Front of so many men of the very type who would have been keenest to turn out for such parades. The review of 27,000 Volunteers at Easter 1915 was virtually the last at which the National Volunteers made a big impression. By the end of 1915, though their nominal roll was still over 100,000, it was as far as members still in Ireland were concerned largely nominal, composed often of totally passive nationalists or even Unionists who had often joined on the outbreak of war as an expression of Irish-tinged Imperial patriotism.

Nevertheless, Nationalist politicians continued to talk as if the sanction of the National Volunteers were still a real factor. Greeted by 150 National Volunteers with rifles and fixed bayonets at a United Irish League Convention at Thurles in August 1915, Dillon argued boldly that 'the 30,000 odd National Volunteers who had left for the front would soon be back, trained and gallant soldiers, and that ... in the final struggle ... if it should be forced upon us, the fact of having a large force of determined organized Volunteers, stiffened by soldiers who have returned from the front, will be a deciding element in the result'.[55]

But it was in the nature of the horror still not fully unfolded in Europe that very many of those thirty thousand would not come back. The cause was coming to have to depend more and more on the moral obligation which Ireland had earned from England. The relevant question became increasingly: would England keep faith? In spite of the provocative statements of die-hard Ulstermen and certain other disconcerting developments in the course of 1915, the general inclination among Irishmen was still to answer that she would.

'Does anyone imagine that Belgium's scrap of paper will be honoured and Ireland's solemn treaty with England repudiated?' asked Joe Devlin at a meeting in Donegal in August 1915. And he added optimistically: 'The Amending Bill, and the Government which proposed it as a basis of common agreement are things of the past.'[56] Exclusion, he maintained, had been put forward as a tactical move in the fight against Home Rule, but now that Home Rule was on the statute book 'the tactical value of exclusion has practically ceased to exist'.[57] And he supported this extremely dubious thesis with the much more tenable argument that the events of the war had considerably mollified the attitude of many English and Irish Unionists with regard to Home Rule.

And yet there were also indications to make Irish nationalists doubt such an optimistic view of England's intentions. One could be found in that very change of government to which Devlin alluded. For, when a coalition had been formed in June 1915 in an attempt to secure a more successful prosecution of the war, not only that English champion of North-East Protestant Ulster, the Conservative leader Bonar Law, had been brought into the cabinet, but Carson himself, in the high post of Attorney General. It was true that Asquith had also offered an unspecified post to Redmond. The Prime Minister had even strenuously urged him to accept it after Redmond had immediately, and with nation-wide approval from Ireland, turned it down. But lack of consideration for the effect in Ireland of Carson's appointment inevitably revived memories of Asquith's own rather ambivalent identification with Irish nationalism in 1914 and earlier. Quite apart from which it seemed unthinkable that Carson and Bonar Law, in such positions of power, would permit the passage of any Amending Bill which contained less than their last demands of 1914. And these, Irish nationalists had already found totally unacceptable.

A further indication that, for all Ireland's participation in the war effort, her national susceptibilities might still not figure particularly high in the priorities of the British Government, was the attempt by Asquith under pressure from his new Tory coalitionists to appoint to the office of Lord Chancellor of Ireland no less a person than J. H. Campbell, Carson's fellow Unionist representative for Dublin University, and one of his most fanatical supporters from before the war. Campbell was actually supposed to have signed the Ulster Covenant in his own blood. He had certainly declared in 1914 that though civil war might be the path of danger, it was also the path of duty, and no other alternative was left to the loyalists of Ulster.[58] As the *Manchester Guardian* of 1915 put it, he was an 'antagonist of everything Nationalist Ireland stood for'.[59] And yet this was the man Asquith proposed for the office which would have to issue writs for an Irish Parliament – a man solemnly pledged to oppose in arms the existence of any such Irish Parliament at all. Thanks to a stubborn stand by Redmond, Asquith was eventually forced to drop the proposal, but the fact that the proposal could have been made produced a profound impression on Ireland. The Bishop of Killaloe, Dr Fogarty, a staunch supporter of the party, wrote to Redmond of 'a great revulsion of feeling' in the country. 'Home Rule is dead and buried,' he wrote bitterly, 'and Ireland is without a national party or national press. What the future has in store for us God knows...'[60]

The bishop was being a little premature in his bitterness. Party leaders like Dillon and Devlin were still laying great emphasis on the need to keep the National Volunteer organization strong as a sanction for Home Rule, and in August another cleric, the Dean of Cashel, declaimed: '... strong and commanding in the British Senate as is the voice of John Redmond, its power will be immeasurably intensified when it re-echoes the thunder of 100,000 Volunteer rifles....' His appeal for the filling up of the ranks of 'the National Army' actually led to a number of Cashel men handing in their names for drill.[61]

But the Bishop of Killaloe's bitter comment revealed at least a growing wariness and political sensitiveness where Irish nationalists had little to build on but trust, and the foundations of that trust suddenly began to seem uncertain. The periodically repeated rumours of the introduction of a conscription scheme which might include Ireland further increased this sensitiveness. Irish nationalist pride insisted that the very considerable contribution Ireland was making to the Imperial war effort should be honoured for what it was – a spontaneous and voluntary gesture with conscious political implications for the future of Home Rule. To ride roughshod over this, turning such contribution into a mere legal obligation exacted ultimately by force from Westminster at a time when an indigenous Irish Parliament was actually on the statute book, seemed not only an insult recalling all the other insults Ireland had received from Britain in the past but also a direct threat to Home Rule itself. In December 1915 the party summed up the attitude of the whole of Ireland when it passed a resolution declaring that 'any attempt to bring into force a system of compulsory service will meet with our vigorous resistance'.[62]

The conscription threat also had one other important effect. An RIC intelligence report from Limerick was not unrepresentative in stating that opposition to conscription brought a number of recruits to MacNeill's small secessionist group of Irish Volunteers in the form of farmers' sons of military age 'who believed that by becoming Sinn Feiners they would not be compelled to serve in the army'.[63]

Indeed, in the climate of mild uneasiness generated by the advent of the Coalition Government at a time when the potential strength of the National Volunteers had been dispersed in Flanders and elsewhere, often for ever, the small rump of the original Volunteer organization, known since the split of a year before as the Irish Volunteers or, by the public, 'Sinn Fein Volunteers', began to attract some attention in its own right.

15

The 'Sinn Fein' Volunteers

By far the most important characteristic of the Irish (or 'Sinn Fein') Volunteers was something quite unknown not only to the public at large in Ireland (in any case little interested in them at this date) but also unknown to the very great majority of the Irish Volunteers themselves. This was the fact that they were secretly under the control of that small group of young men who, with the former dynamiter Tom Clarke, had recently been re-animating the near-defunct Irish Republican Brotherhood.

In August 1914, very soon after the outbreak of war, the grandiloquently titled Supreme Council of this tiny secret society had met and had taken, in principle, the decision to apply the long classic separatist doctrine that England's difficulty was Ireland's opportunity.[1] They pledged themselves sometime in the course of the war to rise in arms for an Irish republic totally independent of Britain. When taken, this decision might reasonably have been regarded as of a largely academic nature, for to the overwhelming majority of the Irish people it would have seemed impractical and childish nonsense.

Although the IRB under Hobson's and MacDermott's guidance had been largely responsible for the successful foundation of the National Volunteer movement, the movement had soon grown into something much too big for them. Its strength and its wide popular support came almost entirely from those who saw in the Home Rule Bill an adequate satisfaction of national aspirations. Redmond's demand for control of the movement merely ratified a *fait accompli*, the assumption by his supporters of a new militancy in their determination to defend a Home Rule Act.

It had been Bulmer Hobson's argument at the time of the party take-over that the IRB's one chance of making any impact at all was by keeping the foothold it had acquired in popular opinion, and his acceptance of Redmond's nominees had been based on this. His argument was reasonable in the context of the time. But the outbreak of war changed everything in the Irish situation. Since the vast majority of the Volunteer movement supported the British war effort under Redmond's leadership, the IRB was unlikely to be able to use that movement as it stood to implement the decision they had just taken to strike at Britain. Thus although the split of the Volunteers in September 1914 – brought about by the original committee members' rejection of Redmond's recruiting drive – left only some thirteen thousand men, or less than a twelfth of the whole Volunteer movement, under any sort of IRB control, these thirteen thousand were at least a more compact force for the IRB to be able to manipulate.

Not that the vast majority of the thirteen thousand had then any inkling of the direction in which they were to be manipulated. Their President, Eoin MacNeill, had a clear idea of what *he* considered the purpose of the Irish Volunteers. It was not so very different from that envisaged by the National Volunteers, namely to be sure that there would be an effective force available to insist on the implementation of Home Rule at the end of the war.[2] The chief difference between his view and that of the Nationalist Parliamentary Party leaders was one of tactics. He and most of his supporters in the Irish Volunteers simply thought it unwise to commit Irishmen to the war effort without being sure that Home Rule would be implemented. They feared that their potential strength would be dissipated in the British Army – a fear which by the latter part of 1915 was beginning to look well founded.

Bulmer Hobson, who had resigned from the Supreme Council of the IRB after the appointment of Redmond's nominees, but remained a member of the organization, had more than an inkling of the Supreme Council of the IRB's theoretical decision to start an insurrection. But he may well have thought at first that the likelihood of it being put into practice was remote. Events certainly showed that he was on the alert against any attempt to implement it which he thought unreasonable. His own views were basically those of MacNeill.

MacNeill considered that the only justification for an actual rising lay in a reasonable chance of positive military success and of this he saw no possibility whatsoever. He specifically rejected the thesis which the military school-master Patrick Pearse, a member of the IRB since 1913 and now in its inner councils, consistently proclaimed to the effect that a blood sacrifice, however hopeless its chances of military success, was necessary to redeem Ireland from her loss of true national pride, much as Jesus Christ by his blood sacrifice had redeemed mankind from its sins.[3] Sometimes this mystical dedication to bloodshed of Pearse, personally one of the gentlest and tender-hearted of men as events were soon to prove, seemed to reach heights of near-insanity. Writing in December 1915 of the Great War which had then lasted sixteen months, he declared: 'It is good for the world that such things should be done. The old heart of the earth needed to be warmed with the red wine of the battlefields.'[4]

For MacNeill the only circumstance other than a real chance of military success which would justify the Volunteers' use of physical force would be if an attempt were made to disarm them. Otherwise they must simply preserve their strength to defend Ireland's legal rights at the end of the war. 'If,' he wrote in a private memorandum in February 1916, 'we can win our rights by being ready to fight for them but without fighting, then it is our duty to do so and we shall not be ashamed of it ... the Irish Volunteers, if they are a military force, are not a militarist force, and ... their object is to secure Ireland's rights and nothing else but that.'[5]

But MacNeill and the bulk of the Volunteers he commanded were unknowingly a tool in the hands of the IRB. In May 1915 the executive of the IRB formally appointed a 'Military Committee' of three to plan the insurrection on which they had decided. This consisted of Patrick Pearse, the St Enda's schoolmaster, Joseph Plunkett, a twenty-four-year-old poet and sometime editor of the literary *Irish Review*, and Eamonn Ceannt, a thirty-three-year-old employee of the Dublin Corporation who had been a founder member of the Gaelic League. All three of them had already had some discussion of insurrectionary plans together. These were mainly the brainchild of the poet Plunkett, and were to cover the whole of Ireland. In September 1915 Tom Clarke, together with Sean MacDermott, who had been imprisoned for a time under the Defence of the Realm Act for his anti-recruiting activities, were co-opted on to this committee which became known as the 'Military Council'.[6]

The extreme secrecy with which the IRB plan for a rising was elaborated, and the extent to which it represented the work of a minority inside a veritable Chinese box of other minorities, is evidenced by the fact that until September 1915 not even the full Supreme Council of the IRB knew of the existence of the military committee. It had been formed only on the authority of a smaller executive. When it is considered that the whole IRB itself was only a tiny minority within the 'Sinn Fein' Volunteers, the extent to which the Dublin rising of 1916 was unrepresentative of the people of Ireland can be properly gauged.

Pearse, in addition to his key position in the IRB's military council, also held the post within MacNeill's Volunteer organization of Director of Operations. Ceannt was appointed to the headquarters staff of the Volunteers in August 1915 as Director of Communications. Director of Training was another poet, Thomas MacDonagh, who was to be co-opted on to the military council for the insurrection at the last moment in April 1916. But though other members of the IRB held positions on the General Council of the Volunteers, Pearse, Plunkett and Ceannt were the only members of the headquarters staff who knew what was really being planned for the Irish Volunteers. Other members of the IRB, like Bulmer Hobson and The O'Rahilly were, together with MacNeill himself, until the very eve of the insurrection quite in the dark, like the vast majority of the thirteen thousand Volunteers they commanded.

The Volunteers had virtually had to reorganize themselves from scratch after seceding from the main organization in September 1914. It is an indication of how lacking in identity the rank and file must have felt at first that their own newspaper, the *Irish Volunteer*, carried as late as three weeks after the split a leader maintaining that in the war Ireland was 'as warmly on England's side as Belgium'.[7] Only in the following week did the *Irish Volunteer* become representative of the minority view and a new Volunteer paper, the *National Volunteer*, make its appearance to continue representation of the majority. The formal reorganization of the minority body of the Volunteers itself took place at a Convention at the end of October 1914, when some 160 delegates were addressed by their president Eoin MacNeill. He declared that their new Volunteer force might 'yet be the means of saving Home Rule from disaster and of compelling the Home Rule Government to keep faith with Ireland without the exaction of a price in blood'.[8] And it was not until the last week of December 1914 that a scheme for the military reorganization of these secessionist Irish Volunteers was published.[9] In spite of the understandable pride taken in the successful landing of some 1,500 rifles at Howth and Kilcoole earlier in the year, the outbreak of war had made that success virtually irrelevant, for there was now no difficulty in obtaining rifles at all, provided the money for them could be found. The Irish Volunteer executive even announced in November 1914 that it was 'anxious that it should be generally understood that rifles and ammunition are available for all duly affiliated Volunteer companies and that rifles would be despatched by return against a remittance from the Company's treasurer'.[10] Again in July 1915 Pearse himself proclaimed that there were quite enough arms and that it was only a question of the Volunteers paying for them.[11]

But the Irish Volunteers themselves were a pathetically small body of men. There was no sign of an increase in their numbers as month followed month after the split, though a London journalist gave it as his opinion at the end of November 1914 that papers like Griffith's *Sinn Fein* and the *Irish Worker* (now edited by James Connolly) were 'producing some effect among a credulous and ignorant peasantry in the South and West'. The next month, however, Griffith's paper was suppressed by the government as was the IRB paper *Irish Freedom*. Griffith replaced *Sinn Fein* by *Scissors and Paste*, composed chiefly of excerpts from British and neutral sources, sometimes containing German wireless news, and of quotations from Grattan, Davis and Parnell. It too was banned in March 1915. It is difficult to say in retrospect to what extent such papers, though their circulation was very small, were in fact preparing the ground for eventual shifts in opinion. The news of their suppression may have been as effective as anything in their content in encouraging new thoughts about the government and the Imperial war effort. Certainly there was little reflection of their influence in an access of numbers to the Irish Volunteers.

But as early as the beginning of December 1914 John Dillon was sounding an alarm that 'Sinn Fein' – by which he meant the Irish Volunteers, for

Griffith had virtually no political organization at this time – needed to be taken seriously. It was, he said, 'a most critical period in the history of the national movement'[12] and police intelligence reports from County Cork early in 1915 said the Irish Volunteers were beginning to 'assume an importance altogether out of proportion to their numbers'.[13]

It was some time before the 'Sinn Fein Volunteers', as they were by now almost universally called, made any effective impact on the public as a military body. And they were not popular. At one of their very first appearances as a separate force in Galway in October 1914, when about forty of them attempted to march through the town with dummy rifles, they had been much booed and jeered by a local crowd, including men on leave from the Connaught Rangers who had been among the first troops into Belgium with the British Expeditionary Force.

It was not in fact until August 1915 that the Irish Volunteers made any very obvious impression at all compared with the main body of Volunteers under Redmondite leadership. The occasion was the funeral of the old Fenian Jeremiah O'Donovan Rossa who after a long, stormy and not always dignified life in Irish-American politics had died in America. The IRB seized on the occasion to manufacture a large public national demonstration out of his funeral rather as Stephens had done with the funeral of the Young Irelander, McManus, over fifty years before. And though Redmond's National Volunteers claimed actually to have the largest numerical representation at the Rossa funeral on 1 August 1915, it was the Irish Volunteers who supervised the marshalling of the crowds and the arrangements generally and who alone appeared not only in uniform – as did the National Volunteers – but also armed with rifles – as the National Volunteers did not.[14] The poet, Thomas MacDonagh, now a 'Commandant-General' in the Irish Volunteers, took charge of the funeral arrangements while the mathematics teacher, Eamon de Valera, promoted from Captain to Commandant in the Volunteers in March 1915, supervised the arrival of seventeen special trains. Over Rossa's grave a guard of honour of Irish Volunteers actually fired their rifles in a solemn last military salute and Patrick Pearse gave a stirring oration, claiming to be speaking on behalf of a new generation that had been 're-baptized in the Fenian faith and that has accepted the responsiblity of carrying out the Fenian programme'. He pledged hate to English rule in Ireland and concluded: 'Life springs from death; and from the graves of patriot men and women spring living nations. The Defenders of this Realm ... think that they have pacified Ireland ... but the fools, the fools, the fools! – they have left us our Fenian dead, and while Ireland holds these graves, Ireland unfree shall never be at peace.'[15]

The fact that Rossa in his latter years had been a supporter of Redmond's United Irish League, and had actually been on the platform to welcome Redmond to New York on the occasion of his last visit there, was of no consequence to Pearse who was busy myth-making. What, however, was of interest, as if almost suggesting a growing willingness to listen to myths on the part of people normally concerned with the reality of politics, was the fact that the *Freeman's Journal*, the party paper, printed Pearse's speech without comment.

Sir Mathew Nathan, the intelligent and well-informed Under-Secretary at Dublin Castle who was the real man in charge of day-to-day administration in Ireland during the not infrequent absences in England of the Chief Secretary, Augustine Birrell, wrote even before the funeral: 'I have an uncomfortable feeling that the Nationalists are losing ground to the Sinn Feiners and that this demonstration is hastening the movement.'[16] And yet the Irish Volunteers' numbers had actually dropped off since the end of 1914,[17] in spite of the employment by the IRB of regular organizers like Sean MacDermott and Ernest Blythe working regularly on a salary provided by Clan-na-Gael funds from America. In fact, Irish Volunteer numbers showed no regular increase until after the Rossa funeral and then only at an average rate of a few hundred a month right up to the Rising of April 1916 itself.[18] This relative failure to attract much support is all the more remarkable, given the drop in emigration from Ireland which had taken place since the beginning of the war.* None of the new stay-at-home population seemed yet attached to the Irish Volunteers in any significant quantity. Recruitment for the British Army on the other hand was proceeding at the rate of over six thousand per month.†

As for Griffith's political organization proper, Alderman Kelly, one of its representatives on the Dublin Corporation, declared frankly in October 1915 on the anniversary of Thomas Davis's death that Sinn Fein was 'on the rocks' and that he did not see what could be done about it. It had kept the light of nationality alive for the past eight or ten years, he claimed, and without it there would be no Volunteers of any kind, yet 'We are now left in this position that we cannot pay the rent or taxes of these premises' (the headquarters at 6 Harcourt Street, Dublin).[20]

Nevertheless, the 'Sinn Fein' Volunteers, and even the hundred-or-so strong Irish Citizen Army of James Connolly with whom they were usually on bad terms because of their refusal to give any priority to labour problems, could hardly help increasingly attracting some attention, however contemptuous, as the other active Volunteers became absorbed by the British Army.

On 19 September Pearse led some 1,500 Volunteers, 600 of whom were armed, through the streets of Dublin and out into manoeuvres at Stepaside, the scene of one of the Fenian victories of 1867.[21] On 6 October James

* Only 8,176 Irishmen had emigrated to countries other than Britain in 1915 compared with 19,267 in 1914 which itself had seen the first annual increase in population since 1851.[19]

† Official figures, *Freeman's Journal*, 2 July 1915. There were 71,494 Irish Catholics alone from Ireland in the armed forces by 20 June 1915 – 49,247 Protestants.

Connolly and his minute Irish Citizen Army, with the Countess Markievicz in uniform as one of his lieutenants, even carried out a mock attack on Dublin Castle.[22] When the anniversary of the Manchester Martyrs' death came round in November that year it was the Irish Volunteers who organized the celebrations.[23] The fact that the reprieved companion in arms of 'the noble-hearted three', Edward O'Meagher Condon, the man who had in fact first shouted the immortal 'God Save Ireland' from the dock, was still alive, and had been a staunch supporter of Redmond for many years and an optimistic enthusiast for the Home Rule Act, troubled Pearse and his colleagues no more than had the United Irish League affiliations of O'Donovan Rossa.* They were working quite consciously with historical myth in a climate that was becoming subtly favourable to it.

The mounting pressure from Conservative quarters in England, as the war situation deteriorated, for a system of conscription which might well include Ireland sharpened the edge of the Volunteers' activity. And under the threat of conscription, they began to receive some support not only from parish priests but also indirectly from at least one member of the Roman Catholic hierarchy. When some Irish emigrants, trying to leave Liverpool for the United States, were attacked as shirkers by the mob and given white feathers, the Bishop of Limerick, the Most Reverend Dr O'Dwyer, wrote publicly in protest: 'It is very probable that these poor Connacht peasants knew little or nothing of the meaning of war.... They would much prefer to be allowed to till their own potato gardens in peace in Connemara.... Their crime is that they are not ready to die for England. Why should they? What have they or their forbears ever got from England that they should die for her? Mr Redmond will say: "A Home Rule Act is on the Statute Book." But any intelligent Irishman will say: "A Simulacrum of Home Rule with an express notice that it is never to come into operation".'[24]

'Any intelligent Irishman' was a gross exaggeration, but it was an exaggeration with a grain of substance in it which any intelligent Irishman would recognize. There was something of a vacuum in Ireland, with the better part of Volunteers off at the war and the attention of most of Ireland directed outwards into Flanders. And in this prevailing situation it was easy for both the Citizen Army and 'the Sinn Fein Volunteers' to acquire an exaggerated significance.

Their opposition to recruiting for the British Army, their insistence on an Irish patriotism which did not, like that of the majority of Ireland, involve identification with the Empire's war effort, made many Unionists in particular indignant at the liberty of action allowed them. But the Chief Secretary, Augustine Birrell, acting in close cooperation with Redmond and John Dillon, consistently refused to yield to the clamour to have them suppressed.

* He died in America the following month. (*Freeman's Journal*, 8 April 1915, 17 December 1915.)

Redmond and Dillon continued rightly to advise Birrell that these extremist forces represented only a minute proportion of Irish opinion and that so delicate were Irish sensibilities that the only danger lay in making martyrs of them. It is to Birrell's credit that he learnt to understand clearly the peculiar nature of an Irish nationalism which, for reasons of history, could so easily be stimulated into something far more extreme than it was. Under Redmond's and Dillon's guidance he correctly saw it as the main task of his wartime secretaryship to prevent emotive influences from unsettling that mass patriotic nationalism which had consolidated into the demand for Home Rule.

Thus, in spite of occasional Unionist outbursts, it became quite a common sight to see the Irish Volunteers and men of Connolly's Citizen Army marching through the streets of Dublin in their uniforms with rifles on their shoulders or wheeling in mock attacks on public buildings. There was not necessarily any sinister objective in all this. The Volunteers' Director of Organization, Patrick Pearse, had written publicly in May 1915 when calling for more recruits that military action was not envisaged by the Irish Volunteers in the near future. 'But,' he had continued, 'what if Conscription be forced upon Ireland? What if a Unionist or a Coalition British Ministry repudiate the Home Rule Act? What if it be determined to dismember Ireland? What if it be attempted to disarm Ireland?'

These seemed the objects for which the Irish Volunteers were parading. If they chose to think them of primary concern while most people gave priority to the war, then that was their business, if faintly ridiculous. The great majority even of this minority of the Volunteers saw it much this way too. They could be accused of excessive zeal but they were proud of it, proud to be emphasizing the priority of the green flag over the Union Jack rather than waving them both simultaneously. The fact that there was an immediate serious practical purpose in this activity was known only to a handful of men in the inner conclave of the IRB. And since this did not even include Eoin MacNeill, the actual President of the Volunteers, it is hardly reasonable to blame the government's Chief Secretary for having known only very little more. What they did know did not seem to substantiate serious fears.

The government and Birrell had in fact known since the beginning of the war that there was some apparently hare-brained scheme to bring about an Irish rebellion. They had learnt of it through messages intercepted between the German Embassy in Washington and the German Government in Berlin, the code of which had been broken by the British Admiralty.[25] The scheme appeared to centre round the old ex-Fenian John Devoy, who presided over the extreme nationalist American organization, Clan-na-Gael, and the curious figure of the British Consular official from the Glens of Antrim, Sir Roger Casement.

16

Casement in Germany

On the same day at the beginning of July 1914 as Erskine Childers had sailed in the *Asgard* to collect his share of the arms shipment for Howth, Casement who had done so much to set the event in motion had sailed for America to try to procure more arms.* He was followed a few days later by a letter from Eoin MacNeill dated 7 July, describing him as the 'accredited representative of the arms sub-committee' of the Irish Volunteers.[1]

On arrival in New York on 19 July he immediately got in touch with John Devoy, head of the secret revolutionary directory of Clan-na-Gael. Casement and Devoy had never met before, though they had corresponded occasionally, and Casement was a subscriber to the newspaper of which Devoy was the editor, the *Gaelic American*. But they knew something of each other through their mutual friend, Bulmer Hobson, and this friendship was to make for awkwardness at their first meeting. Devoy was courteous, but explained that Casement's part in allowing Redmond's nominees on to the Volunteer Committee made him unacceptable to Clan-na-Gael. Casement felt too tired to attempt a full justification of his and Hobson's point of view that evening. But the next day he wrote a long explanatory letter to Devoy which Devoy showed to the other members of the revolutionary directory. 'All,' wrote Devoy afterwards, 'were impressed by the downright sincerity of the man.'[2]

The other prominent members of the revolutionary directory were Judge Dan Cohalan of New York and Joe McGarrity, a naturalized Irish-American of Philadelphia who had made a fortune in the liquor trade. Casement was soon in touch with them. He had also within a few hours of arriving in New York been accosted in the street with a hard-luck, down-and-out story by a clever, disreputable young Norwegian sailor, named Adler Christensen, whom he 'befriended'.[3]

Little attempt seems to have been made to do anything very practical about securing supplies of arms for Volunteers from America. Large public meetings were held at which money was raised and Irish-American morale boosted. This was the sort of thing that had been going on happily in America

* He sailed from Ireland to Glasgow on 2 July and from Glasgow to Montreal on 4 July.

at varying pitches of intensity for more than fifty years. Casement, though he had explicitly said to Devoy that what was wanted were arms and not dollars,⁴ spoke at meetings, contacted public men outside revolutionary circles, published pamphlets and wrote letters to newspapers. At this period of his life he was a man easily distracted from the main task in hand by the bustle of his own activity.

But in any case the need to arm the Volunteers was becoming obscured by the larger shadow rapidly spreading over Europe. And the week which brought to Casement and McGarrity, desperate with excitement in Philadelphia, the wonderful news of the safe landing of the rifles at Howth also brought word that Europe was at war.

The war with Germany was something which Casement had expected though he had not expected it to come so soon. He was clear in his mind how it could be turned to what he saw as Ireland's advantage. In an article published in the magazine *Irish Review* in July 1913 he had already opposed the orthodox view that Ireland and Britain must stand or fall together in the event of war with Germany. The very opposite was the case, he maintained. A war with Germany in which England was defeated might bring about Ireland's separation from England and her establishment as an independent sovereign state: an independent Ireland would be a guarantee for Germany of the freedom of the seas from British control. This view had penetrated to the IRB and Devoy through Casement's friend Hobson as early as 1910 and 1911. In March 1914 Devoy had shown a Casement memorandum to this effect to the German ambassador.

Devoy again got in touch with the German ambassador in New York on the outbreak of war and gave him the message he had received from the IRB in Ireland to the effect that they intended to take advantage of the war to bring about an armed rebellion, and that they wanted arms. Soon afterwards the idea that Casement should go to Berlin in person to facilitate German cooperation was in the air.

Much later Devoy criticized Casement severely for his 'utter impracticability' and described him as an 'honest but visionary' meddler.⁵ The impression has thereby grown up that Casement's mission to Germany was a self-styled one, not really endorsed by the revolutionary bodies either in Ireland or America. But this is incorrect.

It is not clear at what date the idea that Casement should go to Germany was first broached. On Sunday, 2 August, Casement and Devoy were riding together in an open carriage at a meeting held to protest against the shooting of the civilians at Bachelor's Walk. A press photographer rushed up to the carriage and before Casement could turn his face away had clicked the shutter of his camera. Casement was very worried because he thought the wide publication of his photograph might prejudice his chances if he should undertake any secret mission in the future. But he did not then say anything more definite to Devoy.[6] Certainly the two main points which he eventually went to Germany to try and secure (a German declaration of sympathy with Irish national aims, and the formation of an Irish Brigade from prisoners of war) were agreed as objectives between himself and Devoy within a matter of weeks. On 14 September Casement wrote from 'c/o John Devoy' to Joe McGarrity:

'I saw a friend yesterday. They are keen for it – keener now than ever before as they realize its moral value to their case. Also the other matter you and I discussed I put forward, and that too they like and think can be done – they will discuss and let me know.'[7]

On 18 September von Papen, then German military attaché in Washington, wrote to Casement: 'As a result of our last interview I repeated yesterday the cabled request concerning formation of a special Brigade ...'[8]

An emissary from the IRB had been in New York and had discussed Casement's mission. He was Dr Patrick McCartan, editor of the IRB paper *Irish Freedom*, and, after his return, the following letter in a simple general code was sent from Dublin:

My dear Sister,

You will be anxious to hear that I arrived safely without even being questioned ...

Things look fairly good regarding the establishment of the Mission which we all discussed. . . . The Fathers here think Father Rogers should go to Rome at once as he can do most there. They say a capital of five thousand would be useless. It must be at least twenty-five thousand and better fifty thousand. Better they think have as few converts as possible along as they would be safer on the foreign Mission. . . . Father Rodgers [sic] must rush the Superior into making the public statement we spoke of. It will clear the air considerably. . . . Urge him to go at once.

Your fond sister,
Mary.[9]

Casement's mission to Germany was thus clearly approved by both the IRB in Ireland and Devoy.

On 3 October Devoy wrote in a letter to McGarrity describing 'Rory's [Casement's] trip' as 'the most important step we have yet taken'.[10]

On 15 October Casement, having washed his face in buttermilk to try to give himself a fair complexion,[11] and travelling on a borrowed American passport in the name of James Landy, sailed in the Norwegian ship *Osker II* for Germany via Norway. He was accompanied by the young Norwegian, Adler Christensen.

Christensen claimed to have a wife called Sadie living in Philadelphia, habitually used make-up, was soon to be in trouble with the Berlin police, admitted later to spying for the American Government and was finally thought by Casement himself, after a warning received from John Devoy, to be quite possibly in the pay of the British Government.[12] Whatever Christensen's later affiliations, and money seems always to have been his only interest in forming them, there is no doubt at all that at this stage he had decided that his interests lay primarily in being loyal to Casement. When the ship on which they sailed was stopped on the High Seas by the British Navy and detained for two days at Stornaway, Christensen did not give him away, although it is tempting to suspect that he had something to do with the 215 dollars stolen from Casement during the voyage.[13] And again when, after arriving safely in Oslo, the British Ambassador to Norway, Findlay, made a reasonable enough attempt to capture Casement by suborning Christensen, Christensen remained loyal. In fact Christensen was probably the type of man quite commonly thrown up in wars, who considers himself sharp enough to play both sides off against each other in his own interest. From long entanglement in such a game he probably sincerely thought himself to be on whatever side he happened to be getting money from at the moment.*

Historically Christensen is of interest only in showing the amateurish and makeshift nature of the Irish revolutionaries' practical arrangements. Casement was indeed, as Devoy later pointed out, a very poor conspirator, but that is as much a reflection on Devoy and the IRB themselves who, after all, claimed to be professional conspirators whereas Casement did not, and who should therefore have chosen a more suitable agent than Casement for carrying out 'the most important step' they had yet taken. Devoy later said that Casement's 'impracticability' in Germany had necessitated his being by-passed in negotiations between the revolutionaries and the Germans. But as late as 12 November 1915 Devoy wrote to the Germans:

'We have the fullest confidence in Sir Roger Casement; there has never been since he went to Germany any lack of confidence in him on our part. ... Sir Roger Casement has authority to speak for and represent the Irish Revolutionary Party in Ireland and America.'[14]

A few days earlier Devoy had been complaining to McGarrity that it was Casement who was by-passing *him* and that he was 'much disappointed that Casement did not write' and that he was 'evidently not to be considered any more ...'.[15] There is no evidence until 10 February 1916 of Devoy taking any initiative with the Germans independently of Casement. Then he did so for two very good reasons apart from any personal impatience with him. The first was that he was passing on a message of the IRB to the effect that they were definitely on the point of rising in Ireland and he knew that Casement was opposed to such a move. Casement had informed him as long

* The Irish KC Serjeant Sullivan, who defended Casement later at his trial for treason, in old age thought he remembered being told by the British Director of Prosecutions that the compromising Casement diaries of which the British Government made some use both before and after Casement's trial were bought from Christensen who had stolen them from Casement in the course of this journey. (Personal interview with author.)

ago as 20 June 1915 that 'a "rising" in Ireland would be a futile form of force ... and a crime too so I never have and shall not counsel that'.[6] The second reason was that Casement had written to McGarrity on 20 December 1915 to say that he was too ill to act as envoy any more, and that no more instructions should be sent to him.

Whether the revolutionaries in America and in Ireland subsequently liked to admit it or not, Casement was the only permanent direct link that was ever forged with their 'gallant allies in Europe'.*

What had happened in the thirteen months in Germany before Casement had virtually opted out of his mission through illness? The stagnation which was to settle over the mission did not make itself apparent at once. Three weeks after his arrival, on 20 November, 1914, the German Government issued the following official statement:

... The Imperial Government formally declares that under no circumstances would Germany invade Ireland with a view to its conquest or the overthrow of any native institutions in that country. Should the fortune of this great war, that was not of Germany's seeking, ever bring in its course German troops to the shores of Ireland, they would land there, not as an army of invaders to pillage and destroy, but as the forces of a Government that is inspired by good-will towards a country and a people for whom Germany desires only a national prosperity and national freedom.

Casement had written the Declaration himself. 'It breaks new ground in Europe and clears the air,' he wrote to McGarrity the next day, adding that he was spending money faster than he had expected, and that he badly needed a fur coat. '... I got nearly frozen to death going to the battle front in a motor-car 200 miles at a high rate of speed ...' He added cryptically: 'I have not seen the poor friends yet. They are still scattered but are being brought to one place.'[17]

This referred to what he saw as the second main objective of his mission, the organization of an Irish Brigade from British prisoners of war. And it was on this point that, in an attempt to turn into reality the ideal of Irish nationality for militant independent Irishmen, the mission broke down.

The Germans never concealed from Casement that their chief interest in the cause of Irish freedom was in its possible military advantage to themselves. They knew nothing about Ireland and Irish nationality, and therefore at first naturally accepted the Devoy–IRB–Casement interpretation at its face value. And, on the strength of that, it was not unreasonable to expect that many Irishmen captured with the British armies would be ready to change sides and fight against their 'traditional enemy'. The Central Powers knew something of the incipient disloyalty of oppressed nationalities, and a Czech Legion of several thousand men was to be fighting on the allied side

---

* Words of Republican Proclamation of 1916.

before the end of the war. Although the way to Ireland itself was blocked to any large force so long as the British Navy controlled the seas, a successfully organized Irish Brigade in Europe might, they imagined, very possibly encourage a situation in Ireland which would force the British to withdraw a substantial number of troops from the Western Front.

Soon after Casement's arrival the Germans started collecting all Irish prisoners of war together into a separate camp at Limburg. And on 3 December 1914, Casement, a dignified bearded consular figure with a hat and an umbrella, went down there for the first time, accompanied by a German prince who had been educated at Harrow,[18] to talk to the simple country boys of Munster and Connaught.

Those among the prisoners who had imagined themselves to be fighting for anything had imagined themselves to be fighting in the cause of Ireland against Germany and had received some remarkably unpleasant treatment from the Germans in the process. Their curious visitor now suggested to them that they should come out and fight in the cause of Ireland *with* Germany instead. He went there again on 4 December and again on the 6th and again – there were now about two thousand Irishmen in the camp altogether – on 6 January 1915. At the same time he had been negotiating at the German Foreign Office a treaty laying down the conditions on which an Irish Brigade was to be raised and employed. Its members were to be Volunteers, equipped and fed but not paid by the German Government; they were to have Irish officers; to fight under the Irish flag alone, to fight solely in the cause of Ireland and under no circumstances to be employed for any German end, and in the event of a German naval victory, to be landed on the Irish coast with a supporting body of German officers and men.[19] This treaty which was a distinct diplomatic achievement for Casement was signed by himself and the German Secretary of State at the German Foreign Office on 27 December 1914. But by this date he must already have suspected that it was a dead letter.

He himself later tried to minimize the bad reception he got from the prisoners of war (the 'poor friends' or 'poor brothers' as he called them in letters to McGarrity) and certainly the very most of this reception was later made, possibly to the extent of some invention, by his enemies. But even Casement himself only claimed that he had a friendly reception from 'more than half' the fifty men he talked to on 6 January, adding that 'only some of the men (a very few) showed any sign of unfriendliness'.[20] A letter he wrote to Father J. T. Nicholson, an Irish-American priest whom Devoy sent over later in January to help with recruiting for the Brigade, probably gives a clearer hint of what went on. 'I will not,' wrote Casement, 'return to Limburg to be insulted by a handful of recreant Irishmen.... I cannot meet insults from cads and cowards with insults. I can only avoid the cads and cowards.'

At any rate the figures speak plainly enough. He returned to Berlin in January with only one man out of the two thousand Irishmen at Limburg committed. This man was Sergeant Timothy Quinlisk of the Royal Irish Regiment, whom Casement noted in his diary as looking a rogue.*

Faced with Casement's utter failure to bring about the one thing to which they really attached importance, the Germans naturally began to revise their view of him and the Irish situation as he and his friends had painted it. Their disillusionment must have been accelerated by Casement's own behaviour. It was not only that the Berlin police were receiving unsavoury reports about his man, Christensen's, moral character. Casement himself, humiliated by his experience with the prisoners of war, desperately aware of the sudden futility of his presence in Germany, now set about trying to deceive himself that he was doing some good there by building up into what he imagined was a superb propaganda story his account of the British Minister in Oslo's, Mr Findlay's, attempt to capture him on his way through to Berlin. His voluminous writings on this subject reveal a mind temporarily unbalanced. In view of the deep shock not only to his pride from the failure with the Irish Brigade but to all he had ever believed in about Ireland, this temporary loss of balance is understandable. He sought as far as possible to shift the blame for his predicament on to the cynicism of the Germans, but their failure to keep up their enthusiasm after the immediate failure of the Brigade was reasonable enough.

'I am at the end of my tether,' he wrote in June 1915, 'because I see no way out. I have been in that frame of mind for months.... The truth was forced on me in January and February that I had misjudged greatly and made a mistake.'

He would have liked to return to America,[21] but the British Navy controlled the seas. He remained in Germany 'a virtual prisoner'. In the circumstances he did the only thing possible. Encouraged by the persuasions of Father Nicholson, the Irish-American priest at Limburg, and the reports of Sergeant Quinlisk and two other prisoners, Kehoe and Dowling, who had since committed themselves, he embarked on a final attempt to make the Irish Brigade a reality. He knew that only by making the Irish National movement a military reality could he get the Germans interested in it again.

In a post-mortem on this second attempt which he wrote on 30 June, he said: 'I had to go on for so much depended on the possibility of the Agreement coming off' [i.e., the treaty signed on 27 December 1914 which, with only three men in the Brigade, naturally had remained unpublished] ... 'but I went on like a man going to execution *because I had lost faith*†.... They

---

* He was to be shot by the IRA in 1920 for an attempt to betray Michael Collins to the British.
† Casement's italics.

[the Germans] want a show of physical force.... Now a "rising" in Ireland would be a futile form of force – more futile even than de Wet's in South Africa – and a crime too so I never have and shall not counsel that. But a force here on the Continent, under our flag, allied with these armies would give us the right to share in the fight and its results ...'

He knew now that he could not get an effective force together from British prisoners of war, but he hoped to get a sufficient nucleus to persuade the Germans to publish the treaty and then with the help of Devoy and McGarrity in America to raise a force of Irish Americans who would come to Germany and join it (for America had not yet entered the war on the allied side). After everything that Irish Americans had been saying they were prepared to do for the last fifty years or so this was not altogether unrea·· sonable, and Casement pointed this out in a very strong letter to McGarrity written on 29 April 1915, which he held back for ten days because he knew it might cause trouble but eventually posted on 10 May. After outlining his plan he wrote:

I want help. I am here alone. I want officers. I want men. I want a fighting fund.... I came here for one thing only, to try and help national Ireland – and if there is no such thing in existence then the sooner I pay for my illusions the better.... This will be really a test – probably a final one – of the sincerity of Irish nationality. So far the mass of the exponents of Irish nationality have contented themselves for over a century with words not deeds. When the moment came to fight there were either no fighters or no guns.... Unless the Irish in Ireland and most of all in America – where they are free and can act as they will – come forward now and give effective proof of their patriotism then they may bury the corpse of Irish nationality for ever, for no one will want to look at the stinking carcase any longer.... While we are saying that a German victory over England will bring Ireland freedom, we, the most vitally concerned in that result, are not fighting for Ireland, or for Germany – but many thousands of Irishmen *are* fighting ... in the ranks of the British army.... The action so far taken by Irish Americans is contemptible – they have talked – floods of talk – but they have not even contributed money,* much less attempted any overt act for Ireland.... If today, when all Europe is dying for national ends, whole peoples marching down with songs of joy to the valley of eternal night, we alone stand by idle or moved only to words, then are we in truth the most contemptible of all the peoples of Europe.

The hysteria in this letter is that of a man shocked by the truth. At the end of it Casement drops a hint that if no help is forthcoming he will go out alone and face the English as a form of expiation. Perhaps it was this

---

* This, of course, was untrue. A typewritten account sheet found among McGarrity's papers shows that the Clan-na-Gael Treasurer handed over to John Devoy between 31 August 1914 and 2 April 1917, 98,297 dollars for the 'Home Organization' (i.e. IRB). Casement himself had up to this time been financed with some four thousand dollars of Irish-American money.

250

mood which, just over a year later, enabled him to face the appalling sentence, delivered by a twitching judge with black cap clumsily awry,[22] with a self-assurance and courage that impressed all who watched him.

Casement failed in his renewed effort to form a nucleus of the Brigade large enough to persuade the Germans to publish the treaty. In the end only fifty-five men were collected altogether from among the prisoners of war in Germany and one Irish American, John McGooey, came from the States to join them. The IRB, responding to Casement's request for officers relayed by Devoy, sent in October via the States and escorted by Christensen an ex-British NCO and Irish Volunteer instructor called Robert Monteith, to take command of the sad contingent. The fifty-five were kept at Zossen, seventeen miles from Berlin, 'practically as prisoners of war'. They went out on occasional route marches, sometimes pathetically accompanied by Casement, who had always been a great walker. But they were not allowed to carry rifles as Casement proposed, because, in the words of the German general who turned down the suggestion, they consisted 'of individuals proving themselves addicted to drink and opposing the laws of military discipline ... and good order'.[23] Certainly Monteith records one incident in which they came to blows with their German 'allies', and on 22 February 1916 he wrote to Casement to say that he had had to pay out 143·50 Marks (about £8) for 'blankets which some of the boys made away with'.[24] Monteith stood by them loyally in his book published fifteen years later, but when in April 1916 there was some question of sending the Irish Brigade to Ireland to take part in the Rising and Casement asked Monteith to draw up a list of the men in it who could be trusted, Monteith listed eleven, not including Quinlisk. One of the eleven turned king's evidence against Casement after he had landed with him in Ireland from a German submarine.

Thus, out of the two thousand or so Irishmen at Limburg, ten at most proved to be true Irish nationalists in the sense in which the leaders of the 1916 Rising meant the word. And perhaps the proportion of one in two hundred even over-represents the number of such nationalists in Ireland itself at the same time that rising was made.

For a few more months Casement, wandering restlessly round Germany, continued to have some hope of filling up the Brigade with Irish Americans. On 26 October 1915 he wrote to McGarrity: 'If we can get two hundred all told and two officers we have a chance here.'

Monteith, permanently at Zossen, was a great stand-by to him, for his conscience was troubled by the situation of the fifty-five men whom he had called out to commit treason with him in a gamble to convince the German Government, which had failed. Their treason he saw was utterly pointless.

In December he accepted defeat. 'Send no more,' he wrote to McGarrity after the one man from America, McGooey, had arrived. He added that he was trying to get the fifty-five men of the Brigade sent to the East, Syria, where they could fight with the Turks. And the failure to bring off even that mad-cap scheme was a fitting conclusion to the whole disastrous enterprise.

'Write instructions,' he concluded, 'to Monteith now, not to me. I am too sick. . . . Monteith is very good. . . . Meantime M. will send the old man [Devoy] news.'

Four days later, on Christmas Eve 1915, he was signing off altogether.

'Better not write me again as I fear I shall not be able to attend to it. . . . I can never forget all your careful work and thought and kindness, may He keep you still to see some hope dawn on the cause you have so faithfully worked for. You were worthy of a far better agent here than poor broken me. What I did may have been good but I can do no more now I fear all the rest of my days, for the seat of power is giving way . . .'

But meanwhile the 'military council' of the IRB in Dublin had been hoping for German help.

17

The Dublin Rising, 1916

On Easter Sunday, 23 April 1916, John Dillon, who had gone over to Dublin for the parliamentary recess, wrote to Redmond, who had stayed in London:

'Dublin is full of the most extraordinary rumours ... you must not be surprised if something very unpleasant and mischievous happens this week.'[1]

The issue of the *Freeman's Journal*, the party paper, which appeared the next day, Monday, 24 April, was a routine one and fairly dull. Its first leader was about a by-election pending in Queen's County between two Home Rule Nationalists standing on an identical policy of loyalty to Redmond, and competing simply because no candidate had been selected for the constituency by the party convention. Only two items in the paper hinted at unusual events and both were mysteriously imprecise. One concerned the arrest of a prominent member of the Tralee Irish Volunteers, a Mr Austin Stack, on a charge of importing arms from Germany. The other reported that a collapsible boat with arms and ammunition had been found on Currahane strand, County Kerry, and that a stranger of unknown nationality had been arrested in the vicinity and conveyed under escort to Dublin.[2] Only later that day was it announced that the stranger was Roger Casement, and by that time the people of Dublin themselves had been caught up in extraordinary events.

The next issue of the *Freeman's Journal* to appear bore the comprehensive dates 26 April to 5 May, and its first leader began:

'The stunning horror of the past ten days in Dublin makes it all but impossible for any patriotic Irishman who has been a witness of the tragedy enacted in our midst to think collectedly or write calmly of the event.'

The event which took not only the ordinary population of Dublin but most of the rank and file of the Irish Volunteers wholly by surprise had started in an almost dreamlike way on Easter Monday morning, while devotees of the *Freeman's Journal* were still calmly perusing the leader about the election in Queen's County.

Around noon a number of odd things had begun to happen in Dublin. A party of some hundred or so Irish Volunteers and Citizen Army men marching through the streets of the city, as they had been in the habit of doing for months past – and attracting particularly little attention on a Bank Holiday when more normal holiday-makers had gone to the races – stopped opposite the General Post Office in O'Connell Street, then turned and ran into the building.* Within a few minutes, flourishing revolvers and even firing some shots into the air, they had cleared out both customers and officials. Soon two flags were flying from the building: one the traditional green flag with the gold harp, with the words 'Irish Republic' now inscribed on it in gold; and the other a new flag strange to most people, a tricolour of orange, white and green. The Post Office had become the headquarters of the new 'Republic'.

A little later, amazed by-standers saw Patrick Pearse emerge on to the steps of the portico and read a proclamation from 'the Provisional Government'. This stated that in the name of God and of the dead generations, from which Ireland 'received her ancient tradition of nationhood', she was summoning her children to her flag and striking for her freedom.³ The proclamation spoke of the long usurpation of Ireland's right to control her own destinies by 'a foreign people and government', and stated most inaccurately that in every generation the Irish people had asserted their right to national freedom and sovereignty, adding 'six times during the past three hundred years they have asserted it in arms'. It referred to 'gallant Allies in Europe' who were supporting Ireland, thereby blandly dismissing the fact that the flower of Ireland's manhood had been fighting those allies in Europe for the past twenty months. Indeed, almost within the hour Irish men of the 3rd Royal Irish Rifles and the 10th Royal Dublin Fusiliers, themselves the product of the most recent British Army recruiting drive in Ireland, were the first to move against this self-styled republic in the Post Office.⁴ Small wonder that Pearse's words fell among a largely uninterested crowd and that the principal sounds to greet them were not cheers but the crash of breaking glass as a Dublin mob, taking advantage of the absence of the police, began to loot the fashionable shops in O'Connell Street.⁵ The proclamation was signed by Clarke, MacDermott, MacDonagh, Pearse, Ceannt, Plunkett and James Connolly.

Meanwhile, the 'Republic' had already drawn first blood. A party of Volunteers had set out before noon on an audacious expedition to blow up the large ammunition dump at the Magazine Fort in the Phoenix Park. They had skilfully tricked the sentry, gaining entry by pretending to pursue a football, and after wounding another sentry and taking the rest of the guard prisoner, cut the telephone wires and successfully placed a gelignite charge in part of the fort. They had, however, been unable to find the key to the main ammunition dump, for it had been taken by the officer in charge to

* O'Connell Street was then officially Sackville Street, but already popularly known by the name which it assumed officially on the creation of the Irish Free State.

Fairyhouse Races for the day. The subsequent explosion was not very great and did little important damage. The Volunteers made off with some captured rifles, but as they were hurrying away spotted a boy leaving the fort to give the alarm. He was the seventeen-year-old son of the Fort's commandant, who was then away in France, serving with an Irish regiment. The boy was shot with a revolver before he could reach a telephone and died within twenty-four hours.[6]

Another early casualty had been an unarmed middle-aged constable of the Dublin Metropolitan Police, named O'Brien. He had been on the gate of Dublin Castle when men of the Irish Citizen Army had appeared and tried to gain entrance. In the best traditions of the force he put up his hand, and was shot dead.[7] The party entered the Castle yard and, after throwing into the guardroom a home-made bomb which failed to explode, made the six soldiers they found there prisoner. Unknown to the Citizen Army men this was the only guard in this part of the Castle at all and the usual substantial garrison normally to be found round the corner in Ship Street mustered twenty-five men. The traditional seat of British rule in Ireland for many centuries lay within the rebels' power. Undoubtedly the news of its capture would have produced a psychological shock throughout Ireland. But almost inexplicably the Citizen Army men seem to have taken fright at their easy early victory and, evacuating the Castle itself, preferred to occupy some buildings opposite. More blood began to flow as they were engaged there by men of the Royal Irish Rifles and the Dublin Fusiliers who reached the Castle in the early afternoon.[8]

Over much of Dublin it was still quite difficult to appreciate that a coordinated attempt at rebellion had broken out. A young Irish writer, emerging an hour later for lunch from the National Gallery where he worked as registrar, knew nothing of what had happened until, approaching St Stephen's Green, he noticed crowds standing about in curiously silent inquiring attitudes as if there had been an accident. Physically, what had happened was that the 'Sinn Feiners' (detachments of the Irish Volunteers and the Irish Citizen Army plainly acting in harmony for once) had occupied some two dozen strong points – including St Stephen's Green – throughout the city, dominating barracks, railway stations, key approaches, and other prominent public thoroughfares. From the Post Office Pearse, now calling himself Commandant-General of a joint Irish Republican Army, exercised a rather static command with Connolly, Clarke and Plunkett. Commandant Thomas MacDonagh, the poet and university English lecturer, had occupied Jacob's Biscuit Factory behind Dublin Castle. A Citizen Army group to which Countess Markievicz, wearing green uniform and flourishing a revolver, was attached, had occupied the park in St Stephen's Green. There they had dug themselves in, until, coming under fire from the dominating Shelburne Hotel, they recognized that their position was militarily unsound and withdrew to the large distinguished building on the further side of the Green which was the College of Surgeons.

Among several other prominent positions occupied and fortified were the Four Courts under Edward Daly, the nephew of an old Fenian of '67, and Boland's Flour Mills, under the mathematics professor, Eamon de Valera, whose outposts commanded the main road into Dublin from the harbour of Kingstown, along which government reinforcements from Britain might be expected.

Although a quite ambitious plan for a more general rising had at one time been envisaged, involving other parts of Ireland and a more extensive and mobile occupation of Dublin itself, a whole sequence of misunderstandings, muddles and unfortunate disasters prevented it ever being put seriously to the test. Basically the pattern of the rebellion which unfolded over the next five days was that 'the Irish Republican Army' remained in most of the positions it had occupied on Easter Monday, inflicting what casualties it could – and these were sometimes substantial – on Irishmen and others in the British Army, who, backed by heavy artillery fire, inexorably closed in on them and eventually forced them to surrender. Any close study of the activity that took place during these five days in the epic headquarters of the rebellion, the General Post Office, reveals that apart from a brief moment in the afternoon of Easter Monday when Volunteer riflemen shot down and killed four Lancers of a detachment trying to make their way down O'Connell Street, its occupants did almost nothing at all under increasingly accurate shell-fire until they eventually tried to evacuate the burning building on Friday. Though some sixteen of the garrison were wounded, including James Connolly by a bullet in the ankle, none were killed until this attempted sortie on the Friday, when The O'Rahilly was one of those who fell, as they made a dash down Moore Street. In the meantime Pearse, Clarke, Plunkett and Connolly talked away the days, encouraging the men, issuing occasional over-confident dispatches about other parts of Ireland rising and German help being on the way, even once speculating among themselves on the advisability of appointing a German prince King of Ireland after the war, but always supremely confident that the assumption on which they had allowed the Rising to go ahead was justified.[9] This assumption was that success or failure was irrelevant and that it was the action itself which would stir old slumbering fires of fierce nationalism within the hearts of the Irish people, and eventually make the new green, white and orange flag now flying defiantly from the roof of the Post Office the flag of a truly national Ireland.

'We thought it a foolish thing for four score to go into battle against four thousand, or maybe forty thousand,' protested an ancient Gaelic hero in a play Pearse wrote late in 1915.[10]

'And so it is a foolish thing,' had come the super-heroic response. 'Do you want us to be wise?'

For years Pearse had been pining to see the mystical 'red wine of the battlefield' on Irish soil.[11] He gave the rank and file of the Volunteers no chance to challenge the rhetorical question of his play. But even Pearse, planning insurrection on the assumption that wisdom was irrelevant, had taken steps to make it as effective as he could. When, however, a series of events in the few days before the Rising caused it to be not only less effective than he and the IRB could make it, but downright disastrous, neither he nor the IRB were particularly worried. When at Liberty Hall on Easter Monday morning Connolly was assembling his men for the march to the Post Office, he told his friend William O'Brien: 'We are going out to be slaughtered.' O'Brien asked him if there were any chance of success at all. 'None whatever,' replied Connolly.[12]

In the interval between the funeral of O'Donovan Rossa in August 1915 and Easter Monday 1916 the Irish Volunteers had shown a slight but perceptible increase in their numbers for the first time since their split with the main body. This was due to a combination of practical and political factors. Among these were: the growing awareness that Redmond's own Volunteers were becoming ineffective as they were drained off to the war; the simultaneous feeling that the prospect of Home Rule, like the prospect of an end of the war itself, was receding into obscure mists of time in which a British Government might find it easier not to keep faith; the retention of a higher proportion of young farmers' sons on Irish soil than usual, owing to the halt in normal emigration; and the growing Irish determination that the threatened Conscription Act should never be applied to Ireland. The Conscription Act finally went through in January 1916. It was totally opposed by Redmond and the Irish party and in fact excluded Ireland. But the threat of an extension of conscription to Ireland was thereafter always present, and now that the main parliamentary battle on the subject had been won, such a threat was very much easier to implement quickly.

Yet, in these circumstances, the remarkable fact was not so much that the numbers of MacNeill's followers slightly increased but that they did not increase more significantly. According to police intelligence reports the increase was some 3,800 in eight months from August 1915 to April 1916.[13] But the British Army was able to obtain from Ireland over three times that number of recruits in the same period, 1,827 of them in the single month ending 15 April alone.[14] Though the Irish Volunteer parades became better attended and their and the Citizen Army's activity increasingly noticeable, resulting in a particularly good turn out both in Dublin and Cork for St Patrick's Day, 17 March 1916, they were still also noticeably out of tune with the vast mass of public opinion in the country. An Irish Volunteer of the time from Enniscorthy, County Wexford, has recorded how the farmer who lent him and his companions a hay-loft for drilling ran a serious

risk in obliging them, because of their unpopularity.[15] Ernest Blythe, one of
the principal Volunteer organizers of the day, has written of the 1914–15
period: 'The attitude of the majority of the people towards the Irish Volunteers and their independent nationalist stand was one of incredulity, suspicion
or dour hostility.'[16] On 22 March 1916 an anti-Sinn Fein demonstration
took place in Tullamore, when fourteen Irish Volunteers were besieged
by a hostile mob in the local Sinn Fein hall. Feeling that they were inade-
quately protected by the police they fired revolvers to keep the mob away,
and when the police moved in to disarm them resisted arrest, wounding a
Sergeant Aherne seriously.[17]

The professions of the young men finally arrested in the Tullamore case
give a useful cross-section of the social stratum from which the Irish Volunteer rank and file of the day were drawn. They consisted of a clerk, a barber's
assistant, an apprentice, a malt-house workman, a blacksmith's assistant, a
drayman, a painter, a cycle mechanic and a labourer.[18] Local police elsewhere
described the Volunteers as being composed principally of shop assistants,
artisans and, in the country districts, of small farmers' sons, while an English
eye-witness of the occupation of the Post Office in Dublin a month later –
who, incidentally, had the nerve to go in and ask for stamps before the
Republic could be officially proclaimed – also commented on the fact
that the rebels seemed drawn from the poorer classes. 'There were
no well-dressed men amongst them,' he explained a few days later to fellow
Englishmen, totally bewildered by events, 'although the Sinn Fein
movement has within it a great number of better-class people.'[19] In other
words they were of the same class as those who for twenty months had been
dying in Flanders and at the Dardanelles, though as yet unrepresentative of
them.

A marching song written some years earlier had recently become popular
with the Irish Volunteers. The words had a rather artificial stagey ring,
characteristic of the histrionic attitude the Volunteers often seemed to
embody.

> I'll sing you a song, a soldier's song,
> With a cheering rousing chorus
> As round our blazing camp-fires we throng
> The starry heavens o'er us.
> Impatient for the coming fight
> And as we watch the dawning light
> Here in the silence of the night.
> We'll chant the soldier's song.
>
> Soldiers are we, whose lives are pledged to Ireland,
> Some have come from the land across the sea . . .*

* Written in 1907 by Peader Kearney. The tune had been composed by his friend
Paddy Heaney. (O'Dubghaill, *Insurrection Fires*, p. 227.)

It was called 'The Soldier's Song' and though still almost unknown to most of the country was, within six years, to become the National Anthem of Ireland.

But although in this pre-Rising period the 'Sinn Feiners' were unrepresentative and even unpopular, the delicacy of national sensitivity in the prevailing situation was shown at the end of March when a public meeting was held in Dublin to protest against the ordered deportation of some ten Sinn Fein organizers from Ireland. The idea of banishment from Ireland was an ugly one in many Irish minds, and the hall was full and an overflow meeting was held outside it. It was this emotional area in Irish minds, with roots deep in Irish history, that Pearse and other members of the IRB's military council were determined to affect. Myth and reality had interacted on each other throughout Irish history. With a personal courage amounting almost to mania, Pearse and his fellow conspirators set out to turn the myth into reality by living it out in cold blood.

Up to a week before the Rising Eoin MacNeill, the nominal head of the Volunteers, had had no knowledge that it was being planned. He had, however, had certain misgivings, derived largely from the writings and utterances of people like Pearse and Connolly that some such action might one day be contemplated. Therefore in the middle of February 1916 he had made a deliberate point of attacking the living myth theory.

We have to remember [he wrote, in a memorandum designed to lay down the policy for the Irish Volunteers] that what we call our country is not a poetical abstraction, as some of us, perhaps all of us, in the exercise of our highly developed capacity for figurative thought, are sometimes apt to imagine – with the help of our patriotic literature. There is no such person as Caitlin Ni Uallachain or Roisin Dubh or the Sean-bean Bhoct, who is calling upon us to serve her. What we call our country is a concrete and visible reality. Now we believe that we think rightly on national matters ... if we are right nationally, it is our duty to get our country on our side, and not to be content with the vanity of thinking ourselves to be right and other Irish people to be wrong. As a matter of patriotic principle we should never tire of endeavouring to get our country on our side. ... I do not know at this moment whether the time and circumstance will yet justify distinct revolutionary action, but of this I am certain, the only possible basis for successful revolutionary action is deep and widespread popular discontent. We have only to look around us in the streets to see that no such condition exists in Ireland. A few of us, a small proportion who think about the evils of English government in Ireland are always discontented. We should be downright fools if we were to measure many others by the standards of our own thoughts.

I wish it then to be clearly understood that under present conditions I am definitely opposed to any proposal that may come forward involving insurrection. I have no doubt at all that my consent to any such proposal at this time and under these circumstances would make me false to my country besides involving me in the guilt of murder.[20]

Bulmer Hobson, who shared these views with MacNeill and was particularly anxious about Pearse's intention, had been instrumental in getting MacNeill to draw up the memorandum. After it had been discussed with the Volunteer leaders at MacNeill's house, Pearse categorically denied that he was planning an insurrection or that his view of the Volunteers' function was any different from their publicly declared defensive aims. In fact Pearse was lying, for the date for the Rising had already been decided on as Easter Sunday 1916. It had been notified as such to Devoy in America on 5 February and subsequently passed to the Germans. Another deception of MacNeill by Pearse concerned the labour leader James Connolly.

Since the beginning of the war Connolly, who became the outstanding Irish labour figure after Larkin's departure for America in October 1914, had been writing more and more outspoken denunciations of the British Government and of the recruiting campaign in Ireland, and hinting more and more openly at the need for someone in Ireland to rise in arms against Britain while the war lasted. He had, as early as 9 September 1914, been present at a meeting in the Library of the Gaelic League in Dublin at which the desirability of a rising was discussed, together with important members of the IRB such as Clarke, Pearse and Ceannt, and another outsider, Arthur Griffith. But it seems that the IRB members at this meeting did not let Connolly or other outsiders into the full secret of their own decisions or of their contacts already made with the Germans through Devoy.[21] Connolly appears to have had little real knowledge of the IRB's existence at the time, and, as the war continued, he became more and more impatient with and even contemptuous of the Volunteers. The IRB told him nothing of their own appointment of a secret Military Council and he judged the Volunteer organization at its face value.

Larkin's paper, the *Irish Worker*, had been suppressed in December 1914, and Connolly who had been editing it started a successor, the *Worker*, which in turn was suppressed after its sixth issue in February 1915. Thereafter he printed and published the *Workers' Republic* with his own plant at the Transport Workers' Union headquarters in Dublin, Liberty Hall, also the headquarters of the hundred or so strong Citizen Army. Across the front of Liberty Hall hung a bold banner proclaiming: 'We Serve Neither King nor Kaiser – but Ireland'. In itself it was an expression of sentiment which MacNeill would have found unexceptionable. But towards the end of 1915 MacNeill was being made increasingly anxious by talk of Connolly's intention to bring out the Citizen Army in a rising on its own account.[22]

The two utterly different temperaments of Connolly and MacNeill were illustrated in the respective issues of the *Workers' Republic* and the *Irish Volunteer* for Christmas Day 1915. Connolly, after reminding his readers of the price Wolfe Tone had paid for inaction at Bantry Bay in 1796, concluded with the words:

260

> The Kingdom of Heaven [Freedom] is within you.
> The Kingdom of Heaven can only be taken by violence. Heavenly words with a heavenly meaning.
> Christmas Week, 1796; Christmas week, 1915 – still hesitating.[23]

Connolly's frequent attacks in the *Workers' Republic* on the Volunteers for their lack of aggressiveness not only alarmed MacNeill and irritated many rank-and-file of Volunteers but also caused considerable anxiety to Pearse and his fellow IRB manipulators behind the scenes. They began to fear that Connolly would be as good as his printed word and start an individual insurrection with the tiny Citizen Army which would prematurely wreck their own plans.

On 19 January 1916 Connolly disappeared for three days, and his where-abouts remained unknown even to his closest friends. When he reappeared at Countess Markievicz's house on 22 January he seemed like a man with a load off his mind. The next issue of the *Workers' Republic* carried a new solemn determined note, the reason for which was not disclosed. He had in fact spent the three days in conclave with Pearse and the other IRB leaders, and had been made party to the secret of the Rising. He was himself appointed a member of the IRB's military council. He knew now that an insurrection was on for Easter Week.*

But Pearse used this incident to lull MacNeill's suspicions still further. A short while earlier, at the official request of the official Volunteer executive, MacNeill had arranged a private meeting with Connolly at which he heard him at first hand put forward his view that an immediate insurrection was necessary, and declare that whether or not the Volunteers came out the Citizen Army would fight in Dublin. Pearse, who was present at this meeting, assured MacNeill afterwards that he agreed with his point of view and that he would persuade Connolly to abandon his project. 'Very shortly afterwards', that is to say, presumably just after Connolly had spent his three days in conclave with the Military Council of the IRB, Pearse told MacNeill that he had got Connolly to abandon his project.[24] Though this, unlike his earlier statement that he was of MacNeill's point of view, was literally true in the sense that Connolly had now abandoned his project of a *separate* rising, it was deliberate deception of MacNeill who was thus led for the time being at any rate to believe that no 'act of rash violence' was being planned. In any case, shortly afterwards MacNeill received further assurances not only from Pearse but also from Plunkett that no insurrection was being planned.[25] MacNeill's own concept of the Volunteers' purpose

* For many years it was generally thought that Connolly had been 'kidnapped' by the IRB and held forcibly during his three days' absence, but most recent evidence suggests that he took part in the secret meeting of his own free will. William O'Brien, one of Connolly's closest colleagues at Liberty Hall, became satisfied many years ago that Connolly had not been kidnapped (*Sunday Press*, 17 April 1955). See also a methodical analysis of the incident in O'Dubghaill, *Insurrection Fires*, pp. 109–115.

remained, so it appeared, the only accepted one, namely that they would only take to arms if an attempt were made by the government to disarm them or to introduce conscription.

However, MacNeill's anxieties did not stay lulled for long. Several instances had already come to his notice of military dispositions being made for the Volunteers by Pearse, without his own authority, and early in April he actually received through the post a letter from America (that had incidentally been opened by the censor) containing a review article to the effect that a rising aided by Germany was planned for Ireland in the early summer by an extremist group in the Irish Volunteers. MacNeill publicized the fact and strongly disclaimed any such thing in the last issue of the *Irish Volunteer* to appear, which was dated Saturday, 22 April 1916. But by then MacNeill's peace of mind had been shattered by other events, and within twenty-four hours both he and the majority of the Volunteers themselves were in a state of considerable turmoil.

On Wednesday, 19 April 1916, a Sinn Fein alderman at a meeting of the Dublin Corporation read out a document, allegedly stolen from Dublin Castle, detailing instructions for the arrest of the Volunteer leaders and other national figures and for the suppression of the Volunteer organization. MacNeill had been shown the document at the beginning of the week. Although the arrest of the leaders was in fact under consideration at Dublin Castle, and contingency plans for it had doubtless been prepared, it seems virtually certain that this particular document was a bogus one, prepared, possibly on the strength of some information received from the Castle, by Joseph Plunkett and Sean MacDermott. Though it was suspect in some quarters at once, it served its purpose at first so far as MacNeill was concerned, for he accepted it and its menacing implications for the Volunteers as genuine. The secret design of Pearse, Plunkett and the rest of the IRB's Military Council was that MacNeill should openly and unwittingly undertake for them a large part of their undercover mobilization for insurrection.

The defensive conditions in which MacNeill had always been prepared to consider some action for the Volunteers, namely an impending attempt to be made by the government to disarm them, now seemed fulfilled. He ordered the Volunteers to prepare themselves against suppression by the government. His orders for this were made out in consultation with the other members of the Volunteer executive but, in MacNeill's own words, 'neither then nor at any previous meeting was the policy of insurrection adopted or proposed in any form'.[26] On Thursday night, 20 April, MacNeill learnt for the first time that in addition to his own order, other orders had also gone out unknown to him which were 'only intelligible as parts of a general scheme for insurrection'.[27] Appalled, he, Bulmer Hobson and another member of the Volunteer executive, J. J. O'Connell, went round at midnight to Pearse's school, St Enda's, to confront him with what they had discovered and there for the first time Pearse admitted that a rising was intended. MacNeill told Pearse he would do everything in his power, short of informing the government, to prevent the rising and would issue countermanding orders. A few hours later, on Friday morning, Sean MacDermott came to MacNeill's house and told him for the first time that a large quantity of arms was about to be landed from Germany. MacNeill, who still believed on the strength of the Castle document that a government swoop on the Volunteers was in any case imminent, realized that with the arrival of the arms the die would be firmly cast and agreed to accept what looked like the IRB's *fait accompli*.

'Very well,' he finally said to Sean MacDermott. 'If that is the case I'm in with you.'²⁸

From this moment onwards MacDermott, wishing doubtless to simplify the IRB chain of command in the Volunteers as the crisis approached, and assuming that MacNeill would prove no further trouble, began to suggest privately that MacNeill had resigned as Chief of Staff of the Volunteers. He had already been suggesting earlier in the week that MacNeill was sanctioning all the secret preliminary orders for the insurrection. But there was as little truth in the new report as in the earlier one, and MacNeill, in spite of his new awareness that so much had already been going on behind his back, does not seem to have doubted that he again held authority over the Volunteers.

To prevent any possible further disruption of the Rising's plans the IRB also took the precaution of neutralizing the one other man who it seemed might seriously make things awkward for them. On the Friday evening they kidnapped and held prisoner over the next few crucial days Bulmer Hobson, the man who a few years before had done so much to give their organization life. However, unpleasant surprises were still in store for them.

On the following morning, Saturday, 22 April, two Volunteers arrived in Dublin from the south-west of Ireland to see MacNeill with dramatic information. In the first place, they were able to enlighten him that the 'Castle Document' on the strength of which he had based his initial orders to the Volunteers to prepare for mobilization was a bogus one, designed to get him to do just that. More important still, they brought news that the arms ship on which the leaders were depending and on the strength of which he had reluctantly agreed to go into an insurrection with them had been captured by the British Navy and had sunk itself in Queenstown harbour. The 20,000 rifles and hundreds of thousands of rounds of ammunition Pearse was expecting were at the bottom of the sea. Roger Casement, a link between the insurrectionists and the Germans, had landed from a German submarine and had been captured almost immediately.

MacNeill at once sent messengers all over Ireland cancelling any orders the Volunteers might have received for special action. He also arranged for a notice to appear in the largest circulation Sunday newspaper, *The Sunday*

Independent, rescinding any orders that might have been issued to the Volunteers for Easter Sunday and forbidding every individual Volunteer from taking part in any parades, manoeuvres or other movements. On the very morning therefore of the day on which Pearse, Connolly and the rest of the military council had planned to come out in arms for an Irish Republic, they found the men they hoped to command paralysed by an order from their official leader telling them not to move.

This was a severe enough blow, but that caused by the capture and destruction of the arms ship had been even worse.

For almost a year now negotiations of a rather desultory and unprofessional sort had been going on between the IRB and the Germans for some form of military help. The situation had been rendered opaque by the fact that their chief resident representative in Germany was Casement, a man embittered since early 1915 by the failure of the Irish Brigade to fulfil his hopes, and by what he increasingly considered the cynical exploitation of the Irish cause by the Germans.

In April 1915 the IRB had sent Joseph Plunkett to Germany to make its first direct contact with Casement. He had taken a month getting there via neutral countries, but when he arrived had nothing to tell that Casement did not know or had not guessed already.[29] There was to be a rising some time before the end of the war and he had come to see what sort of military help was available. Casement himself was at this time already doubtful that any effective scheme of active cooperation with the Germans could be worked out.[30] The Germans after all had had their eyes opened to the limited appeal of Irish separatism by the failure of the Irish Brigade. And the thin, ailing, poetical Plunkett made a poor impression on them as a specimen of Irish revolutionary militancy.[31] However, Casement took Plunkett along to see the German General Staff, where he could personally put forward the IRB request for fifty thousand rifles with ammunition for the Irish Volunteers. The Germans turned this down, telling Plunkett in so many words that there were millions of Irish in the United States and he should get the arms from them.[32] When, about 25 June, Plunkett eventually left Germany, he took with him a message from Casement for Dublin to the effect that it was not going to be possible to get an Irish Brigade together, that Casement saw no way of getting German help and that he regarded his own mission as ended.[33] Whether Plunkett delivered this message and in what terms is not known.

Casement was left behind, admiring Plunkett personally for the effort he had made but feeling that he had done little but add to the ridicule of his (Casement's) own situation. For once he even saw the German position quite tolerantly. 'In our own land,' he wrote, 'they see only that no force exists, that talk expresses the extremity of Irish nationalism – and that if I represent anyone it must be a mighty small handful.'[34]

A renewal of the request for arms came in October 1915 through the German military attaché in Washington passing on a message of Devoy's. It was proposed that rifles and ammunition should be sent in submarines to the coast of Kerry, and Fenit pier in Tralee Bay was suggested as a suitable landing point.[35] But the German Admiralty informed the General Staff in December 1915 that submarines were not practical. And Casement wrote to New York later in the month that arms could not be supplied.[36] His efforts now were concentrated on getting the Germans to send the tiny group of the Irish Brigade to fight for the Turks, finally securing an assurance from the German General Staff to this effect on 4 January 1916.[37] They were to be sent to Syria. Three weeks later he retired for a 'nerve rest'[38] to a nursing home in Munich, leaving Robert Monteith, the ex-British NCO and Irish Volunteer instructor sent out via New York in October to help with the Irish Brigade, to take over in Berlin as a direct link for Devoy and the IRB with the German government.

But although Pearse and the military council were about this time perfecting their final arrangements for the Rising, they seem to have shown little sense of urgency or devotion to detail on the question of a supply of arms from Germany. It was something they were hoping for and for which they made provisions in their plans for the rising in other parts of Ireland than Dublin, and yet paradoxically something to which they hardly gave the detailed priority it might seem to have deserved.

On or about 5 February 1916 Devoy in New York received a coded message from the IRB in Dublin, brought personally across the Atlantic by a seaman named Tommy O'Connor, to the effect that an insurrection would break out in Ireland on Easter Sunday, 23 April. The decoded message was passed to the German Ambassador in Washington who in turn passed it on by radio to Berlin on 10 February.[39] Devoy sent a cable to Berlin confirming this and asking rather vaguely for arms to be delivered 'between Good Friday and Easter Sunday, Limerick West Coast'.[40] This was followed by a letter setting out the request in greater detail and specifying a need for 100,000 rifles, and for artillery, together with German officers and artillerymen.

Casement, still unwell in his nursing home at Munich, was visited there early in March by Monteith with news of the cable, and sent a memorandum back to Berlin stressing that the Germans must notify the Irish clearly about landing places and times before sending the arms. On 16 March he and Monteith went to the General Staff in Berlin, and on the next day to the German Admiralty to hear the arrangements made with Devoy: 20,000 rifles, 10 machine guns and 5,000,000 rounds of ammunition were to be sent, together with 55 men of the Irish Brigade. The ship was to be met off the Inishtookert lightship in Tralee Bay beween Friday, 20 April and Sunday, the 23rd, and the pilot boat meeting it was to show two green lights after dark. Devoy had sent a cable agreeing these details.⁴¹

Both Monteith and Casement were appalled by what they considered the inadequacy of German help in the circumstances. And yet they were in an awkward position, for the Rising was clearly going ahead, and even this amount of help would be better than nothing. After protesting to the Germans bitterly against the inadequacy of the arrangements, they concentrated on two objectives: first, to prevent the dispatch of the fifty-five members of the Irish Brigade, and second, secretly to get a message through to Dublin strongly urging that no rising should take place in the circumstances.

After some argument with the Germans, in which Monteith and Casement maintained that no more than twelve out of the fifty-five members of the Irish Brigade were reliable, the Germans finally agreed not to send them.⁴² Casement also managed to persuade the German Admiralty to let one member of the Irish Brigade – the only Irish American to have joined it, named McGooey – over the frontier into Denmark to try and get a ship to Scotland and then to Ireland. His ostensible purpose was to tie up the final arrangements for the arms landing. His real instructions from Casement, however, were to say that Casement 'strongly urged "no rising" …' and to 'get the heads in Ireland to call off the rising and merely try to land the arms and distribute them'.⁴³

When the German General Staff heard of McGooey's departure they were furious, accusing Casement of sending him off to try and stop the Rising. No word of McGooey seems ever to have been heard again. If he had reached Ireland it seems possible that, though he would almost certainly not have deflected the leaders from their intention to start an insurrection, what he had to say might have had some material bearing on events, for he may also have carried the information that the arms ship had no wireless.*

Devoy's letter to the Germans suggested that Casement should remain in Germany as 'the accredited representative till the end of the war of the Irish Revolutionary Body'.⁴⁴ But Casement persuaded the Germans to let him go with the arms to Ireland together with two companions, Monteith and another member of the Irish Brigade named Bailey. They were to travel by submarine. Casement's hope was to get ashore in time to dissuade the leaders from going through with the Rising. If unsuccessful in this he would identify himself with what he knew to be a desperate cause.

Things were even more desperate than he knew. In spite of Devoy's

* In a letter intended for the leaders of the rebellion written by Casement in Germany in April but never delivered, he specified among much other information that the ship, 'carries no wireless, I believe'. He added that he had sent John McGooey, 'a Clan-na-Gael man from Chicago, to try and reach Dublin and tell them all this', on 19 March. (Casement to a friend of James Malcolm at Berne, 6 April 1916. McGarrity Papers, NLI.)

agreement to the arrangements with the Germans given in the middle of March, the IRB in Ireland seem to have been rather inconsequential about their arrangements for the arms landing. At the beginning of April they sent Joseph Plunkett's father, an elderly Papal Count, to Switzerland. Through the German Embassy at Berne on 5 April he transmitted a message to Casement in Berlin, reiterating that the Rising was fixed for Easter Sunday (evening), that the arms ship should arrive in Tralee Bay 'not later than dawn of Easter Monday' and that the dispatch of German officers was imperative. Casement tried desperately to convey to his mysterious informant that all was not well, but could make no contact. In any case, four days later the arms ship, a former ship of the British Wilson line captured by the Germans and renamed the *Libau* but disguised for this occasion as a Norwegian trawler, the *Aud*, had sailed for Tralee Bay. Three days later Casement, Monteith and Bailey set out on the same journey by submarine.

Meanwhile, incredibly it only now seems to have occurred to the Military Council in Dublin that if the ship arrived any time *before* Sunday, 23 April in the bracket of three days originally agreed, it would alert the British and seriously compromise the chances of the Rising starting undetected on the Sunday evening. They therefore at that late stage sent Plunkett's sister to America with a message which she delivered to Devoy on 14 April, five days after the *Aud* had sailed. It stated that on no account must the arms be landed before the night of Easter Sunday. Devoy sent the message to Berlin, but the Germans had in fact no way of communicating with the *Aud* since she was without wireless.

In these circumstances it might have been expected that the rebel leaders would at least inquire whether the *Aud* carried a wireless or not. At the very least it might have been expected steps would be taken to meet the ship on the three earlier days originally agreed in case she arrived earlier than Easter Sunday. No such steps were taken. The most charitable explanation is that the leaders, weighing the risk of the arms ship's early arrival against the possible loss of the arms, decided that the former was the most serious. Their top priority after all was the occurrence of the rebellion, not its military success. In fact the *Aud* arrived in Tralee Bay after a journey through the British blockade on the afternoon of Thursday, 19 April. She was even seen there by the pilot, who, having received orders to expect nothing until Sunday, merely wondered what ship she was and went home. She remained there nearly twenty-four hours without signal from the shore, whereupon the captain, feeling that he could not risk waiting there any longer, moved away. His luck then ran out for he was intercepted by the Royal Navy, escorted into Queenstown and there with some skill succeeded in scuttling his ship and its cargo, raising the German colours just before he did so.

On the early morning of the same day, Good Friday, Casement, Monteith and Bailey landed from their submarine in a rubber dinghy on Banna strand, County Kerry. The dinghy overturned in the water and they were soaked to the skin. After walking some distance Casement, exhausted, hid in some brambles on the site of an ancient fort while the others pressed on to Tralee to try to make contact with the Volunteers. Early in the afternoon he was found there with sand on his trousers and a used railway ticket from Berlin to Wilhelmshaven in his pocket by a sergeant and constable of the RIC. He spent that night in Tralee gaol from which he might possibly have been rescued by the Volunteers if their leader, Austin Stack, had not been under strict instructions not to take any premature action until the Rising broke out in Dublin. However, through a priest, who was allowed to visit him, Casement managed to get out a verbal message which was taken to Dublin by a Volunteer. Pearse heard it from the messenger himself the next day, Saturday. It ran simply: 'Germany sending arms, but will not send men.'[45] But Pearse, who up to the last moment seems to have been hoping not only for troops but also some naval and air diversion to help the Rising, knew by then that even the arms would not be coming, for the news of the sinking of the *Aud* had also reached him.[46]

The disasters and errors of judgement had not been all on one side. The British Government had known since early in the war a good deal about the movements and intentions of Roger Casement in New York and Germany.[47] Early in 1915 British Naval Intelligence had broken the German diplomatic code and had been intercepting messages between the Embassy in Washington and Berlin, including those from Devoy which retailed information about the projected rising. This information and its source seems never to have been passed as a matter of urgency directly to Dublin Castle.

The possibility of some German invasion of Ireland had naturally been in the minds of the administration in Dublin Castle in a routine way. They were well aware that splinter elements in Ireland, like the Irish Volunteers, besides opposing recruiting might in certain circumstances favour an insurrection with German support. But they were also aware of what a minute section of Irish opinion these splinter elements represented. They knew that the vast majority of the Irish population were loyal to the Crown and behind the imperial war effort. Still, they kept their ears open. As always in Irish history the government had informers in the Irish radical quarters of the day, but for the first time in Irish history these appear themselves not to have been really well informed.[48] Clearly the government was given no proper concept of the IRB's role or effectiveness at the time. An intercepted letter from Casement in Germany to MacNeill even made it appear that MacNeill himself was one of the most dangerous men they had to face. In these circumstances the Liberal Chief Secretary, Augustine Birrell, understandably saw as his paramount task the need to keep a balance between prevention of a nuisance and the inflation of nuisance value into something more important than it was.

In this he was much encouraged and supported by the Parliamentary Nationalist Party's leaders, Redmond, Dillon and Devlin. Unionists were often outraged at the latitude allowed to the anti-recruiting activities of the Irish Volunteers and the relative freedom with which they paraded and manoeuvred. But the party leaders, who had as much to lose as anyone at their hands, always insisted that the only real danger the Irish Volunteers presented was as potential martyrs. Thus, although there was sporadic suppression of the various splinter 'seditious' organs of the press and some prosecution and deportation of individuals under the Defence of the Realm Act, Birrell and his Under-Secretary, Sir Matthew Nathan, in amicable consultation with the Nationalist Party leaders, pursued what might be called a 'soft line' towards the small dissident minority. Though Birrell, as early as November 1914, had recognized 'the danger of a real street row and sham rebellion in Dublin',[49] his chief concern was not to turn this small minority into traditional Irish martyrs. What he could hardly be expected to know without better sources of information was that a small minority within this small minority was determined that it should turn itself into martyrs at all costs.

The third member of an administrative triumvirate at Dublin Castle was the new viceroy who had replaced Lord Aberdeen in 1915, Lord Wimborne, formerly Sir Ivor Churchill-Guest, who had been created a peer in 1910 to swell the Liberal minority in the House of Lords. Wimborne was more orthodox in his view of authority's responsibilities than Birrell or Nathan and more naturally sensitive to the insistence of the Southern Unionist leader, Lord Midleton, that something should be done about the Irish Volunteers. And it was Wimborne who, at the last moment, very nearly prevented the Rising from breaking out altogether.

In November 1915 Birrell, in reply to a remonstrance of Midleton's about the Irish Volunteers, said that they could not be disarmed nor could their parades be forbidden because to take notice of speeches made by crack-brained priests and other enthusiasts would only halt the growth of loyalty in Ireland. 'I laugh at the whole thing,' he added.[50]

On the other hand, both he and Nathan were quite aware that winter of the perceptible increase in the numbers of the Irish Volunteers. Nathan was the less cocksure of the two. In November 1915, with the possibility of conscription for Ireland looming, he even described the situation as 'bad and fairly rapidly growing worse'.[51] With what was, for that time, almost uncannily premature foresight, he actually told Birrell that the Nationalist Party had lost control of the country, and Lord Midleton that 'Sinn Fein' were edging out Redmond.[53] Given such an appreciation, the coolness with which the administration was able to receive some of the reports from informers, and, in a roundabout way, British intelligence in the early months of 1916, seems remarkable.

British intelligence certainly behaved almost casually with the knowledge at its disposal. In the middle of March both Nathan and Wimborne saw a report from the Inspector General of the RIC in which he stated that information had been received 'from an informant in Ireland to the effect that the Irish Volunteer leaders have been warned to be in readiness for a German landing at an early date'.[53] Nathan continued to insist that he did not believe that the leaders of the Volunteers meant insurrection.[54] A strong recommendation from the GOC Irish Command, General Friend, that the Volunteers ought to be proclaimed had been turned down the month before.[55] And Birrell wrote to Midleton at the end of March that 'to proclaim the Irish Volunteers as an illegal body would be in my opinion a reckless and foolish act and would promote disloyalty to a prodigious extent'.[56] Midleton replied that the Castle was shirking its responsibility, and though the charge was unfair, for Birrell and Nathan's policy was carefully thought out, their continued unruffled confidence in the developing circumstances was certainly surprising. Wimborne himself was becoming anxious and was relieved to hear that at least a number of Sinn Fein organizers were being banished from Ireland at the end of March, speculating personally whether 'Clarke, Connolly and others whom I don't remember' might not soon follow them.[57] In justification of Birrell's and Nathan it must be said that even the deportations caused nationalist ripples beyond mere Sinn Feiner circles. Dillon himself noted anxiously: 'To me it appears that the tension has been seriously increased.'[58]

The military continued to wish to play safe regardless of political considerations, and a proposal was made that the garrison in Ireland should be reinforced by one or more infantry brigades from England.[59] The officer in charge of Irish intelligence reported that there was undoubted proof that Sinn Fein Irish Volunteers were working up for rebellion, if ever they had a good opportunity.[60] Reports from informers inside the ranks of the Volunteers sometimes confirmed this, but others said that in spite of the impatience of some young men in the Volunteers, backed by Connolly and the Citizen Army, the leaders were against a rising at present. Nathan's nerve held. He had again been momentarily disconcerted after St Patrick's Day, 17 March, when uniformed Volunteers with rifles and bayonets had manoeuvred in the centre of Dublin and held up traffic for two hours.[61] But on 10 April he wrote to Lord French, now GOC Home Forces in Britain: 'Though the Volunteer element has been active of late I do not believe that its leaders mean insurrection or that the Volunteers have sufficient arms if the leaders do mean it.'[62]

A week later he was handed a letter from the general in charge of the defence of the South of Ireland which relayed information that a landing of arms and ammunition was expected on the south-west coast, and a rising fixed for Easter Eve. And two days later an informer reported that Mac-Donagh, the Volunteer Commandant, had said to his men: 'We are not going out on Friday [Good Friday], but we are going on Sunday.... Boys, some of us may never come back.'[63] A time had been fixed for a general Volunteer march out on Sunday.

All this naturally put even Nathan on his guard. Birrell was in London. Nathan saw that the police were in a state of alert. But on the Saturday morning he heard of the capture and sinking of the *Aud*, and also that the man who had been arrested the previous day after landing from a German collapsible boat was Sir Roger Casement. The news seemed immensely reassuring both to himself and to Wimborne. The military, too, shared the view that Casement was the key man in the business. When on Sunday morning they read in the *Sunday Independent* that all movements ordered for the Volunteers for that day had been cancelled, they drew the reasonable conclusion that such plans as there were for a rising had been totally ruined.

However, such overwhelming evidence now existed of the Irish Volunteers' connection with the German enemy that, after some insistence from Wimborne, Nathan agreed on Sunday morning to cable Birrell in London for permission to arrest them. At lunch he assured his host and fellow-guests that all danger of a rising had been averted with Casement's arrest and that they could go to Fairyhouse Races on the following day, Easter Monday, quite happily.[64]

But there was work to be done, for a load of gelignite had been stolen that morning and taken to Liberty Hall. A police raid to recover this had to be planned and dispositions made for the projected arrest of the Volunteer leaders when permission arrived from Birrell in London. A conference was held that Sunday evening with senior army and police officers and the viceroy himself. Wimborne pressed for the arrest of from sixty to one hundred of the leaders that very night (Sunday).[65] Nathan, however, insisted on waiting for permission from Birrell to arrive the next day.

Birrell sent it the next morning. Nathan was in his office making final practical arrangements with the Senior Intelligence Officer and the Secretary of the Post Office, having just told the latter that the telephone and telegraph services in south-western Ireland must be temporarily confined to naval and military use, when rifle fire rang out below the window. It was the policeman on the gate being shot dead by the Citizen Army. The Rising had begun.

The shooting of fellow Irishmen in more or less cold blood continued sporadically for the rest of the day. There was an unpleasant scene near Beggar's Bush barracks shortly after four in the afternoon. A detachment of

what was confusingly called the Irish Volunteer Defence Corps, a reserve
training body of the *British* forces, consisting of middle-class Irishmen over
military age, returned at that time from a route march in the countryside
where they had been oblivious of events in Dublin. They carried rifles but no
ammunition. Some sniping was in progress round the barracks at the time.
The rebels, seeing the reserve corps (known as the Gorgeous Wrecks, from
the GR they wore on their arm bands) marching down the road towards
them, understandably did not stop to ask questions but poured a withering
fire into the khaki ranks. They killed five and wounded nine. A little later
that evening the writer James Stephens witnessed the shooting by a Volunteer
of a civilian trying to extricate his cart from a barricade the Volunteers had
built at St Stephen's Green.[66] Stephens noted that at that moment the crowd's
mood, which earlier in the day had been one of bewildered curiosity, was
one of hate for the Volunteers. At just about the same time fifty miles away
at Castlebellingham in County Louth, an Irish constable named McGee and
an English grenadier guards officer named Dunville were shot when lined
up against some railings with other prisoners by Volunteers under the command of a Belfast electrical engineer named John MacEntee. MacEntee
himself had until only the year before been a supporter of Redmond's and
trying to get a commission in the British Army.[67] The Irish constable, who
had been shot at least twice, died within a few hours; the Englishman, though
shot through the chest, subsequently recovered.

But the shooting of the defenceless was not to be confined to the rebel
side. On the evening of the next day an Irish officer of the Royal Irish Rifles,
who was by nature excitable and eccentric and who had been in the retreat
from Mons and wounded at the Battle of the Aisne, arrested three journalists
in the Dublin streets, Thomas Dickson, Patrick MacIntyre and the well-
known pacifist Francis Sheehy Skeffington.[68] The next morning without any
sort of trial and entirely on his own initiative he had them shot by a makeshift firing squad in the barracks yard. The firing squad did its work so
badly that a second party had to be assembled a few minutes later to finish
Sheehy Skeffington off.[69] Later in the week some civilians were killed by the
military in a house in North King Street while prisoners in their custody.[70]
Such incidents on both sides were not significantly representative of the
character of either, only of the nature of the situation for which anyone
initiating a cold-blooded insurrection in these circumstances must take
responsibility.

The Catholic Church, of which Patrick Pearse was a devout member,
sanctions violent rebellion only when the government is a tyranny, ruling by
force against the will of the governed, and the insurrection is approved by the
community as a whole. As MacNeill had already emphasized, by no stretch of
the imagination could it be maintained that such a state of affairs prevailed

272

in Ireland in 1916.*⁷¹ But Pearse had transcended mundane Church teaching
with a vision of morality which equated what he saw as Ireland's redemption with the work of the Redeemer himself. Since, as a good Catholic, he
knew that in the last resort, whatever the Church's rules, the final judgement
on his action lay elsewhere, he had no moral doubts. It was hardly a coin-
cidence that the date of the Rising had been fixed for Easter.

Though opinion continued to harden against the Volunteers during the
course of the week, particularly when the British Army's heavy shelling of
rebel strongholds in Dublin caused increasing destruction and casualties,
James Stephens, who kept a day-to-day record of impressions and events,
noted that as late as Wednesday when the heavy shelling started there was a
strong ambivalence in public feeling, a reluctance, particularly among men,
to express much more than curiosity or astonishment at what had happened.
One part of people's minds was even grateful that the Volunteers had managed to hold out for as long as two days and avoid total humiliation.⁷² Women
were on the whole more condemnatory, often saying that all the rebels ought
to be shot. 'Civil war' was how a nurse in Dublin Castle typically thought of
what was going on, and many of the emotions at work were those that invariably accompany civil war.⁷³ And yet at the same time there was something special about this one, for the same Irishman was sometimes on both
sides at once. Myth and reality were themselves warring in Irish minds. It
was the very development on which Pearse and Connolly with their conscious
reactivation of the myth had been counting.⁷⁴

Wednesday, 26 April, saw the Volunteers achieve their greatest military
success of the rebellion. On that morning the first British reinforcements
from England landed at Kingstown, welcomed as deliverers by the local
population, and marched towards the centre of the city.⁷⁵ They were men of
the Sherwood Foresters from the English midlands, few of whom had been
in the army more than three months. Advancing down Northumberland
Road towards Mount Street Bridge to cross the canal which rings the centre
of the city at this point they ran into extremely effective fire from de Valera's
outposts, and it was only after many hours of bitter fighting that they succeeded in crossing the canal. The Sherwood Foresters' casualties here were
four officers killed and fourteen wounded and 216 other ranks killed or
wounded, and these amounted to more than half the entire British Army
casualties in the rebellion. The essentially static and defensive nature of the
rebel command's psychology was, however, once again manifested in this
situation, for although de Valera's men in the outposts round Mount Street
base fought with great bravery against overwhelming odds, the headquarters

* Other theological conditions required are that the tyranny should be irremovable
except by bloodshed, that its evil be greater than the effects of the revolt and that it
should have serious probability of success.

battalion in Boland's Mills remained virtually inert throughout the engagement.

Such psychology undoubtedly made things easier for the Army Commander, General W. H. M. Lowe. It was his strategy to tie a cordon round the area in which the rebel strongholds were situated, and then methodically reduce this by artillery fire – supported by the gun-boat *Helga* on the Liffey – and infantry pressure. To many people the Army's progress seemed slow, but given the extent to which it had been caught off guard on the Monday, with less than two thousand troops in Dublin altogether, and the need to bring reinforcements not only from other parts of Ireland but from England, the plan was carried out with methodical efficiency.

By Thursday evening the words Irish Republic on the green flag above the Post Office had been scorched to a deep brown by flames.[76] The building was on fire and no longer tenable as rebel headquarters. The O'Rahilly led the sortie to establish new headquarters elsewhere, in which he was killed by machine-gun fire as he dashed with his men up Moore Street. Pearse and Connolly – now on a stretcher with his ankle broken – were the last to leave the building, and after a temporary halt in a grocer's they knocked their way through the walls of a number of buildings to a fishmonger's shop in Great Britain Street.[77] From there Pearse witnessed the shooting down in the street of a publican and his family trying to leave their burning house under a white flag. In the circumstances the sight was too much for this gentle man who had longed for red war in Ireland. In any case his work was done. He had shown that the myth could be made to live. Now, to ensure its survival there was need in his eyes only for that death, which in the words of the greater Myth in which he was also a believer, would confer eternal life.

Connolly, a very different kind of man from Pearse, subscribed to the same fundamental belief in surprisingly similar terms. '...In all due humility and awe,' he had written in an editorial in the *Workers' Republic* in February 1916, 'we recognize that of us, as of mankind before Calvary, it may truly be said "without the shedding of Blood there is no Redemption."'[78]

Blood had been shed but the Calvary image had still to be completed.

At 3.30 p.m. on Saturday, 29 April, Pearse, wearing his Volunteer uniform with its Boer War style slouch hat, surrendered to Brigadier General Lowe on the steps of the burnt-out Post Office, ceremonially handing over his sword. For the rest of that day and on the following Sunday morning Pearse's and Connolly's orders to surrender were carried round to the various isolated Volunteer strongholds by a nurse who had been in the Post Office during the week, Elizabeth O'Farrell, now under British escort. Some of these strongholds were still virtually untried and intact. A Volunteer posted in a window overlooking St Stephen's Green had not even fired a shot, and when the order for surrender came round on Sunday there was a cry from the garrison there: 'Surrender! We haven't started yet.'[79] Other garrisons, such as those in the

South Dublin Union Workhouse under Eamonn Ceannt, and in the Four Courts area under Edward Daly, were hard pressed after bitter fighting in which they had conducted themselves with chivalry and courage.

The rebel casualties were not particularly heavy: 64 killed altogether during the week.[80] But casualties among civilians were high from sniping and artillery fire. Civilian casualties altogether were at least 220 killed, and an unknown number in excess of 600 wounded.[81] Total casualties among all Crown forces were 134 killed or died of wounds and 381 wounded. The killed included 35 officers and men of Irish regiments,[82] 5 GR's and 17 Irishmen of the RIC and Dublin Metropolitan Police. Most of the police casualties occurred not in Dublin at all but at a fight near Ashbourne, County Meath, on Friday, when a party of forty RIC men under a chief inspector, on their way by motor-car to relieve the police barracks at Ashbourne which had been reported occupied by Volunteers, were skilfully ambushed by rebels under Volunteer Commandant Thomas Ashe. The fight lasted for five hours, and when the police had run out of ammunition they surrendered. Eight of them had been killed and fifteen wounded.[83] The same group of rebels had been moving fairly freely over both eastern County Meath and northern County Dublin during the week, raiding police barracks and disturbing communications. The fate of the rebellion was, however, totally unaffected by their activity or by the 'Battle of Ashbourne', and it was in a different though also tragic role that Commandant Ashe the next year was to make a contribution to the success of Irish republicanism.

Elsewhere in Ireland, thanks to the double disaster of the loss of the German arms ship and the conflicting orders of MacNeill and Pearse, the Volunteers' efforts were either of less significance still, or, in most cases, nil. The town of Enniscorthy was actually taken over by the local Volunteers for three days from early Thursday morning, 27 April, while the police sat in a state of uneasy siege in their barracks, but no fighting took place, and when the leaders of the rebels sent an offer of help to the beleaguered garrisons in Dublin James Connolly turned it down. After a military armoured train moving up from Wexford had sent them into a defensive position on Vinegar Hill the rebels, who numbered about six hundred altogether, surrendered unconditionally having barely fired a shot.[84] John MacEntee, one of the leaders in County Louth of the party which had shot Constable McGee, made his way to Dublin and pluckily joined the besieged Post Office three days before the surrender.[85] In County Louth his men had dwindled to fourteen as the news reached them of British troop movements in their direction.

In Limerick, an old centre of Fenianism, two bodies of Volunteers over a hundred strong had been mobilized on the Sunday before the outbreak but then disbanded on receipt of MacNeill's countermanding order. The next day they actually received another order, from Pearse this time, telling them to go into action all the same but, understandably perhaps in view of their own disarray and the known loss of the arms ship, they did not obey.[96]

In 'rebel' Cork which had seen a very strong turn-out of armed and uniformed Irish Volunteers on St Patrick's Day only a month before, there was a similar story. Over a thousand men were in fact successfully mobilized for Easter Sunday, their task being to hold the military forces in the area while the arms from the *Aud* were being distributed. They received the countermanding order and dispersed, only to receive another order from Pearse the next day telling them that the action in Dublin was on and that they were to carry out their original instructions. However, since in the course of these days they actually received no less than nine separate dispatches from Dublin altogether, some of them contradictory, they eventually decided to do nothing. After the Rising the IRB held an inquiry into this activity and found, perhaps rather leniently by strict military standards, that 'Cork could not have acted other than it did'.[87]

In Belfast 132 Volunteers were mobilized in the Falls Road. But no countermanding order was needed here to throw their plan into confusion. This had been worked out by Pearse and Connolly in Dublin and provided for them to cross Ulster without engaging in any action and, together with other Volunteers from Tyrone, join up with the larger bodies due to rise in County Galway. However, the Tyrone men when they heard this plan flatly refused to leave their own county and the plan disintegrated. The leader of the Volunteers in Ulster, refusing to commit the Belfast men alone, was thus driven into total inaction.[88] Ironically, he was none other than Denis McCullough, the young pioneer of the new IRB with Hobson a few years before, and by right of his position as President of the Supreme Council technically, under the IRB constitution, 'President of the Irish Republic'. But Pearse, in taking on responsibility for the Fenian myth through the secret Military Council had appropriated this title for himself, although whether or not with McCullough's acquiescence is not clear.

In Galway, Liam Mellows, one of the Sinn Fein organizers who had been deported by Nathan and Birrell the previous month but who had made his way back to Ireland in disguise, managed to mobilize a thousand or so men. They had no more than sixty rifles and 350 shotguns between them and had been particularly dependent on the anticipated arms from the *Aud*. Some even carried pikes in the '98 tradition. They captured one police barracks and its five Irish policemen but failed to capture another defended by a similar handful. They cut some telegraph wires and uprooted some railway lines but eventually, after moving for some days desultorily round the county, harassed by troop movements and even some shells from a warship in Galway bay, dispersed on receiving news of the insurrection's collapse in Dublin.[89] Their failure was reminiscent of similar Fenian activity in 1867.

Except for the factual element of defeat the same could by no means be said of the rising in Dublin as a whole. Ineffectual as it had been in terms of military achievement, mustering altogether only about 1,500 rebels unsupported and even strongly condemned by the populace, it had brought about the only serious and disciplined fighting that had ever been conducted by Irishmen in single-minded pursuit of Wolfe Tone's aim of a totally independent Irish Republic. Something quite new had happened in Irish history. The centre of Dublin lay in ruins to prove it. Although the rebellion had come as a shattering surprise to ninety-nine per cent of Irishmen of all classes and political beliefs, being unexpected even by most of those who carried it out, such an event could not leave any nationally-minded Irishman's attitude to events in the future unaffected.

References

PART ONE

1 Beginnings of the Fenian Movement

1 Sullivan, *New Ireland*, pp. 36ff.
2 ibid.
3 *Cork Constitution*, 4 November 1858.
4 ibid., 16 November 1858.
5 *Cork Examiner*, 29 November 1858.
6 See letter to the Lord Lieutenant, Lord Naas, from the priest, Father John O'Sullivan of Kenmare, dated 5 October 1858 in John Rutherford, *The Fenian Conspiracy*, 2 vols., London, 1877, vol. i, p. 118.
7 *Cork Examiner*, 10 December 1858.
8 *Clare Journal*, 14 March 1859.
9 ibid.
10 Lord Abercorn, 6 February 1866, Hansard, 3rd series, vol. 181, col. 68.
11 *Clare Journal*, 14 March 1859.
12 *Cork Examiner*, 14 March 1859.
13 See *Irishman*, 1 January 1859, in Belfast; *Irishman*, 8 January 1859, in Westmeath; *Irishman*, 26 February 1859.
14 *Westmeath Guardian*, 3 March 1859.
15 ibid.
16 *Irishman*, 12 February 1859; Sullivan, op. cit., pp. 201–2; *Cork Examiner*, 24 December 1858.
17 *Kilkenny Moderator*, 8 January 1859.
18 See, e.g., *Irishman*, 12 March 1859.
19 See letter from John O'Mahoney to O'Doheny, autumn 1856, cited in Ryan, *Fenian Chief*, pp. 51–3. Also Stephens himself, *Weekly Freeman*, 15 November 1883.
20 Cited in Ryan, op. cit., p. 48.
21 Ryan, op. cit., p. 56.
22 Stephens, Reminiscences, *Weekly Freeman*, 13 October 1882.
23 *The Tribune*, 17 November 1856.
24 ibid., 19 January 1856.
25 ibid.
26 Stephens, *Weekly Freeman*, 13 October 1882.
27 ibid.
28 ibid., 8 December 1883.
29 ibid., 1 December 1883.

30 ibid., 17 November 1883.
31 ibid., 15 November 1883.
32 ibid., 17 November 1883.
33 ibid., 3 November 1883.
34 ibid., 9 February 1884.
35 Ryan, op. cit., p. 84.
36 Stephens, Reminiscences, *Weekly Freeman*, 9 February 1884.
37 Joseph Denieffe, *A Personal Narrative of the Irish Revolutionary Brotherhood*, New York, 1904; William D'Arcy, *The Fenian Movement in the United States*, 1947, p. 2.
38 D'Arcy, op. cit., p. 5.
39 ibid., p. 8.
40 Denieffe, op. cit., p. 3.
41 ibid.
42 Cited in Ryan, op. cit., p. 62.
43 ibid.
44 Stephens, Reminiscences, *Weekly Freeman*.
45 Ryan, op. cit., p. 82.
46 Denieffe, op. cit., pp. 156–7.
47 Ryan, op. cit., p. 90.
48 Denieffe, op. cit., p. 22.
49 John O'Leary, *Recollections of Fenians and Fenianism*, vol. ii, p. 81.
50 Rutherford, *The Secret History of the Fenian Conspiracy*, pp. 62–5. Rutherford, a Unionist journalist from the West of Ireland, allowed his book to become full of small inaccuracies but he was clearly writing, in 1877, with much authentic material provided by the authorities at his disposal, and it is not nearly so worthless as nationalist sources have usually suggested. For an account of the IRB organization in 1880 see article by A. Chester Ives, the *New York Herald*, 12 August 1880. The article was based on information from first-hand sources. (See O'Brien and Ryan, *Devoy's Post Bag*, vol. ii, pp. 546–7.)
51 Ryan, op. cit., p. 279. O'Leary, op. cit., p. 65.
52 Cluseret, *Fraser's Magazine*, July 1872, new series, vol. vi, p. 54.
53 O'Leary, op. cit., vol. i, p. 123.
54 'Derivation of the Fenians', *Irish People*, 16 August 1865.

2 James Stephens at Work

1 Ryan, *Fenian Chief*, p. 159.
2 Ryan, op. cit., p. 160, from Denieffe, *Personal Narrative*, pp. 46ff.
3 Ryan, op. cit., p. 161.
4 ibid., p. 161.
5 ibid., p. 165.

6 William D'Arcy, *The Fenian Movement in the United States*, Washington, 1947, pp. 25, 27, 52.

7 *Irish People*, 5 March 1864.

8 O'Leary, *Recollections*, pp. 124, 148.

9 Ryan, op. cit., p. 175.

10 Regulations for Lent read in all Catholic churches in the Dublin diocese, Sunday 28 February 1859 – see, e.g., *Drogheda Argus*, 5 March 1859.

11 All details of McManus's funeral from *Freeman's Journal*, 11 November 1861.

12 ibid.

13 O'Leary, op. cit., p. 180.

14 Sullivan, *New Ireland*, p. 249.

15 e.g., 29 July 1866.

16 *Irish People*, 2 January 1864.

17 ibid., 13 February 1864.

18 ibid., 26 December 1863.

19 ibid., 9 April 1864.

20 D'Arcy, op. cit., p. 30.

21 ibid., p. 27.

22 ibid., p. 40.

23 ibid., p. 46.

24 ibid., p. 47.

25 Denieffe, op. cit., p. 91.

26 D'Arcy, op. cit., pp. 56–7.

27 ibid., p. 57.

28 John Devoy, *Recollections of an Irish Rebel*, New York, 1929, pp. 21, 25.

29 *Report of Dublin Special Commission for the Trial of T. F. Bourke*, 1867, p. 211.

30 *Report of Dublin Special Commission for the Trial of T. C. Luby*, 1865, pp. 141, 156, 221.

31 ibid., p. 148.

32 See, e.g., arrests in Belfast reported *Irish People*, 23 March 1864 and 3 May 1864.

33 D'Arcy, op. cit., pp. 46ff.

34 ibid., p. 72.

35 ibid.

36 ibid., pp. 74–5.

37 ibid, p. 87.

38 Ryan, op. cit., p. 208, gives the text of these letters.

39 Denieffe, op. cit., pp. 97ff.

40 *Report of Dublin Special Commission for the Trial of T. C. Luby*, 1865, p. 1043.

41 *Munster News*, quoted by *Irish People*, 16 September 1865.

42 ibid.
43 ibid.
44 ibid.
45 Ryan, op. cit., p. 207.
46 *Report of Dublin Special Commission for the Trial of T. C. Luby*, 1865, p. 182.

3 Stephens In and Out of Trouble

1 D'Arcy, *The Fenian Movement in the United States*, p. 79.
2 Sullivan, *New Ireland*, p. 257.
3 *Irish Liberator*, quoted in *Irish People*, 13 February 1864.
4 *Report of Dublin Special Commission for the Trial of T. F. Bourke and others*, pp. 601–11.
5 Ryan, *Fenian Chief*, p. 212.
6 D'Arcy, *The Fenian Movement in the United States*, p. 72.
7 ibid., p. 99.
8 ibid.
9 Ryan, op. cit., p. 212.
10 Sullivan, op. cit, p. 265.
11 D'Arcy, op. cit., p. 101.
12 Parliamentary Papers. Accounts and Reports, 1876, vol. lviii, pp. 495, 497, 499.
13 Ryan, op. cit., p. 216.
14 D'Arcy, op. cit., p. 114.
15 ibid., p. 139.
16 D'Arcy, op. cit., p. 159.
17 ibid., p. 166.
18 ibid., p. 165.
19 ibid., p. 169.
20 ibid., p. 214.
21 ibid., p. 218.
22 Cited in Ryan, op. cit., p. 247.
23 Massey's evidence at, for example, the trial of J. F. X. O'Brien, *Cork Examiner*, 20 May 1867. Also at the trial of T. F. Bourke, *Report of Dublin Special Commission*, p. 173.
24 Massey's evidence, *Cork Examiner*, 30 May 1867. Also Stephens' own statement, cited Ryan, op. cit., p. 249.
25 Ryan, op. cit., p. 249.
26 ibid., p. 252.
27 *Cork Examiner*, 30 May 1867. Massey's evidence at trial of J. F. X. O'Brien.
28 Ryan, op. cit., p. 244.

29 *The Times*, 29 April 1868. Trial of Richard Burke.
30 Trial of T. F. Bourke, *Report of Special Commission*, p. 169. Trial of J. F. X. O'Brien, *Cork Examiner*, 30 May 1867.
31 Officially confirmed in this designation, 15 February 1867, D'Arcy, op. cit., pp. 251–2.
32 Ryan, op. cit., p. 238.
33 ibid.
34 Article by Cluseret in *Fraser's Magazine*, July 1872, new series, vol. vi, p. 32.
35 ibid., p. 39.

4   1867: Bold Fenian Men

1 *The Times*, 29 April 1868, Trial of Richard Burke.
2 ibid., 30 April 1868, Trial of Richard Burke.
3 ibid.
4 Ryan, *Fenian Chief*, p. 239.
5 *Cork Examiner*, 24 May 1867, Trial of McClure. Evidence of Corydon.
6 See letter of Kelly from Ireland, 19 March 1867, D'Arcy, *The Fenian Movement in the United States*, pp. 240–41. See also evidence of Massey, *Report of Special Commission for Trial of T. F. Bourke*, etc., pp. 178–9; also Trial of J. F. X. O'Brien, *Cork Examiner*, 30 May 1867
7 Denieffe, *A Personal Narrative of the I.R.B.*, pp. 278–80.
8 *The Times*, 30 April 1868, Trial of Richard Burke.
9 ibid., Corydon.
10 *Report of Special Commission for Trial of T. F. Bourke*, etc., pp. 201, 501, 563–78.
11 Evidence of Massey, Trial of J. F. X. O'Brien, *Cork Examiner*, 30 May 1867.
12 *Report of Special Commission 1867*, Trial of Bourke, p. 535.
13 ibid., p. 502.
14 *Freeman's Journal*, 13 February 1867.
15 *Report of Dublin Special Commission*; Trial of T. F. Bourke, etc., p. 502.
16 ibid., p. 503.
17 ibid., p. 209.
18 *Freeman's Journal*, 15, 16 February 1867.
19 *Cork Examiner*, 12, 16 February 1867.
20 ibid., 30 May 1867. Trial of P. J. Condon.
21 ibid.
22 ibid.
23 ibid.
24 Cluseret, *Fraser's Magazine*, July 1872, p. 37.
25 ibid., pp. 38, 41.

26 ibid., p. 38.
27 These and subsequent details, *Cork Examiner*, 30 May 1867. Trial of P. J. Condon. Evidence of Massey.
28 The proclamation is given in full in *The Times*, 8 March, 1867.
29 Letter published in the *Irishman*, quoted *The Times*, 13 January 1868.
30 *Report of the Dublin Special Commission, 1867*, Trial of T. F. Bourke, etc., pp. 186–7.
31 *The Times*, 1 June 1867. *Cork Examiner*, 30 May 1867.
32 *The Times*, 15 July 1867.
33 *Report of the Dublin Special Commission*, 1867, pp. 244–50.
34 ibid.
35 ibid., pp. 154–5.
36 ibid., Trial of T. F. Bourke, etc., pp. 248–9. The Report here gives the figures as 'between 40,000 and 50,000', but Lennon was a fairly hard-headed man and we know from elsewhere (Trial of P. J. Condon, *Cork Examiner*, 30 May 1867) that 14,000 men were organized for Dublin. I am assuming that the larger figures were a mis-hearing.
37 ibid., p. 152.
38 ibid., p. 224.
39 ibid., p. 164.
40 This and subsequent details, *Report of the Special Commission*, Trial of T. F. Bourke, p. 221.
41 ibid.
42 *Drogheda Argus*, 9 March 1867.
43 *Cork Examiner*, 9 March 1867.
44 ibid.
45 ibid., 25, 27 May 1867.
46 *Report of Special Commission*, p. 271.
47 These and subsequent details, *Report of Special Commission*, pp. 288–92.
48 ibid., pp. 465–6.
49 J. J. Finnan, *Patriotic Songs*, Limerick, 1913, pp. 136–7.
50 *Cork Examiner*, 24 May 1867.
51 D'Arcy, op. cit., p. 243.
52 ibid., p. 245.
53 *The Times*, 4 November 1867. Trial of Colonel Warren.
54 ibid.
55 Listed among those named in *The Times*, 17 June 1867.
56 D'Arcy, op. cit., p. 246.
57 *The Times*, 14 November 1867.
58 D'Arcy, op. cit., p. 247.
59 *The Times*, 4 November 1867.

60 ibid., 15 June 1867.
61 ibid., 19 June 1867.

5 *The Manchester Martyrs*

1 Anthony Glynn, *High Upon the Gallows Tree*, Tralee, 1967, pp. 30–1. This competent compilation of the available facts is the most recent and extensive study of the Manchester Rescue.
2 Glynn, op. cit., pp. 94ff.
3 *The Times*, 2 November 1867.
4 Glynn, op. cit., p. 104.
5 ibid., p. 125.
6 *The Times*, 25 November 1867.
7 Hansard, H.C. Debates, 3rd series, vol. 230, col. 808.
8 *The Times*, 29 May 1867.
9 ibid., 27 May 1867.
10 ibid., 28 May 1867.
11 e.g., *The Times*, 23 May 1867.
12 ibid., 14 January 1868.
13 ibid., 11 January 1868.
14 ibid., 18 January 1868.
15 ibid., 14 January 1868 (Queen's evidence from Patrick Mullany).
16 ibid., 18 January 1868.
17 ibid., 14 January 1868.
18 ibid., 8 January 1868.
19 ibid., 14 January 1868.
20 ibid., 2, 6 January 1868.

PART TWO

1 *Beginnings of Home Rule*

1 Parliamentary Reports, 1881, vol. lxxvii, 725.
2 ibid.
3 David Thornley, *Isaac Butt and Home Rule*, London, 1964, p. 25.
4 *The Times*, 23 January 1868.
5 ibid., 29 January 1868.
6 Quoted in *The Times*, 3 March 1868.
7 Evelyn Ashley, 'Mr Gladstone – Fragments of Personal Reminiscence' in *National Review*, vol. xxxi, no. 184, June 1898.

8   Hansard, H.C. Debates, 3rd series, vol. 191, col. 491.
9   ibid., col. 471.
10 ibid., col. 515.
11 ibid., col. 711.
12 ibid., col. 853.
13 ibid., col. 864.
14 ibid., col. 505.
15 ibid., col. 507.
16 ibid., vol. 304, col. 149.
17 ibid., vol. 199, col. 333.
18 ibid., col. 1761.
19 Thornley, op. cit., p. 92.
20 ibid., p. 112.
21 ibid., p. 127.
22 Parliamentary Papers, 1871, vol. xxxii, p. 14.
23 ibid., p. 369.
24 Thornley, op. cit., p. 71.
25 ibid., p. 18.
26 ibid., p. 71.
27 ibid., p. 154.
28 ibid., p. 161.
29 ibid., p. 168.
30 ibid., p. 179.
31 ibid., p. 215.
32 ibid., p. 230.
33 ibid., p. 81.
34 ibid., p. 251.
35 W. J. O'Neill Daunt's *Journal*, cited in Thornley, op. cit., p. 254.

2 Parnell and the Land Crisis

1   For biographical details, see Bibliography.
2   Michael Davitt, *The Fall of Feudalism in Ireland*, London and New York, 1906, p. 110.
3   William O'Brien and Desmond Ryan (eds.), *Devoy's Post Bag, 1871–1928*, vol. i, p. 269.
4   *Irish World*, 6 March 1880.
5   Quoted P. S. O'Hegarty, *A History of Ireland under the Union, 1801 to 1922*, London, 1952, p. 529.
6   John J. Horgan, *Parnell to Pearse*, Dublin, 1949, p. 39.
7   Hansard, H.C. Debates, 3rd series, vol. 233, col. 1049.
8   *The Times*, 13 April 1877.
9   N. D. Palmer, *The Irish Land League Crisis*, New Haven, 1940, p. 64.

10 Parliamentary Reports, 1881, vol. lxxvii, 275.

11 Palmer, op. cit., p. 93.

12 ibid., p. 105.

13 Thornley, *Isaac Butt*, p. 363.

14 O'Brien and Ryan (eds.), op. cit., vol. i, p. 312.

15 ibid., p. 268.

16 R. Barry O'Brien, *The Life of Charles Stewart Parnell*, 2 vols., London, 1898, vol i., p. 139.

17 *Devoy's Post Bag*, vol. i, p. 298.

18 ibid., vol. i, p. 325.

19 ibid., vol. ii, p. 40.

20 ibid., pp. 89–90.

21 Michael Davitt, op. cit., p. 119.

22 ibid., p. 113.

23 ibid., p. 131.

24 ibid., p. 153.

25 ibid., p. 154.

26 Palmer, op. cit., pp. 141–2.

27 Hansard, H.C. Debates.

28 ibid., vol. 253, col. 1715.

29 ibid., H.L. Debates, vol. 254, col. 1869.

30 Hansard, H.C. Debates.

31 *The Times*, 3 December 1880.

32 Quoted Palmer, op. cit., p. 120.

33 ibid., p. 171.

34 ibid., p. 168.

3 Parnell and Home Rule

1 Conor Cruise O'Brien, *Parnell and His Party, 1880–1890*, Oxford, 1957, p. 137.

2 Palmer, *The Irish Land League Crisis*, p. 205.

3 O'Brien, op. cit., p. 61.

4 ibid., p. 64.

5 ibid., p. 67.

6 Thomas Corfe, *The Phoenix Park Murders*, London, 1968, p. 176.

7 P. J. Tynan, *The Irish National Invincibles and Their Times*, New York, 1894, p. 272.

8 ibid., p. 444.

9 Corfe, op. cit., p. 142.

10 *Cork Examiner*, 8 June 1886.

11 ibid., 18 July 1886.

12 ibid., 1 July 1886.

13 ibid., 14 July 1886.
14 *Freeman's Journal*, 14 July 1886.
15 Hansard, H.C. Debates, 3rd series, vol. 304, cols. 1195–6.
16 ibid., col. 1330.
17 ibid., col. 1253.
18 ibid., vol. 306, col. 1173.
19 ibid., vol. 305, col. 1707.
20 ibid., cols. 627, 625.
21 O'Brien, op. cit., p. 67.
22 e.g., Leader in *The Times*, 9 June 1886.
23 *I.H.S.*, vol. viii, no. 31, p. 141.
24 Hansard, H.C. Debates, 3rd series, vol. 306, col. 683.

4 The Orange Card

1 Hansard, H.C. Debates, 3rd series, vol. 306, col. 388.
2 ibid., vol. 304, cols. 1081–2.
3 E. R. R. Green, 'The Beginnings of Industrial Revolution', in *Ulster since 1800* (edited T. W. Moody and J. C. Beckett), British Broadcasting Corporation, 1954, p. 37.
4 Parliamentary Papers, 1857–8, vol. xxvi, p. 10.
5 ibid., pp. 292, 270.
6 ibid., p. 180.
7 Quoted by Sir Charles Russell during the second reading of the first Home Rule Bill, Hansard, H.C. Debates, 3rd series, vol. 306, col. 63.
8 ibid.
9 *The Times*, 6 February 1868.
10 ibid., 7 February 1868.
11 ibid., 9 November 1868.
12 ibid., 10 July 1869.
13 ibid., 30 April 1868.
14 ibid., 8 May 1868.
15 ibid., 10 June 1868.
16 ibid., 20 July 1868.
17 ibid., 6 February 1868.
18 ibid., 5 February 1869.
19 ibid., 14 December 1868.
20 ibid., 15 July 1868.
21 Reginald Lucas, *Colonel Saunderson, M.P.*, London, 1908, p. 67.
22 *The Times*, 13 July 1883.
23 Lucas, op. cit., pp. 71, 101.
24 *The Times*, 14 July 1884.
25 Cited *I.H.S.*, vol. xvi, no. 62, September 1968, p. 167, fn. 39.

26 *The Times,* 2 January 1885.
27 W. S. Churchill, *Lord Randolph Churchill,* 2 vols., London, 1906, vol. ii, p. 59.
28 D. C. Savage, 'The Origins of the Ulster Unionist Party' in *I.H.S.,* vol. xii, no. 48, September 1961, pp. 194–5.
29 *The Times,* 15 February 1886.
30 ibid.
31 Cited in *I.H.S.,* vol. xii, no. 47, March 1961, p. 185.
32 *The Times,* 24 February 1886.
33 *I.H.S.,* vol. xii, no. 47, p. 201; *The Times,* 14 May 1886.
34 *The Times,* 12, 14, 25, 28 May 1886.
35 ibid., 8 May 1886.
36 *I.H.S.,* vol. xii, no. 47, p. 208.
37 Hansard, H.C. Debates, 3rd series, vol. 305, col. 659.
38 ibid., col. 1342.
39 ibid., vol. 306, col. 62.
40 ibid., vol. 305, col. 1353.
41 ibid., cols. 1053–4. The committee stage, of course, was never reached.
42 Sir Charles Russell.
43 Figures quoted by John Redmond from Parliamentary Return, Hansard, H.C. Debates, 3rd series, vol. 305, col. 970.
44 Churchill, *Lord Randolph Churchill,* vol. ii, p. 59.
45 Hansard, H.C. Debates, 3rd series, vol. 304, cols. 1385, 1395.
46 ibid., vol. 306, col. 1179.
47 ibid., col. 1180.

5 Parnell's Fall

1 *The Times,* 17 November 1890.
2 F. S. L. Lyons, *John Dillon,* London, 1968, p. 109.

6 Second Home Rule Bill: Orangemen at Play

1 *The Times,* 22 June 1892, quoting a report of the sermon in the *Irish Daily Independent* of 20 June 1892.
2 Hansard, H.C. Debates, 4th series, vol. 10, col. 1864.
3 ibid., 3rd series, vol. 364, cols. 1419–20.
4 ibid., cols. 1315–18.
5 ibid., 4th series, vol. 11, col. 44.
6 ibid., 3rd series, vol. 364, col. 1467.
7 ibid., cols. 1862–3.
8 ibid., 4th series, vol. 15, col. 1742.
9 ibid., 4th series, vol. 15, cols. 1504–6.

10 *The Times*, 10 August 1893, 13 September 1893.
11 Hansard, H.C. Debates, 4th series, vol. 15, cols. 1656–8.
12 *Freeman's Journal*, 12 September 1893.
13 These and subsequent details from *The Times*, 15, 17, 18 June, 1892.
14 ibid., 18 June 1892.
15 Lucas, *Saunderson*, p. 102.
16 ibid., pp. 180–1. Also *The Times*, 31 May 1892.
17 *The Times*, 20 December 1892.
18 ibid., 18 January 1893.
19 Hansard, H.C. Debates, 3rd series, vol. 363, col. 185.
20 ibid., col. 1338.
21 ibid., col. 550. Quotation of a report from the *Derry Sentinel*.
22 *The Times*, 5 April 1893.
23 ibid., 17 March 1893.
24 ibid., 3 March 1893.
25 William Johnston, MP.
26 *The Times*, 10 August 1892.
27 Quoted Lyons, *Dillon*, p. 190.

7 Nationalists at Ease

1 *Freeman's Journal*, 14 September 1893.
2 ibid., 9, 11, 12 September 1893.
3 ibid., 5 July 1895.
4 ibid., 19 July 1895, 25 June 1895, 31 July 1895.
5 Denis Gwynn, *Life of John Redmond*, London, 1932, p. 84.
6 *Freeman's Journal*, 22 July 1895.
7 A speculative but interesting comment on this action of Parnell's may be found in the Epilogue by Owen Dudley Edwards to Desmond Ryan's *Fenian Chief*.
8 *Freeman's Journal*, 7 June 1898.
9 ibid.
10 ibid., 9 June 1898.
11 ibid., 17, 29 June 1898.
12 These and subsequent details of this day from the *Freeman's Journal*, 15 August 1898.

8 Growth of National Consciousness

1 *United Irishman*, 12 October 1901.
2 See M. O'Dubghail, *Insurrection Fires at Eastertide*, Cork, 1966, p. 20; also David Greene, 'Cusack and the G.A.A.', in *The Shaping of Modern Ireland*, edited by Conor Cruise O'Brien, London, 1959.

3 Quoted – from *Representative Irish Tales* – by H. Krans, *W. B. Yeats*, London, 1905, p. 10. See also W. B. Yeats, *Autobiographies*, London, 1926, p. 245.

4 W. B. Yeats, *The Celtic Twilight*, London, 1893, p. 25.

5 ibid., p. 83.

6 ibid., p. 6.

7 ibid.

8 Yeats, *Autobiographies*, p. 267.

9 ibid., p. 268.

10 Myles Dillon, 'Douglas Hyde', in C. C. O'Brien (ed.), *The Shaping of Modern Ireland*, p. 51.

11 See reprint of lecture in *The Revival of Irish Literature*, London, 1894, p. 160.

12 ibid., p. 161.

13 ibid., p. 158.

14 ibid., p. 157.

15 ibid., p. 123.

16 Douglas Hyde, *Beside the Fire*, London, 1890, Preface, p. xlv.

17 *The Revival of Irish Literature*, pp. 137–8.

18 ibid.

19 George A. Birmingham (The Reverend J. O. Hannay), *An Irishman Looks at His World*, London, 1919, pp. 168–9.

20 O'Dubghail, *Insurrection Fires*, p. 27; Sydney Brooks, *The New Ireland*, Dublin, 1907, p. 27.

21 ibid.

22 Quoted in the *United Irishman*, 22 June 1901.

23 D. P. Moran, *The Philosophy of Irish Ireland*, Dublin, 1905, p. 2.

24 ibid., pp. 4, 96, 10, 13–14, 98.

25 ibid., p. 105.

26 Elizabeth Coxhead, *Lady Gregory*, London, 1963, p. 59.

27 ibid., p. 58.

28 Robert Brennan, *Allegiance*, Dublin, 1950, p. 11.

29 Yeats, *Autobiographies*, p. 254.

30 W. B. Yeats, 'The Literary Movement in Ireland', *Ideals in Ireland* (ed. Lady Gregory), London, 1901.

31 Moran, op. cit., pp. 108, 114.

32 Donal McCartney, 'Hyde, D. P. Moran and Irish Ireland', in F. X. Martin (ed.), *Leaders and Men of the Easter Rising: Dublin 1916*, London, 1966, p. 46.

33 Myles Dillon, 'Douglas Hyde', in C. C. O'Brien (ed.), *The Shaping of Modern Ireland*, pp. 55, 57.

34 George Moore, *Hail and Farewell*, London, 1937, p. 256.

35 Sir Horace Plunkett, *Ireland in The New Century*, London, 1905, p. 192.

36 ibid., pp. 228, 288.
37 ibid., pp. 310–11.
38 Lyons, *Dillon*, p. 288.

9 *Arthur Griffith and Sinn Fein*

1 Gregory (ed.), *Ideals in Ireland*, pp. 65–8.
2 Louis Marcus, 'The G.A.A. and the Castle', *Irish Independent*, 9–10 July 1964, cited by O'Dubghaill, *Insurrection Fires*, p. 20.
3 O'Brien and Ryan (eds.), *Devoy's Post Bag*, vol. ii, p. 347.
4 ibid., pp. 340–1.
5 In 1900. George Lyons, *Some Recollections of Griffith and His Times*, Dublin, 1923, pp. 9, 44.
6 *United Irishman*, 11 March 1899; 1 April 1899.
7 ibid., 3 June 1899.
8 ibid., 25 March 1899; 8 April 1899; 1 April 1899; 3 June 1899: 30 September 1899; 18 August 1900; 22 September 1900.
9 See letter from George A. Lyons, *United Irishman*, 23 September 1899.
10 *United Irishman*, 8 April 1899.
11 ibid., 30 September 1899.
12 ibid., 7 October 1899.
13 ibid., 14 October 1899; 30 December 1899.
14 ibid., 14 October 1899.
15 ibid., 18 November 1899.
16 ibid., 23 December 1899; Nora Connolly, *Portrait of a Rebel Father*, London and Dublin, 1935, p. 60.
17 George Lyons, op. cit., p. 24.
18 L. Paul-Dubois, *Contemporary Ireland*, London, 1908, p. 178.
19 *United Irishman*, 9 December 1899.
20 ibid., 16 March 1901.
21 ibid., 22 December 1900.
22 ibid., 16 March 1901.
23 ibid., 7 October 1899; 9 December 1899.
24 ibid., 1 September 1900; 31 January 1903.
25 ibid., 7 April 1900.
26 ibid., 24 February 1900.
27 ibid., 3 March 1900.
28 ibid., 6 October 1900.
29 ibid.
30 ibid., 17 November 1900.
31 ibid.
32 ibid., 6 April 1901.
33 ibid., 1 November 1902.

34 ibid., 18 May 1901.
35 ibid., 19 October 1901.
36 Circulation figures given in *United Irishman.*
37 ibid., 9 March 1901.
38 ibid., 30 March 1901.
39 Padraic Colum, *Arthur Griffith*, Dublin, 1959, p. 3.
40 *United Irishman*, 14 September 1901.
41 ibid., 15 February 1902.
42 ibid.
43 ibid., 18 January 1902.
44 ibid., 10 May 1902.
45 ibid., 1 November 1902.
46 ibid.
47 ibid., 28 February 1903.
48 ibid., 18 April 1903.
49 ibid., 6 June 1903.
50 Denis Gwynn, *Edward Martyn and the Irish Revival*, London, 1930, p. 63.
51 *Cork Examiner*, 3 August 1903. See also Horgan, *Parnell to Pearse*, p. 102, confirming this.
52 *United Irishman*, 8 August 1903.
53 ibid., 2 July 1904.
54 ibid.
55 ibid., 10 September 1904.
56 For other reactions to articles see ibid., 23 July 1904.
57 ibid., 18 February 1905.
58 George A. Birmingham, *An Irishman Looks at His World*, p. 43.
59 James Stephens, 'In the Morning of His Triumph', in *Arthur Griffith, Michael Collins, A Memorial Album*, Dublin, 1922.
60 *United Irishman*, 28 January, 4, 11 February 1905.
61 ibid., 21 January 1905.
62 ibid., 1 April 1905; facsimile of letter in Griffith's handwriting in W. G. Fitzgerald (ed.), *The Voice of Ireland*, Manchester, 1924. For earlier uses of the words Sinn Fein in Irish history see above pages of this book.
63 Article by Mary Butler in Fitzgerald (ed.), op. cit.
64 P. S. O'Hegarty, *The Victory of Sinn Fein*, Dublin, 1924, p. 30.
65 *Sinn Fein*, 17 October 1906.
66 *Leader*, 8 June 1907.
67 Denis Gwynn, *Life of John Redmond*, London, 1932, p. 115.
68 *Freeman's Journal*, 8 May 1907.
69 ibid.
70 ibid., 9 May 1907.
71 ibid., 15 May 1907.

72 ibid., 18 May 1907.

73 Lyons, *Dillon*, p. 288.

74 ibid., p. 289.

75 O'Brien and Ryan (eds.), *Devoy's Post Bag*, vol. ii, p. 359. He lived until 1965.

76 T. M. Healy, *Letters and Leaders of My Day*, 2 vols., London, 1928, vol. ii, p. 482; *Sinn Fein*, 29 February 1908.

77 *Sinn Fein*, 8 October 1910; 14 October 1911; 18 February 1911.

78 ibid., 27 November 1912.

79 'Standing down' and 'cessation of activity' were Griffith's own terms — see *Sinn Fein*, 7 October 1911.

80 Sean O'Faolain, *Constance Markievicz*, London, 1934, p. 29.

81 Jacqueline van Voris, *Constance de Markievicz*, Massachusetts, 1967, pp. 56, 51.

82 ibid., p. 58.

83 ibid.

84 *Sinn Fein*, 5 September 1908.

85 ibid., 4 September 1909.

86 See his poem: *On a Political Prisoner*.

87 Casement to Alice Stopford Green, 24 April 1904, N.L.I.

88 *United Irishman*, 25 February 1905.

89 Casement to Bulmer Hobson, 10 September 1905, N.L.I.

90 Casement to Alice Stopford Green, 8 September 1906, N.L.I.

91 Casement to Alice Stopford Green, 21 September 1906, N.L.I.

92 Casement to Bulmer Hobson, 10 August 1905, N.L.I.

93 Casement to Bulmer Hobson, 13 August 1907, N.L.I.

94 Bulmer Hobson, *Ireland Yesterday and Tomorrow*, Tralee, 1968, p. 35.

95 ibid., p. 8.

96 O'Brien and Ryan (eds.), *Devoy's Post Bag*, vol. ii, pp. 347, 350.

97 ibid., p. 350.

98 *Sinn Fein*, 2 February 1907.

99 ibid., 30 March, 1907.

100 ibid., 14 March 1908. *Sinn Fein*, 18 March 1908.

101 *Sinn Fein*, 18 March 1908.

102 ibid., 15 February 1908.

103 O'Brien and Ryan (eds.), op. cit., vol. ii, p. 383.

104 ibid., p. 390.

10 Asquith and the Third Home Rule Bill

1 For full details of these transactions see H. W. Macready, 'Home Rule and the Liberal Party 1899–1908', in *I.H.S.*, vol. xii, no. 52, September 1963, pp. 316–48.

2 ibid., p. 322.
3 ibid., p. 323.
4 ibid., p. 328.
5 ibid., p. 324.
6 ibid., p. 333.
7 ibid., pp. 333–4.
8 ibid., p. 342.
9 For some details of attempts, before the introduction of the third Home Rule Bill, to explore the possibility of a compromise with the Conservatives which might release the Liberals from their dependence on the Irish see Montgomery Hyde, *Carson* (London, 1953), pp. 277–80, and Roy Jenkins, *Asquith* (London, 1964), pp. 246–7. The attempts were conducted by Lloyd George.
10 Denis Gwynn, *Life of John Redmond*, London, 1932, p. 169.
11 Cited by F. S. L. Lyons 'The Irish Unionist Party and the devolution crisis of 1904–5', in *I.H.S.*, vol. vi, no. 21, March 1948, p. 10.
12 ibid., p. 13.
13 *Freeman's Journal*, 30 November 1910.
14 Hyde, *Carson*, pp. 158, 209.
15 ibid., p. 329.
16 ibid., p. 14.
17 ibid., p. 89.
18 ibid., p. 329.
19 ibid., p. 157.
20 Hansard, H.C. Debates, 5th series, vol. xxi, col. 1157.
21 Hyde, op. cit., p. 283.
22 ibid., p. 286.
23 ibid., p. 291.
24 A. T. Q. Stewart, *The Ulster Crisis*, London, 1967, p. 69.
25 Hyde, op. cit., pp. 310–11.
26 ibid.
27 *Belfast Evening Telegraph*, 9 April 1912.
28 ibid., 19 April 1912.
29 ibid., 9 April 1912.
30 Sir J. B. Lonsdale, MP for Mid Armagh and Member of the Ulster Unionist Council, Hansard, 5th series, vol. xxi, col. 89.
31 Ian Malcolm, MP for Croydon, Hansard, ibid., col. 1082.
32 Hyde, op. cit., p. 316.
33 ibid., p. 311.
34 *Belfast Evening Telegraph*, 10 April 1912.
35 Robert Blake, *The Unknown Prime Minister*, London, 1955, p. 130.
36 ibid., p. 133.
37 Hansard, H.C. Debates, 5th series, vol. 36, col. 1437.

294

38 ibid., vol. 21, cols. 1103–6.
39 ibid., cols. 1156–7.
40 ibid., col. 1117.
41 ibid., cols. 1134, 1145.
42 ibid., col. 1424.
43 ibid., col. 41.
44 *Freeman's Journal*, 12 April 1912.
45 ibid., 24 April 1912.
46 Hansard, H.C. Debates, 5th series, vol. 22, col. 91; vol. 21, col. 1161.
47 See Macdonald's speech on Parliament Bill, Hansard, H.C. Debates, 5th series, vol. 25, col. 1380.
48 Lecky, *History of Ireland in the Eighteenth Century*, vol. ii, p. 182.
49 Hansard, H.C. Debates, 5th series, vol. 29, cols. 826–7 (7 August 1911).
50 ibid., vol. 37, col. 2162; see also vol. 39, col. 771.
51 For full details of the ceremony see Stewart, *Ulster Crisis*, pp. 61–6.
52 *Daily News*, quoted in *Freeman's Journal*, 21 December 1910.
53 Hansard, H.C. Debates, 5th series, vol. 46, col. 468.
54 ibid., vol. 46, col. 478.
55 ibid., cols. 2125–6. Author's italics.
56 ibid., col. 2150.
57 ibid., col. 2191.

11 Ulster Volunteers

1 Stewart, *Ulster Crisis*, p. 71.
2 Hansard, H.C. Debates, 5th series, vol. 46, cols. 2324–5.
3 Hyde, *Carson*, p. 339.
4 *Freeman's Journal*, 5 June 1913.
5 Gwynn, *Redmond*, p. 228.
6 For details see Blake, *The Unknown Prime Minister*, pp. 161–7.
7 Gwynn, op. cit., p. 232.
8 ibid., p. 231.
9 ibid., pp. 234–6.
10 ibid.
11 Blake, op. cit., pp. 161–2.
12 ibid., pp. 164–5.
13 Roy Jenkins, *Asquith*, p. 292.
14 ibid., p. 290.
15 Gwynn, op. cit., pp. 234–6.
16 ibid., pp. 237–8.
17 ibid., p. 250.

18 ibid., pp. 250–1.
19 ibid., pp. 267–73.

12 The Liberal Nerve Begins to Fail

1 Stewart, *Ulster Crisis*, pp. 119–20.
2 ibid., pp. 130–40. See also A. M. Gollin, *Pro-Consul in Politics*, London, 1964.
3 ibid., pp. 126–7.
4 *The Times*, 16 March 1914.
5 Two excellent authoritative accounts of these events are to be found in Sir James Fergusson, *The Curragh Incident* (London, 1964) and A. P. Ryan, *Mutiny at the Curragh* (London, 1956). The former, written by the son of one of the principal participants, is the more detailed, and, like the latter, admirably objective.
6 Fergusson, op. cit., p. 67.
7 ibid.
8 ibid., pp. 56, 69.
9 ibid., pp. 84, 88.
10 ibid., pp. 106–13.
11 ibid., pp. 145–6.
12 ibid., pp. 150–51.
13 ibid., pp. 125, 146–7, 153.
14 ibid., p. 152.
15 Lyons, *Dillon*, p. 335.
16 Emmet Larkin, *James Larkin*, London, 1968, pp. 56–7.
17 Quoted from *Sinn Fein*, 28 November 1908, in Larkin, op. cit., p. 57.
18 *Report ... Into the Housing Conditions of the Working Classes in Dublin*, Parliamentary Papers, 1914, vol. xix, p. 66.
19 ibid., p. 68.
20 ibid., pp. 68–9.
21 ibid., p. 70.
22 ibid., p. 69.
23 *Report on Local Government*, Parliamentary Papers, 1914, vol. xxxix, p. 628.
24 Parliamentary Papers, 1914, xix, p. 79, pp. 76–9.
25 C. Desmond Greaves, *The Life and Times of James Connolly*, London, 1961, pp. 14–20.
26 ibid.
27 ibid., p. 69.
28 *Irish Worker*, 11 May 1912. Quoted Larkin, op. cit., p. 74. For circulation figures see ibid., p. 71.

29 *Report of the Dublin Disturbances Commission*, Parliamentary Papers, 1914, vol. xviii, p. 647.
30 ibid., p. 645.
31 ibid., p. 647.
32 ibid., pp. 651-2.
33 ibid.
34 Larkin, op. cit., p. 53.
35 ibid., p. 160.
36 ibid., p. 155.
37 ibid., p. 162.

13 Volunteers and Home Rule

1 *Sinn Fein*, 21 February 1914.
2 Gwynn, *Redmond*, p. 307.
3 *Westmeath Independent*, 18 October 1913.
4 ibid.
5 *Freeman's Journal*, 26 September 1914; *Westmeath Independent*, 25 October 1913.
6 *Westmeath Independent*, 13 December 1913.
7 ibid., 18 October 1913.
8 Martin, *The Irish Volunteers*, p. 71.
9 ibid., p. 59.
10 ibid., pp. 33-40.
11 ibid.
12 ibid., pp. 119-20.
13 Horgan, *Parnell to Pearse*, p. 229.
14 ibid., pp. 228-9.
15 Lyons, *Dillon*, p. 350.
16 *Freeman's Journal*, 27 March 1914.
   (eds.), *Devoy's Post Bag*, vol. ii, pp. 456, 463, N.L.I.
17 Casement to Alice Stopford Green, 20 June 1914, Ryan and O'Brien (eds.), *Devoy's Post Bag*, vol. ii, pp. 456, 463, N.L.I.
18 Hobson to Casement, 30 June 1914, N.L.I.
19 Clarke to Devoy, 7 July 1914, N.L.I.
20 O'Brien and Ryan (eds.), op. cit., p. 456.
21 Hobson to Casement, 14 July 1914.
22 Casement to Alice Stopford Green, 8 September 1906, N.L.I.
23 *Irish Freedom*, December 1910.
24 ibid., August 1911.
25 ibid., January 1911.
26 Statements by Ernest Blythe and Cathal O'Shannon respectively, *Irish Freedom*, July 1912.
27 ibid., June 1913.

28 ibid., October 1913.
29 O'Brien and Ryan (eds.), op. cit., vol. ii, pp. 403–4.
30 Martin, op. cit., p. 15.
31 Hobson, *Ireland Yesterday and Tomorrow*, p. 43.
32 ibid., pp. 37–9; Martin, op. cit., p. 17.
33 Van Voris, *Constance Markievicz*, p. 82.
34 *Freeman's Journal*, 26 November 1913.
35 P. H. Pearse, *Political Writings and Speeches*, Dublin 1952, pp. 91–9.
36 O'Brien and Ryan (eds.), op. cit., pp. 425, 450, 466.
37 ibid., pp. 42–5.
38 ibid., p. 427.
39 ibid., p. 445.
40 *Irish Freedom*, July 1913.
41 Darrell Figgis, *Recollections of the Irish War*, London, 1927, pp. 10–11.
42 Martin, op. cit., p. 32. Gwynn, *Redmond*, p. 311.
43 See Bulmer Hobson's account in Martin, op. cit., pp. 32–3.
44 See A. S. Green, *Irish Nationality*, London, 1912.
45 Casement to Mrs A. S. Green, 24 April 1904, N.L.I.
46 Casement to Mrs A. S. Green, 24 August 1906, N.L.I.
47 Figgis, op. cit., p. 15.
48 ibid., p. 18.
49 F. X. Martin, *The Howth Gun-Running* (Dublin, 1964), p. 38. Figgis, *Recollections*, pp. 22–37.
50 Martin, *Howth Gun-Running*, p. 129.
51 Martin, *Howth Gun-Running*, pp. 79–80 (extract from Mary Spring Rice's diary).
52 ibid., pp. 128–63.
53 ibid., top photograph facing p. 150.
54 *Report of the Royal Commission on the circumstances connected with the landing of arms at Howth on 26th July 1914*, Parliamentary Papers, 1914–16, xxiv, p. 805. '... The proceedings of the police and military were tainted by fundamental illegality.'
55 These and other details of this event from *Royal Commission*, Parliamentary Papers, 1914–16, vol. xxiv, pp. 824–89 (minutes of evidence).
56 ibid., p. 892.

14 Volunteers and the European War

1 Gwynn, *Redmond*, p. 330.
2 Jenkins, *Asquith*, p. 321.
3 ibid., p. 323.
4 Gwynn, op. cit., p. 354.
5 *Freeman's Journal*, 1 August 1914.

298

6 Gwynn, op. cit., p. 355.

7 ibid., p. 356.

8 ibid., p. 353.

9 ibid., p. 357.

10 ibid., p. 353.

11 T. P. O'Connor to Dillon, quoted Lyons, *Dillon*, p. 357.

12 *Freeman's Journal*, 2 September 1914.

13 ibid., 12 September 1914.

14 ibid., 15 September 1914.

15 Gwynn, op. cit., p. 383; *Freeman's Journal*, 19 September 1914.

16 *Freeman's Journal*, 22 September 1914; *Irish Independent*, 23 September 1914.

17 *Freeman's Journal*, 19 September 1914.

18 ibid.

19 Quoted Gwynn, op. cit., pp. 380–81.

20 ibid., p. 385.

21 *Freeman's Journal*, 21 September 1914.

22 Breandán Mac Giolla Choille, *Intelligence Notes 1913–16*, Dublin, 1966, p. 175.

23 *Freeman's Journal*, 26 September 1914.

24 ibid.

25 *National Volunteer*, 24 October 1914.

26 ibid., 7 November 1914.

27 *Freeman's Journal*, 28, 29 September 1914; 7, 16, 17 October 1914.

28 ibid., 29 September 1914.

29 ibid., 1 October 1914.

30 ibid., 5 October 1914.

31 ibid.

32 ibid.

33 ibid., 12 October 1914.

34 ibid.

35 ibid.

36 ibid., 15 October 1914.

37 ibid., 18 October 1914.

38 ibid., 19 October 1914.

39 ibid.

40 See *Freeman's Journal* and *Irish Independent*, September 1914, *passim*.

41 *Freeman's Journal*, 19 November 1914.

42 ibid., 21 December 1914; *Irish Independent*, 20 December 1914. The former gives the numbers at this meeting as 14,000, the latter as upward of 12,000. Police reports placed them lower at about 5,000, Mac Giolla Choille (ed.), *Intelligence Notes*, p. 80.

43 *Freeman's Journal*, 18 March 1915.

44 ibid.
45 ibid., 26 August 1915.
46 ibid., 23 August 1915.
47 Gwynn, *Redmond*, pp. 397, 404–5, 407.
48 Quoted Gwynn, op. cit., p. 390.
49 ibid., p. 401. Also quoted by John Dillon, *Freeman's Journal*, 26 October 1914.
50 *Freeman's Journal*, 16 October 1915.
51 ibid., 29 October 1915.
52 ibid., 8 March 1915.
53 ibid., 4 April 1915.
54 ibid., 2 July 1915.
55 ibid., 4 August 1915.
56 ibid., 18 August 1915.
57 ibid.
58 Gwynn, op. cit., p. 274.
59 Quoted *Freeman's Journal*, 4 June 1915.
60 Gwynn, op. cit., pp. 431–2.
61 *Freeman's Journal*, 18 August 1915.
62 ibid., 22 December 1915.
63 Mac Giolla Choille (ed.), *Intelligence Notes*, p. 149.

15 The 'Sinn Fein' Volunteers

1 O'Hegarty, *Victory of Sinn Fein*, p. 18. The strength of the IRB in January 1914 was approximately 2,000. See Diarmuid Lynch, *The I.R.B. and the 1916 Rising*, Cork, 1957, p. 24.
2 See F. X. Martin, 'Eoin Macneill on the 1916 Rising', *I.H.S.*, vol. xii, March 1961, p. 226, particularly pp. 234–40.
3 Pearse, *Political Writings*, p. 91.
4 ibid., p. 216.
5 Martin in *I.H.S.*, vol. xii, pp. 236ff.
6 Lynch, op. cit., pp. 25, 102, 113, 131.
7 *Irish Volunteer*, 15 October 1914.
8 Martin, *Irish Volunteers*, p. 169.
9 ibid., pp. 170ff.
10 *Eire*, 17 November 1914.
11 *Irish Volunteer*, 20 March 1915; 10 July 1915.
12 *Freeman's Journal*, 5 December 1914.
13 Mac Giolla Choille (ed.), *Intelligence Notes*, p. 147.
14 *Freeman's Journal*, 2 August 1915; *National Volunteer*, 14 August 1915; *Irish Volunteer*, 7 August 1915.
15 Pearse, op. cit., pp. 133–7. Rossa: *Freeman's Journal*, 31 July 1915.

16 Leon O'Broin, *Dublin Castle and the 1916 Rising*, Dublin, 1966, p. 53.
17 Mac Giolla Choille (ed.), op. cit., p. 176.
18 ibid., p. 176. Also *Freeman's Journal*, 2 July 1915.
19 Official figures quoted in *Freeman's Journal*, 12 January 1916; see also *Freeman's Journal*, 11 May 1915.
20 ibid., 14 October 1915.
21 Mac Giolla Choille (ed.), op. cit., p. 224.
22 O'Broin, *Dublin Castle*, p. 53.
23 Mac Giolla Choille (ed.), op. cit., p. 224.
24 Dorothy Macardle, *The Irish Republic*, Dublin, 1951, p. 138; *Freeman's Journal*, November 1915.
25 *Documents Relative to the Sinn Fein Movement* (Cd 1108), 1921; Sir William James, *The Eyes of the Navy*, London, 1955, p. 43.

16 Casement in Germany

1 McGarrity Papers.
2 Devoy, *Recollections*, p. 411.
3 Casement's own word. See C. E. Curry (ed.), *Sir Roger Casement's Diaries*, Munich, 1922, p. 25.
4 Casement to Devoy, 21 July 1914. Devoy, *Recollections*, p. 411.
5 *Documents Relative to the Sinn Fein Movement*, 1921.
6 Devoy, op. cit., p. 417.
7 McGarrity Papers, N.L.I.
8 ibid.
9 Moloney Papers, N.L.I.
10 ibid.
11 Devoy, op. cit., p. 419.
12 See Desmond Ryan, *The Rising*, p. 18, footnote, and Casement's Brief to his Counsel, Casement microfilm (1) and Maloney Papers (Box 182), N.L.I.
13 Casement to McGarrity from Berlin, 21 November 1914, McGarrity Papers, N.L.I.
14 Herbert O. Mackey, *The Life and Times of Roger Casement*, Dublin, 1954, pp. 77–8.
15 McGarrity to Casement, 9 November 1915, McGarrity Papers, N.L.I.
16 See Memorandum by Patrick McCartan quoted in *Documents Relative to the Sinn Fein Movement* (C1108), 1921.
17 Casement to McGarrity, 21 November 1914, McGarrity Papers, N.L.I.
18 Fürst von Leiningen. Casement's Brief to Counsel, Casement microfilm (i) and Maloney Papers, N.L.I.
19 For facsimile copy of this treaty in Casement's handwriting see Denis Gwynn, *The Life and Death of Roger Casement*, London, 1930.

20 Brief to Counsel, N.L.I.
21 Letter to McGarrity, 23 March 1915.
22 See René MacColl, *Roger Casement*, London, 1956, p. 268.
23 Cited MacColl, op. cit., p. 190.
24 Moloney Papers, N.L.I.

17 *The Dublin Rising, 1916*

1 Gwynn, *Redmond*, p. 471.
2 *Freeman's Journal*, 23 April 1916.
3 For a full page facsimile of the proclamation see Macardle, *Irish Republic*, or Max Caulfield, *The Easter Rebellion*, London, 1964.
4 Sir John Maxwell's Dispatch. *Sinn Fein Rebellion Handbook*, Dublin, 1916, p. 93.
5 E. R. Dodds (ed.), *Journal and Letters of Stephen MacKenna*, London, 1936, p. 51.
6 *Rebellion Handbook*, pp. 29–30. Caulfield, *Easter Rebellion*, p. 70–4.
7 *Rebellion Handbook*, pp. 15, 17. Caulfield, *Easter Rebellion*, p. 2.
8 *Rebellion Handbook*, p. 93.
9 Desmond Fitzgerald, *The Memoirs of Desmond Fitzgerald*, London, 1968, pp. 140–1.
10 Patrick Pearse, *The Singer*, Dublin, 1915.
11 Patrick Pearse, *Political Writings*, p. 216.
12 Ryan (ed.), *Labour and Easter Week*, p. 21.
13 Mac Giolla Choille (ed.), *Intelligence Notes*, p. 176.
14 *Rebellion Handbook*, p. 154.
15 Robert Brennan, *Allegiance*, Dublin, 1950, p. 2.
16 Cited F. X. Martin, '1916 – Myth, Fact and Mystery', in *Studia Hibernica*, 1968, p. 98.
17 *Freeman's Journal*, 24 March 1916.
18 *Rebellion Handbook*, p. 193.
19 Roger McHugh, *Dublin 1916*, Dublin, 1966, pp. 81, 87.
20 F. X. Martin (ed.), *I.H.S.*, vol. xix, pp. 239–40.
21 Ryan, *Labour and Easter Week*, Dublin, 1949.
22 F. X. Martin (ed.), *I.H.S.*, vol. xii, p. 245.
23 Cited in Ryan (ed.), *Labour and Easter Week*, p. 13.
24 F. X. Martin (ed.), *I.H.S.*, vol. xii, p. 246.
25 ibid., p. 247.
26 ibid., p. 248.
27 ibid.
28 Eoin MacNeill, *Memoirs*, Dublin, 1935, p. 115.
29 Casement to McGarrity, 5 May 1915, 10 May 1915, McGarrity Papers, N.L.I.

30 ibid., 5 May 1915.

31 ibid., 20 June 1915.

32 ibid.

33 Casement's Brief to Counsel, 20 June 1915, N.L.I.

34 Casement to McGarrity, 30 June 1915, McGarrity Papers, N.L.I.

35 Karl Spindler, *The Mystery of the Casement Ship*.

36 Casement to McGarrity, 20 December 1915, McGarrity Papers (microfilm), N.L.I.

37 Diary of Casement entitled *The Last Page*, N.L.I. microfilm.

38 ibid.

39 Devoy, *Recollections*, p. 458.

40 *Documents Relative to the Sinn Fein Movement*, H.M.S.O. (Cmd. 1108), p. 9.

41 Casement, *The Last Page*, N.L.I. microfilm.

42 ibid.

43 ibid.

44 Devoy to German General Staff, 16 February 1916, McGarrity Papers, N.L.I.

45 MacColl, *Casement*, p. 212.

46 See German documents cited from microfilm at St Anthony's College, Oxford, by MacColl, op. cit., p. 199.

47 Admiral Sir William James, *The Eyes of the Navy*, London, 1955, pp. 43ff.

48 For some evidence of informers see Leon O'Broin, *Dublin Castle and the 1916 Rising*, Dublin, 1966, p. 81; and Mac Goilla Choille, *Intelligence Notes*, p. 278.

49 O'Broin, op. cit., p. 40.

50 ibid., p. 54.

51 ibid.

52 ibid., p. 55.

53 Mac Goilla Choille, op. cit., p. 278.

54 O'Broin, op. cit., p. 73.

55 ibid., p. 62.

56 ibid., p. 75.

57 ibid.

58 ibid., p. 72.

59 ibid., p. 70-1.

60 ibid., p. 74.

61 ibid., p. 70.

62 ibid., p. 73.

63 ibid., p. 85.

64 ibid., p. 87.

65 ibid., p. 88.

66 Stephens, *Insurrection in Dublin*, p. 18.
67 Rebellion Handbook, pp. 109–12; *Freeman's Journal*, 19 June 1916.
68 *Rebellion Handbook*, pp. 102–8.
69 ibid., p. 104.
70 ibid., p. 29.
71 Martin, '1916 – Myth, Fact and Mystery', in *Studia Hibernica*, no. 7, p. 108.
72 Stephens, op. cit., pp. 35–6.
73 ibid., p. 39.
74 McHugh, *Dublin 1916*, p. 97.
75 Max Caulfield, *Easter Rebellion*, p. 223.
76 ibid., p. 332.
77 ibid., p. 344.
78 Cited Greaves, *Connolly*, p. 319.
79 *Capuchin Annual*, 1966, pp. 232, 234.
80 Lynch, *I.R.B. and the 1916 Rising*, p. 143.
81 *Rebellion Handbook*, pp. 59–61. The death figure is a compilation of the cemetery interments resulting from the rebellion.
82 ibid., pp. 52–8.
83 ibid., pp. 112–15; also p. 57.
84 *Rebellion Handbook*, pp. 178–9; Wells and Marlowe, *A History of the Easter Rebellion*, pp. 184–7; but see also Brennan, *Allegiance*, pp. 72–3.
85 Sean MacEntee, *Episode at Easter*, Dublin, 1966, pp. 107–35.
86 *Capuchin Annual*, 1966, pp. 353–68.
87 ibid., pp. 376–80.
88 ibid., pp. 382–4.
89 *Rebellion Handbook*, pp. 175, *Capuchin Annual*, 1966, pp. 324–6.

Index

320

FOR THE BEST IN PAPERBACKS, LOOK FOR THE

In every corner of the world, on every subject under the sun, Penguin represents quality and variety – the very best in publishing today.

For complete information about books available from Penguin – including Puffins, Penguin Classics and Arkana – and how to order them, write to us at the appropriate address below. Please note that for copyright reasons the selection of books varies from country to country.

In the United Kingdom: Please write to *Dept E.P., Penguin Books Ltd, Harmondsworth, Middlesex, UB7 0DA.*

If you have any difficulty in obtaining a title, please send your order with the correct money, plus ten per cent for postage and packaging, to *PO Box No 11, West Drayton, Middlesex*

In the United States: Please write to *Dept BA, Penguin, 299 Murray Hill Parkway, East Rutherford, New Jersey 07073*

In Canada: Please write to *Penguin Books Canada Ltd, 2801 John Street, Markham, Ontario L3R 1B4*

In Australia: Please write to the *Marketing Department, Penguin Books Australia Ltd, P.O. Box 257, Ringwood, Victoria 3134*

In New Zealand: Please write to the *Marketing Department, Penguin Books (NZ) Ltd, Private Bag, Takapuna, Auckland 9*

In India: Please write to *Penguin Overseas Ltd, 706 Eros Apartments, 56 Nehru Place, New Delhi, 110019*

In the Netherlands: Please write to *Penguin Books Netherlands B.V., Postbus 195, NL-1380AD Weesp*

In West Germany: Please write to *Penguin Books Ltd, Friedrichstrasse 10–12, D–6000 Frankfurt/Main 1*

In Spain: Please write to *Alhambra Longman S.A., Fernandez de la Hoz 9, E–28010 Madrid*

In Italy: Please write to *Penguin Italia s.r.l., Via Como 4, I-20096 Pioltello (Milano)*

In France: Please write to *Penguin Books Ltd, 39 Rue de Montmorency, F-75003 Paris*

In Japan: Please write to *Longman Penguin Japan Co Ltd, Yamaguchi Building, 2–12–9 Kanda Jimbocho, Chiyoda-Ku, Tokyo 101*

VOLUME I AND III OF HIS HIGHLY ACCLAIMED TRILOGY

Robert Kee's *The Green Flag* stands as the most comprehensive and illuminating history of Irish Nationalism yet published.

THE GREEN FLAG: VOLUME I
THE MOST DISTRESSFUL COUNTRY

In this opening volume he asks the question, 'Who are the Irish?', and ranges from Ireland's earliest beginnings to the Great Famine of 1845.

THE GREEN FLAG: VOLUME III
OURSELVES ALONE

The third and final volume of Robert Kee's monumental history concentrates on the years 1916–23, from the Easter Rising to the creation of the Irish Free State.

'Shrewd and penetrating . . . this is an important book and should start a timely revaluation of Irish history' – *Observer*

'The really significant thing about this book is not just that it is a sympathetic epic, but that it is also a highly intelligent and critical one . . . Mr Kee writes out of a long affection for this country, but he remains in the best sense an outsider, and he brings to the most volatile ingredient of our history the detachment which his subject so desperately needs' – *Irish Times*

'As a blow-by-blow account of the Irish Nationalist movement it is a marvel of industry and organizational skill' – *Sunday Telegraph*